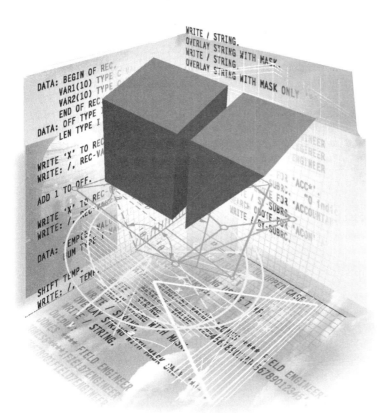

Thomas Teufel

Monika Nguyen
Nam

Roland Heun

SAP®
Business One

THOMSON

COURSE TECHNOLOGY

Professional ■ Trade ■ Reference

ISBN: 1-59200-591-8

Library of Congress Catalog Card Number: 2004114411

Printed in the United States of America

05 06 07 08 09 BH 10 9 8 7 6 5 4 3 2 1

THOMSON

COURSE TECHNOLOGY

Professional ■ Trade ■ Reference

Thomson Course Technology PTR, a division of Thomson Course Technology
25 Thomson Place
Boston, MA 02210
http://www.courseptr.com

Publisher and General Manager of Course PTR:
Stacy L. Hiquet

Associate Director of Marketing:
Sarah O'Donnell

Marketing Manager:
Heather Hurley

Manager of Editorial Services:
Heather Talbot

Senior Acquisitions Editor:
Emi Smith

Senior Editor:
Mark Garvey

Developmental Editors:
John Gosney,
Thomas Boehm

Marketing Coordinator:
Jordan Casey

Project Editor:
Estelle Manticas

Copy Editors:
Estelle Manticas,
Gene Redding

PTR Editorial Services Coordinator:
Elizabeth Furbish

Interior Layout Tech:
Marian Hartsough

Cover Designer:
Abby Scholz

Indexer:
Sharon Shock

Proofreader:
Kim V. Benbow

About the Authors

THOMAS TEUFEL has more than 11 years' experience working with SAP. He has worked as an SAP consultant on several international projects and currently owns a consulting company in Germany.

MONIKA NGUYEN NAM has participated in the implementation of group-wide standard software SAP/R3 in five countries, as well as in the migration of three new business units to SAP in a four-month period. She has also participated in the implementation of SAP Business One in Japan.

ROLAND HEUN has 15 years' experience in the IT field. He has extensive experience in business development, marketing, and product management for SAP Business One.

Contents

Chapter 4 Business Process Design. 53

Chapter 5 Model Company A: Sales of Capital Goods. . . 63

Introduction

The enterprise story of SAP proves that success is programmable—what can be programmed can be repeated. For a new product like SAP Business One—with a new target market—this does not mean programmed with the same lines of code but with the same know-how that made SAP the world market leader for ERP software. The simple and easy-to-understand SAP Business One product is extremely efficient in its support for all the normal business transactions of small and medium-sized enterprises. Its functionality is expanded by add-ons provided by SAP's highly qualified partners.

For enterprises that already use SAP software such as R/3 or mySAP, integration of new sales or production facilities with SAP Business One will be easy and smooth, ultimately saving your company both time and money.

With SAP Business One, SAP is on track to repeat their successes with small and medium-sized enterprises. Your company can now participate in this success—*SAP Business One* will show you how.

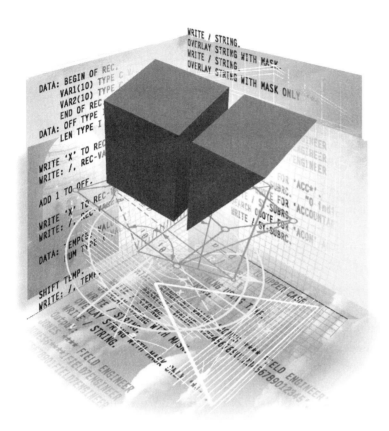

Chapter 1

Inside SAP Business One

Mid-size customers (that is, companies with between two and 250 employees) are increasingly uncertain as to which enterprise software is suitable for their company. This uncertainty is due to the consolidation of the ERP market as well as to the rising number of smaller software companies closing their doors.

SAP continues to be the enterprise solution package of choice for such customers. SAP Business One has gained favor in the mid-size market because it is both cost-effective and compact in size. Like larger enterprises, small and mid-size companies need an integrated software solution that adapts the overall document/process flow to the larger operational processes of the company. Indeed, most of mid-size customers can cover 85 percent of their ERP requirements using the built-in functions in SAP Business One. The remaining 15 percent can be customized via the SAP Business One SDK.

This chapter will focus on the "small but powerful/Less is More" aspect of the SAP Business One suite. It will give you an introductory look at the product and show you why it can be such a powerful solution for the small- to mid-size customer. Along the way, we'll also examine the positioning of SAP Business One in the SAP family and discuss the underlying technology that is implemented in the product (this includes more detailed look at the SDK referenced above).

SAP Business One: A Compact ERP Solution

A major component of the "compact solution" aspect of SAP Business One is the SDK. SAP has been proactive about distributing the SDK as widely as possible. Indeed, the availability of the SDK add-ons can greatly reduce the overall development and implementation time of an SAP Business One solution, as additional functionality that would have to be developed from scratch can quickly be implemented via the SDK. Utilization of the SDK guarantees an integration of SAP Business One with other SAP solutions. For example, SAP Business One could be used for a subsidiary in a decentralized system, where other functional operations (such as data comparison/analysis) could be carried out via SAP NetWeaver.

A good analogy for the benefits of the SDK is to think of the entire organization as a seaport. If you use the SDK to build your "ships," then they can "dock" at the larger "port" (that is, the larger organizational infrastructure being managed by, in this example, SAP). This development is then under the larger quality seal of SAP.

 NOTE

Given that SAP has become the gold standard in the ERP arena, it is not unusual for larger customers to demand that their suppliers develop to and implement SAP standards, in the same manner that they would require quality certification via ISO9001. With SAP Business One (and taking advantage of the SDK) the small- to medium-sized company can afford SAP and fulfil such quality requirements.

By again drawing on the benefits of the SDK, a powerful integrated solution can be developed for specific company needs. Figure 1.1 offers a functional overview of an integrated solution.

FIGURE 1.1 *SAP Business One offers a compact yet powerful ERP solution.*

SAP Business One is equipped with the standard functions that are demanded by the small to medium-sized enterprise. The performance spectrum of SAP Business One covers the following areas:

- **Contact Management and Opportunity Analysis (CRM).** With this function, you can administer your contacts as gathered from telephone calls, conventions, or any method of customer contact you practice.

- **Administration** (Customizing SAP SAP Business One). This functionality is maintained by an administrator and covers general functions within the system, such as user administration, system initialization, workflow definitions, and so on.

- **Financials.** The arrangement and maintenance of accounts, including general budgeting, journal entries, and so on, are managed within this function.

- **Sales/Order Processing.** Sales offers, customer orders, master record and discount structures, returns, and other functions are all included here.

- **Purchase and Procurement.** Within this function, the buyer may locate the order process, and goods receipt and incoming invoices are maintained.

- **Business Partner.** Included here are the uniform structures for the business partner vendors, as well as customer and prospective customer information (that is, "leads"). For example, specific data fields will be visible to sales and purchasing depending on the specific business case as highlighted by the information contained.

- **Cost Accounting/Cost Calculation.** Within this function, the profit center is created based on cost center structure, and in turn is evaluated and tracked according to typical P&L statements.

- **Inventory Management.** Item master management (that is, raw material and finished and semi-finished goods), item management, standard price lists, and inventory transactions (goods issued, receipt and transfer posting, and so on) are handled here.

- **Production.** Here, bill of materials are defined, production orders are applied, and material availability is examined and guaranteed.

- ◆ **Invoicing/Payment**. The electronic payment transactions are handled in this area. Both domestic and foreign payment transactions are supported.

- ◆ **Material Resource Planning (MRP)**. MRP calculates gross requirements for the highest-level bill of materials, according to sales orders and forecast demands; order recommendations are scheduled according to a defined lead time.

- ◆ **Service**. The Service area optimizes the potential of Sales and Service departments; also included here is service contract management and planning, customer interaction tracking, customer support, and sales opportunities management.

- ◆ **Human Resources**. Integration interfaces are available for HR; these can be used depending on the requirements of the existing personnel system in mySAP.

- ◆ **Reports**. The Reports area includes a variety of reports, namely business, accounting, warehouse, and financial reports as well as account reports/statements.

- ◆ **Internet Sales**. Integration interfaces are available to the B2C or B2B Internet sales system of SAP.

This list of process areas shows that most enterprise processes—with the exception of production control and planning (PPS) functions—can be facilitated with the SAP Business One standard. While the functional range of SAP Business One is clearly not as extensive as that of the conventional SAP-R/3, SAP Business One is intended as a compact solution for the mid-sized customer and has been designed to meet the specific needs of this level of customer. While SAP Business One may not possess the full capabilities of SAP R/3, it is still most certainly a complete ERP package.

 NOTE

For more information on PPS function, see Chapter 3, "SAP Business One SDK."

The Less Is More Approach

A major design feature of SAP Business One is the intuitiveness of the user interface. As an end user works within the various process areas, only those functions that are required for his or her daily work are presented, thus making a large and potentially very complex environment easier to navigate and utilize. This is the Less is More approach, and can be found throughout SAP Business One.

SAP Business One offers easy integration with the Microsoft Office suite. Given that the vast majority of end users are familiar with the applications found in that product (Word, Excel, and so on), this further decreases the learning curve and anxiety involved with working with SAP Business One.

Management reports can be made simple and interactive with the innovative "Drag and Relate" technology. For example, a user can use his mouse to drag a specific field from one area and drop it in another, immediately creating a relationship between the two areas. This not only allows for quick report generation, but also a powerful level of transparency between the various process areas of SAP Business One. Users can build and see data relationships that might not otherwise have been possible.

Relevant Costs for Decision Making

The costs of implementing new software can be divided into implementation costs and operating costs. Figure 1.2 highlights these two areas as they impact a new implementation.

The first major implementation cost to be considered is client licensing. As with most ERP solutions, discounts for sales partners are available for SAP Business One.

 NOTE

It's important to note that the adjustment costs for the initial implementation can easily increase by a factor of 1.5-2 in comparison with the initial software license costs. That said, medium-sized enterprises often implement SAP Business One in stages. In cases where cost adjustment becomes an issue, a power user can be trained to do the larger process operations. To facilitate this type of rollout, SAP offers various SAP Business One courses, with SAP consultant certification available.

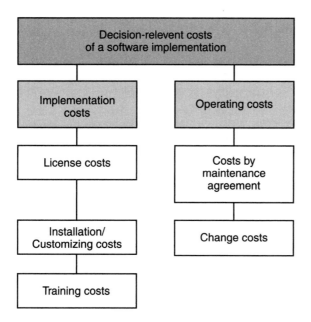

FIGURE 1.2 *Decision-making costs of a new implementation* (Source: Clasen, 2003)

Other implementation considerations include the following:

◆ For the typical user workstation, a Pentium III (or higher) PC with at least 256MB RAM is required.

◆ The architecture of SAP Business One is based on a typical client-server concept. A license key is generated for each client workstation.

◆ As noted previously, with the Less is More approach, initial implementation also includes individual client configuration so that only required forms/specified fields are imported.

◆ Another critical aspect of implementation is, of course, support. Usually, support is contained within the tier 1/first-level support; however, as part of the initial installation, so-called Hot Packages are provided that allow for site-specific customization and error correction.

NOTE

All of the items in this list are potential cost considerations, based primarily on how they affect system performance or the ability of the user to interact with the system to the highest degree possible. For example, in the second bulleted item, an initial system rollout design may call for licensing 50 users; however, in practice, it is found that only having 50 license keys is not sufficient, as there are (for example) 75 users who need access to the system. Clearly, then, this becomes a cost-implementation issue, as funds must be allocated to purchase the additional 25 licenses. Put simply, all of the issues listed here can have a potential cost component if—because of system performance and/or user interaction—they must be upgraded, extended, developed, and so on.

Return on investment (ROI) is, of course, the most critical initial implementation cost concern. Generally speaking, SAP Business One installations must (and do) adhere to the following requirements for ROI eligibility:

♦ Customization/add-on programming available via an SDK.

♦ Scalability via integration with other products, especially Web-based solutions.

♦ Adherence to open standards (for example, XML).

NOTE

ROI eligibility is defined here as meaning that the solution is built to conform to specific standards (the standards being the three items listed here), such that accurate and positive ROI benefits are possible, assuming a proper initial installation.

Specific adjustments (that is, adjustments that "fine-tune" the application) can be made to SAP Business One during the ongoing operational phase.

Position of SAP Business One in the SAP World

As part of its focus on small and mid-sized customers, SAP has developed industry-specific solutions under the name All in One. In the past, these solutions were known separately by the names Ready to Work and Ready to Run.

The SMB solutions are based on the larger mySAP (R/3). The advantages of SMB solutions when compared to the larger R/3 product are that, for the small and middle size enterprises, the full R/3 solution was often oversized (on all levels, from cost to implementation complexity) with the business requirements of the customer. SAP Business One provides an attractive answer to this problem (again, on all levels) without sacrificing the functional requirements of the customer, again illustrating the Less is More philosophy behind the product. Figure 1.3 illustrates the overall position of SAP Business One in regard to SAP.

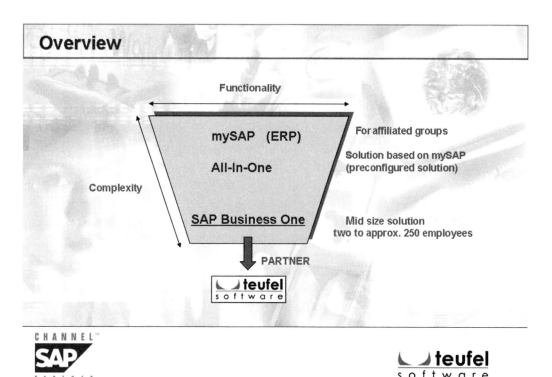

FIGURE 1.3 *Positioning of SAP products relative to SAP Business One*

Another key differentiator of SAP Business One is that it is programmed differently from past SAP products. SAP Business One uses C++, not the proprietary ABAP language of R/3. Therefore, customer extensions (for example, add-ons developed through the SDK) are not carried out in the standard source code but through pre-defined interfaces via the component object model (COM) objects. At this time, the SAP implementation partner has 52 COM objects available. All of these can be modified and/or refined with the data record structures (DATA-API). If add-on functionality is used in conjunction with SAP Business One, the COM objects remain unaffected with a new product release, as they are based on object interfaces.

 NOTE

Do not underestimate the focus on COM functionality. If modifications to SAP Business One are necessary, you don't need to find a R/3 specialist with detailed ABAP expertise to make them—a C++ programmer can do the job. Given the large pool of C++ programmers (that is, any college computer science major!) that exists, it is easy to see how ongoing support costs associated with program modifications can be significantly easier to absorb with a SAP Business One solution as compared to a more complex, ABAP-proprietary R/3 implementation.

We should mention a couple of additional considerations concerning the structural programming differences between R/3 and SAP Business One. The overall, ongoing support cost for an R/3 solution has been difficult to measure, because each customer represents a unique installation, and modifications will be required. That said, it has proven difficult to obtain a truly accurate cost for a SAP R/3 All-in-One solution. While some SAP partners offer fixed prices, the consultation fees (for example, for ABAP modifications) present a large and potentially costly contingency during implementation planning.

Ongoing support and implementation are issues that businesses of all sizes must keep in mind when considering an ERP-based solution. Certainly, it is risky to implement such a solution without a trusted partner. As this chapter has shown, there are significant implementation and ongoing support costs to consider with these types of software solutions. Small and mid-sized business are traditionally more vulnerable to the risks of an ineffective ERP solution because of their more limited resources.

The SAP brand has become an industry-wide accepted seal of security. The real difference between SAP and other, larger software companies is that SAP focuses on business processes first and technology next, rather than on the technology alone. Given the business processes that must be facilitated and—ideally— enhanced by an ERP solution, SAP has earned its reputation as a software vendor that has the operational components of business as its primary focus. With SAP Business One, that focus has been extended to the small and mid-sized customer.

Technology of SAP Business One

The technology behind SAP Business One further illustrates the Less is More concept, as it neatly integrates with technologies that the typical end user is already familiar with. Moreover, the larger operational structure of the product utilizes proven technology processes. Figure 1.4 diagrams SAP Business One's general technology structure.

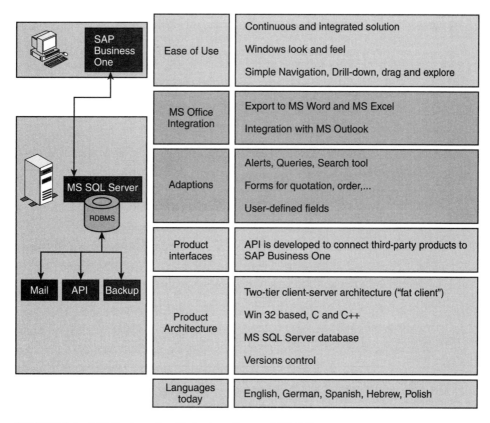

FIGURE 1.4 *SAP Business One Technology (Source: SAP AG).*

The advantages offered by the SAP Business One technology structure include the following:

- Integration
- Openness
- An intuitive user interface (MS Windows)
- The capability to export to MS Word and Excel
- Expandability (industry-standard development)
- Multinational functions (country-specific accounting systems)
- Multilingualism (it's available in more than eight languages)
- Migration ability/scalability (growth path to mySAP R/3)
- Connection to mySAP applications via XI

SAP Business One integrates easily and extensively with Microsoft Office. As mentioned earlier in this chapter, this greatly facilitates the training of those users who need to use SAP Business One.

Moreover, typical client/server technology provides SAP Business One with an appropriate and stable load sharing of system resources. SAP Business One is a "fat client" application, meaning the business logic runs on the user's workstation PC. The entire application is installed on the object bridge server, which in turn can be accessed from other applications.

Also, SAP Business One—as of this writing—only uses the Microsoft SQL Server enterprise database product; an automatic administration version of SQL Server is utilized to aid the consistency of the client/server application. SAP Business One supports an automatic upgrade process in which the new client software is loaded by the server database. Moreover, backup services provide necessary data security. The database offers protection from data loss and unauthorized access. SAP Business One provides a comprehensive user authorization concept, so that users can be assigned specific data access to different areas of the system (for example, the buyer cannot access audit transactions).

 TIP

This "user synchronization" aspect of SAP Business One should not be understated. All users can concurrently access the system and receive the most complete and up-to-date information as it is stored within the application.

NOTE

E-mail services and the license administration also run on the server side of SAP Business One.

SAP Business One supports an open architecture. Each voucher statistic can be exported into Microsoft Word and/or Excel, for example, when a sales employee would like to download his price list from SAP Business One into Excel for further calculation. This flexibility is ideal for the typical SAP Business One customer and further demonstrates the focus on interoperability with programs (especially the MS Office suite) with which most users are comfortable.

Finally, the use of a relational database (SQL Server) with SAP Business One allows for a tremendous variety of possible reports. In conjunction with the Drag and Relate technology described earlier, report generation is made much easier, too. Information from other process areas within the application can be easily obtained and manipulated according to standard customized reports. A query assistant supports the user with the generation of his or her own customized reports. Also, standard Application Programming Interfaces (APIs) provide integration with internal and external data sources, such as handheld PDAs and mobile phones.

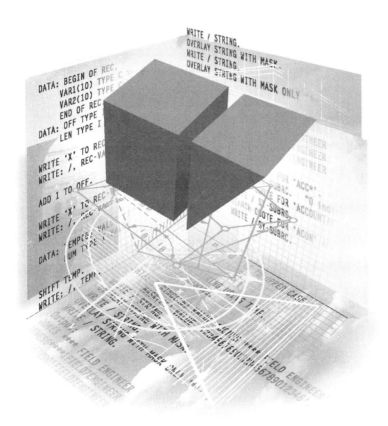

Chapter 2

Overview of SAP Business One

S AP Business One delivers an integrated software solution for the small- to mid-sized enterprise and is equipped with all the functionality necessary to address the majority of business-process requirements of the mid-sized enterprise—the software contains all the required functionality, including purchase, sales, integration of business partners, inventory, production and accounting.

This chapter will provide a brief overview of Business One functionality, including a preview of the user interface.

The Business One Interface

When a user logs in to Business One, he is presented with a menu bar listing his areas of access. Figure 2.1 shows the Business One interface.

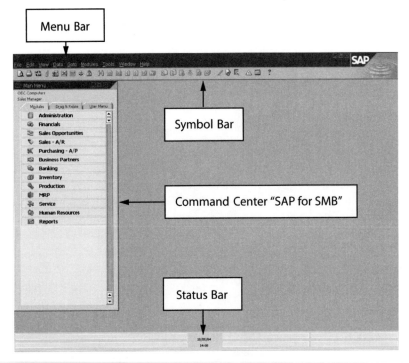

FIGURE 2.1 *Elements of the SAP Business One Interface*

Each application in the system can be accessed through the menu. As the user selects the specific applications described in this chapter, the menu bar presents additional functionality specific to the program's operation.

The Business One system is subdivided into 13 modules; these, along with their most important functions, are described in the following sections.

TIP

You can quickly activate individual applications and functions from the user-specific menu area; this eliminates frustrating (and time-consuming) searching through the menu structure. You can also find general information (like error messages and information about all input fields) in the status bar; for example, if the cursor is positioned over a specific field, information specific to that field is indicated at the bottom left-hand corner of the status bar.

The Administration Module

The Administration module contains all of the basic configuration settings of the system, including currency conversion, system initialization, definitions, data import/export, utilities, approval procedures, license add-ons, and alert management functions. In this module, the general company data is stored and access to information from other vendor's software systems is possible.

SAP Business One allows you to administer several instances of different companies. You can switch between the individual companies in the system by using the Choose Company function and maintain business transactions separately for each company. The Choose Company window (see Figure 2.2) is used to select the company that you want to view or for which you want to create or update data.

Administration
Choose Company
Define Foreign Currency Exchange Rates
System Initialization
Definitions
Data Import/Export
Utilities
Approval Procedures
License
Add-Ons
Alerts Management

FIGURE 2.2 *The SAP Business One Main Navigation Area (Administration)*

An essential component of the Administration module is the system initialization, which must be executed after a new company is defined in the system. The most important functions of the system initialization are:

- Company details
- General settings
- Authorizations
- Document settings and numbering
- Opening balances
- Print preferences

NOTE

Think of system initialization as the critical first step when preparing to administer a new company in SAP Business One. The functions listed here provide the application with basic operational parameters, and will in turn influence nearly every functional aspect of the application, including (of course) how information is stored, manipulated, and accessed. Although SAP Business One functions can operate without certain settings being defined, you should take the time to perform a complete system initialization in order to more efficiently use the application.

CAUTION

The system initialization functions should be configured only for user defined companies. Each company that is defined in Business One must be initialized separately.

The Financial/Cost Accounting Module

The Financial module enables the user to perform all the accounting transactions typically generated by the daily activities of a company, including making journal entries, reconciling tax issues, and generating all the reports required for users at different levels within the company.

SAP Business One provides a variety of tools for easily performing your company's required financial activities. SAP Business One's Financial module includes:

- A Chart of Accounts and Edit Chart of Accounts
- Journal Entry and Journal Voucher Exchange Rate Differences and Conversion Differences
- A Budget function
- Cost Accounting

The Chart of Accounts is an index of all General Ledger (G/L) accounts that are used by one or more companies. A chart of accounts must be assigned to every company. This chart of accounts becomes essential after carrying postings for these companies in daily business. For every G/L account, there is an account code, an account description, and information that determines the functions of the G/L account. The Chart of Accounts in SAP Business One has a tree structure with five levels that differentiates between an active account and a title (see Figure 2.3).

All vouchers produced in an company must be booked in one of the accounts defined in the chart of accounts. If this is not handled carefully, errors can occur. You can avoid such errors with the option in Business One that allows you to place a journal voucher in a draft state so that it creates no values in the general ledger. Then, the journal voucher can be checked and completed, and then recorded.

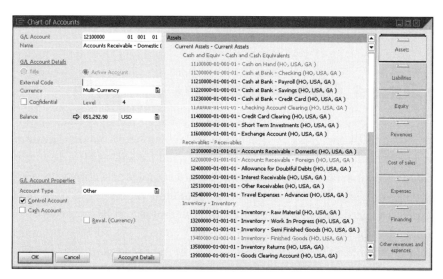

FIGURE 2.3 *Example of an SAP Business One Chart of Accounts*

Every business has transactions that recur monthly or weekly. For example, personnel accounts are paid by the bank every month. For such recurring transaction procedures, SAP Business One includes the Standing Instructions function. You can use the Standing Instructions function to indicate how Business One should handle individual recurring transactions and also to handle them automatically. When you have different reports in the Financials module, the bookings you've created can be accurately checked and recorded.

The Budget function is used to track company expenses, and it allows the blocking of transactions when the budget is exceeded. The Budget function is defined by setting maximum limits on specific accounts. During daily work, the system will check the accounts against budget limit information and, depending on the settings chosen, will either sound an alert on accounts that have been exceeded or will block the posting of transactions.

In addition to conventional financial accounting (wherein the values of all business transactions are recorded), many companies also perform cost accounting. The aim of cost accounting is to determine how profitable a company's business activities are. Cost accounting allows you to define the profit center and distribution rules, which offer important information about costs and revenues and are sorted by area and department. Some expenses and revenues can be assigned to one specific business area or activity; such expenses and revenues are called *direct costs* and *direct revenues*. In cost accounting, indirect costs like administration, advertising, and financial costs (and indirect revenues) are allocated to business activities by means of distribution keys.

The Sales Opportunities Module

The Sales Opportunities module is used to track and analyze sales opportunities according to the progress of sales activities. A number of reports, from different business operational viewpoints, can be generated for analysis. These activities can include meetings and negotiations, or other activities, as defined by the user, in the sales pipeline. You can enter the total amount expected if a particular sale is completed successfully, so that the earning potential can be estimated. A closing percentage for each sales stage can also be entered. The forecasting system uses comprehensive and complex methods for projecting the earning potential and prioritizing the sales activities.

To process a sales opportunity, choose Business Partners and Sales Opportunity from the main menu. You can use the Sales Opportunity window to add, update, delete, and close Sales Opportunities. The system opens the Sales Opportunity window in Add mode. The general data for a sales opportunity is displayed in the upper part of the window. Several tabs containing detailed information are displayed in the middle part of the screen. The lower part of the screen contains the sales opportunity table, in which you enter the sales pipelines for the specific sales activity.

Sales Opportunities reports are used for analysis of sales opportunities. Reports can be based on all parameters or can be filtered according to certain parameters. Choosing a parameter often opens one or more windows, from which different options can be selected. Certain reports can be displayed in graph or table formats.

You can open Sales Opportunities reports by selecting Sales Opportunities, Sales Opportunities Reports from the Reports module. Different options can be selected in each of the Details windows (see Figure 2.4). These windows are selected by the choosing the Details icon in each of the report windows.

FIGURE 2.4 *Order of the Sales Receipts in the Main Navigation Area*

The Sales—A/R Module

The Sales—A/R module covers the entire sales process, from creating quotes for customers and potential customers to invoicing. Business One provides the user with a wide variety of sales documents; each document refers to a different stage in the sales process.

The Sales—A/R module provides several different options, including Sales Quote, Sales Order, Delivery, Returns, A/R Invoice, Dunning Wizard, and Sales Reports. All of these functions can be originated with reference to a preceding document.

The different sales documents and their functions are potentially unique (in how they can be configured, the data/system areas they draw from, and so on) depending on which area of the application you are working within. All of the sales documents can be customized for the user's special requirements. As these options are supported only in the generic print templates of A/R Invoice and Sales Quotation, in order to have them printed in the other sales documents, the Print Layout Designer must be used.

Different sales documents present different functional views of the data as stored within the application.

- **Sales Quote.** The Sales Quote, as it is displayed in Business One, is not a legally binding document. It is generally used for informational purposes only, and can be the first link in the sales process chain. Entering a quotation does not result in any postings that alter quantities or values in inventory management or accounting.

- **Sales Order.** Whether the Sales Order is a legally binding document or not depends on your line of business. For example, your company might not manufacture products or ship items before an order has been created. When you enter orders, no value-related changes are posted in accounting. If the order calls for specific items, then the order quantities are listed in Inventory Management as reserved for the customer. You can view the ordered quantities in various reports, such as the Inventory Status. This information is also available for viewing in other areas of the application. This information is important for optimizing ordering transactions and stockholding.

- **Delivery.** The Delivery Note is a legally binding document. Without a Delivery Note, goods can only be delivered if an invoice has already been created. When you enter a Delivery Note, the corresponding goods issue is also posted. The goods leave the warehouse and the relevant stock changes are posted. When the stock is changed, the values in accounting also change—this is a continuous stock system.

- **Returns.** When you enter Returns, you can reverse the posting of a delivery. When you create Returns, the stock quantities are corrected.

If your company runs a continuous stock system, then creating a return automatically generates a journal entry that updates the stock value. The Return is the clearing document for a delivery; therefore, if an A/R invoice has not yet been created for the delivery you want to reverse, you would use the Returns document.

◆ **A/R Invoice**. The A/R Invoice is a legally binding document. When the A/R Invoice is received, the postings are made to the related customer account in accounting. If a Delivery Note did not precede the A/R Invoice and you are selling items that are in stock, the stocks are also corrected accordingly when the A/R Invoice is issued. When you must create both a Delivery Note and an A/R Invoice for a sales process, you must enter the Delivery Note first and then the A/R Invoice. In this case, however, it is probably sufficient just to create the A/R Invoice, as that's all that is required for the delivery.

NOTE

If the goods were delivered to the customer and an A/R Invoice has already been created, you can partially or completely reverse the transaction by entering a credit memo. In addition, the Dunning Wizard enables you to create and send reminders to customers who have not paid their open invoices within a given time range.

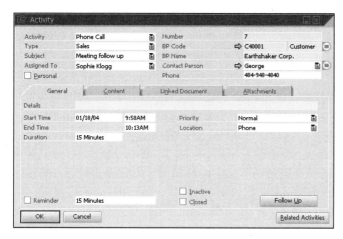

FIGURE 2.5 *Example of Return Receipts in SAP Business One*

Purchasing—A/P Module

The Purchasing module allows you to control the entire purchasing process, from negotiations with vendors and purchase requisitions to delivery of the ordered goods and incoming invoice processing.

If a purchasing transaction—such as a purchase order or an incoming invoice— is entered in the system, it is generally referred to as a *purchasing document*. The following are some of the purchasing documents that SAP Business One supports:

- ◆ **Purchase Order.** When a purchase order is entered, no value-based changes are posted in accounting. The order quantities are, however, listed in inventory management. You can view the ordered quantities in various reports and windows, such as the inventory status report and the item master data window.

- ◆ **Receiving PO.** Receiving documents should be created as soon as the enterprise receives goods from the vendor. When a Receiving PO is entered, the goods are accepted into the warehouse and the quantities are updated. For a company that runs a continuous stock system, SAP Business One creates the relevant postings to update the stock values as well.

- ◆ **A/P Invoice.** When an incoming invoice is received, the related accounts for the vendor are posted in accounting. If a delivery for a purchase order has not preceded the incoming invoice in the system and if you are purchasing items managed in the warehouse, the stocks are also increased when the invoice is posted. If inventory is active and incoming invoices are updated without a previous receiving, then a message is sent when a posting is made indicating that no goods have been received.

The data for purchasing documents that is stored in the system must be identical to the data in the documents that you receive from the vendor. Accounting data must be exactly the same as that in the vendor's invoice. If there is a difference between the data in your system and the data in the vendor document, these differences must be clarified with the vendor. This may be the case if a vendor invoices you for an amount other than the one entered in the purchase order (for example, to account for additional shipping charges that weren't anticipated in the original PO). The details in the vendor's document are legally binding.

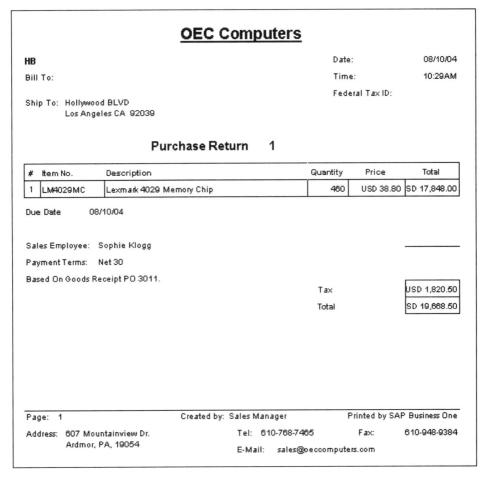

FIGURE 2.6 *Example of a Goods Return Document in SAP Business One*

 NOTE

Additional business transactions can be managed using the other purchasing documents, Goods Return and Credit Memo. The Goods Return document is the clearing document for a Receiving PO. When a Goods Return is entered, the goods are issued from the warehouse and the quantities are reduced. If a company runs a continuous stock system, SAP Business One creates the relevant postings to update the stock values as well. The A/P Credit Memo is the clearing document for the incoming invoice. If the vendor has delivered the goods and has already entered an A/P Invoice, the transaction can be reversed either partially or completely by entering a Credit Memo.

The Business Partners Module

This module allows for the data management of all business partners. It also contains all relevant information about customers and vendors. This information is required for handling business transactions and for preparing business documents.

 NOTE

In SAP Business One, both customers and vendors are referred to as *business partners*. The system does differentiate automatically between a customer and a vendor for the relevant business processes.

Leads, or potential customers, are also viewed as business partners. You can also enter data for these business partners into the system in order to control marketing and sales activities. Sales activities involve contact with interested parties in the form of discussions and meetings; such contacts can be entered in to the system. You can also enter sales opportunities involving potential customers in order to evaluate the overall sales pipeline.

Information specific to a business partner and recorded within the system is called *master data*. The following types of information represent master data:

- Company name, addresses(s), and telephone number(s)
- Contact person's name, telephone number, e-mail address, and so on.
- Payment terms/price list
- Payment system
- Accounting-related data

SAP Business One can automatically analyze master data in view of larger business processes. For example, terms of payment defined for a customer can be used for further calculations (orders) and embedded in the collection papers.

 NOTE

Master records of a potential customer are not required for accounting procedures (no value-changing transactions are entered in the system for potential customers). However, quotations and orders for potential customers can be entered; as these do not result in value-changing postings, they do not affect your accounting procedures.

The Banking Module

The Banking Module facilitates complete financial transactions, including incoming payments, deposits, outgoing payments, payment system, bank statements, and reconciliations. It is currently not possible to carry out a data medium exchange in SAP Business One. For bank transactions, a fundamental differentiation takes place between an incoming payment and an outgoing payment. The Incoming Payment function is used to enter all the payments from your customers and link them with the corresponding invoices you sent out. Conversely, the Outgoing Payment function assigns your outgoing payments to the open invoices that have been received from your vendors. Both incoming and outgoing payments can be made via bank credit transfers, checks, or cash, as well with credit cards.

NOTE

A distinction is made between cash checks and predated checks: Cash checks become predated checks on a current account and become cash checks automatically as soon as the due date is reached.

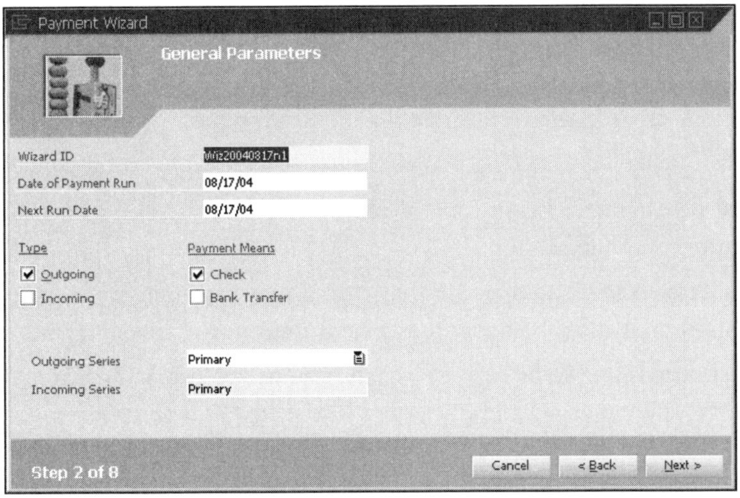

FIGURE 2.7 *The Payment Wizard*

You can define different payment methods, such as check or bank transfer, within the system. You can also select different payment methods for each business partner. During the payment run process, the payment method selected for a business partner affects how the system clears invoices.

The Banking module also contains a Reconciliation option. Bank account data can be entered or imported directly into this module. Credit and debit postings or data can be synchronized with those of your bank.

TIP

The Reconciliation Wizard allows you to perform this synchronization quickly and efficiently. The reconciliation parameters are entered so that the system can search for matching options using a defined algorithm, greatly reducing the time it spends locating matching entries.

The Inventory Module

In the SAP Business One Inventory module, a company can manage all items it purchases, sells, produces, or holds. The Inventory module contains all information about your company's item master data, item management, inventory transactions, price lists, pick/pack, and inventory reports.

In the Inventory module there are three distinct item types:

- ◆ **Purchase item.** A purchase item is one that is procured from a vendor. To be able to purchase an item, it must be defined as such within the Inventory module.
- ◆ **Sales item.** A sales item is one that is sold to a customer. To be able to sell an item, it must be defined as a sales item in the Inventory module.
- ◆ **Warehouse item.** To be able to use an item in inventory management, it must be defined as a warehouse item in the Inventory module.

NOTE

Services can also be defined as an item within the system.

FIGURE 2.8 *Item Master Data*

A further classification of an item in the Inventory module allows for classification of the item as a fixed asset. A fixed asset item is one that is merely used within the enterprise—it is neither sold nor scalable for further production processing. Such items could be, for example, computers or furniture that are meant exclusively for in-house use.

SAP Business One allows for direct data correlation, throughout the system, for all data that directly relates to the item. Such data can range across all system areas, including Purchase, Sales, Production, and so on.

The Production Module

The Production module defines bills of material (BOM) for your products, creates and maintains Production Orders, controls receipts from and issues orders to production, generates production reports, and can update parent item prices globally. In the bill of materials for a finished product, you can specify the various components that make up that product and the appropriate quantities of the components. The information in the BOM can be used for ensuring that the appropriate quantities of the required components are on hand.

A Production Order is a command to produce or repair a production item. The Production Order supports the planning and assembly of a production item, and it also tracks all the material transactions and costs that are involved in the production process.

In some cases, a *finished product* is defined as the end result of an entire production process. In other cases, though, a finished product might simply be a collection of items that are sold as a unit but are not the output of a production or assembly process.

The product structures within the Production module can be differentiated as follows:

- ◆ **Production Bill of Materials (PBOM).** This function is used to define multilevel BOM. Such a structure has a hierarchical arrangement of components. The PBOM represents a finished product made up of different inventory components. During the production process, the components are turned into the finished product. The PBOM is the only type of BOM used in the MRP run and it is always used in standard production orders. Components in the PBOMs can be physical items (such as a screw or a wooden board) or virtual objects (such as one work hour).

- ◆ **Assembly Bill of Materials (ABOM).** In the ABOM, the finished product appears in the Sales Order document (for example, let's say the finished product is a set of garden furniture). You can use the ABOM to define the finished product. The finished product is not stored as an entire set in the warehouse; however, the individual components of the set (such as garden chairs, tables, and umbrellas) are items in stock.

- ◆ **Sales Bill of Materials (SBOM).** The SBOM and the ABOM represent a finished product that is assembled at the Sales stage. The difference between the Assembly BOM and the Sales BOM is that with the Assembly BOM, the finished product appears in the Sales Order document and with the Sales BOM, both the finished product and the components appear as separate items in the Sales Order document.

You can use templates for BOMs to make changes to components when you create a sales document for the finished product. You can update the quantity of a component, swap components, or delete components in the BOM.

FIGURE 2.9 *A Defined BOM (Bill of Material)*

NOTE

If a component is deleted from a BOM, then the components only appear as a list of items in the sales document. In other words, as they were not included in the finished product, the components will not be listed as such on that finished product.

With the Production Order function, you can choose the product from the existing BOM for a standard or disassembly production order, or you can specify the kind of product you plan to produce for a special production order. The product component items that make up the product, the type of the production order, and the production order due date, can be defined in the system as well. The materials required to assemble the product can also be described. The Production Order entry combines the BOM with the manufacturing plan to create a finished product. The Production Order window enables you to keep track of materials, quantity, and cost, as well as product completion in the manufacturing process.

MRP Module

The Material Requirements Planning (MRP) module enables you to plan material requirements in the manufacturing process. MRP calculates gross requirements for the highest BOM level according to sales orders and forecast demands. Furthermore, it estimates gross requirements of the lowest BOM levels according to parent demands. The lowest levels might be required by independent demands, such as sales orders and forecasts.

Running an MRP report gives a company new planned recommendations that fulfill gross requirements through consideration of the existing stock and the existing purchase and production orders. The MRP run also takes into account defined planned rules, such as multiple orders, order intervals, and so on. Finally, new planned recommendations are scheduled backward according to the defined lead-time.

Forecasting can provide an additional source for the MRP run. Sales orders are often received with no or very short notice; while the time to manufacture the product includes the time to order and receive parts, the actual manufacturing process and the assembly time, which all together tends to take a lot longer. Therefore, the product for the forecast is produced when the actual sales orders arrive so that goods can be delivered on a timely basis. Forecasting can be managed on a daily, weekly, or monthly basis.

The Order Recommendation report is used to display the list of all MRP recommendations according to the defined selection criteria. It enables you to see what items must be purchased and what items must be manufactured. In addition, the report runs according to the results of the MRP recommendations. It allows you to automatically create Production and Purchase Orders. Quantities and items can also be changed and recommendations can be deleted.

Important features of the MRP module include a wizard to set up the forecasting process, support for multiple "what-if?" scenarios, and the sales forecasts for predicting demand.

The MRP Wizard guides you through the five-step process of defining new MRP scenarios and analyzing the MRP results. MRP recommendations are presented in an intuitive and user-friendly way, directly on screen or via a printed report. The Wizard allows you to

- Create and maintain MRP scenarios
- Save a MRP scenario
- Update and/or define individual forecasts
- Attach an individual forecast to a specific scenario
- Run MRP

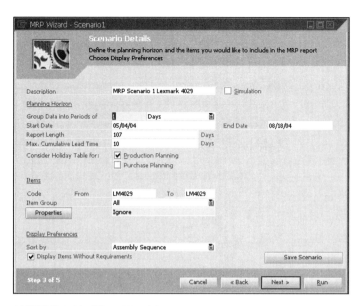

FIGURE 2.10 *The MRP Wizard*

The MRP module enables continuous planning based on re-evaluation of demand and on changing planning parameters (such as lead time determination, make or buy decisions, lot sizing, and so on).

The Service Module

The Service module optimizes the potential of the Sales and Service departments, providing support for service operations, service contract management, service planning, tracking of customer interaction activities, customer support, and management of sales opportunities.

Sub-functions provided by the Service module include the following:

- ◆ **Service Call.** The Service Call feature enables you to resolve customer questions and deal with item-related problems. If the customer does not have a valid contract or warranty for the item, he can purchase a contract, pay for the service call, or terminate the service call. A service call is opened as a result of a complaint or inquiry received by telephone, e-mail, fax, or any other means the company uses. The Service module includes a solution knowledge database that helps solve customers' service problems. Service call expenses can be tracked and all of the transactions created during the service call can be analyzed.

♦ **Customer Equipment Card.** The Customer Equipment Card is the database that contains information on all of the items for which service can be provided. To provide service on an item, details about the item must be entered into a Customer Equipment Card. It is then possible to create a service contract and respond to service calls for the item. Information on the contracts (for example, the item with the serial number and the history of the service calls) can all be easily viewed. All inventory transactions and sales details can also be analyzed.

♦ **Service Contract.** A Service Contract is a formal or legally binding agreement that enables a customer to receive service for items during a specified period of time. The Service Contract contains information specifying the service for which a customer is eligible. SAP Business One supports the following service contract types:

- *Customer.* Covers the service for all the items the customer has purchased from the company, regardless of the group or serial number.

- *Item Group.* Covers the service for the item groups defined in the Service Contract.

- *Serial Number.* Covers the service for the serial numbers defined in the Service Contract.

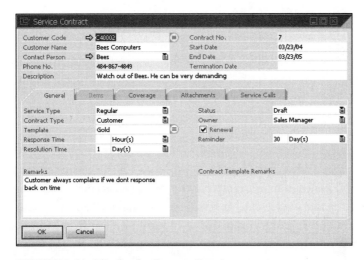

FIGURE 2.11 *The Service Contract Database*

◆ **Knowledge Base Solution.** The Knowledge Base Solution includes key solutions to solve various problems and cases. It helps streamline service, speeds up service representatives' performance, and allows external sources to view questions and solutions regarding the organization's products.

◆ **Service Reports.** Service Reports enable you to view and analyze data related to service contracts, customer equipment, and service calls. Details about service calls made by individual sales representatives and those reported by certain customers can be checked. Efficiency and performance can be also be evaluated using these reports.

The Human Resources Module

The Human Resources module allows you to enter and maintain information on company employees and to perform the following related tasks:

◆ Enter and maintain general and personal employee information, such as age, marital status, passport number, ID number, phone number(s), and home and work addresses.

◆ Manage information regarding customer education, previous job records, results of professional reviews, and days absent.

◆ Analyze employee costs and salaries.

◆ Create various reports and employee lists to (ideally) allow for more efficient business operation.

The Employee Master Data function allows you to enter and display personal and financial information about an employee. In addition, you can track an employee's performance and number of sick or vacation days available, as well as keep a history of the employee's previous employment and education.

The Human Resource reports allow you to retrieve data according to the selection criteria you enter. For example, you can generate reports that show an employee's attendance record in comparison with other employees in the entire organization or in a particular department(s). The contact details for every employee in the company can also be displayed. You can also print phone books, absence reports, and various employee listings.

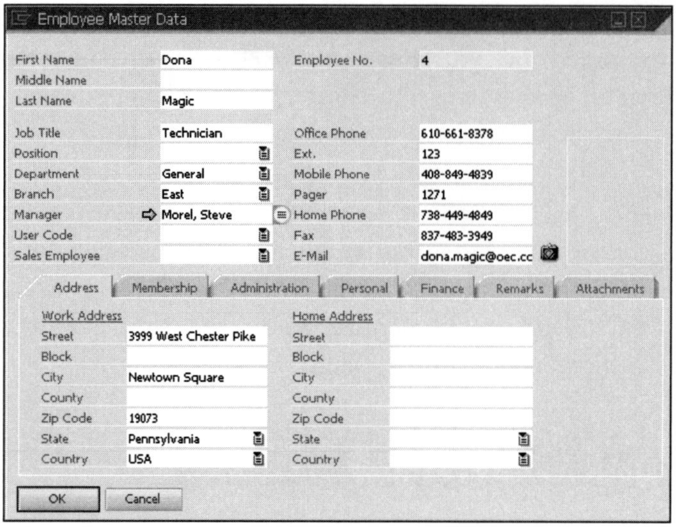

FIGURE 2.12 *Employee Master Data*

The Reports Module

Business One contains an integrated and extensive Report module. It includes a wide variety of reports, such as business reports, accounting reports, warehouse reports, financial reports, and account statements. In short, you can compile reports containing business data in almost any fashion imaginable.

The Report module contains many predefined reports that can be analyzed in various ways by using the selection and sort functions. Simple navigation through a report enables you to quickly access the detailed information it contains. Any number of reports can be easily created to fit individual needs and requirements. To help in creating reports, the module includes a Reports Wizard. This wizard offers step-by-step instructions for defining a query.

It is also possible to export all reports to a Microsoft Excel or Microsoft Word document, which in turn allows access to critical data outside of the system.

Figure 2.13 shows the organization of the Report functions in the main navigation area of Business One.

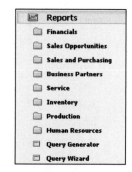

FIGURE 2.13 *Report Navigation*

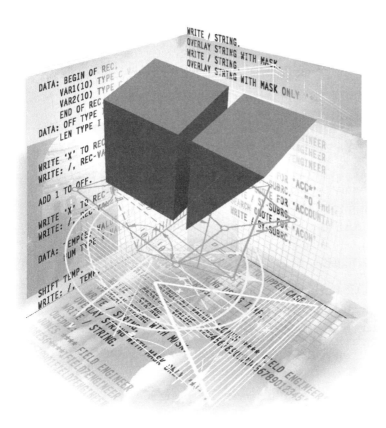

Chapter 3

SAP Business One SDK

A dd-ons are supplementary product lines for SAP Business One that were developed through its own SDK (Software Development Kit), which was first discussed in Chapter 1. SAP Business One can be customized to meet the customer's specific functional requirements with these add-ons. This customization process can be likened to building blocks, as illustrated in Figure 3.1.

Depending on the specific SAP Business One implementation, additional functional solutions may be required. These solutions are often referred to as add-ons, and the advantages they offer are significant.

- By using add-ons, you can achieve a customized SAP Business One solution.
- During the implementation of SAP Business One, using add-ons can result in significant time and cost savings.
- As add-ons are made available to future customers with the same business requirements, the cost of initial development is reduced through repeated sales of the custom add-on. This means that there is a possibility that the additional functionality your company requires has already been achieved by another company—and that an add-on already exists

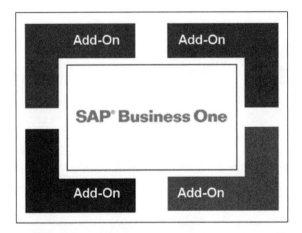

FIGURE 3.1 *Bottom-up Approach with SAP Business One Add-ons*

that can meet your specific business requirements. Thus, you can avoid having to build the add-on from scratch.

◆ As mentioned in Chapter 1, add-on functionality is independent of new releases via the use of the COM object from the Business One SDK (DATA API). You can be sure that the resources you utilize in developing an add-on will continue to pay off in the future, as the add-on will remain compatible with new releases of SAP Business One.

This chapter will review some of the major Business One add-ons in light of their functionality and level of customization in a customer-specific solution environment.

The B1-PPS Add-On

The B1-PPS add-on extends the functionality of the standard Production module in Business One, allowing for the fulfilment of more business production requirements. Specifically, the order of operations can be fixed and managed with non-order-related routings. Forward-scheduled completion dates can be calculated based on production criteria, as determined by placing machines (and machine capacity), shifts, factory calendars and other factors within the B1-PPS.

Target Group for B1-PPS

All enterprises that don't need an oversized PPS (Production Planning System) but still need a simple and easy-to-use PPS in addition to SAP Business One are target groups for B1-PPS.

The B1-PPS add-on is suitable for production companies, which need routing with operations and need to keep a close eye on resource planning. When the add-on is integrated with Microsoft Outlook, a simple graphic planning table becomes available to the workshop leader, once he has assigned the production orders automatically and the B1-PPS determines the completion date of that order.

 TIP

B1-PPS is ideal at facilitating a company's manufacturing processes that are dependent on customer orders.

Work Centers/Machines

Work centers in the B1-PPS add-on can be defined as follows:

- ◆ **Type 1**. Machines and plants
- ◆ **Type 2**. Machines with human operators
- ◆ **Type 3**. Manual work centers

Every work center is assigned to a profit center in the add-on and contains a location key (factory membership). If there are work centers of Types 2 and 3, then there is a connection to HR (Human Resources), according to the details of the personnel number in the work center master data. The determination of a work center's capacity is usually based on the available use time; work centers are therefore assigned to a Factory Calendar, which describes the shift models and decreased-capacity times, such as holidays. The normal available capacity usually differs from the actual (effective) available capacity. In practice, this deviation is the result of employee illness, machinery breakdowns, and so on.

For the calculation of normal capacity and capital requirements, the following formulas are used:

- ◆ *Normal capacity = shift number × shift duration – capacity reductions*
- ◆ *Capacity requirements = (order quantity × job time × setup time) × performance degree*

Using the data in the work center, it is possible to specifically identify which machines or persons shall be used; moreover, specific investigations can be made regarding costs, capacity, and scheduling of operations.

The future capacity requirements in the manufacturing process are determined by assigning work centers to the work plans. The concepts of work center and resource do not always match in production companies: A work center is usually found in a manufacturing facility, while the term resource has a higher-level meaning, which not only includes work centers but also production facilities, processing units as well as other manufacturing tools (such as tankers, storage containers, transport vehicles and others).

Relationship between normal and efficient capacities B1-PPS possesses the same "look and feel" as SAP Business One; it can be found in the Production module

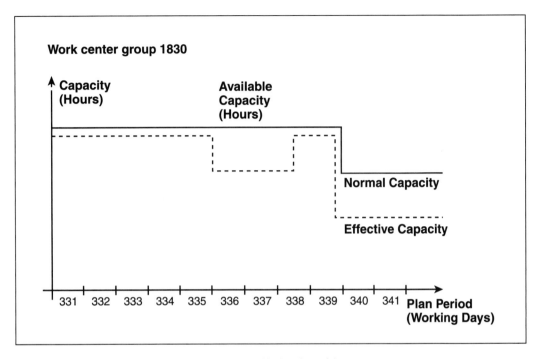

FIGURE 3.2 *Relationship between Normal and Effective Capacities*

navigation menu. The work center master correlates directly to the larger work center data of mySAP, so that integration of the B1-PPS data can take maximum advantage of the data processing/analysis features of the mySAP suite.

The detail data of a work center contains its available capacity. The types available are machine, personnel and pool capacities that are all associated with dates. It must be created before the assignment to the work center and is identified by a key in the work center. The whole capacity need can be divided between different operation steps such as set-up time, working time, tear down time. Certain master data can be entered into the work center for the scheduling of a production order (for example following a control post add-on). The scheduling base specifies which capacity determines the basis for the scheduling. Further formulas can be stored to calculate the execution time. This means the time for each individual process step such as set-up time, working time and tear-down time is calculated via formulas.

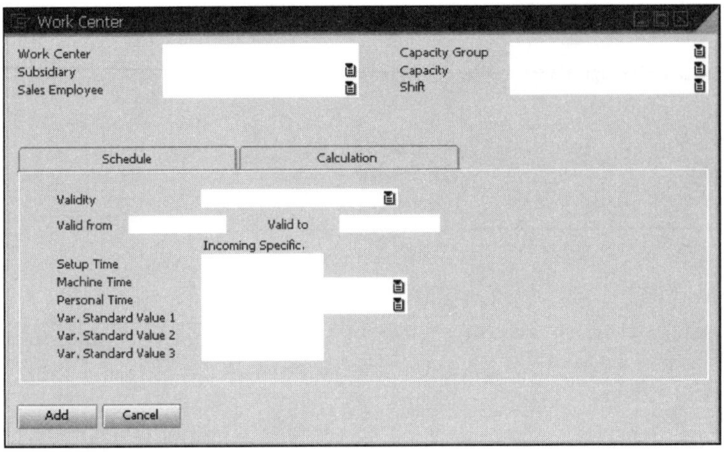

FIGURE 3.3 *Functionality of Work Center*

> ### TIP
>
> You can use the larger SAP Business One HR functions to connect to the functionality of a work center in B1-PPS; you can combine with HR objects like persons, positions, profiles, qualifications, and so on. Another possible option is to connect the work center with the profit center (to also include rendered services). As the work centers themselves are assigned in the routing on an operation level, this connection can determine at which work center-specific operations or sub-operations are executed. The formula for calculating execution time is based on the work center, and takes every operational section (set-up, production, and teardown) into account.

Routing

The routing operation shows the production processes of a product, along with the Production Order and the bill of materials. Features of routing include the following:

- ◆ The ability to view routing status
- ◆ The ability to view the validation time period
- ◆ Alternative routings
- ◆ Associated working times based on the assigned work centers

Operations in the routing process describe the individual steps that are necessary for a product to be manufactured (and can reference how different work centers interface with a specific routing process). The operation number, description, and supplies are tracked for overall operation information.

The routing is "order neutral"—that is, it can be reviewed for different production orders. The tracked times (the duration of the work step execution) in the routing process serve as default values for a later runtime scheduling of a production order. Planned times (default values) are tracked in the routing for the execution of the individual operation.

Routing coordinates all of the individual operations necessary to produce a finished product. You should think of this coordination linearly, so you can decide how the routings are placed. If the operation sequences are fixed, then sub-operations can be included, based on the requirements of the specific step in the routing. For example, sub-operations may be necessary if several machines or employees are used for the same operation.

 NOTE

Sub-operations cannot be individually scheduled.

Sub-operation descriptions are required, whether the sub-operation runs through internal or external processing (in other words, a prolonged workbench). For a sub-operation that requires payment processing, the material components are defined automatically as provision of materials. Note that the overall assignment of production resources and tools (operating resources) requires the existence of production resources and tools master data specific to the operation, in the form of master data in Business One.

Factory Calendars

The Factory Calendar defines working days of an extended time period. Different factory calendars that govern different locations are created as master data. Holidays can, as required, be included specific to the location.

Tracking Shifts

In addition being tracked by the Factory Calendar, company shifts are tracked as a master records in relation to work capacity. Shift models can be constructed based on traditional work weeks (Monday through Friday) or include Saturday and Sunday. The shifts represent a company calendar and can be changed, depending on production utilization (that is, consideration of "special shifts").

Scheduling/Dispatching

B1-PPS allows for forward scheduling, so that the earliest completion date can be determined. If the completion date falls after the promised delivery date, the capacities (hour quota) can be increased—for instance, by providing overtime and/or special shifts. In the dialog with the MRP controller, these capacity mountains (capacity leveling) can be modified accordingly. With this capacity customisation, you can determine a suitable closing date by renewed forward scheduling.

The Planning Table in MS Outlook

The Planning Table is an important aid for the MRP controller and workshop leader. The dispatched production orders are shown graphically in the table. Bottlenecks in production can be more easily recognized in the table's graphical representation.

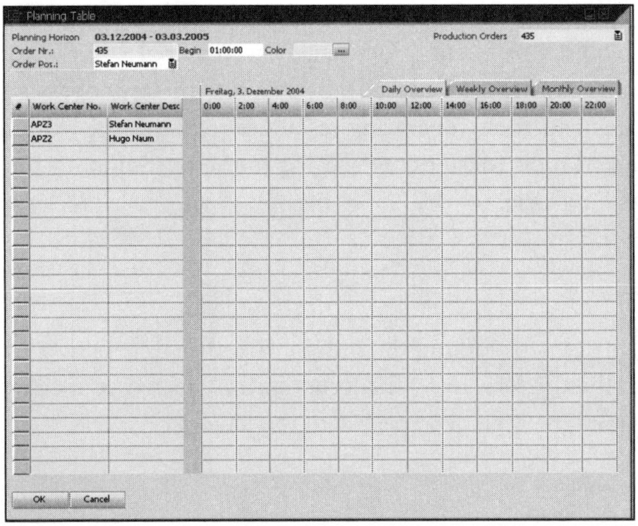

FIGURE 3.4 *A Graphic Planning Table as Viewed in MS Outlook*

Partial Confirmation

The partial confirmation is an important step for the controller, as it allows supervision of in time order completion dates. In SAP Business One, only a final confirmation is available, while the B1-PPS add-on allows for multiple partial confirmations to be added.

The B1-Cash (POS Solution) Add-On

The B1-Cash add-on functions as a complete cash register when used with a PC-based integrated merchandise management system that is also integrated with SAP Business One. The GUI of the Point-Of-Sale (POS) terminal can be adapted and/or extended according to the requirements of the individual user; the appearance and functionality of the cash register can also be customized to specific user needs as well.

The add-on can be installed on a typical desktop PC, a notebook computer, or even a PDA. Data input is possible via mouse, keyboard, touchscreen, or in connection with a bar code reader.

FIGURE 3.5 *B1-Cash with Cash Box and Touchscreen*

Cash Register Functions

With the B-1 Cash add-on software, the cashier has access to a variety of functions. The following shows the available functions for the cashier. Following are both the functions available standard in SAP Business One and the ones added by the B1-Cash Register add-on:

- ◆ Cashier login and logout (B1) + add-on (cashier = sales employee)
- ◆ Cashier settlement (B1-Query) by sales employees
- ◆ Break (B1-Query) by sales employees
- ◆ Multi-cashier system (B1) sales employee
- ◆ Change settlement-interface to the register
- ◆ Cash check (by means of payment)
- ◆ Deposit/proceeds/payment/expenditure (B1)
- ◆ Advance/final payment, paid invoice (B1)
- ◆ General cashier reports (B1)

Registration

The registration is used to tell the system which employee is logged on. An additional function of the registration is the security aspect to restrict access to functions of the cash register from unauthorized users.

- ◆ Seller and customer number
- ◆ Services (studio, repair, service)
- ◆ Coupon sale (coupon management)
- ◆ Register item/items group
- ◆ Multi-box booking
- ◆ Price level, final- and sub-total
- ◆ Quantity/multiplication, item return/exchange, account for VAT
- ◆ Additional item texts

Revenue Detractions

Revenue detractions are often negotiated between business partners as part of their business transactions. These detractions can be directly managed through the B1-Cash add-on. Percentage discounts/variable amounts, as well as staff discounts, are possible.

Corrections and Cancellation Types

If the cash register is to be used on a daily basis, its functions must, of course, be easy to learn and use. Nevertheless, errors can—and will—occur. Therefore, the B1-Cash add-on offers the following cancellation functions:

◆ Immediate cancellation

◆ Lines and voucher cancellation

◆ Sums and discount cancellation

Means of Payment

Every mode of payment can be specifically categorized. In SAP Business One, every known means of payment is available for use via the register. Mixed payment—that is, through more than one method of payment—is also possible. The most frequent and best-known modes of payment are cash, check, credit card, and debit advice transactions. Foreign currencies can also be accepted, which is useful in areas close to international borders.

FIGURE 3.6 *The Operating Area (Touch Screen) of B1-Cash*

Printing with B1-Cash

It is also possible to generate a printout covering selected document numbers (backward-calculated for the whole day) with B1-Cash. Additionally, the document design can be individually adapted to the requirements of the user.

If necessary, the delivery note and invoice print can be integrated.

 TIP

B1-Cash also contains additional features that are often necessary for a complete cash register solution. These features include no sale, value-added tax refund, a training mode, and additional function management processes.

The B1-CTI (Telephone Interface for CRM) Add-On

B1-CTI is the complete telephony solution for Business One. In the typical medium-sized business (or any-sized business, for that matter), contact information is often contained across multiple databases and applications (for example, Business One itself, marketing databases, MS Outlook, and so on). Searching through these multiple locations to find a desired contact can be an exercise in frustration, not to mention needlessly time-consuming. Worse still, such disorganization can make a bad impression on callers—for example, when they are repeatedly asked to update their contact information by different individuals in an organization who are using different contact lists.

The solution for these problems is the BI-CTI add-on. The CTI Connector integrates the Business One software with various contact management systems. The result is optimized contact operations throughout the entire company. Information about an incoming call (company, partner, customer number, and so on) can be directly displayed in SAP Business One. With a few mouse clicks, detailed information about the caller and associated processes within the organization can be quickly and efficiently displayed onscreen. The ideal result is that the caller receives a detailed and personal welcome, and the discussion can quickly move forward, as all necessary details are immediately available.

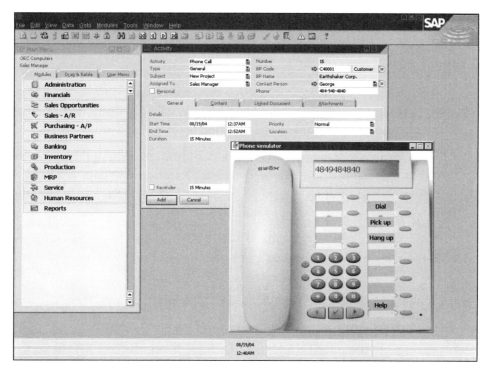

FIGURE 3.7 *B1-CTI (the CRM Telephone Interface to SAP Business One)*

 NOTE

The B1-CTI Add-On is not limited to a certain CTI server, but rather integrates with all TAPI-capable CTI servers or telephones. Call detection is always active, regardless of whether the SAP Business One system is running. Even with outgoing calls, the add-on can determine what number is being called (that is, what customer is being called) and display information specific to that customer.

The B1-CTI add-on can also

♦ List all incoming calls

♦ List all outgoing calls

♦ Display the duration of a telephone call

♦ Differentiate between incoming and outgoing calls.

The B1-Mobile Add-On

With Business One, you can easily mange your new contacts (or leads), your existing customers, and your suppliers. Moreover, the ability to quickly and confidently store this information guarantees that this critical data won't be lost. However, as you can't carry SAP Business One with you, your ability to remain in constant contact with your customers and suppliers is limited.

With the newly developed Mobile-PDA add-on, though, you can carry this critical contact information wherever you go. By porting your data to a PDA, you are freed from the confines of your PC (that is, only having access to customer contact information when you're sitting in your office).

The following sections describe how the B1-Mobile add-on allows for the integration of Business One and a PDA.

PDA Data Input via Keyboard and Character Recognition

Most PDAs allow for input both through special "handwriting" character recognition and via a mini-keyboard. To facilitate input, the B-1 Mobile program has been developed specifically so that Business One can record customers' personal data for later transfer from a PDA back into the Business One suite. After opening the input form, individual fields are chosen with the stylus and the appropriate entries per person are entered. The data is saved on the PDA by selecting the Add Prospective Client field. Following the typical PDA synchronization (that is, placing the PDA on its cradle, which is connected to a PC), information is transferred into Business One.

FIGURE 3.8 *Transferring Data into SAP Business One*

CAUTION

Business One should also be running during the PDA synchronization process, in order to avoid errors in data transmission.

Data transferred into Business One can be accessed in the business partner master data record from the Business Partner application. Once added, appropriate changes to the displayed data (based on new data input) are visible.

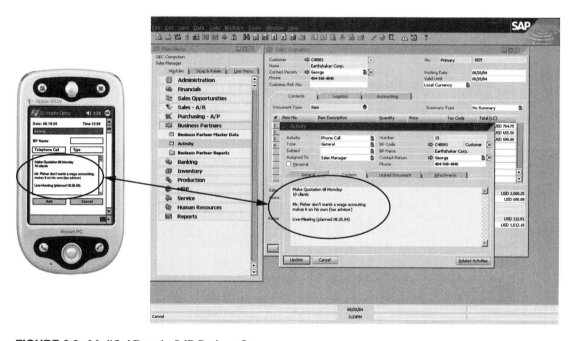

FIGURE 3.9 *Modified Data in SAP Business One*

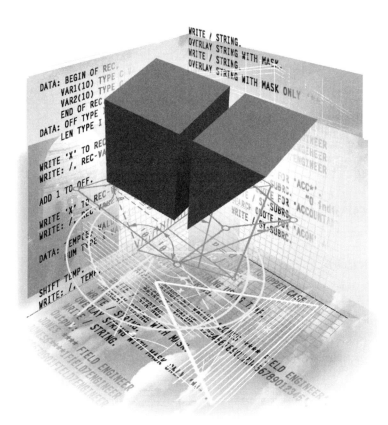

Chapter 4

A strong business process design (BPD) is an essential requirement for a business of any size. It is wrong to assume that a medium-sized enterprise would have simpler processes than a larger organization. The size of the company is not the critical factor in determining the complexity of business process design—the number of divisions, the depth of the organization structure, and the handling of relationships between suppliers and customers, to name just a few, are all major issues to consider when determining the complexity of a company's processes. A small to mid-sized company could, in fact, be more "complex" (at least in terms of the BPD) than a larger company.

Companies that implement qualitative systems like SAP Business One have, as their primary goal, the streamlining of the BPD, with a focus on allowing a greater sense of operational cohesion and thus more organization. As the implementation moves forward, modifications to the original process flow (if there was one) inevitably change, as areas for improvement and areas in which efforts are being duplicated are discovered. It's important to realize that this process of re-evaluating, or "tweaking," the BPD is ongoing—the benefits of business process "reengineering" will be discovered again and again. Indeed, this process of re-evaluation is an attractive (and often initially overlooked) benefit of working with a solution like SAP Business One.

This chapter will briefly explore the concepts of business process design and reengineering, and will include a discussion of value-added chains and trigger process chains.

 NOTE

The relationship between the BPD and SAP Business One is reciprocal—issues impact either one, modifications will be required for each. However, rather than viewing this as a negative, time-consuming, "never-ending" process, you should instead realize that SAP Business One is continuously fine-tuning the BPD (and thus the operational efficiency of the organization).

Renaissance of Business Reengineering

During the 1990s, operational process design was most frequently referred to as *business reengineering*. Research on the topic was carried out extensively in Europe (by Scheer, Oesterle, and Thome) and in the United States (most notably by Michael Hammer in his 1994 book *Reengineering the Corporation: A Manifesto for Business Revolution*).

SAP developed a reference-processing model for the SAP R/3-System in the period between the 1992 and 1997 that was based on the Event-Driven Process Chains (EPC) methodology. The EPC approach was applied for the first time at the Institute of Wirtschaft (see Kellar, Nüttgens, Scheer, *Semantic Process Modelling* 1992).

EPC is extensively applied today; however, it is highly time-consuming, especially for the illustration of business processes for mid-sized companies. As a result of this extensive resource allocation necessary for EPC, the method was further simplified to the Trigger Process Chain (TPC) method. Using TPC, companies can quickly illustrate (or determine) their workflow processes, removing the need for extensive methodological analysis This simplicity makes TPC ideal for mid-sized companies. Figure 4.1 is an illustration of the "renaissance" period of business reengineering, as described above.

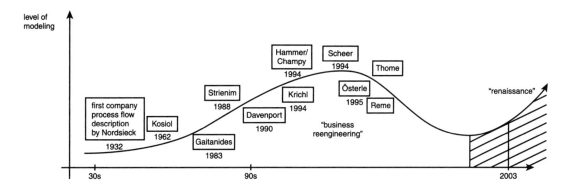

FIGURE 4.1 *The renaissance of business reengineering*

Value-Added Chains

Value-added chains (VACs) have proven to be a critical requirement at the start of an enterprise-modelling project. Simply put, they offer a baseline of understanding of any process modelling to the entrepreneur, the co-worker, and the project manager, all whom have the task of introducing a new data processing system that revolves around the financial component of an organization. The value-added chain diagram of Porter (see Figure 4.2) subdivides the process chain into primary and secondary activities. Further classification of process chains can be carried out in leadership, performance, and support processes (see Österle, _Business Engineering: Process and System Development_ 1995, chap.5.9.1.).

For our discussion (and for simplicity's sake), we'll focus on only the primary areas of responsibility. A value-added chain of the kind discussed in this section is a representational form that contains several process components that should be adapted, depending on various enterprise scenarios. Some value-added chains can be used as "best practice" models after the project reaches completion, and if made available, can save other medium sized business time when dealing with similar situations. Moreover, value-added chains can be understood and analyzed even by those who were not directly involved in their initial introduction.

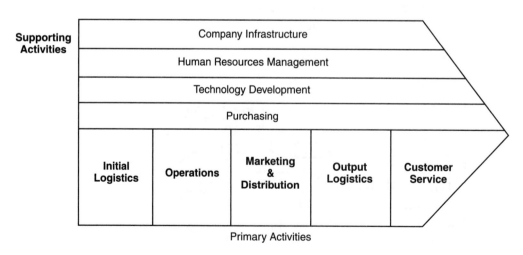

FIGURE 4.2 _Value Chain According to Porter (Porter,_ Wettbewerbsvorteile _1992, S.62)_

Some well-known authors in this arena don't distinguish between business processes and value-added chains—they use the terms interchangeably. Others consider a business process to be a part of the value-added chain that can cross organizational borders like divisions (cf. Davenport/Short 1990, p.12-13).

The following list illustrates the modelling of a business process/value-added chain, with specific emphasis on highlighting common terminology:

1. A *value-added chain* (VAC) is the adaptation of different process components over enterprise process areas, as illustrated in Figure 4.3.

2. An *enterprise process division* (EPD) is an organizational unit of an enterprise. As a project is initiated, the project framework can be defined as the selection of the enterprise process divisions. Note, however, that at this point the individual processes are not yet analyzed in detail.

3. A *process element* (PE) consists of workflow descriptions of one or more functions, and is illustrated in Figure 4.4. The process element can contain triggers (that is, events that access other process elements in a parallel or subsequent fashion). A process describes a business management task that an employee can execute in an uninterrupted workflow. Examples include customer sales order processing, delivery processing, invoice order processing, and the processing of incoming goods.

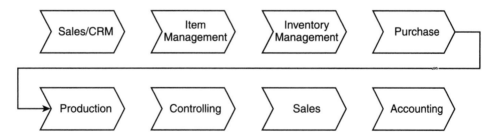

FIGURE 4.3 *Value Chain Example Structure*

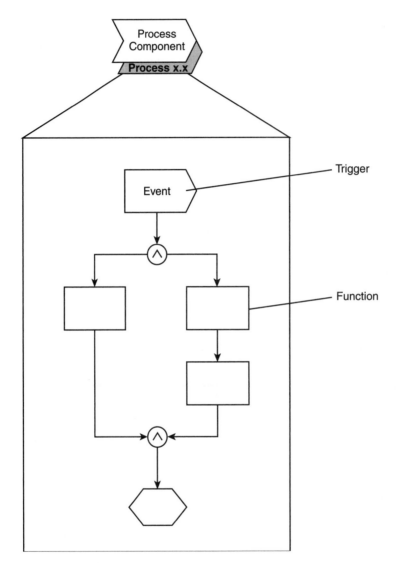

FIGURE 4.4 *Process Component of an Example Structure*

4. The adaptation of individual process elements depends on the characteristics of an enterprise. With this in mind, the *enterprise scenario* now
must be considered. An enterprise scenario is primarily dependent on:

- The branch of an organizational unit
- The category (trade, service, production)

- The processing form (retail without manufacturing, standard order manufacturing, shop production, batch production, series production and so on)

Figure 4.5 illustrates the business scenario.

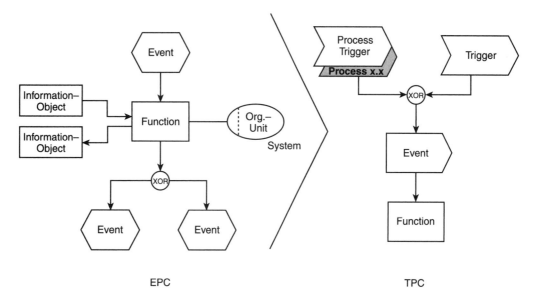

EPC   TPC

FIGURE 4.5 *Business Scenarios*

The Trigger Process Chain (TPC) Method

The trigger process chain method (TPC) is a simplification of the well-known event-driven process chains (EPC). Redundant events are omitted in this method and the entire process flow can be represented more clearly and simply. Events necessary for the process flow are shown as triggers and process-triggers in the process chain.

The TPC method describes the logical operational sequence of tasks (functions) that are activated by trigger events (starting events). Further simplification involves the non-graphical representation of organizational units and entities to their respective function. This operational sequence information is identified as text in the footer line of a function.

A TPC contains the following elements, and is further illustrated in Figure 4.6:

- ◆ **Process triggers.** Triggers within the time-controlled processes, functions, or events.
- ◆ **Triggers.** Functions at the beginning of a time-controlled process.
- ◆ **Functions.** Descriptive operational processes for the events necessary for the process flow.
- ◆ **Organizational unit.** Describes which employee role executes the function in which organizational division.
- ◆ **Entity (data object).** Describes which table is addressed with the execution of the function.
- ◆ **Control line.** Illustrates the temporal-logical operational sequence (line with arrow, which runs down and connects trigger functions with above functions).
- ◆ **Relation.** The relations AND, OR, and XOR can connect functions logically.

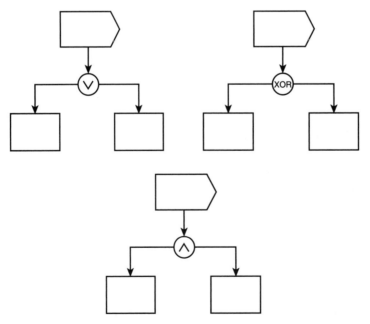

Allowed concatenations in the TPC

FIGURE 4.6 *Simplification of the TPC Basic Structure with the TPC Basic Structure*

When using TPC during initial process design, events are linked using different types of connectors. For example, a function can follow another function or an event without the need for a logic element. A connection element is only necessary to connect process components between levels. The operators OR, AND, and XOR are used with the TPC.

OR, AND, and XOR operators provide all possible combinations of connection types between elements. The only difference is in regard to whether a element is a distributor (one incoming and several outgoing control lines) or a collector (several incoming and one outgoing line). A connection of several incoming to several outgoing lines isn't permitted.

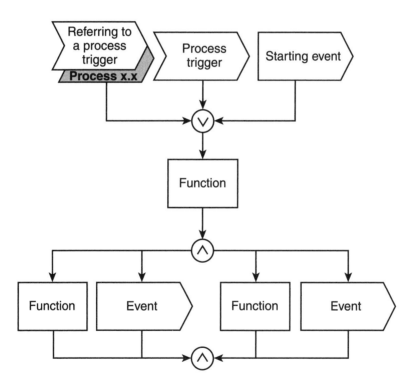

FIGURE 4.7 *TPC Connectivity Possibilities*

The biggest difference between the TPC and EPC methods concerns the starting event. With the TPC method, the starting event is a process trigger and corresponds to a preceding process component. With the EPC method, events are defined within the process and do not necessarily correspond to the processes of the higher level. All proven process components in the value-added chain are trigger events in the TPC representation. Therefore, the forbidden connections of the EPC method are permitted within the TPC method, as the starting events have a separate meaning and reflect the process component.

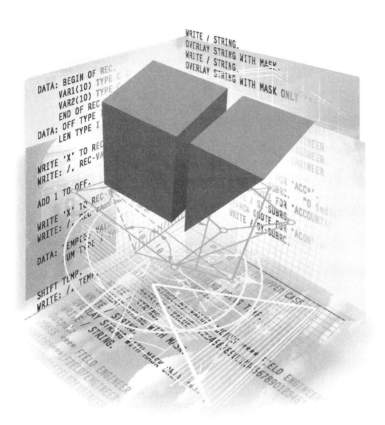

Chapter 5

**Model Company A:
Sales of Capital
Goods**

The model company described in this chapter is a marketing-based company without its own production plant. The model company, Carwash Marketing, sells car washes in Europe for exclusive distribution at gas stations and independent dealers. The products are assembled, packed, and delivered exclusively in Germany by a second model company, Carwash Assemblers. The assembly company receives an order from the marketing company and triggers the actual production. Carwash Marketing works with sales BOM and production BOM, as there are different product models available. The customers are primarily individually owned gas stations and larger companies; however, additional customers include rental-car companies and even new-car dealers who wish to have an onsite washing facility. When there is a need to order individual or "spare" parts, the marketing company can refer directly to the manufacturers of the components without directly consulting Carwash Assemblers.

The structure of Carwash Marketing is as follows: The corporation management, represented by Mr. Carter, is responsible for directing the activity of the marketing, sales, purchasing, and accounting areas. However, the processes that will be described here primarily concern the employees in the Sales, Purchasing, and Accounting departments. Per SAP Business One authorization concepts, assignments are made on an individual basis, allowing employees to work independently (the exception is where higher-level process management decisions are concerned). (See Figure 5.1)

The primary activity of Sales is the successful marketing (and selling) of the car wash units. The Washing Bay product is a portable "washing box" in which one vehicle can be washed at a time (see Figure 5.2). It contains covered steel racks that move forward and backward alongside the vehicle. The brushes used in the product are moveable so that they can adapt to an individual vehicle's form. These car washes are assembled in different areas and are delivered directly to the respective customer by Carwash Assemblers.

Employee List

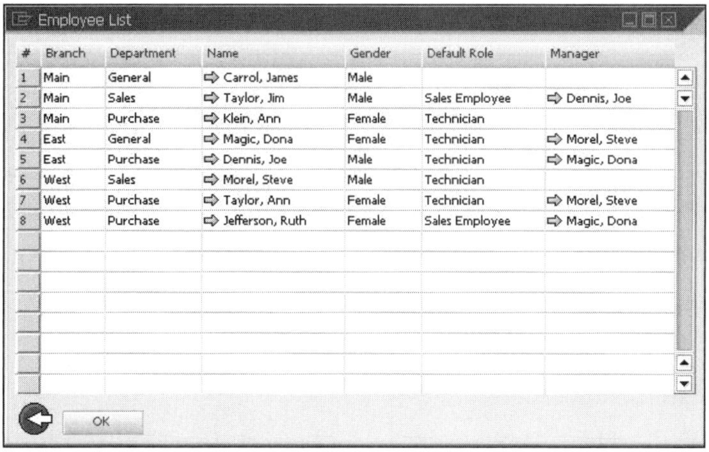

#	Branch	Department	Name	Gender	Default Role	Manager
1	Main	General	Carrol, James	Male		
2	Main	Sales	Taylor, Jim	Male	Sales Employee	Dennis, Joe
3	Main	Purchase	Klein, Ann	Female	Technician	
4	East	General	Magic, Dona	Female	Technician	Morel, Steve
5	East	Purchase	Dennis, Joe	Male	Technician	Magic, Dona
6	West	Sales	Morel, Steve	Male	Technician	
7	West	Purchase	Taylor, Ann	Female	Technician	Morel, Steve
8	West	Purchase	Jefferson, Ruth	Female	Sales Employee	Magic, Dona

OK

FIGURE 5.1 *Carwash Marketing employee list*

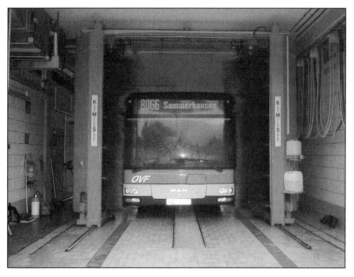

FIGURE 5.2 *The Washing Bay product*

NOTE

In cases where the customer cannot immediately accept delivery, Carwash Assemblers maintains a temporary storage location (this location also houses spare parts and other individual components).

The main components of the product include the following):

- ◆ Steel framework with hot-dip galvanizers
- ◆ Two side brushes and one roof brush
- ◆ Two wheel scrubbers
- ◆ Drying unit (fan)
- ◆ Rails
- ◆ Control desk
- ◆ Various optional components (such as entry/exit signals, underbody wash device, payment gates, or card-scanning terminals)

Sales of the drive-through car washes are completed in much the same fashion except that once Carwash Assemblers builds the drive-through carwashes, it dismantles the washes for more efficient transport to the customer location. Other than requiring disassembly for transport and some unique component parts, the drive-through carwashes are sold and delivered in much the same manner as the Washing Bays are.

If additional marketing companies (especially those abroad) are to be brought online in the future, SAP Business One can offer several possibilities for integration of these companies into the larger system. For example, the system offers rich CRM functionality to allow for more effective marketing. In addition, every sales employee can record his activities within the system, allowing for more efficient forecasting (and ideally, more efficient production). (See Figure 5.3.)

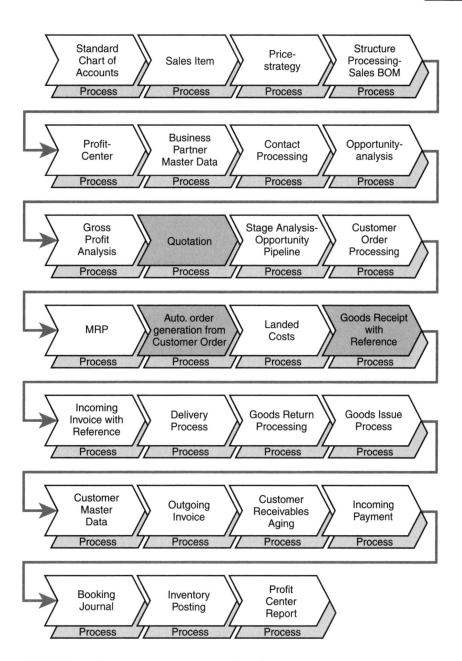

FIGURE 5.3 *Carwash Marketing Process Flow Chart*

The Sales Process

In accordance with a larger "pyramid description" of the sales process, an item is assigned in a systematic arrangement to a material group. Usually this is done by placing the product in question into a larger material group, such as clothing, foodstuffs, metal goods, and so on.

Business Description

There can be similarities in how products are organized. Everyday items are often labeled as *material*; however, the economic definition usually provides the differentiation. For example, beer might be classified as a foodstuff (beverage). Among beers are a variety of types, such as ale, lager, porter, and stout. Each type of beer can then be subdivided among the various brewery labels such as Brand A, Brand B, Brand C and so on. Each brand can then be subdivided further based on packaging options: bottles, cans, cartons, and so on. At this point, the beer is defined in the most exact commercial manner. How an item is defined is based on the production process flow or on the service-rendered process for service-based industries.

SAP Business One: Specific Description

The core information in SAP Business One is the material master data. Without it, no illustration of the sales process can be made because this data represents all information that is purchased, stored, and manufactured (and finally sold) by the enterprise. For example, quantity units, catalogue numbers, price lists, and so on are stored as master data. In connection with this, the allocation of the price list represents very important information in the material master collection.

In the context of the larger sales viewpoint, the following questions often arise:

- Are item numbers to be generated automatically by the program or manually allocated?
- Do you assign your items with fixed catalog numbers?
- Do they work with EAN codes and/or bar codes?
- Is there a preference for items from certain brands?
- For which items are you responsible?

Process Application

In order to create a sales item, you must first select the Inventory module from the menu. The Item Master Data function must be selected in order to enter an item, as doing so opens a new window. You cannot create an item right away because the function is in Search mode, identified by the gray FIND in the Symbol menu. Activate the Add mode symbol, located next to the Find symbol, in the Symbol menu. Now you can create a sales item.

In the yellow field, you must first enter the item number. This can be adapted completely to your enterprise defaults. If your items have an EAN code, enter it in the intended field. Next, enter the description and source of the item (you can later select a suitable price list for your item). Following these steps is necessary to specify the regulation markings for the kind of item; therefore, you must set the appropriate indicator for the sales item. These are in the active window on the top right. You can also set further indicators, such as Purchased Item, Inventory Item, or Fixed Asset as your default values.

In the bottom area on the screen are the fields for the detailed definition of the item. In the Sales Data field, you can specify the dimensions of the item. Define the volume and weight and enter the unit of measurement and the item quantity per sales unit. When you click the Add button, the item will be created in the system.

Navigation Information

- ◆ **Menu Path:** Inventory > Item Master Data.
- ◆ **Tables:** AITM, AIT1, CUMI, OITG, OITM.
- ◆ **Incoming Trigger:** This includes the decision-making processes regarding the admission of a new item into the product portfolio, the creation of market products by catalog numbers, and so on.
- ◆ **Outgoing Trigger:** This includes the price strategy, purchase item, fixed assets, inventory items, and sales item.

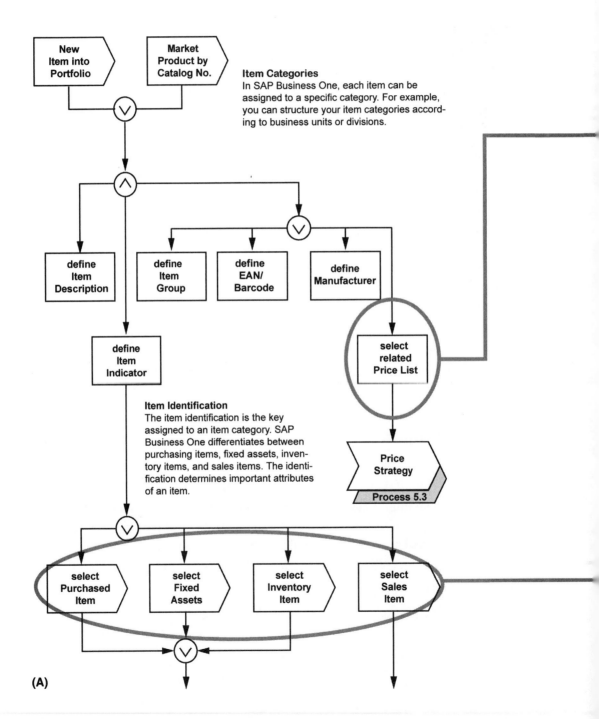

Item Categories
In SAP Business One, each item can be assigned to a specific category. For example, you can structure your item categories according to business units or divisions.

Item Identification
The item identification is the key assigned to an item category. SAP Business One differentiates between purchasing items, fixed assets, inventory items, and sales items. The identification determines important attributes of an item.

(A)

FIGURE 5.4 *(a) List of price lists, (b) Identification of the product types*

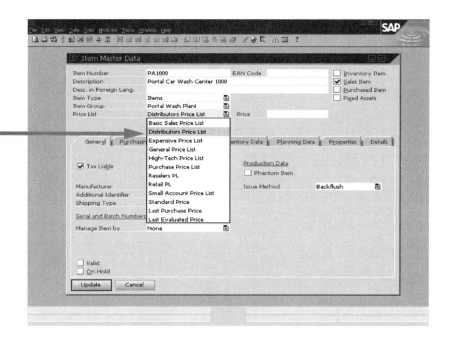

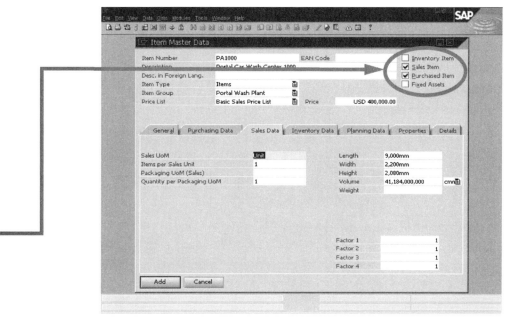

(B)

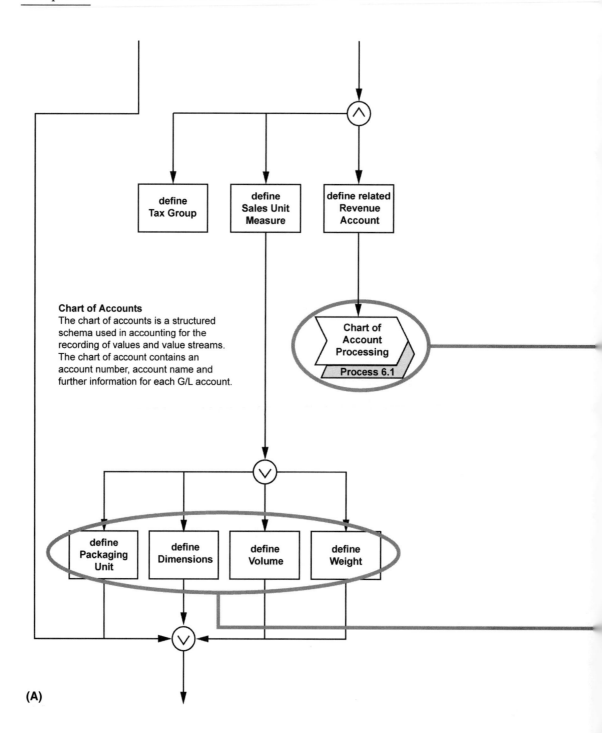

FIGURE 5.5 *(a) Detail description of the chart of accounts, (b) Product measurements*

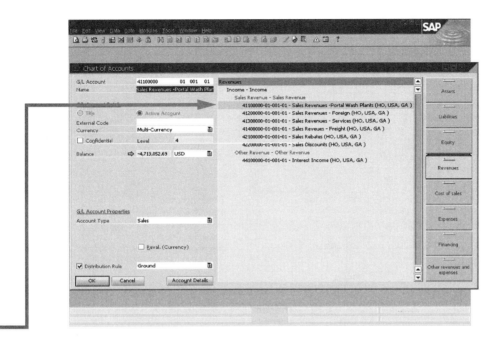

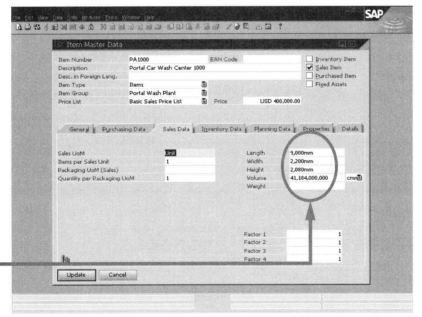

(B)

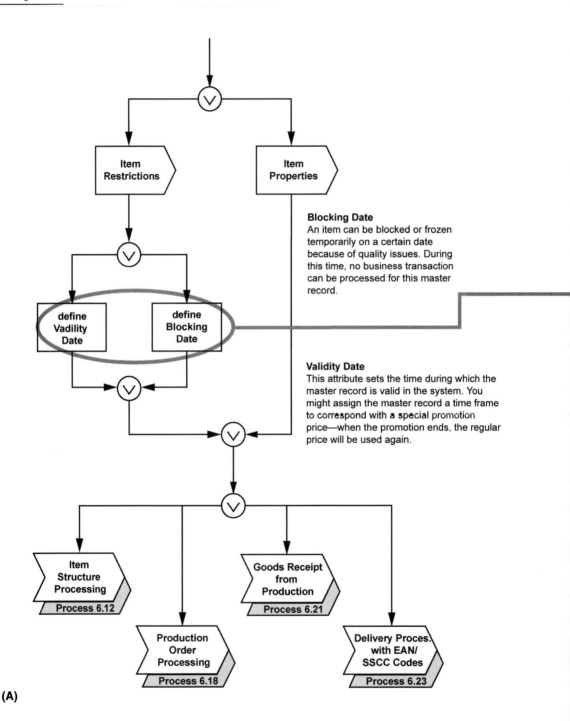

Blocking Date
An item can be blocked or frozen temporarily on a certain date because of quality issues. During this time, no business transaction can be processed for this master record.

Validity Date
This attribute sets the time during which the master record is valid in the system. You might assign the master record a time frame to correspond with a special promotion price—when the promotion ends, the regular price will be used again.

(A)

FIGURE 5.6 *(a) Detail description of the inventory management, (b) Product details*

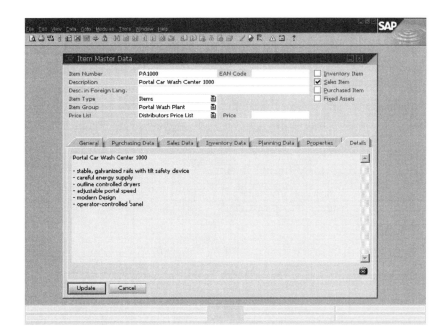

(B)

The Price Strategy Process

An enterprise defines procurement and sales price ceilings. The sales price strategy does not necessarily reflect a direct correlation between price and sales volume. The sales price strategy can also be determined by market share.

Business Description

The procurement price ceilings are based on costs at the time of purchase. Procurement price ceilings can be derived from considering the effect of reducing net revenue by the costs of individual procurement goods.

SAP Business One: Specific Description

By defining a price strategy for the enterprise, the pricing model data can be stored directly within SAP Business One. Within the system, the prices appear in the form of price lists. Different price lists can be defined (for customers and suppliers, price lists are assigned to specific business partners under the category Terms of Payment).

As soon as a voucher is created for a business transaction, the prices for the stored items are gathered from the price list. The price list updates itself according to different methods. For example, fixed purchase price and/or selling price can be set according to a price strategy or the method utilized for earlier price strategies (last purchase price and/or last selling price). You can also define base price lists and assign additional price lists with a purchase factor.

Thus, different prices for different business partners can be created. Infrequent customers can be assigned a 1.2 factor and would therefore pay 20 percent more than the standard price. Such modification of basic prices is carried out only in the base price list.

In the context of the price strategy, the following questions should be answered:

- How do you define your pricing logistics (base prices, factors for customers)?

- Do you work with sales price and/or purchase prices that are drawn from the price lists or with previously defined purchase and selling prices that result from the last business transaction?

- ◆ Do you work with special prices?

- ◆ Will you permit price list rounding? If yes, will you round to the nearest tenth or to the nearest full number?

- ◆ Do you make an allocation of groups within the price lists so that you can differentiate between each authorization assignment for each user (that is, who maintains the list and which lists do they maintain)?

- ◆ Do you manually enter pricing data that should not be changed by automated price settings?

- ◆ Are the prices of an assembly/final item determined by a specific product structure/purchase price?

Application of the Process

In the model company, all item prices are based on price lists. These price lists are defined differently, as there is a distinction between purchase price lists, sales price lists, and lists for special customers.

In the system, you can create price lists with the function of the same name in the Inventory module. At the beginning, at least one base price list must be stored in which all item prices are included. All other price lists can refer to this base list. The differences in prices result from the assignment of factors for the individual lists. When selecting the Price List function, a new window opens in which 10 price lists are pre-specified by default.

You can update these price lists by assigning new names with respect to your default values. Navigate to the field for the name of the price list. If you click the left mouse button, the field changes to Input mode and you can enter a name.

In the next field, you can select the basis for your price list from the selection list. This selection opens if you select the symbol at the right edge in the Base Price List field. Now you must define another factor by which the item prices of the base price list should be multiplied. Select a factor greater than 1 if you want to increase the price or a factor less than 1 if you want to decrease the price.

In the Rounding Method field, specify the type of rounding used in your calculations. You have two options here: round to the nearest full number or round to the nearest tenth. If you click on the Update button in the active window, the price list will be created.

NOTE

Only persons with appropriate authorization can work on the price list. See Chapter 7 for more information on SAP Business One's authorization concept.

Price lists can also be manually changed at a later date: Select the Price Lists function and double-click on the number of the price list to be changed. This opens a new window in which the items of the price list are displayed with the purchase prices. Now you have the option to remove different items from the list or reduce or expand it with assistance of a filter. When using a filter, you can make an item selection by supplier, number, group or characteristic of an item.

 CAUTION

To delete an item price, you must highlight the appropriate line; otherwise, all prices of the price list are deleted. To mark the desired item, click on the line number.

Sometimes a price list must be updated (such as when a supplier's prices increase or due to changes in marketplace conditions). SAP Business One offers two options for updating a price list:

- The first option allows you to update the complete price list. If you are in the Price List function, choose the Update Entire Price List option. Now you can assign another factor with which the prices will be calculated in the price list. Confirm the changes by clicking on Update. If you want to update only a selected group of item prices, then you must use the second option, Update By Selection. However, if you select Update, a window opens in which you can select your criteria, such as a selected supplier. After confirming, the system updates the prices of the chosen items.

- You can also manually execute price changes in the different price lists. There is a column in the price lists in which an indicator can be set, marking the price as manual entry. This price is then bypassed in regard to changes for the complete price list. An example of such a manual change could be a special action for a particular item that is sold at special terms.

In SAP Business One, you can also delete from the system price lists that are no longer used. You should confirm, of course, that the price list you wish to delete will no longer be used within the system (that is, will not be used as master data for a business partner). Only those price lists that don't refer to other price lists can be deleted. Therefore, to delete such a list you would have to delete all additional referenced lists.

Delete the price list by selecting a field in the row of the list and then going to the menu bar and selecting the Data menu and then the Delete Row function. Confirm the process by selecting Update.

You may also need to add an additional price list. To do so, select the Add Row function in the Data menu.

The Previous Purchase Price list includes only items and prices related to transactions that already exist in the system. The prices on this list are automatically updated by the system when one of the following transactions is executed:

- The entry of an A/P invoice
- The entry of a delivery
- The entry of a positive opening balance for an item
- The entry of updated available inventory data
- The production of an item with a BOM, in which the price of the produced item results from the last purchase prices of the components
- A data import

Manual changes cannot be made in this price list. When you click on the Form Settings button in the Symbol menu, a window opens wherein you can specify the defaults for the display of the fields and the entry activation of the table price lists.

Navigation Information

- **Menu Path:** Inventory > Price Lists
- **Tables:** OPLN
- **Incoming Trigger:** Sales item, inventory item, purchase item
- **Outgoing Trigger:** Business process master data process, A/P invoice, goods issue, inventory and stock booking, product structure processing

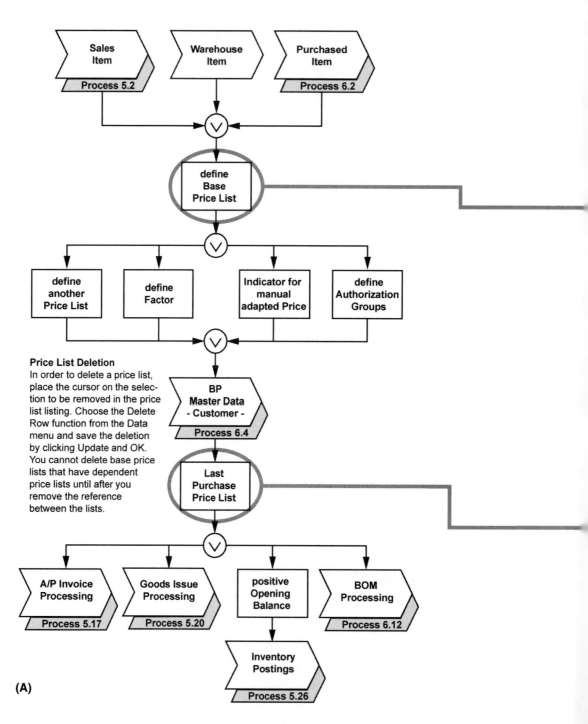

FIGURE 5.7 *(a) Designation of a base price list, (b) Price list menu in the business partner line*

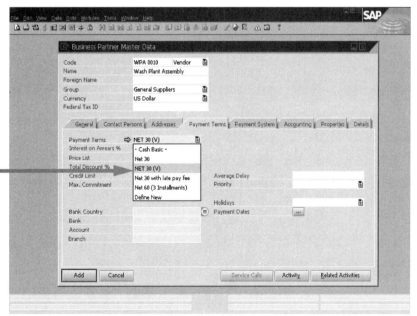

(B)

Product Structure Processing: Sales BOM

A product structure must be equated to the Bill of Material (BOM) item. A *BOM* is a quantitative list of the products coming into an end product or an assembly. In turn, the products can be assembled kits or individual component parts.

Economic Description

To achieve the most analytical view of this process, the individual parts and assembled kits that are required to complete a customer order must be identified. The accuracy of this assessment of demand depends on the breadth and depth of the product assortment in the commercial enterprise. In turn, this depth is dependent on the number of different variants of a product type.

A BOM can be structured or unstructured. An unstructured BOM is the gross-requirement BOM, while the multilevel bill of materials and the single-level bill of materials represent structured BOMs. Since the BOMs are relatively similar—despite differing structural approaches—they can be seen as variances of each other. The respective BOM levels are linked within the attributes of the structural relationship. For example, consider the quantity of a product. If the quantity equals 0, the product will not appear on the BOM. Data can be viewed in more than one report due to the structural relationship.

SAP Business One: Specific Description

In SAP Business One, you can create additional single-level bills of material. A single-level bill of materials contains only the assembled kits or individual parts that are placed directly into a product. The single-level BOM is a single-step list. For a multilevel BOM, further single-level bills of materials must be defined if a product again consists of assembled kits.

The following are questions related to a sales BOM:

- Do you have special sales that you incorporate into your BOM?
- Do you base your pricing strategy for assembled kits on BOMs?

- Is your sales BOM different from the assembly or production BOM or do you use a universal BOM?

- Will you permit rounding in the price list and, if so, will you round to the nearest number or round to the nearest decimal place?

- Do you use the allocation of groups within the price lists so that you can differentiate with the authorization assignment for the users who work with these price lists?

- Do you manually enter pricing data that should not be changed by automated price settings?

- How are the prices of an assembly or an end product developed— through purchase prices or by means of a product structure?

- Do you sell final items that require service (such as introduction or consultation), and do you display these working hours as a component in the sales BOM?

- Would you like to use the BOM as collection assistance in the customer order with variants?

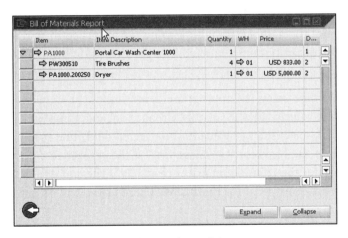

FIGURE 5.8 *Single level parts of materials*

Application of the Process

In the model company, the structure of a portable car wash is illustrated with a simple bill of material. The entry of a bill of material (BOM) takes place in the Define Bill Of Material function in the Production menu.

In the Define Bill of Material screen, a window appears in which the BOM can be created. In order to create a new BOM, you must switch first into Add mode. If you want to change an already-existing BOM, you can access it in Find mode and modify it according to your default values. By selecting Update, you replace the existing BOM with the modified one.

Before a new BOM can be created, you must make sure that all necessary items are already present in the system. If this is not the case, then first enter the missing items (see "The Sales Process" earlier in this chapter for more information).

The first input in the Define Bill of Material window is the item number of the final item. As per the naming convention in our model company, a portable car wash with the product number PA1000 is specified as distribution channel. You can enter the number directly or select it from the item list. An item selection list opens if you press the Tab key or enter the (*) symbol and confirm instead of making an entry. The name for the product is selected automatically if you confirm the entry or the selection of the number. If multiple items are produced from the same component parts, this quantity can be entered into the field right beside the item number.

You define the BOM type using the appropriate definition of the item type. You can select four possible values: Sales, Assembly, Production, and Template. To create a dispatch item list, select the sale value in the selected field. The specification of a price list serves as the basis for the calculation of the respective component prices. You can also enter the component prices manually if the component prices are not stored in the price list used for the BOM. These prices will be automatically transferred to the price list.

In the next screen, you can enter all components that are used in the finished item by specifying the quantity used. To do so, either enter the item numbers of the components or use the selection list.

NOTE

You'll receive a multilevel distribution channel if you insert a defined BOM as a component into the finished item.

Click the Update button, and the new BOM is created in the SAP Business One database.

Navigation Information

- ◆ **Menu Path:** Production > Define Bill of Materials
- ◆ **Tables:** ITT1, OITT
- ◆ **Incoming Trigger:** Sales Item, Price Strategy
- ◆ **Outgoing Trigger:** Product Structure Processing, Quotation Processing, Date Order Processing, Delivery Processing, A/R Invoice

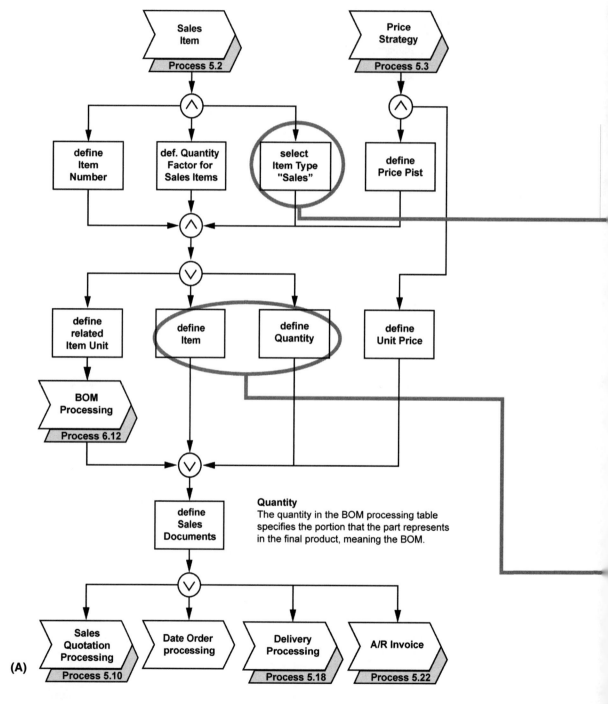

FIGURE 5.9 *(a) List of structure types, (b) Determine product structure*

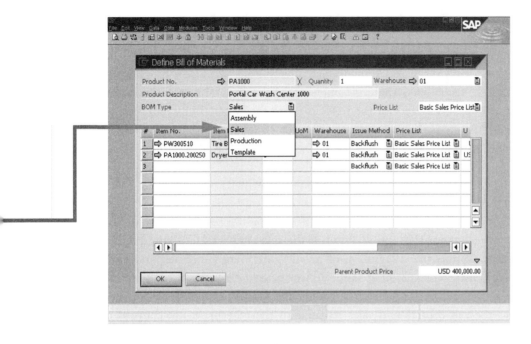

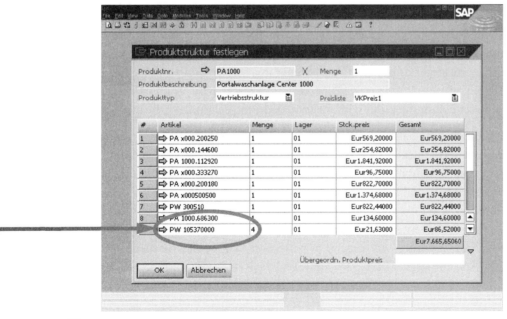

(B)

Business Partner Master Data

In the past five years, customer relationship management (CRM) has become more intensively discussed and supported technically with new programs. Companies have recognized that customers should be brought into the system not when an order is entered for the first time into the system but when they become *potential* customers. For example, after a trade show, all contact addresses of interested customers (or *leads*) should be entered into the CRM system.

Business Description

Customer relationship management is a tool for the reorientation of customer focus as well as for the optimization of the sales impact of an enterprise. CRM programs support the integration of business partners, processes, and technologies, particularly the customer- and service-focused divisions of the business. The Sales (inside and in the field), Marketing, and Customer Service departments, as well as the call centers and sales partners of the enterprise, are concerned with CRM.

The functionalities of a CRM system are extensive, but the main emphasis is on contact and data management, as well as on prospective customers (leads) and customer administration. Data regarding a lead considers the general interest of an existing customer or prospective customer in a service or a product. Leads arise in different ways—from marketing (tele-sales, direct mail, trade shows, and so on) to direct communication with customers during sales activities.

Leads represent the base for a continuing sales cycle and are mostly pre-qualified. Promising leads are called *hot leads*. These are the ones that are suitable for further processing. If hot leads are generated in the Sales and Marketing departments, then the actual sales activity starts earlier in the process. This results in a shorter sales cycle to reach a business transaction, which crucially reduces distribution costs. Most enterprises work with a one- or two-stage selling strategy: Leads are further processed directly or passed on to a reseller/partner.

SAP Business One: Specific Description

In SAP Business One, the customers, suppliers, and prospective customer (leads) are combined into the term *business partner*. For these business partners, you can register the marketing opportunities and store the respective contacts, and of course, track all contact information for the prospective customer.

To evaluate leads, you assign an internal group of those who are best suited to address the sales potential of the lead, as well as additional marketing information you may have that is specific to the customer and their interest. Note that you can track several contacts for a potential customer and determine a main partner/contact.

In the Remarks field, you can store up to 100 types of data for each potential customer, and this information is readily available. For example, if the lead calls, you can open the master record manually or over the Telephone Data Processing Interface (TAPI), and the master data appears on the screen automatically. Notes you might have made during a previous contact with the lead are also available. If you want to enter more text, you can store several notes under Detail in the master record.

To structure your lead administration, the following questions should be asked of Sales:

- Would you like to group your leads (more interested, less interested, and so on)?
- Which sales personnel have access to the lead master records?
- Do you assign your sales personnel to specific leads so that you can measure the performance of individual sales teams?
- Do sales personnel contact your leads through a TAPI interface with your telephone system?

 TIP

The customer master data is augmented with additional data, such as payment terms, payment system, accounting data, and so on.

Application of the Process

The master data of a lead or a business partner and how a lead in Business One is designated are administrated in the Master Data Business Partner (BP) function in the main menu of the Business Partner module. In the window that opens when you select the function, you specify all data that is relevant to the lead. First, however, you must switch to the Add mode because the function is in the Find mode by default. You must also select the appropriate symbol from the Symbol menu. Then, within the upper area of the window, you can specify the general master data relevant to the business partner.

In the Code field, enter a key code of up to 15 characters that clearly identifies the business partner. This code is unique in the entire system. If an account in the system already has this code, you will receive an error message telling you that the code already exists. In the field right beside the code, you define the type of business partner. Because we want to add to the system a prospective customer for our model company, the Lead type must be selected. In the two name fields you can enter the exact description of the lead.

If you want to assign the business partner to a certain group, you can classify it accordingly in the Group field. The assignment of a business partner to a group simplifies later analysis and reporting. If you don't assign your lead to a particular group, SAP Business One will assign the lead automatically to the first group of the selection list.

If the new lead is a foreign prospective customer, you can specify a foreign currency in the Currency field, indicating the currency to be used with all business transactions with the business partner. You can select the appropriate currency from the selection list. If you can't find the correct currency in SAP Business One, you can define a new currency using Define New. Including the lead's value-added tax ID number is recommended as well, as it will be included in future reports that you may generate.

In the lower area of the window, you can define additional data concerning the business partner, such as the partner's contact information, in the General field. In the right part of the field, you can enter information for a specific contact person, assign a further ID number, enter remarks, and assign to the business partner a buyer who is responsible for this lead.

Using the Active and On Hold fields, you can specify the period for which the master data is valid. If necessary (for example, if a customer does not pay), you can close the master data for further business transactions. The lock can be in effect for a limited time, or it can be used for an unlimited period starting on a certain date.

In the Contact Persons field, you can add one or several contact persons for the new business partner. Enter the data for the individual contact person into the specific fields and confirm the entry with Add.

Another field is intended for the entry of addresses. In this field, you define the pay-to address and, if it differs, the ship-to address of your business partner. Click on the field Define New and enter the data in the right area. Pay-to and ship-to addresses can later be selected from lists in different sections of the system.

Navigation Information

- **Menu Path:** Business Partners, Business Partner Master Data, Select Lead from Business Partner Code
- **Tables:** ACRD, ACPR, ACR1, CRD1, OCRD
- **Incoming Trigger:** Tip, Sales Promotion by E-Mail, Catalog Discounts, Fairs, Mass-Mailings, Promotional Events
- **Outgoing Trigger:** Contact Processing (CRM), Quotation Processing, Business Partner Master Data (Customer), Customer Order Processing

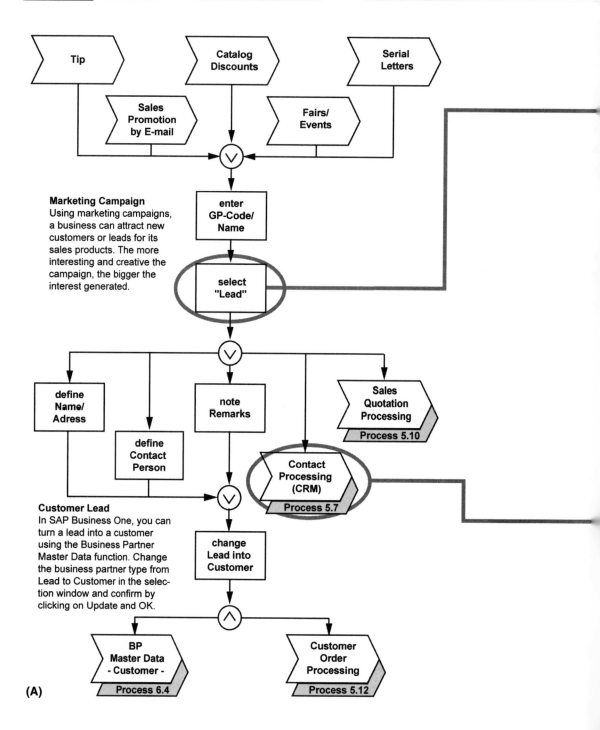

Marketing Campaign
Using marketing campaigns, a business can attract new customers or leads for its sales products. The more interesting and creative the campaign, the bigger the interest generated.

Customer Lead
In SAP Business One, you can turn a lead into a customer using the Business Partner Master Data function. Change the business partner type from Lead to Customer in the selection window and confirm by clicking on Update and OK.

(A)

FIGURE 5.10 *(a) Choose a business partner type, (b) Contact management*

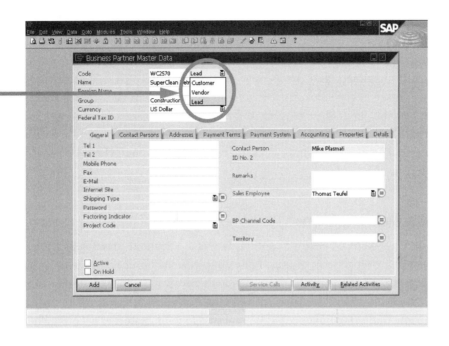

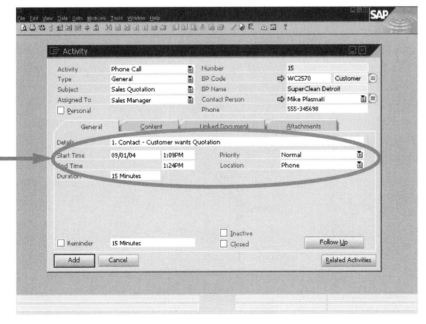

(B)

Contact Processing

Contact processing is important for sales representatives who are in regular contact with customers and prospective customers. The reps can record details on every contact in the sales support section of the system (Customer Relationship Management), and all employees in the enterprise can access this collected information. Then, if necessary, this information can serve as the basis for further sales activities. The organization of customer relationship data is based on the concept of customer life cycles.

Business Description

The management of partner contact data is a continual process, as the relationship evolves over time in phases. For example, a customer relationship is based on the personal relationship of the individuals involved—perhaps today your company has a solid relationship with the buyer at your customer account; however, tomorrow that same buyer could be replaced at your customer account, thus altering the dynamics of the personal and professional relationship between your companies. Or consider this scenario: Your company develops a new product for your customer to resell. As the product is developed, marketed and sold, the companies' relationship is strong; however, as the product sales fail to meet expectations, the relationship becomes strained. In either scenario, it is important to continually document the changes to the relationships with your partners.

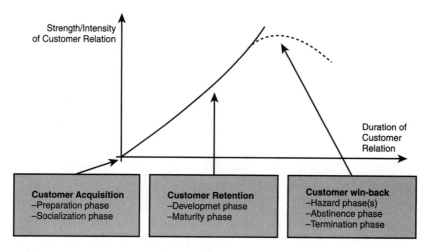

FIGURE 5.11 *Customer relations lifecycle*

Initial contact between the vendor and the buyer takes place in the Customer Acquisition phase. After the Acquisition phase (after an order has been placed)—if further contacts are maintained—this data evolves into the Customer Relation phase and the Development phase. The Development phase fully exploits the customer potential through an expansion of the customer relationship through additional projects, larger orders and so on. The danger of losing customers after the Development phase occurs in the Maturity phase, when the potential is often maximized. Contact must be intensively maintained with an existing customer; otherwise, the customer turns away (the Abstinence phase), resulting in the possible complete loss of business relations (the Termination phase).

SAP Business One: Specific Description

The following questions must be answered during contact processing:

◆ To what extent do you use CRM functionalities (only used by sales or customer service employees, or used by other departments as well)?

◆ Which dialog type/sales activity type have you defined?

◆ Do you attach the contacts to the SAP reports or other documents? If yes, where are these centrally stored?

With the dialog type/sales activity type, the different forms of contact, such as in-person, telephone call, or written, can be represented. Additionally, if a telephone call results in a new sale, you can link directly from the contact information to a new sales voucher or customer order. Also, you can search for recorded contacts with a business partner at any time. You change from the Add mode by hitting Control+S in Search mode.

Another function is to establish customer care reminders. With the appropriate settings on your contacts, you can automatically receive reminder alerts at the times you specify to follow up particular accounts contacts. The status of a contact also can be changed from open to closed if no additional notes are stored in this contact. Additional new contacts can be easily included as well. Finally, contacts can be selected and evaluated within the report system for groups of suppliers or customers using the business partner number.

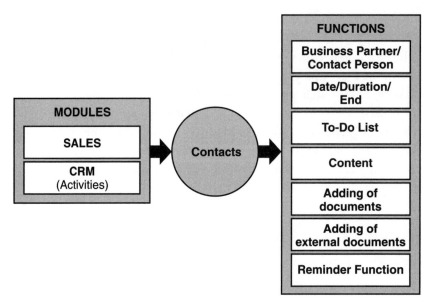

FIGURE 5.12 *Contact management functions in SAP Business One*

Application of the Process

For contact processing, SAP Business One offers two methods: You change contacts directly from the Business Partner Master Data function or by selecting the Contact function in the main menu.

Under normal conditions, you will work on contacts to business partners whose master data is already entered into SAP Business One. You can open the BP code field with the Search function (by entering * into the input field); a selection list appears, and you can select the desired business partner from the list. The business partner also can be brought up by entering the code. The Number field on the right side is updated by the system and gives the number of all contacts to the business partner.

The area is divided into different fields in which the respective contacts can be defined in more detail. In the General field, you first enter the type of the contact and its content. You can select the type of contact from the selection lists or add new inputs if the ones you want are not contained in the lists. You can also enter appointment dates so that you are reminded to periodically contact active accounts. The system configuration can also be set to mark the time when information was received in your mailbox. Once a message is received, you can navigate between the received message and the stored contact information.

With the Active and Closed selection buttons, you can mark whether a contact is open or closed. An active account can be used until it is closed, whereas a closed contact can no longer be utilized. In SAP Business One, when you close a contact, a new window opens for listing data, documents, and attachments that are also associated with the contact.

The window for contact processing is always open in Working mode. In order to search for an existing contact and change it, you must select the Find symbol for the Search mode in the symbol bar.

Navigation Information

- ◆ **Menu Path:** Business Partner > Business Partner Master Data > Activity
- ◆ **Tables:** ACR1, ACRD, OCLG, OCLO, OCLS, OCLT
- ◆ **Incoming Trigger:** Lead—Business Partner Master Data, Customer—Business Partner Master Data, Vendor—Business Partner Master Data
- ◆ **Outgoing Trigger:** Indicated Inactivity, Sales Opportunity, Activity Overview Report

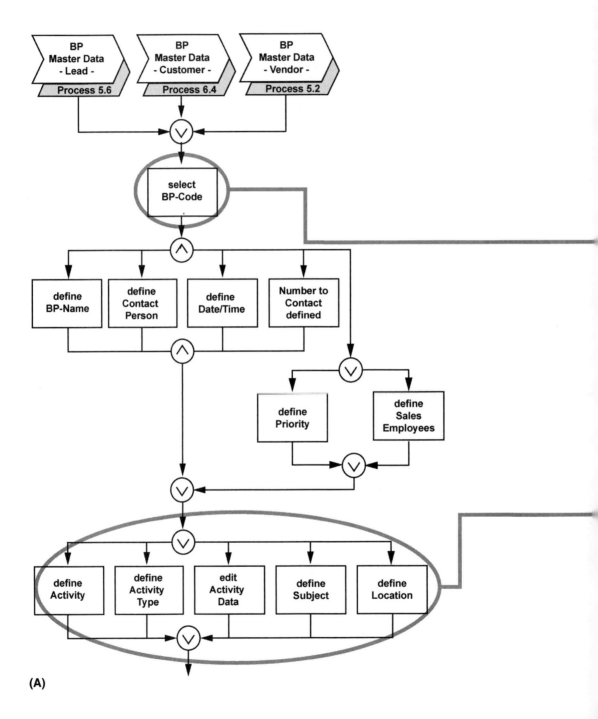

(A)

FIGURE 5.13 *(a) Business partner selection, (b) Detail description of contact with business partner*

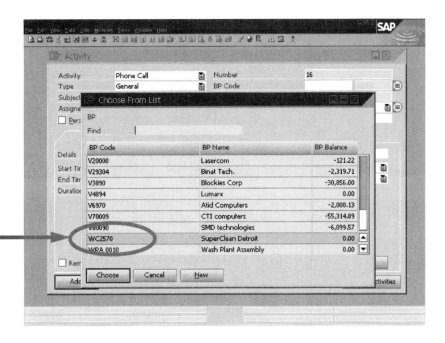

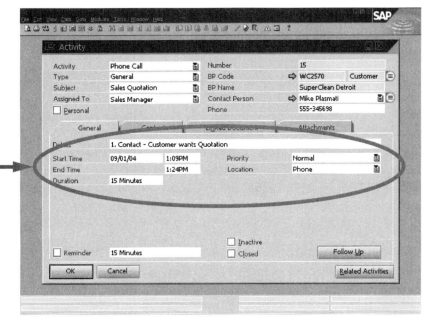

(B)

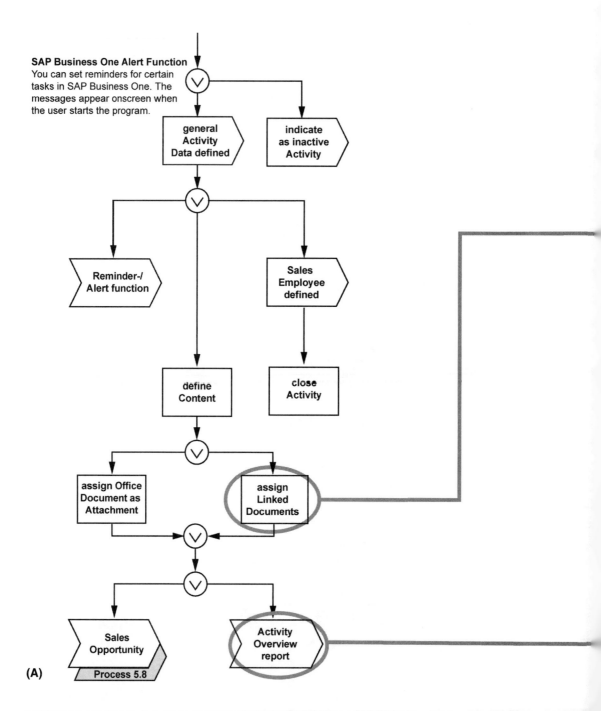

SAP Business One Alert Function
You can set reminders for certain tasks in SAP Business One. The messages appear onscreen when the user starts the program.

FIGURE 5.14 *(a) Selection of receipt types, (b) Contact summary*

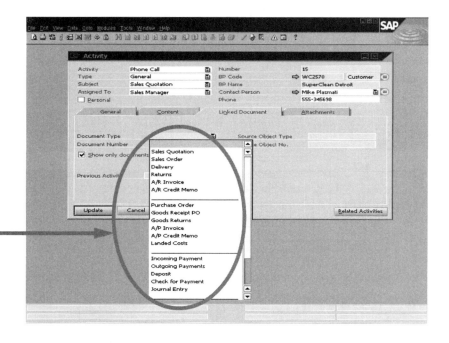

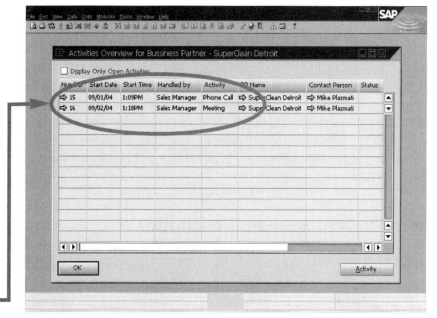

(B)

Opportunity Analysis

The opportunity analysis describes the sales prospects from qualified leads and contains all relevant data that is necessary for best cooperation with the customer. The goal is to provide a business proposal to the customer and/or lead.

 NOTE

The definition for *opportunity analysis* equates to a key axiom of business behavior: appropriateness in the present situation. For example, a salesperson's compensation is set relative to his or her expected sales forecast. An opportunity analysis forecasts the potential revenue a salesperson can be expected to earn in a defined time period.

Business Description

The basis for the opportunity analysis is the probability of success. The more precise the sales forecasting is, the more exact planning can be. In turn, the order forecast is based on fixed, already-received demand quantities and the probability of future demand quantities is based on the opportunity analysis.

In the context of an opportunity analysis, with customers it is meaningful to perform disaggregated analyses. The specified contacts within an opportunity between the salesperson and the customer provide detail about the contact situation. On this basis, the use of CRM tools is meaningful because they can provide these reports to the opportunity analysis in real time. The sales director can see the probability of sales turnover through this report and more accurately judge the effectiveness of the sales team.

SAP Business One: Specific Description

The opportunity analysis focuses on the relationship with potential and established customers by compiling and analyzing potential orders. An opportunity contains the business partner number (code) and the relevant sales stages, as defined earlier in this chapter. However, these stages of a sales cycle are always product- and business-specific. For example, service and consulting businesses have sales stages that don't apply to sales of consumer goods. On the basis of sales experience, the sales stages can be defined very quickly and assigned to respective opportunities. In each stage, it is important to measure the probability of each opportunity becoming a closed sale. Pending sales are noted in SAP Business One reports with the Sales Pipeline symbol.

FIGURE 5.15 *Sales pipeline in SAP Business One*

During the collection of new prospects, such as leads gained from a trade show or from a personal contact, the intent and the interest level can be recorded, among other things. With this general data, the sales stage is represented by a percentage. Then this information can be attached as appendices to the opportunity, including documents that were conveyed to the business partner (such as a Microsoft PowerPoint presentation).

The potential quantity of orders from an opportunity is addressed as an expected maximum sum in which the potential, such as total gross profit, is also forecasted. Often, it is useful to include information about your own partners and marketplace competitors when analyzing the potential of a larger order. This information helps to analyze the strengths and weaknesses of the competitors and to forecast the quantity of potential orders accordingly. When a sales opportunity has been won or lost, it can be noted in SAP Business One by marking the corresponding radio button. As long as the opportunity is pending, the opportunity remains marked as Open.

The following questions arise in the opportunity analysis:

- Which sales stages do you have?
- Do all sales employees work according to the enterprise philosophy of being "sales oriented?"
- Are there different sales stages (sales cycles) in your enterprise, as you have different lines of business with different target groups?
- Did you have ongoing discussions/analyses of the larger sales pipeline?

Application of the Process

An opportunity analysis can be executed for both open and closed opportunities. The Opportunities Report function is in the Sales Opportunities module. When you select this function, the system opens a selection window in which you can edit your analysis according to certain criteria.

 NOTE

In the model company, we will perform an opportunity analysis for a business partner through the analysis of the most important criteria.

There are different ways to limit an opportunity analysis to the desired aspects. In the BP selection, all business partners are included. To limit this selection, click on the Detail icon. There you can decide whether the analysis should take place in detail for each customer or for a whole customer group. The first option for the input of the BP code is to enter a number for one business partner, a range of numbers for a group of customers, or properties connected arbitrarily for business partners that are to be consulted for the analysis.

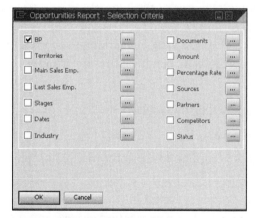

FIGURE 5.16 *Analysis Criteria*

With the selection of the Customer Group field, you can define limitations for a selected group. By selecting Select All, you can include all stored business partners in the analysis. The analysis related to one or more sales employees of your enterprise is created with the Main Sales Employee option.

With Sales Stages, you can select different sales for analysis. A date range is set with the Date option. With the Vouchers option, you restrict the analysis to the connected vouchers of a certain type. The simultaneous selection of several kinds of vouchers is also possible. The Amounts option limits the analysis of opportunities according to amount. For this, you enter the range of the maximum expected sum, a weighted total amount, or the gross profit total. A combination of these criteria is also possible. A further option of this selection is to limit the selection to the percentage of the probability of success. This can be furnished over the sales stages.

The analysis is started when you press the OK button after completion of the details. You get the data of the analysis listed in a table. By clicking the orange arrow in this table, you can retrieve and view the detail information.

Navigation Information

- **Menu Path:** Sales Opportunities > Opportunities Report > Sales Opportunities > Sales Opportunity > Sales Opportunities > Opportunities Pipeline > Sales Opportunities > Won Opportunities Report > Sales Opportunities > Stage Analysis
- **Tables:** OOPR, OPR1, OPR2, OPR3
- **Incoming Trigger:** Contact Processing, Lead—Business Partner Master Data, Customer—Business Partner Master Data, Quotation Processing
- **Outgoing Trigger:** Stage Analysis, Opportunity Pipeline, Customer Order Processing

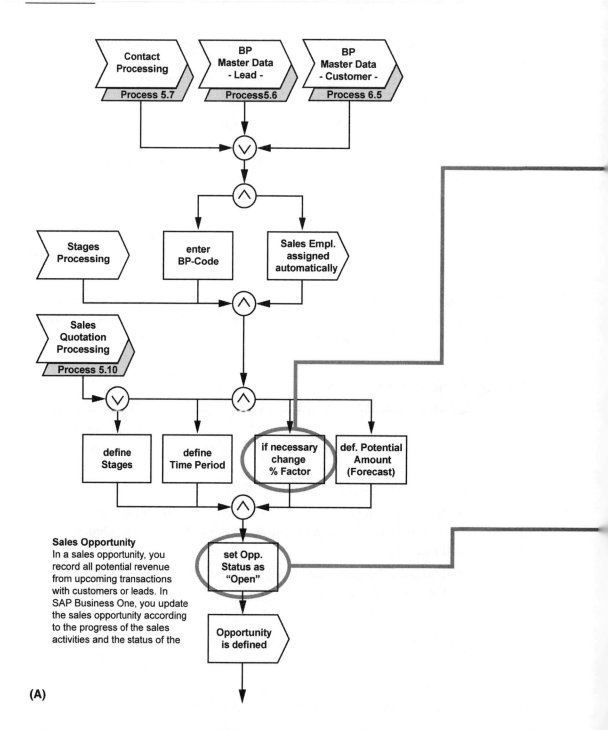

(A)

FIGURE 5.17 *(a) Detailed description opportunity, (b) Summary data for opportunity*

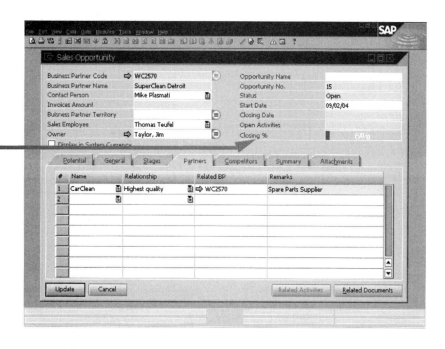

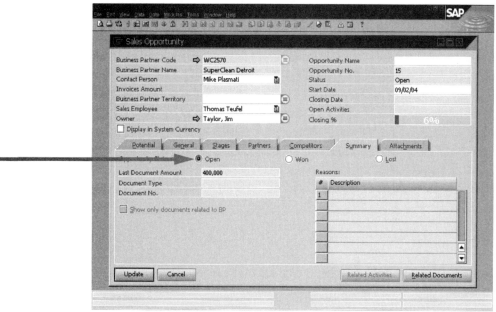

(B)

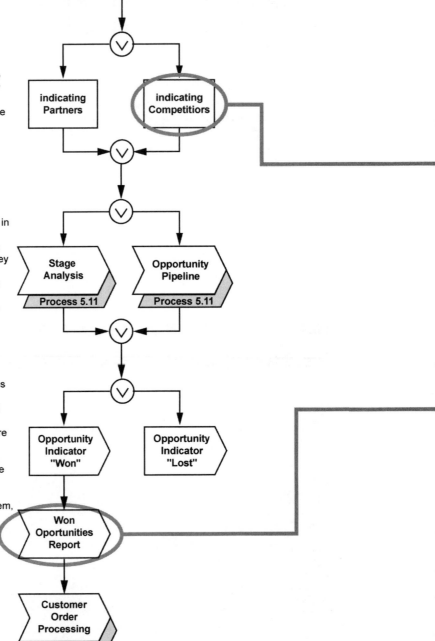

Partner
As a company, you must decide before the start of a sales opportunity whether to carry the project out on your own or partner with another business. SAP Business One allows you to define one or more partners with which to collaborate on a sales opportunity.

Competitors
Companies are often confronted with competitors in the sales process. If these competitors are known for a certain sales opportunity, they can be used for analyses. In SAP Business One, each competitor can be recorded and classified in a risk category in order to calculate a realistic win and loss evaluation.

Tip:
You can ensure that no sales stage is skipped by having each stage assigned to and worked on by a company employee. If sales stages are recorded accurately and detailed in the system, then they can be used to optimize and improve your sales process. The more detailed the data tracked in the system, the more meaningful the subsequent analyses will be.

(A)

FIGURE 5.18 *(a) Competitor for an opportunity, (b) Graphical representation: won opportunities*

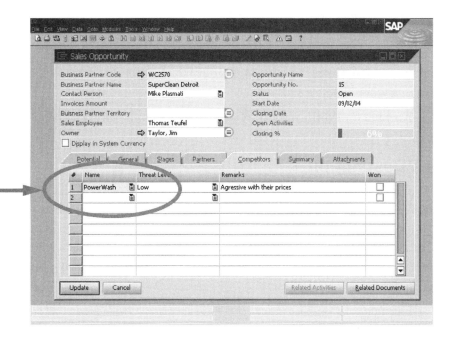

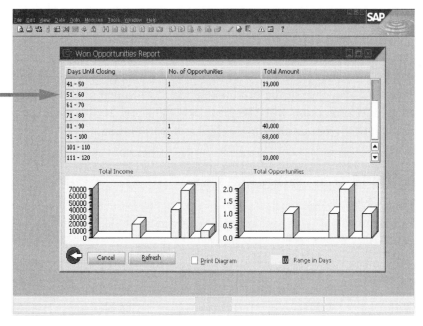

(B)

Gross Profit Analysis

The gross profit of a product can be considered as its profit margin. The profit margin is economically seen as the amount by which revenue of a product exceeds the costs of a product.

Formula for Profit Margin: *Revenue / costs = profit margin*

Business Description

Profit margin, or gross profit, is the value of the difference between the gross sales revenue and the cost of goods sold. The profit margin analysis provides a formula for determining the economic success of selling a product unit. The cost of goods sold, or marginal cost, is the expenses incurred to physically produce a unit of the product. A success product earns gross revenue that exceeds the related marginal costs.

Formula for Purchase Price: *Net reference price of trade goods / all price deductions = purchase price*

Formula for Goods Cost Price: *Purchase price / direct traceable incidental costs = goods cost price*

The gross profit analysis can serve as a decision criteria in bottleneck situations where a decision must be made to move forward with a product. If no bottleneck is present, the sequence of the products can be determined due to its gross profits for product promotion with the gross profit analysis. In this case, the product with the highest gross profit is most eligible for promotion.

SAP Business One: Specific Description

Within SAP Business One, gross profit can be represented as profit above the cost price or as profit above the selling price. This must be defined in the document settings dialog, shown in Figure 5.19.

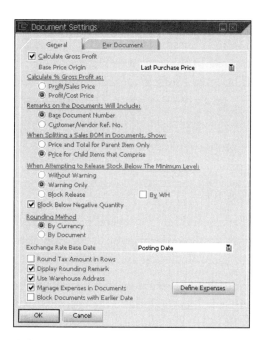

FIGURE 5.19 *The Document Settings dialog.*

Within a gross profit analysis, the purchase price list can be changed at any time; you can do so by pressing the Update button. The system immediately changes the current display in the Price List selection field. The entries defined in the document settings are not changed by it.

For the best analysis results, it is important to use the most recent cost of goods for the current inventory. In performing a gross profit analysis, SAP Business One uses the most recent cost of goods valuation of the current inventory.

Gross profit analyses can be conducted on products that have been either purchased for use or produced for resale. If the profit is billed based on the cost price, the system calculates the absolute gross profit in proportion to the cost price of the item. If the profit is billed based on the sales price, the system calculates the absolute gross profit in proportion to the sales price.

The analyses for profit margin and gross profit, as designated in SAP Business One, would appear as follows: An item is bought at an average cost of $100 per unit. This value represents the cost price. In the sales revenue, an average of $160 per unit is obtained for this item. The gross profit amounts to $60 per item sold. The cost price analysis would show a profit of 60 percent. The gross profit analysis shows a profit of 37.5 percent.

These are the quotients behind the proportional profit card:

Based on cost price: $60/100 \times 100 = 60\%$

Based on sales price $60/160 \times 100 = 37.5\%$

The gross profit analysis can be called up and seen in several places in SAP Business One: during the offer generation, in the order receipt in the case of the supply, and in the sales calculation with the Calculation and Payment function.

The gross profit is calculated individually for every item of a document. Furthermore, SAP Business One adds up all lines and therefore also calculates the absolute and proportional gross profit of the document.

Application of the Process

A gross profit analysis can be accomplished in SAP Business One for the Quotation, Order, Delivery, and Invoice sales documents. If you invoke one of these documents using the search functions in the respective functions in the Sales module or with a procedure, you can indicate the gross profit in the voucher. You invoke this function with the Gross Profit symbol in the symbol bar at the upper edge of the screen, shown in Figure 5.20.

FIGURE 5.20 *Gross Profit icon on the toolbar*

After you select the symbol, a window appears with a table listing all positions that the original voucher contains. In this table, among other things, there are columns that compare purchase price and sales price, list the amount of gross profit, and list the proportional share of profits. The cost price can refer to different price lists, which are defined and stored in SAP Business One. You make this selection above the table in the Base Price By selection list.

Navigation Information

- **Menu Path:** Sales-A/R > Sales Quotation > Gross Profit Analysis, Sales-A/R > Sales Order > Gross Profit Analysis, Sales-A/R > Delivery > Gross Profit Analysis, Sales-A/R > A/R Invoice > Gross Profit Analysis
- **Tables:** ITM1, A1T1, OPLN
- **Incoming Trigger:** Quotation, Order, Delivery, Outgoing
- **Outgoing Trigger:** No outgoing trigger

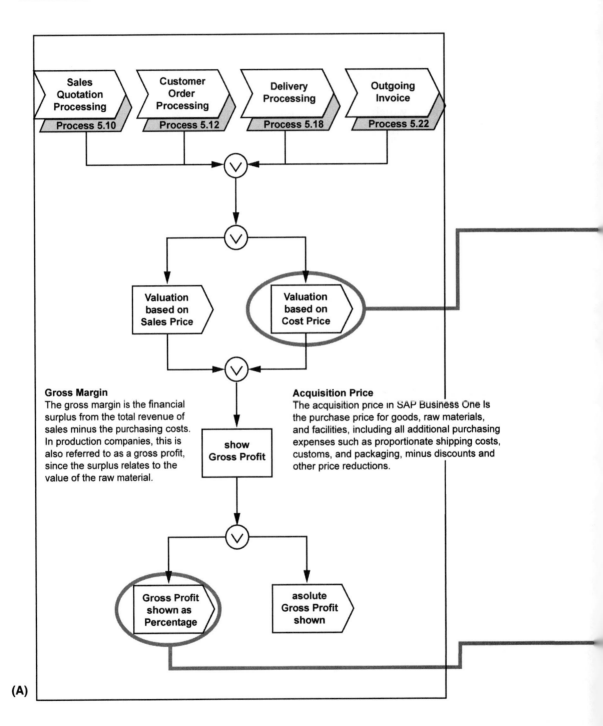

Gross Margin
The gross margin is the financial surplus from the total revenue of sales minus the purchasing costs. In production companies, this is also referred to as a gross profit, since the surplus relates to the value of the raw material.

Acquisition Price
The acquisition price in SAP Business One is the purchase price for goods, raw materials, and facilities, including all additional purchasing expenses such as proportionate shipping costs, customs, and packaging, minus discounts and other price reductions.

(A)

FIGURE 5.21 *(a) Selections of price lists, (b) Gross profit for an order*

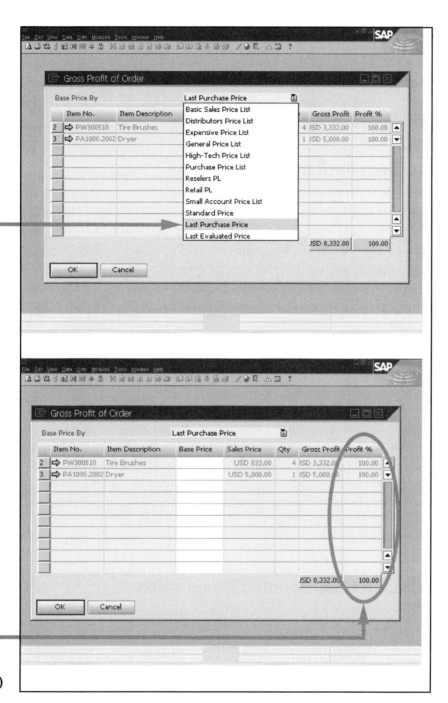

(B)

Quotation Processing

The business transactions in the Advance booking phase contain Inquiry and Quotation documents. An inquiry is usually conveyed by fax or e-mail or verbally via a call-connected system. Based on the inquiry, a quotation is created with inquired product contents for the customer.

Business Description

A quotation is a legally binding document to a customer for the supply of materials or for the contribution of services under fixed conditions. Obviously, a quotation can be quite extensive and ultimately is the result of varying economic scenarios and factors. A stock salesman who sells products to industrial customers handles orders mostly with reference to the quotation. Stock salesmen who deliver products with shipping try to present the quotation spectrum through sales promotion measures, such as a sales catalog, to the final consumer.

In the consumer market, quotation processing takes place by means of quotation catalogs and authorized contract dealers. If it is pure anonymous-customer stock manufacturing, then the customer can select from products in a catalog or purchase them directly from a retail or wholesale outlet. With order-related assembling (as the model company B shows in Chapter 6), the products are offered to the customer from predefined components. In the producer market, quotation processing takes place frequently via sales employees who are in contact directly with the customer (via e-mail, fax, EDI, telephone, and so on). Normally, the trigger for quotation processing is a written inquiry made by the customer. The order-related assembly manufacturer must check the technical requirements for its technological feasibility in prototyping or tooling. Only then can it deliver a qualified quotation.

SAP Business One: Specific Description

A customer offer in SAP Business One has several places that can contain the price quote for the material or service to be sold. At the beginning of the Quotation mask, you can select between the possible items and services above the Position table in the Contents field. If you have made your selection (for instance, in the Item menu option), then you can get the details of the individual item number with the pertinent data in the following positions. If you quote a service, then the Item

Number field disappears and you can
describe the service for the quotation.
Items, which are not included with an
item master in the system, can also be
entered as a service.

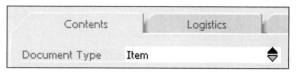

FIGURE 5.22 *Product/Service – Selections area*

 TIP

If you want to create a quotation that contains both items and services, you create
your service specifications as items. Thus, you can include services as items in the
quotation. For example, a consulting firm can list its junior advisor as a Service 1
item, its senior advisor as Service 2, and its project manager as Service 3. These
items have standard prices and therefore can be evaluated again after the business
transaction.

By including a quotation in the SAP system, neither quantitative nor value-based
postings are connected. The quotation can be amended at any time and doesn't
require any adjustment postings. The total amount can be divided into different
subsets by entry of product structures (BOM) as an item. The delivery date can
be found in the entry detail view (double-click on the item number on the left).
The most important entry fields, which are tabular in the Quotation mask, can be
configured using the Form Settings menu option (see the Form Settings icon on
the top right).

New customized fields, such as Type, can be pulled into the Sales Quotation window by selecting the Visible and Active checkboxes in the Table Format Tab field.
A Type field is added in the sales quotation, providing the option to choose Alternative, Text, or Subtotal. The following are the standard fields for the position:

◆ Entry number

◆ Item number

◆ Item description

◆ Quantity

◆ Price

◆ Tax code

◆ Total price

The price of an item is drawn from the price list, which is stored in the Item Master. In the sales quotation, the prices can be adjusted as required. For some business partners, special prices can be agreed upon and stored; then they can be drawn into the quotation.

Deviating from the business partner master data, another address can be indicated in the sales quotation in the Address for Delivery field. You can define this alternative address directly in the sales quotation. If you work with a one-time customer, it is recommended that you create a dummy customer first as a business partner master data before the quotation is created.

The following questions can arise during quotation processing:

- How is your number system defined for quotations (automatic/ manually)?
- Do you need different numbers for service and item quotations? Do you generally work with service items?
- Do you work at different item numbers with different quotation numbers?
- Do you work with different groups of items and thereby different offer numbers?
- Do you generate unique offers for one-time customers or do you use standardized initial offer terms for new business partners?

Application of the Process

In SAP Business One, a quotation serves exclusively for informative purposes. That is, no bookings are carried out or stock changes made in accounting. For the creation of a quotation, you select the Sales Quotation function in the Sales A/R module. The system opens a new window to record the quotation. Open the selection list to select a customer. To enter the customer in the Customer field, you can enter * in the input field that lists the customer or simply click the Tab key. From the list, you can select a customer by double-clicking on the required customer; their master data is then transferred to the Quotation window.

If the customer for whom the quotation is being created is not in the system, then you must enter the customer data manually. A document number automatically appears in the field on the top right. If the Manual field is selected, you must enter this number. Then enter the document date, the inquiry date, and a tax date into the corresponding fields if the default values deviate from these.

If all the data for a particular customer is already in the system, you can begin to generate an offer by entering the item number in the table. Go to the first line of the table and mark either the Item Number field or the Description field.

Now you have the option to pick an item from a selection list or enter an item number or item description. An item list is displayed by pressing the Tab key at a highlighted entry field. Of course, the search function with * also works. You can sort the selection list according to the item description. Enter the first letters of the desired item in the input field of the list; the focus shifts to the list items that begin with the letters you entered. Double-click on the desired item and it is entered into the quotation. If an item is a marketing structure, then all items belonging to the structure are entered in the quotation.

If the quotation is complete, you can enter remarks in the bottom area, assign a sales employee, and determine the terms of payment. In the right section, you can grant another discount by entering a percentage into the input field. When you click the Add button, the quotation will be stored in SAP Business One.

Navigation Information

- **Menu Path:** Sales A/R > Quotation
- **Tables:** OQUT, OUT1, OUT2, OUT3
- **Incoming Trigger:** Price Strategy, Sales Item Master Data, Lead—Business Partner Master Data, Customer—Business Partner Master Data
- **Outgoing Trigger:** Quotation created, Order Processing

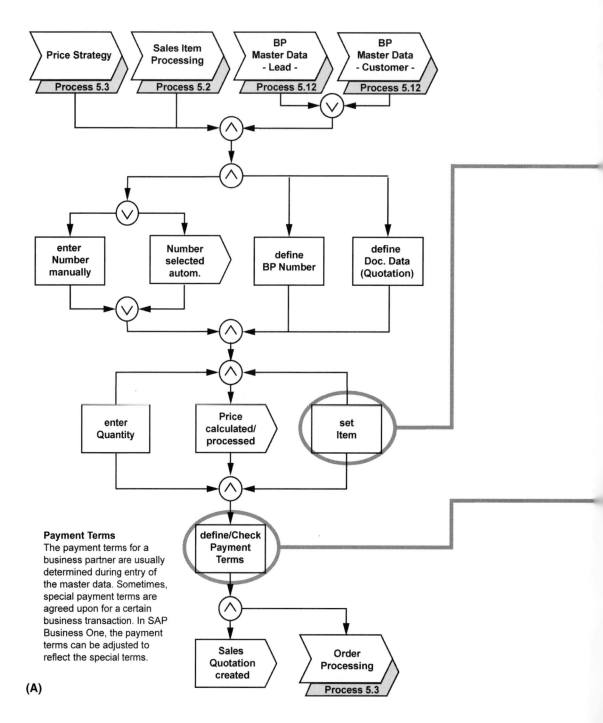

Payment Terms
The payment terms for a business partner are usually determined during entry of the master data. Sometimes, special payment terms are agreed upon for a certain business transaction. In SAP Business One, the payment terms can be adjusted to reflect the special terms.

(A)

FIGURE 5.23 *(a) Initial form for a bid or quote, (b) Specification of the payment terms*

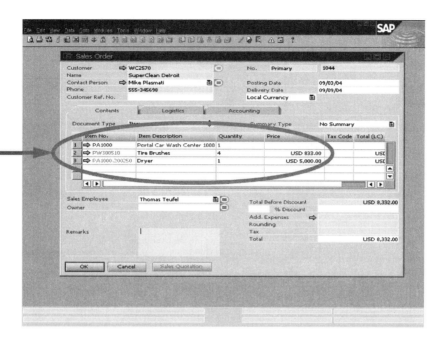

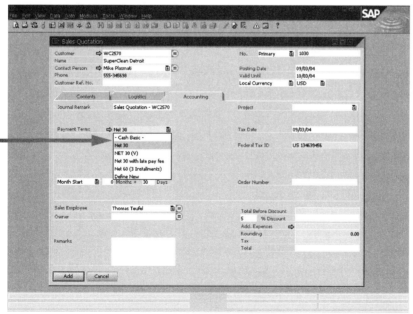

(B)

The Stage Analysis/Opportunity Pipeline Process

Real opportunity management starts with the acquisition of a promising lead in Sales. An opportunity represents a qualified chance for an enterprise to sell products or services. It is a result of the sales process from which a quotation, an order, or even a contract can result. The entire sales cycle is controlled by the permanent continuation of an opportunity.

Economic Description

An opportunity is not necessarily always derived from a lead. An opportunity can arise as a direct result of a sales action, such as an advertising campaign or a conversation at a trade show. The goal is to develop an optimized sales process that identifies different layers of an opportunity and enables an analysis of all sales projects and their progress. With the help of such analyses, evaluations can be created at any time to determine, for example, whether a sales employee is lagging behind, how much money is involved in an opportunity, and what is required to earn that money.

SAP Business One: Specific Description

Within SAP Business One, data can be sorted by lead or by salesperson for evaluation. Furthermore, the data can be filtered to provide a more in-depth analysis by applying limitations on the sales cycle stages or on the salesperson.

A second sales evaluation in SAP Business One is the opportunity pipeline. This report shows the sales pipeline graphically—the orders expected in the future—and the sale stages with the expected total. The analysis of the opportunity pipeline can be displayed through different filters, such as by business partner, by sales employee, and by stages, among others. The sales forecast and activity evaluation reports are only meaningful when multiple opportunities are entered into the system and are continuously updated and maintained.

The stage analysis/opportunity analysis process can be a valuable tool during conferences with sales employees to evaluate potential opportunities.

Application of the Process

In SAP Business One, stage analysis is in the Sales Opportunities Reports folder in the Sales Opportunities module. There is a selection window where you can set the object of your stage analysis. You may enter a date range for the opening or end date of opportunities, select one or more sales employee, or enter a business partner code for analysis.

When you press the OK button, the data is displayed in a new window, and all opportunities are listed according to sales stage. If you want to specify further restrictions concerning a sales stage or an employee, use the Stages or Sales Employee option. With a double-click on the stage line, a detailed stage view is displayed. For the opportunity pipeline, you must open the associated function in the Sales Opportunities module. In a new dialog window, you get an overview of existing open opportunities. The diagram contains a report of all sales stages for the opportunities. Each segment of the pipeline illustrates a sales stage.

Different segment values can be displayed for sales stages by selecting one of the three options: Expected Total, Weighted Amount, or Percentage. The amounts of sales stages are changed accordingly.

If you double-click either of the segments or a line in the lower table, you receive a list of the opportunities contained in the stages. Click or hold the mouse over a segment data, and a message box is displayed with a short summary of the segment data. You can show the dynamic development of the opportunities in a balloon presentation by selecting the Dynamic Opportunity Analysis function in the Go To menu or using the context (right-click) menu. A new diagram appears in the window.

Navigation Information

- ◆ **Menu Path:** Sales Opportunities > Sales Opportunities Reports > Opportunities Pipeline
- ◆ **Tables:** OPR1, OPR2, OPR3, OPR
- ◆ **Incoming Trigger:** Opportunity Analysis, Sales Quotation Processing
- ◆ **Outgoing Trigger:** Sales Employee Meeting

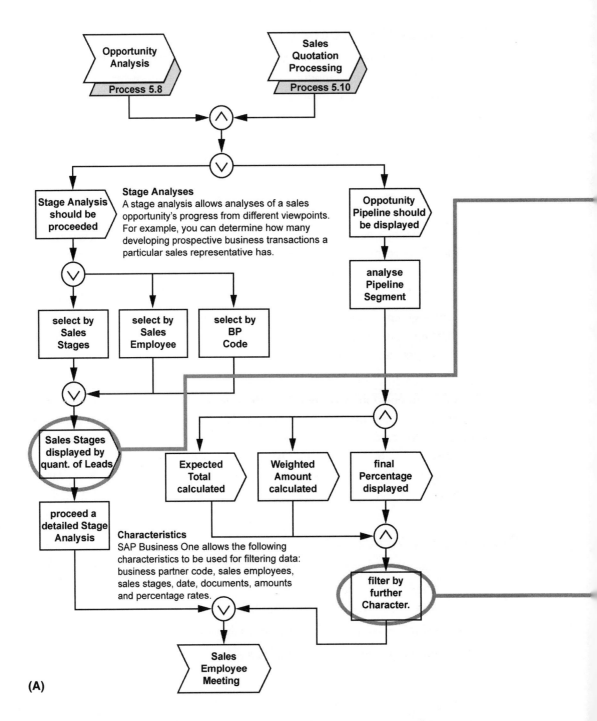

FIGURE 5.24 *(a) Graphical representation: phase analyses, (b) Opportunity pipeline*

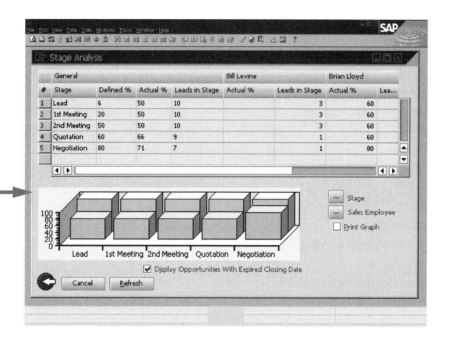

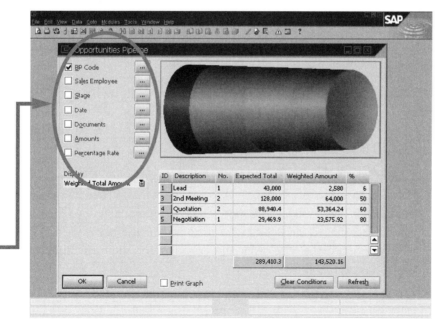

(B)

Customer Order Processing

The customer order is the contractual agreement between a sales organization and a customer regarding the delivery of materials or the provision of services at defined prices, quantities, and times. A customer order contains one or more entries, such as the quantity of a material, an item, or a performance. The total quantity of an order item might be divided into several shipments with different delivery dates. The parts of an order can be hierarchically arranged.

Business Description

Customers place their orders by different methods: telephone, fax, or e-mail or through direct sales contact. Regardless of how the order is placed, it must be manually entered into the system. Web-based ordering is also a possibility, in which case the order (as placed online) is integrated with back-end system processes.

NOTE

One form of order processing that avoids manual entry into the system is the use of EDI (electronic data interchange) contact with customers. Through this method, the customer uses a fixed order declaration, which in turn is converted into an order within the selling enterprise.

Several marketing-relevant scenarios that have an effect on different methods of customer order handling are dependent on the relationship between Sales and Procurement. These scenarios are as follows:

◆ **Direct Sale (Sale from Stock).** Direct sale is concerned exclusively with the sales handling of products, which are sold from a warehouse (series products or mass-produced goods, which were manufactured and procured again due to marketing or a turnover plan). Since there is no direct reference between a sales order and procurement, the turnaround time of the sale is usually short.

◆ **Produce to Order.** With this process, a product is manufactured specifically for a certain customer, in contrast to mass production for an anonymous market. Same or similar manufacturing can be repeated in the course of the order. Usually there is no long-term inventorying of single manufactured products. At the same time, a new cost objective is created with the customer order that considers all flat and actual values belonging to the customer order on both sides of delivery and cost. Evaluation of the profit margin can then be carried out directly from the customer order. Two variants have to be distinguished during produce to order:

- **Assembly to Order.** A product is assembled as the result of a customer order for a product that is not kept as warehouse stock of finished products. The components are prefabricated; however, they are available from the warehouse for single-step assembly. Assembly can be interactively initiated directly from Sales or, if desired, by shifting of the order plan only after requirement planning. The customer order completion differentiates between standard products and single-level, non-standard products without an order BOM (bill of materials).

- **Make to Order.** Production is the result of a customer order included in the sale for a product that is not in warehouse stock of finished products. Unlike assembly to order, there is more than one production stage, and some of the components are kept in inventory but are manufactured or procured specifically for a particular customer order. Production can be interactively initiated directly from Sales (assembly management). Customer order completion differentiates between standard products and single-level or multilevel, non-standard products with or without an order BOM.

SAP Business One: Specific Description

While quotation processing serves only for the preparation of an order, a binding agreement between the enterprise and a customer represents an order in SAP Business One. All Sales documents have the same structure in principle: They consist of the document header and as many document positions as desired, in table form. The document item can be opened to item detail pictures by clicking on the item number. The general data that is valid for the entire document is held in the document header. The following items are also included:

- Number of the ordering party (the customer)
- Address of the delivery receiver
- Document currency and the exchange rate
- Order number
- Delivery date

While the data in the document header applies to the entire document, other entries are valid only for certain positions. The data that is saved on a position level includes:

- Item number
- Item description
- Quantity
- Price
- Tax indicator (tax code)
- Possible granted discounts
- Total

An order item can contain even further data in the item detail picture. The detail data covers all information needed for the delivery of the order. In customer order processing, you can also include service positions for immaterial goods; order-related invoicing of the service items is then carried out. The date of invoicing is explicitly given by the delivery date.

When creating a sales document in SAP Business One for the first time—that is, without reference to a preceding document (such as the offer)—the data is taken from the respective master records. SAP Business One copies the data to the Business Partner document position from the Item Master data and copies from relevant tables (price lists, billing address, and so on). Sometimes the customer master lists different addresses, such as a different ship-to address and invoice address. Each business partner has its own debtor master, and during sales order processing, the data in the receivable account can be navigated with the orange arrow. The data is transferred in to the individual positions from the Item Master record as soon as the number is entered. Further item data, such as weight, length, height, volume, bar code, stock, profit center, and so on, is updated into the position detail data (see Figure 5.25). This data can be changed for an individual process.

FIGURE 5.25 *Example position detail data of a product in SAP Business One*

It is possible to create a new customer order based on an existing document. If a customer accepts one of your quotations during the creation of an order, the system can take all relevant master data that is already included in the quotation. If deviations between the quotation and the order have been agreed upon, these deviations can be changed as necessary. When creating a customer order with reference to another document, a dialog window appears that offers two different options:

- Copy all positions into the new document (take over)
- Transfer only some positions to the new document (position selection)

In the standard design of SAP Business One, the option to create a customer order exists in a quotation, a contract, and a customer order. If you create a new document, you can transfer positions from several documents to the new document.

With or without reference, when an order is created and the individual tasks in the order are executed, it must include sales order processing such as the pricing, credit limit check, determination of delivery date, material reservation, and tax.

Pricing is based on material price lists in the system as well as customer-specific special prices. Both a net value inquiry and a gross value inquiry must be possible. The outgoing gross profit is computed from the gross price of the material and special prices or groups of discounts.

The determination of delivery date is designed to give a realistic delivery date for the goods. In the simplest case, the distribution time must be computed only by the warehouse; in the most difficult cases, production times of certain components must also be considered. Stock production includes monitoring dispatch and invoicing. Furthermore, with customer-related assembly in the producer market, the status of production—planned, approved, or posed—at the supplier and in customer-related batch production must be considered.

During materials reservation at the time of order entry, no changes related to value are posted in Accounting. However, the quantities are reserved for the customer in inventory management. You can see order quantities in different reports such as the stock overview and in other places in the system. This information is important to optimize order procedures and inventorying. You also need this information to make sure that customers' requests can be processed fast and satisfactorily.

With the Tax Indicator, you apply country-specific taxes (in addition, see the predefined tax groups specified under Administration and at Ust. Group in the system). For a tax inquiry for the U.S., the standard design contains terms for sales taxes at the state, county, and city levels, as well as for taxes on the basis of tax jurisdiction code. The customer and item settings, as well as those in the Account Determination General Ledgers window, serve as the basis for calculation. Each line of a document (item or service) contains a tax group for which the system computes the sum of the taxes of the document, and when required, the preparation of different tax reports is possible.

When you edit a document, the system first examines the standard tax group defined in the General Ledger definition window and suggests it. When you select the customer for the document, the system checks again whether the customer is subject to tax, is tax exempt, or EC. If the customer is subject to tax and you have assigned any tax group in the customer's master record, this tax group overwrites the suggested tax group. If no tax group was defined for the customer, the system determines whether a tax group was assigned to any item in the appropriate item master data and uses that group in the appropriate item line of the document. For each document line, you can manually enter a tax group independently from the rules just explained.

The following are special handling situations that might arise with customer orders and need to be addressed in more detail:

- ◆ **Rebate (discount) in Kind:** A *rebate in kind* can be included at any time as its own entry in an order without a price or if you have defined a rebate group for the item. There are two kinds of discounts:
  - • Bonus: The customer pays for only part of the goods requested. The rest of the goods are free. For example, of 10 bottles of champagne ordered, two bottles are regarded as discount in kind.
  - • Extra Bonus: The customer pays for the goods requested and gets additional goods free of charge. For example, the supplier includes an additional coffee machine free of charge when four coffee machines are ordered.
- ◆ **Different Business Partner Roles:** The business partners of a customer order are identified by different partner roles. For every partner role, the kind of partner is fixed, whether as Debtor, Creditor (such as the shipper), Partner (such as the Purchasing Manager at the customer), or Personnel (such as a sales representative in your enterprise). The most important debtor partner roles are ordering parties, Goods Recipient, Invoice Recipient, and Payer. These are mandatory in standard delivery because a customer order cannot be completed without their specification. The different partners in a customer order are taken from the customer master record of the ordering party. This is only a suggestion and can be manually changed at any time.
- ◆ **Release Procedures (for Purchase Requisition):** In preparing a sales document, you can also define a release procedure that is independent of different criteria. For example, if you include an order that exceeds the credit limit of the customer, you can initiate release procedures and have a message sent to the system user. The same applies to a deviation from the proportional gross profit in a sales invoice. If an authorized user approves the document, the sales procedure can be executed. You will find information for the definition of the release procedures and the associated criteria under the heading "Administration (Customizing)" in the SAP Business One manual.

The following questions should be asked as you analyze your own processing of customer orders:

- Do you use products that are defined clearly by material numbers?
- Do you also have products that differ from sales BOMs?
- Are there contracts for the acceptance of certain quantities?
- Do you work with discounts in kind (bonus/extra bonus)?
- Do you work with foreign currencies?

Application of the Process

After a sales quotation for a customer is recorded and its release authorized, an order can be released directly in SAP Business One. The customer must be transferred to the address area with assistance of the Find function, whose symbol is right beside the input field for the customer. Select the customer whose quotation has to be changed to an order.

In our model company, this is client 200110, the Krueger gas station. The customer data is automatically transferred to the order edit window. The Quotation button is located at the bottom of the order input window; when you click on it a window with currently open customer quotations appears. These are quotations that have not been accepted and made into an order. Double-clicking chooses the desired quotation from the list (for example: quotation number 201000005). Now pick the items from the item list of the chosen quotation. Confirm the transfer of the information to the input table of the order by clicking on OK. The transfer can include part of the items or additional items not included in the quotation. The quantity of the items can also be changed from the quotation, if necessary. In order to assure correct processing, a date has to be entered in the tax date field. If the other suggested values are not what you want, then they can be changed here as well. Add the order to the system by clicking the Add button.

Navigation Information

- **Menu Path:** Sales > Sales Order, Sales > Sales Order > Gross Profit
- **Tables:** ORDR, RDR1, RDR2, RDR3
- **Incoming Trigger:** Opportunity Analysis, Order Without Reference to Quotation Arrived
- **Outgoing Trigger:** Automatic PO Generation from CO, Delivery Processing, Customer Dunning after Due Date, A/P Invoice, Production Order Initialization, Customer Order Processing

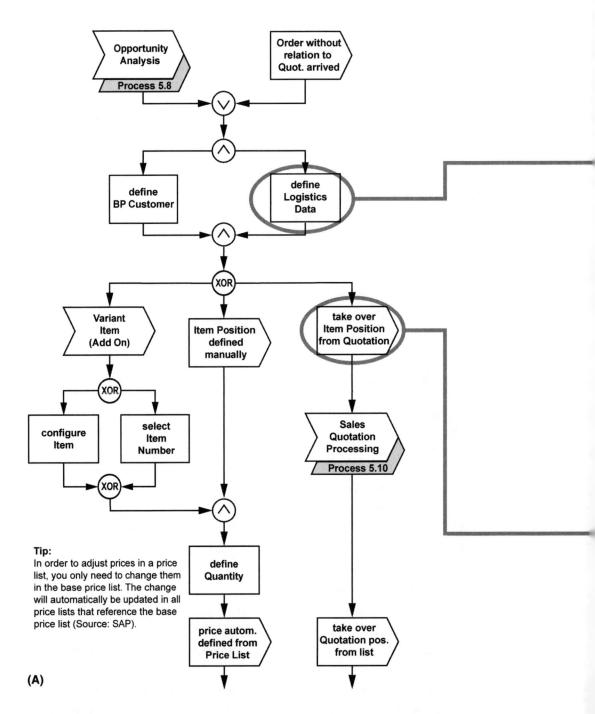

Tip:
In order to adjust prices in a price list, you only need to change them in the base price list. The change will automatically be updated in all price lists that reference the base price list (Source: SAP).

(A)

FIGURE 5.26 *(a) Deliver address in the order, (b) List of the products to be copied*

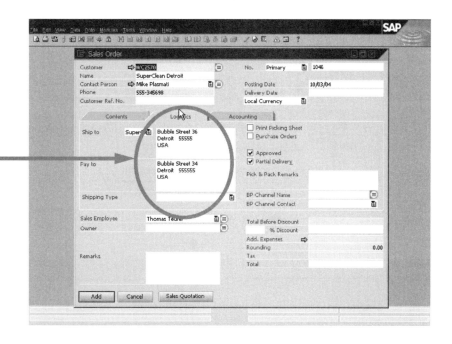

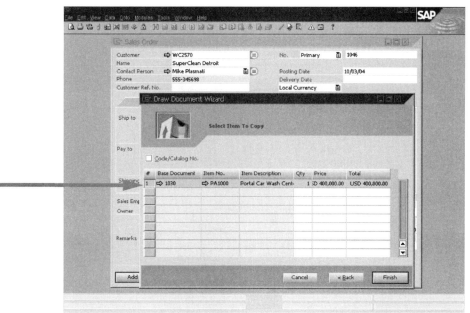

(B)

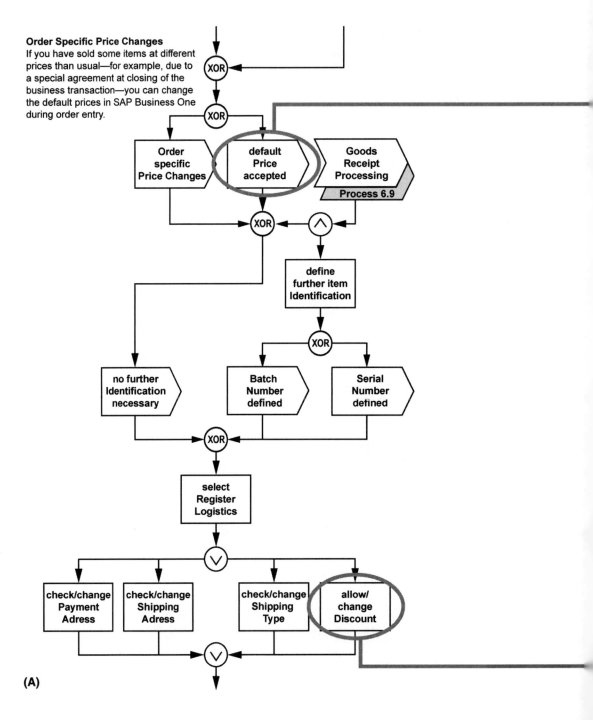

Order Specific Price Changes
If you have sold some items at different prices than usual—for example, due to a special agreement at closing of the business transaction—you can change the default prices in SAP Business One during order entry.

(A)

FIGURE 5.27 *(a) Initial order form, (b) Register representation for logistics data*

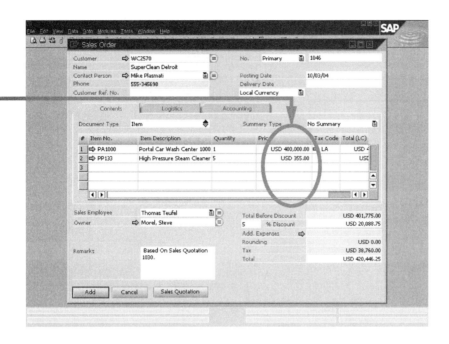

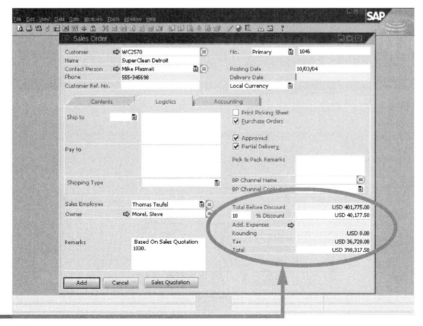

(B)

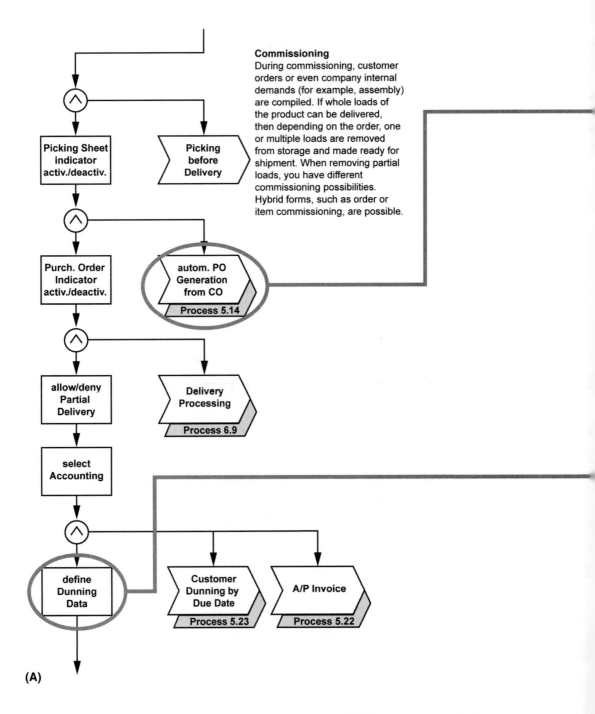

Commissioning
During commissioning, customer orders or even company internal demands (for example, assembly) are compiled. If whole loads of the product can be delivered, then depending on the order, one or multiple loads are removed from storage and made ready for shipment. When removing partial loads, you have different commissioning possibilities. Hybrid forms, such as order or item commissioning, are possible.

FIGURE 5.28 *(a) Initial screen for the automatic order generation, (b) Register representation for accounting criteria*

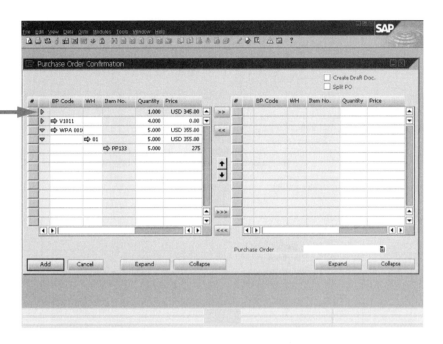

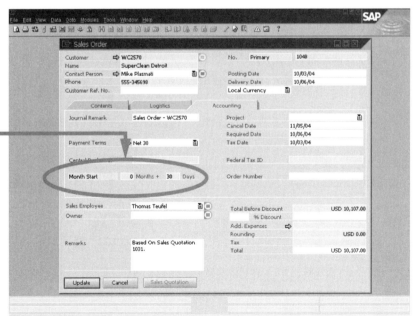

(B)

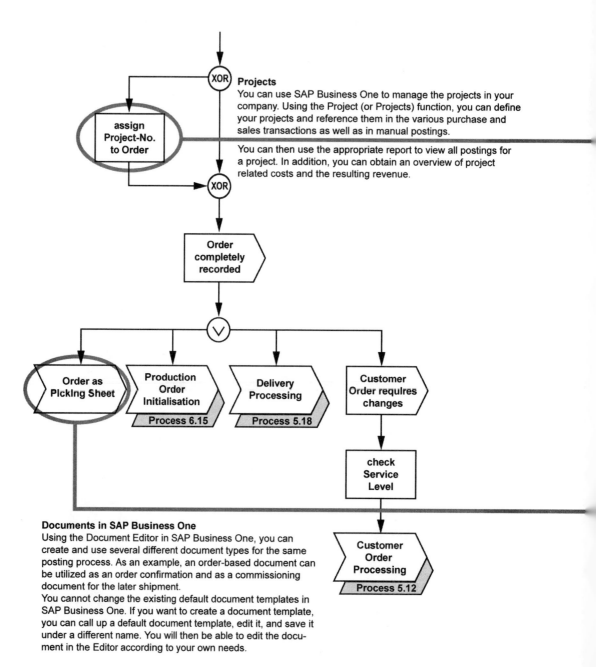

Projects
You can use SAP Business One to manage the projects in your company. Using the Project (or Projects) function, you can define your projects and reference them in the various purchase and sales transactions as well as in manual postings.

You can then use the appropriate report to view all postings for a project. In addition, you can obtain an overview of project related costs and the resulting revenue.

Documents in SAP Business One
Using the Document Editor in SAP Business One, you can create and use several different document types for the same posting process. As an example, an order-based document can be utilized as an order confirmation and as a commissioning document for the later shipment.
You cannot change the existing default document templates in SAP Business One. If you want to create a document template, you can call up a default document template, edit it, and save it under a different name. You will then be able to edit the document in the Editor according to your own needs.

(A)

FIGURE 5.29 *(a) Project assignments in order, (b) Order receipt*

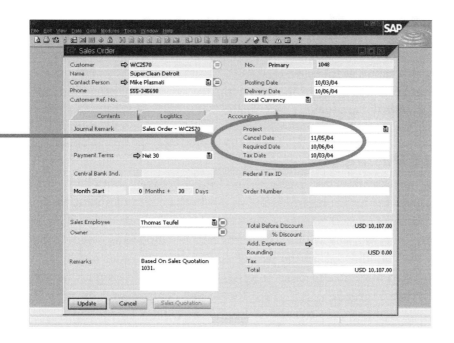

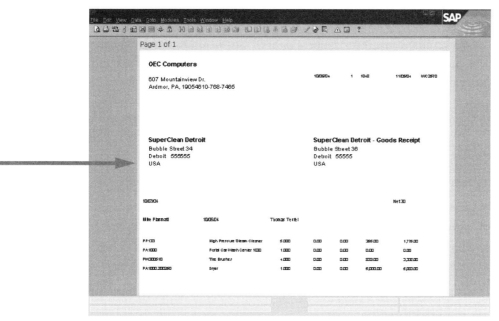

(B)

Inventory Situation Analyses

Usually, a controller will perform the analyses of the inventory; his arrangement list is also known as the *parts-needed* list. Most often, this is a materials list that is split into two separate parts for each item, depending on whether this item is produced internally or purchased externally.

Business Description

These materials lists can largely be subdivided between controllers—each individual receives his list regarding the items. In the electronics industry, for example, both active and passive components must be purchased. This leads to Controller A working with a list for the active components, while Controller B deals with another list for the passive components. In order for the Purchasing department to be able re-order in time, the inventory levels must be defined, at which time a message is sent to the Purchasing department. This inventory level is known as the *re-order point*.

SAP Business One: Specific Description

One of the standard inventory reports in SAP Business One is the inventory status, which can be seen as an arrangement list. This report shows all items with inventory that:

- Are in the warehouse
- Are in the warehouse, but are already reserved for a customer order
- Are on order but have not arrived

In addition, the available quantity is shown.

In the inventory column is shown the free stock, which is stock in inventory that is not already reserved. The inventory management represents the physical inventory resulting from the entry of all inventory changing procedures and the resulting inventory updates in real time. A customer order contains the reserved quantities that are scheduled to be issued at a later time and for a particular reason. This reservation system ensures that the items are available when needed. In addition, the reservation system serves to make the goods issue process to the customer easier and more expedient. It is also important that the materials controller keeps an eye on reservations in order to make sure that materials are ordered in time.

The inventory levels are not only kept by quantity but also by value. The system updates for each inventory movement the quantity and value adjustment for the inventory, allocation for the cost accounting, and G/L accounts in Accounting using the automatic accounting locating. The organizational level on which the material inventory is managed by value is called the Valuation area. The Valuation area is equivalent to a company code/client in SAP Business One.

The inventory management is strictly done on the storage location level. If you enter a goods movement, then you only need to input the storage location of the item. If the material is to be further divided into batches, then each batch can be assigned a number that is then separately tracked in inventory. The inventory management can track several special internal and external inventory types, such as consignment stock, separately from the normal inventory. In this case, multiple inventories that require a reclassification are defined in SAP Business One.

In the context of inventory situation analyses, the following questions should be asked:

- Which organizational units access the inventory situation analyses?
- Do you need a query for reorder levels which lead to planned orders?
- Do you need further divide the inventory for example using batch numbers?

Application of the Process

The Inventory Situation report is used in SAP Business One to call up an arrangement list. You can find this report in the Inventory Reports menu in the Reporting application. In the selection window, you can choose single items or a category of items. Tthe selection of specific vendors is also possible. The item groups and item characteristics serve as further selection criteria. After confirming the selections, a summary view appears, displaying information about how many items are in stock, how many of those are reserved for orders, if there are orders and their quantity, and the total availability of an item. To open a detailed view of an item, double-click on a row.

Navigation Information

- **Menu Path:** Reporting > Inventory Reports > Inventory Situation > Inventory Levels > Items

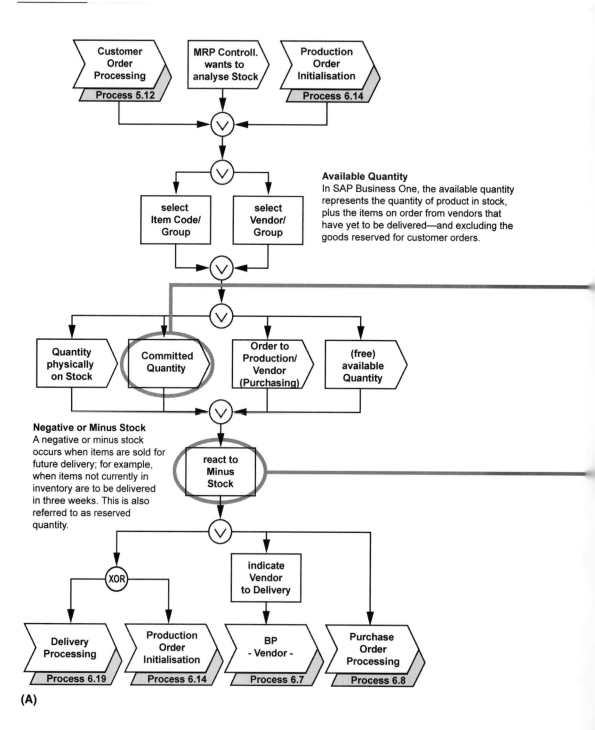

Available Quantity
In SAP Business One, the available quantity represents the quantity of product in stock, plus the items on order from vendors that have yet to be delivered—and excluding the goods reserved for customer orders.

Negative or Minus Stock
A negative or minus stock occurs when items are sold for future delivery; for example, when items not currently in inventory are to be delivered in three weeks. This is also referred to as reserved quantity.

(A)

FIGURE 5.30 *(a) Current inventory table, (b) Minus inventory for drag and relate*

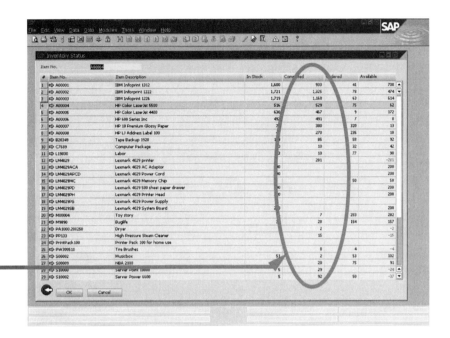

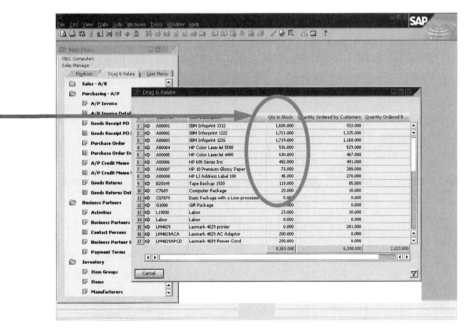

(B)

- **Tables:** OITW, OPDN, ORDR, POR2, POR3
- **Incoming Trigger:** Customer Order Handling, Inventory Analyses, Production Order Opening
- **Outgoing Trigger:** Delivery Handling, Production Order Opening, Vendor BP-Master Record, Order Handling

Automatic Order Generation from the Customer Order

The trend in industry points increasingly toward a flat production model that reduces the creation of value-added chains in the vertical range of manufacturing. The planning and execution of procurement processes always gain significance, since increasing costs of materials are advanced as well as the reduction of stock level. The portion of external parts is increasing and furthermore leads into a close partnership with the supplier/system suppliers.

Business Description

The determination of the optimal quantity and time line of an order has become one of the most important aspects of running a company. Procurement includes the purchasing of materials, parts, and finished products, as well as capital equipment and services. The trigger for the procurement process is the request for materials from a specific department (for example, construction or manufacturing) to Purchasing.

If this request is for a new item, Purchasing sends out requests for information to several vendors regarding their price, quality, and previous record regarding on-time delivery. The offers from the vendors are then compared in an offer comparison spreadsheet. If a vendor exists who is able to deliver the needed material within the requested conditions, an order can be placed immediately after the decision is made. The receipt of an order confirmation from the vendor makes the contract binding. Especially, the delivery conditions and payment terms stated in the order are part of the contract. At the conclusion of the contract it is often also determined whether to make this a one-time order or a long-term relationship between the contract partners.

If this is more than a one-time order, it is called a *fixed-term vendor contract*. A fixed-term vendor contract is a contract agreement with a vendor for a defined time period. The company agrees to deliver a certain quantity of material within a defined time period to the specified conditions. Outline agreements are most often made with manufacturers who receive deliveries on the Just-In-Time principle.

A disruption of the delivery process is always possible due to unforeseen problems; the receiving company needs to monitor the delivery process regarding the fulfillment of the contractually agreed-upon services. This monitoring includes checking the correct delivery date and quality of material. Often, the vendor is queried regarding the ability to keep the agreed upon delivery time in advance. The worst-case scenario is a contract penalty for the vendor, if the receiving company has damages due to production loss.

SAP Business One: Specific Description

SAP Business One now makes it possible (starting with Release 6.2) to automatically generate a supplier order from a customer order. The system tries to map as many entries as possible from the customer to the supplier order during the transfer. The order can also be split into several supplier orders, if different sources (vendors) are involved.

Prices and quantities are contractually obligating after the order is generated. If goods are not received by the agreed-upon date, a reminder must be sent from the buyer to the supplier. SAP Business One uses an open item inventory in the case of partial deliveries of individual order items to track items still missing from the order. The subsequent Goods Receiving process and Incoming Invoice process always relate to the order. Shipments without orders are normally rejected.

Purchase order requests from Production can be listed and converted to orders through the Product Recommendations report. Most companies try to automate most orders using order templates (parked vouchers), especially when they are repeat orders from the same supplier with similar conditions. During the creation of an order, the buyer first has to determine the supplier, which can be done via a match-code search (the icon right next to the input field).

The purchase order header data applies to all following order items, such as the payment terms, delivery dates, journal entry, and certain notes. The order number (whether assigned internally by the system or externally selected) is included as key in the purchase order header and serves as reference number for the supplier. In the Administration module (see Figure 5.31), a number of order versions can be customized with specific parameters using the order numbers. These versions are then available in document processing. This customization of parameters is useful when a company uses different order forms for use with business partners.

In our scenario, an order item requires a material number, which means that the attribute in the order header is set to item instead of service. Further procurement versions, such as consignment, sub-contracting, and so forth are possible through user-defined fields. In our example, the item is assigned to payroll processing in the item detail window using the Provision of Material field, as shown in Figure 5.32.

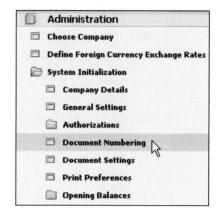

FIGURE 5.31 *Customizing Administration in SAP Business One*

If you include an item on the order that is immediately moved into consumption, a different account number may appear on the item detail screen. The account number (cost center, project, and so on) determines which accounts are charged when the invoice or the goods receipt are posted. Another important entry on the

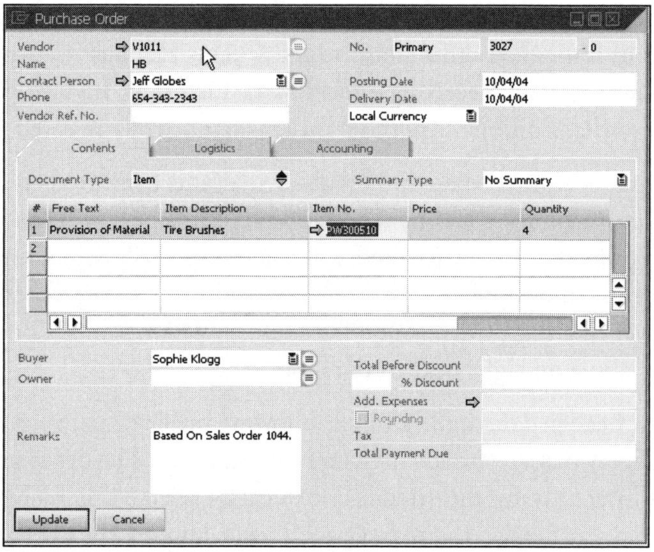

FIGURE 5.32 *Column "Order" for payroll processing*

item line is used for the price determination. You can either determine the price without taxes yourself or by the system automatically using the price lists.

You can specify further information per order item, such as add-on (order reason) or additional notes, which are added in the item detail window. The location of a particular text on an order receipt is determined by the configuration in document processing. This determines both the location and order of the text on the screen and printouts. Fields, images, and text are configured on a purchase order header and a line level. The entry of data in the order form does not necessarily mean that it appears on the printed document. In general, the add-on notes are printed on the purchase order form after the order item data such as item number, quantity and price. SAP Business One has the ability to allow the adding of images for products in the item master record, which can be printed with the order. This allows the business partner to immediately recognize the item.

An important special order form is represented by the internal stock transfer. This type of order causes a transfer of stock from one plant to another. A prerequisite is a transparent inventory structure within the company. This shows which items are stored in the internal warehouses and can be acquired via an internal stock transfer.

Another special order form deals with no-value items such as samples, promotional items, and others. During the monitoring of this ordering, just like with other orders, the delivery date is checked; however, the items are tracked in inventory as a no-value item. The order is entered with a price of zero.

The Third-Party Purchase Order is a special order form that is needed for items that are purchased for a third party and shipped directly to the customer. You place an order and pay the invoice after your customer has received the items directly from your supplier. You place the order by telling your supplier the address of your business partner, who receives the order via a third-party deal.

You can print the order documents manually using the Printer icon in the upper menu bar. The print preview shows the documents the way they will be printed, so that you can examine the correctness of the information. If you would like to print out a batch run of all orders, select the Document Printing option from the Purchase main menu. This will bring up a batch-run selection screen, where you can print, for example, all orders that have not been printed (see Figure 5.33). You can also select a time frame or number range. Afterwards, the orders are printed in batch.

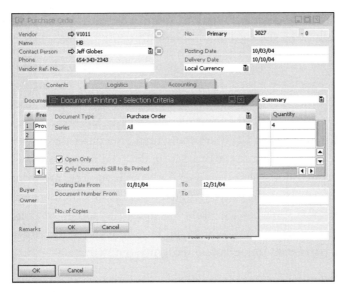

FIGURE 5.33 *Selection to print a receipt*

The following questions should be asked during purchase order processing:

♦ How do you assign purchase order numbers? Do you number different types of purchase orders with different sets of numbers? Do you use automatic number assignment, or do you assign the numbers manually?

♦ What types of purchase orders does your organization use: normal, subcontracting, third party, order with provision of materials (consignment)?

♦ What purchase price lists do you use and how are they arranged? Are there different price lists for finished goods, semi-finished goods, and raw materials?

♦ Which item detail fields would you like to use, and which ones are displayed in the table in the main overview?

Application of the Process

If not all materials are available for a product, then missing parts must be ordered. This is done by using the Purchase Order function in the Purchasing module. Pick a supplier who produces the parts themselves or is a distributor. The model company "Car Wash Assembly" serves as a vendor, which purchases, sometimes refines and assembles, all items sold by the "Car Wash Distribution" company. The supplier master data is taken into the current form using the selection field icon. You can change the Posting, Delivery, or Controlling dates if they are different from the suggested values, and enter the items to be ordered in the table. You can look up items by using the various search functions. In the appropriate fields, enter the quantities for the items and confirm the entries with the Update button. Confirm by clicking OK, which will transfer the order to SAP Business One.

The automatic purchase order is released by making the appropriate selection of the Logistic register in the input window. When you click on Update, it opens a form with which you can automatically generate an order. Transfer the lines of the order from the left to the right side and confirm the entries. The order is released and the window is closed.

When all parts of a product are not available, the missing parts must be ordered. To do so, you call the Purchase Order function in the Purchasing application. Define a vendor that either manufactures or sells the parts. In the model company, our vendor is Car_wash_plant_Assembly, which buys, modifies, and installs all products sold by Car_wash_plant_Distribution. The master data of the vendor is transferred to the current mask with the selection field symbol. If these differ from proposed values, change the date for posting, delivery, and control. Enter the items to be ordered into the table. You can transfer the items with different integrated search functions from SAP Business One to the selection list. Enter the desired quantities into the specific fields. Confirm the input with the Update button and confirm the order by clicking OK. The order is transferred to the SAP Business One system.

You release the automatic purchase order by clicking the appropriate indicator in the input window under the Logistics register. If you click on Update, the mask for automatic generation of the purchase order will open. Transfer the entries of the order from the left side to the right side and confirm the entries. The order is released, and the window closes.

Navigation Information

- **Menu Path:** Purchase > Purchase Order, Sales > Order >Logistics > Purchase Order > Add
- **Tables:** OPOR, POR1, POR2, POR3
- **Incoming Trigger:** BP Vendor, PO without Reference, Purchased Item, Customer Order Processing
- **Outgoing Trigger:** Goods receipt processing with reference to PO

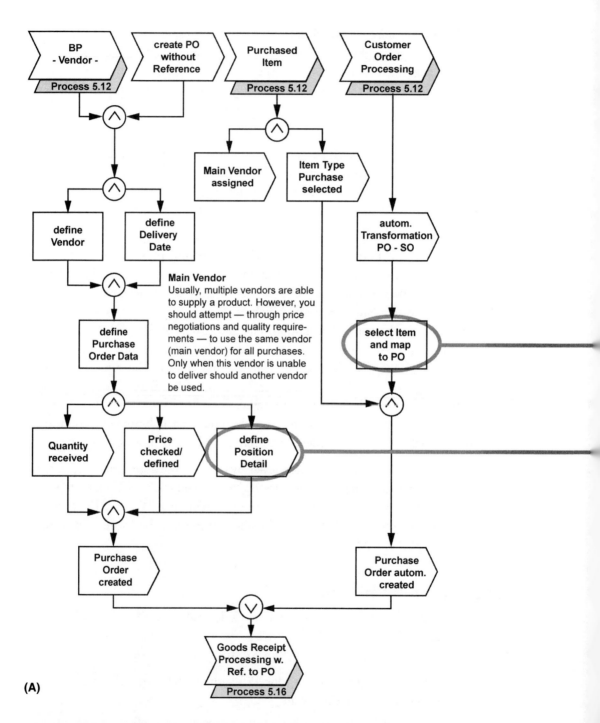

Main Vendor
Usually, multiple vendors are able to supply a product. However, you should attempt — through price negotiations and quality requirements — to use the same vendor (main vendor) for all purchases. Only when this vendor is unable to deliver should another vendor be used.

(A)

FIGURE 5.34 *(a) Purchase receipt for an automatic order, (b) Initial screen for orders*

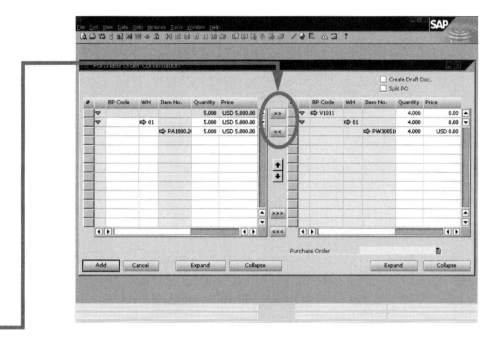

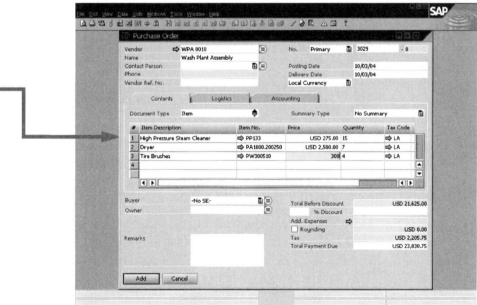

(B)

Import Data

The process of reporting to the authorities after international procurement depends on the respective economic zone. In the ERP system, reported data from purchasing documents must be captured and is stored in a sequential file

Business Description

Only purchasing data, already posted to accounting and therefore finalized, is stored. After reporting, the data can then be updated at any time and overwritten.

SAP Business One: Specific Description

If you import goods from foreign countries, you can administer the associated landed costs of the deliveries with SAP Business One. You can calculate the purchase price to include import tax and other import charges and expenditures within the system. It is also possible to store purchase-related costs such as import fees, taxes, transportation costs, loading charges, and so on. Import costs are distributed according to a predefined formula according to the cost category; for example, transportation costs are distributed according to the weight and volume of the items. First you must enter relevant data about each item, and after delivery of the order from the foreign country has been posted, then you must add the import costs in a separate document. To enter the import costs (reporting data) for an item in the system, you ust enter different data in the master record of the item. The following data must be entered for an item:

- ◆ **Length, Width, Height, Volume, and Weight Fields.** In these fields, the physical characteristics of the item and its weight should be indicated. This data forms the basis for calculating transportation and storage costs of a delivery.

- ◆ **Customs Tax Group Field.** Here, the predefined customs group relevant to the item is determined. Import costs are calculated; these include the import tax, import charges, and other fees based on the purchase price.

The import data is captured after the delivery at the same time as incoming invoice.

The characteristics of the documents concerning the import process include the following:

- **The Process Module, Purchase Order.** No separate import data is recorded at the time of the order. The order probably shows the amount in foreign currency. The creation of an order is recommended with items tracked in inventory, in order to increase the stock by the purchased order quantity.

- **The Process Module, Goods Receipt with/without Reference to Purchase Order.** Receiving can take place with or without a reference to a purchase order. An import procedure does not necessarily have to have an order preceding it. However, to record import costs within SAP Business One, a delivery must exist. With the delivery of the order, the stock levels of the items within the order are increased accordingly. Since the import costs are based on the delivery, you should make sure that prices and quantities are included correctly in the delivery note. The prices indicated in the delivery of an order are the supplier's item prices, without additional transportation costs. This means that the prices are with shipping included or with free shipping. The total amount of the delivery is the amount to be paid to the supplier. It does not include commissions to individual agencies or intermediate suppliers that still must be paid.

- **The Process Module, Purchase Invoice.** The purchase invoice is usually entered after the delivery. It isn't part of the import costs, but it is included in the system so that payment can be made to the supplier.

- **The Process Module, Landed Costs.** Import data is processed based on delivery. Import costs usually are recorded at the same time as the purchase invoice but in a separate document so that the total production cost of an item can be calculated. In the import data, both the purchase price and the import costs are captured. Thus, inventory valuation, gross profit, and other calculations can be done on the basis of inventory values. After import costs are compiled, the price of an item is updated in the last purchase price list to reflect the cost of importing the product. Also, by capturing the import data, the appropriate postings are triggered in accounting to charge the associated accounts for the cost of importing.

In the context of the landed costs for the marketing company, the following question should be asked:

- Is the item number range defined during system initialization for internal (automatic) assignment of sequential numbers or are item numbers assigned manually?

Application of the Process

To record the data for an import procedure in SAP Business One, you must select the Import Costs function in the Purchase application. The system opens the window in the Add mode for recording import data. If you want to display or change an existing import data document, you first must change into Find mode. In the top area of the window, the vendor and customs agency data are indicated. If the imported delivery included shipments from several vendors, you can select them together. You can add additional vendors simply by recalling the list of vendors by clicking the icon to the right of the field. Select one or multiple vendors from the list and confirm the choice by clicking OK. Confirm in the dialog window that appears that you do not want to overwrite the vendors previously selected, and the system transfers the additional vendor to the document. A multiple selection of vendors is indicated by star symbols in the input field.

After choosing vendors, enter the customs agency for information purposes only in the Broker input field, assuming that you have already recorded the agency master data in the system.

You can set the Import Data Processed attribute, if the reporting of the Import to the authorities has been processed and concluded at the time of the delivery. This attribute is also for information purposes only.

You can change the suggested values in the company code, posting date, or due date fields at any time. In the middle of the window, a table contains different registers with information concerning the imported items. In the Items register, you can display a list of open deliveries for purchase orders of the selected vendors by clicking the Goods Receipt PO button at the bottom of the window. Select one or more document and insert them into the table by clicking Add. In the lower area of the register, you can find the data for import costs and the total amount of the delivery, as well as the Notes field, in which the reference document is listed. If differences exist between expected and actual customs, you can adjust the default value to the actual customs.

In the Costs register is the option to distribute the real import costs of an item by fixed and variable costs. To distribute the costs on the items in accordance with their origin, a distribution key is defined using the New Import Costs function.

A list of all vendors is displayed by switching to the Vendors register. Further information about the import is displayed in the Details register. There, detailed characteristics of individual items can be displayed by clicking the arrow at each line.

The Journal register enables you to add the journal entry for the costs of the import directly from the register. To activate this entry, click on the Create Journal Entry button, which opens another window in which you can define the journal entry.

To save the data, add the document by clicking on Add to the System.

Navigation Information

- ◆ **Menu Path:** Purchasing > Landed Costs
- ◆ **Tables:** OARG
- ◆ **Incoming Trigger:** Item Master Data Processing, Purchase Order Processing, Automatic PO Generation from CO
- ◆ **Outgoing Trigger:** Goods Receipt Processing with Reference to PO

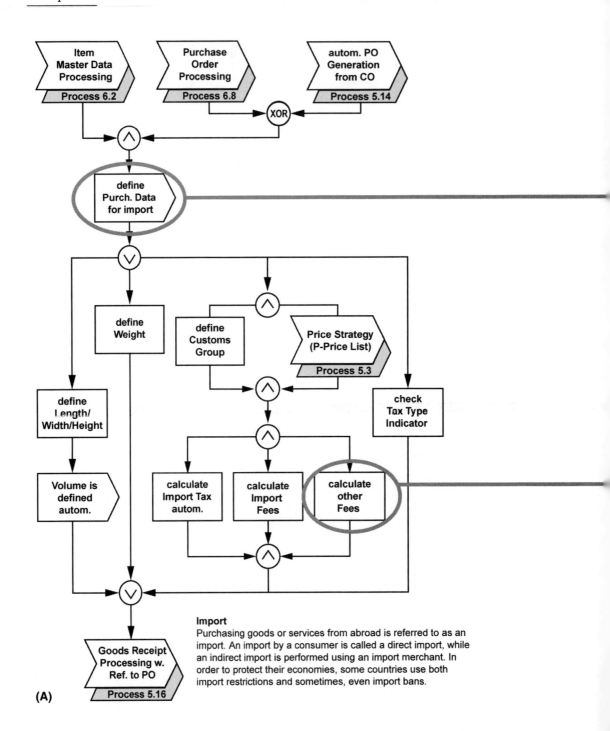

Import
Purchasing goods or services from abroad is referred to as an import. An import by a consumer is called a direct import, while an indirect import is performed using an import merchant. In order to protect their economies, some countries use both import restrictions and sometimes, even import bans.

(A)

FIGURE 5.35 *(a) Purchasing data for the item master data, (b) Detail description of the import costs*

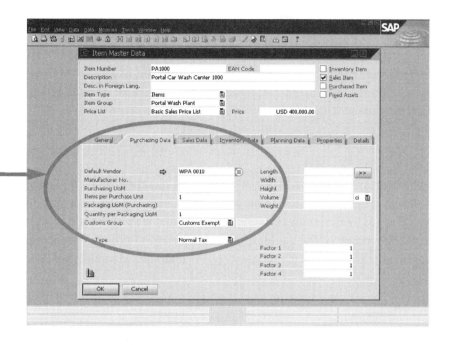

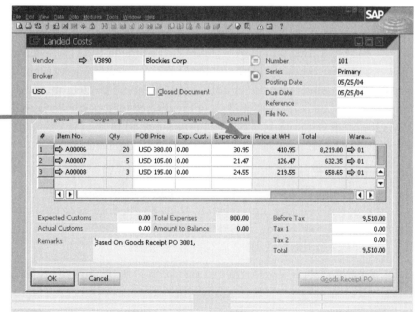

(B)

Goods Receipt Processing

Goods receipt is both part of procurement and also part of inventory management. It can take place as the result of an order or be unplanned. For example, inventory administration must account for the storage of remaining materials, overproduced parts, and so on.

Business Description

Goods receipt processing includes not only item quantities but also quality-relevant and price-relevant factors. The primary purpose of goods receipt processing is to receive products that are delivered by a supplier or an agent and to record and acknowledge receipt of the goods. Quantities, as well as other goods receipt data, are captured with—or if necessary, without—reference to a purchase order.

 NOTE

Unplanned receiving of shipments is closely examined based on legal standards, but often occurs because of samples or returns.

If there is a corresponding purchase order to the shipment, then the receiving data from the delivery is compared to the order. If there are differences, then an over-delivery or under-delivery exists. In both cases, it should be determined whether the supplier should be contacted regarding the discrepancy, particularly with over-delivery. Often, for example with plastic parts, a few additional parts are delivered intentionally to compensate for various product contingencies.

During receiving, it is specified whether the delivered product is to be transferred to quality inspection (incoming control) or delivered directly to the production plant. If the product is used immediately, then an expense account is allocated (and, if necessary, a cost center, an order, and/or a project). Note that all required posting takes place at the time the product is received.

If the delivered product is stored, then at the time of the receipt of goods, a posting takes place on an asset account. The time it takes to process the receiving depends on the quality inspections and whether the procurement is external or internal. Internal goods receipt might be from another production department of the same enterprise. External goods usually are submitted to a quality inspection, and sometimes only a visual inspection at the loading ramp. The quality inspection also determines the process of the incoming invoice, since payment can only be released or stopped after it is complete. The results are stored in the shipping documents.

SAP Business One: Specific Description

Goods Receipt is part of the Procurement cycle in SAP Business One and is an interface to Inventory Management. Usually the delivered materials are posted to the available materials in stock. If the receiving is based on a purchase order, then you can implement several controls to make sure that the vendor is keeping the dates agreed upon in the order (planned receiving). When posting, the open order quantities are the default values, meaning the goods yet to be delivered. This is especially important when accepting partial deliveries. Under-deliveries are allowed in SAP Business One, as the quantity adjustments per item are adjusted automatically for the next receipt of goods. If you receive higher quantities from the vendor, then you can still establish the reference to the purchase order and enter a higher quantity. With goods receipt, the following processes are executed in the background:

- ◆ Updating the quantity fields
- ◆ Updating inventory and consumption costs

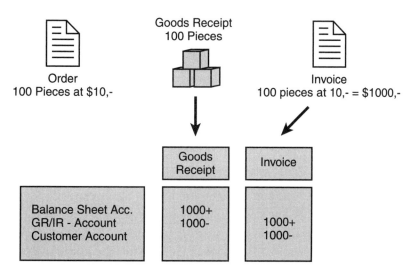

FIGURE 5.36   *Account maintenance (Source: SAP AG)*

The automatic account determination is a major advantage in the system-supported procurement process. The only time an inventory account must be entered is when the stock transaction is to be posted to a different account. Otherwise, the inventory account is automatically determined by the system. The following example describes the posting that is executed for the incoming invoice after the automatic account determination during receiving.

You are receiving 100 items and post a transaction of $1,000 to the asset account, as the price per item is $10. In accounting, it is not customary to create a separate account for each item, but rather to group items with similar properties in an account. A WE/RE offset account is used as an interim account between the inventory and accounts payable. The above posting is then balanced with an offsetting entry on the vendor account with an incoming invoice.

When you're using a continuous inventory with sliding average pricing, the actual inventory of an item is reevaluated after each receipt of goods:

> *Inventory quantity × previous average price = previous quantity price*
>
> *Quantity received × incoming invoice price = price of quantity received*
>
> *Total quantity = total expenditure*
>
> *Total expenditure/total quantity = new average price*

All following issues out of inventory are valued at the new average price. This procedure repeats itself with each acquisition.

The item price is stored in price lists and assigned to the item master data. Inventory posting differentiate according to two price sources: price list (standard costs) and last calculated costs.

Stock lists for the order include the following:

- Warehouse balance report
- Stock valuation
- List of inventory postings

These lists represent proof for the inventory movements. You can find the information by looking in the Accounting area and tracing the postings responsible for the inventory movement. The posting of a receipt of goods increases the current inventory of the item by the delivered quantity (the In Stock column). The inventory situation list provides the current stock levels. After the intake of goods, you can again check whether the item is assigned to inventory or the customer order (reserved items). For additional verification, you may view an inventory report on a per item basis (Stock Balance report) that provides exact information regarding the per warehouse inventory levels of each item (for example, Warehouse 01).

The following questions should be asked for goods receipt processing:

- ◆ Do you permit unplanned goods receipt? Is there goods receipt with purchase order in your enterprise?
- ◆ Which evaluations (stock lists) do you need?

Application of the Process

You will find the Goods Receipt function in SAP Business One in the Purchasing application of the main menu. The general data for goods receipt is entered in the upper area of the window. Select the vendor that supplied the goods from the list using the search functions. You can display all purchase orders from this vendor with the Purchase Order button, and select the order which items were delivered. If not all items were shipped, then mark the lines of items delivered by holding the Control key. Transfer the selected lines to the table by confirming with the OK button. Now you can assign the items to a group and make changes to the default values for Due Date and Tax Date. The document number to reference the purchase order is listed in the Notes field below the table. The text in the Journal Entry field is submitted with the posting to the database. You can name a sales employee in the Buyer field and, finally, specify the payment terms.

Navigation Information

- ◆ **Menu Path:** Purchasing > Goods Receipt
- ◆ **Tables:** O1GN, PODN, IGN1, IGN2, IGN3
- ◆ **Incoming Trigger:** Purchase Order Control, Purchase Order Processing, Automatic PO Generation from CO, Material with Reference to PO Received
- ◆ **Outgoing Trigger:** Returns Processing, Purchase Order Control, WH Management System, Inventory in WH Report, Inventory Valuation Report, Inventory Posting List, Inventory Status, A/P Invoice

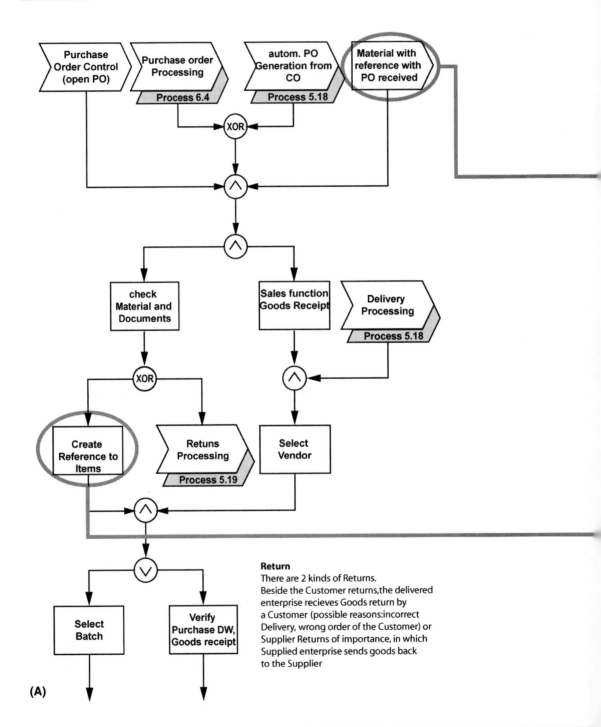

Return
There are 2 kinds of Returns.
Beside the Customer returns,the delivered
enterprise recieves Goods return by
a Customer (possible reasons:incorrect
Delivery, wrong order of the Customer) or
Supplier Returns of importance, in which
Supplied enterprise sends goods back
to the Supplier

(A)

FIGURE 5.37 *(a) Goods receiving for the order, (b) Selections for the delivery receipt*

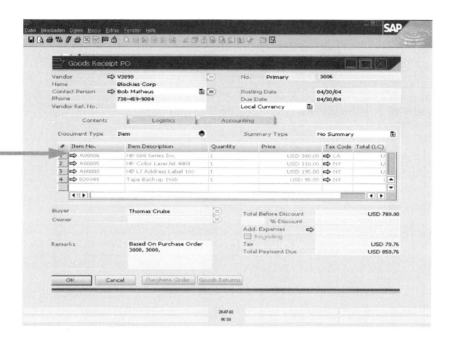

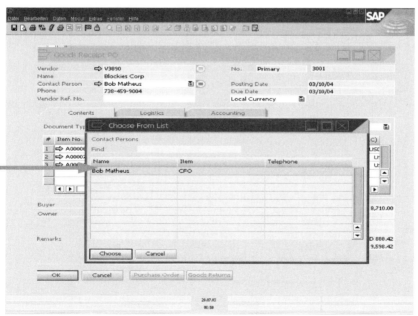

(B)

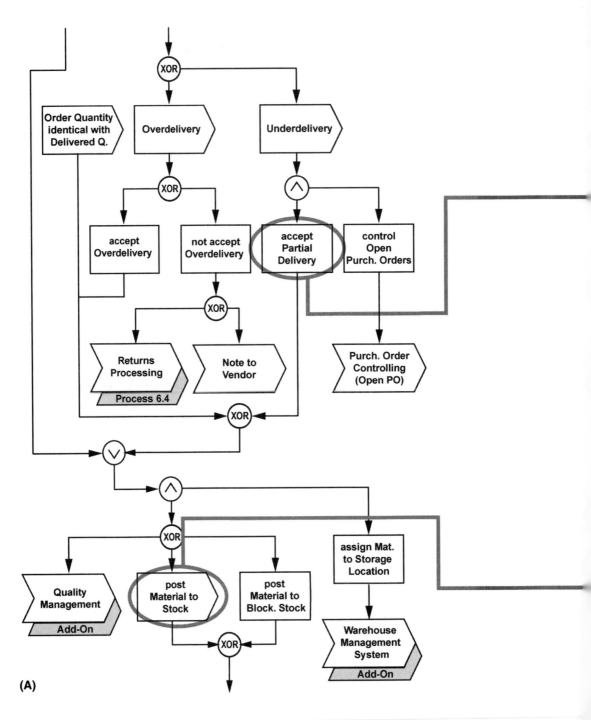

(A)

FIGURE 5.38 *(a) Selection of items to be copied, (b) Image of the booking receipt*

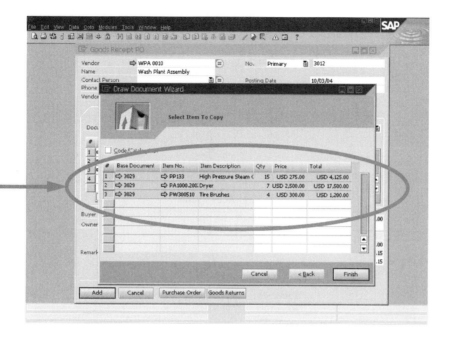

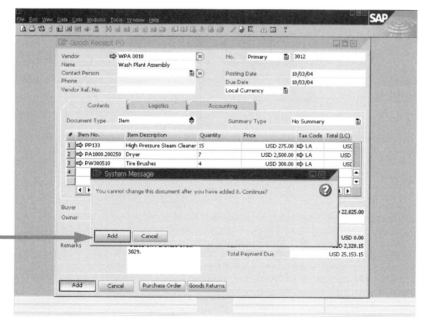

(B)

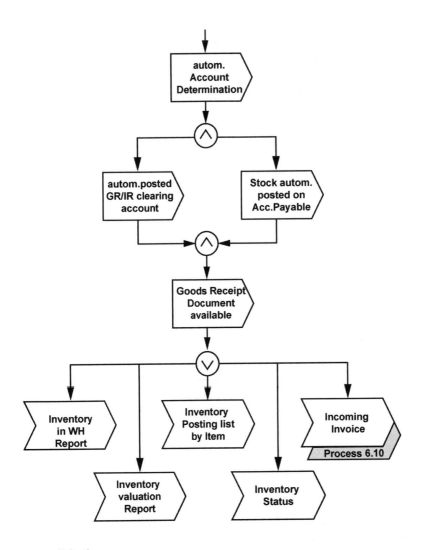

Inventory Valuation
With this report the entire Stock of all Items can be evaluated at a deadline.
Under normal conditions you can accomplish the evaluation of the Stock to the balance sheet date.
You can use each usual standard method for the Inventory Valuation. In addition you can limit
the selection of the Inventory Valuation according to different Criteria. The system evaluates
the Stock, as well as incomings and Outgoings with the method of moving average Price.
You can select another Valuation method for the Inventory Valuation. If you accomplish
the evaluation according to the method of moving average Price, you obtain the same value
as in accounting.

(A)

FIGURE 5.39 *(a) Document processing in the receipt editor, (b) Receipt: Goods receipt for the order*

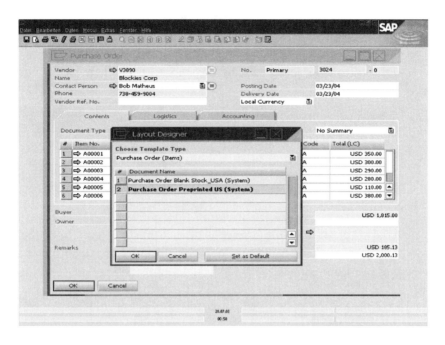

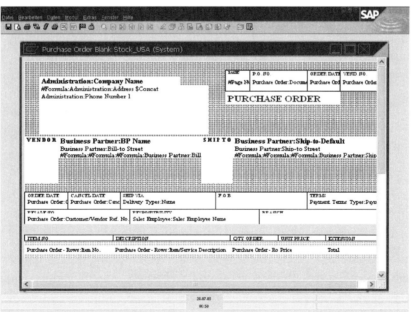

(B)

Incoming Invoice with Reference

The vendor provides the incoming invoice that is checked for accuracy against the order and the documents accompanying the shipment. Three invoice verifications are carried out:

- Material verification (comparison of the invoice items with the order items)
- Price verification (price variance/multi-computation)
- Invoice verification (correct adding of the amounts)

The clerk captures the invoice with the order reference.

The material verification of the invoice is done against the data from the order. Differences between the ordered and delivered quantity are determined and, if necessary, a complaint is filed.

Business Description

Difficulties arise if the vendor makes a partial delivery but bills for the full amount of the order or if the invoice arrives before the delivery. In these cases, the procurement process is interrupted, and a lot of time is spent in straightening out the circumstances with the supplier. In selecting a vendor, the company must not only pay attention to the lowest price, but also to how well the business partner will support the planned operational process in the long run. Over- and under-deliveries usually can be queried and automatically accepted based on fixed tolerance limits. Even if these limits are exceeded, a correction can be made during invoice verification.

Receiving checks the incoming invoice to assure that the quantity of the items delivered and the invoice data match. A material verification of the incoming invoice is confirmed, usually by initials or signature on the invoice. Purchasing then compares the prices and conditions of the incoming invoice with the order data.

In most enterprises, Purchasing is responsible for allocating the incoming invoice to an account (based on process flow charts) because only they know which cost centers, projects, or orders needed the order. In most companies, Purchasing will release the invoice for payment by signing it. Then Accounting formally examines the invoice and, if at least two signatures and a complete account assignment are present on the invoice, then it is posted in the system.

Pricing variances usually happen to currency and price fluctuations between the order and the invoice date. The buyer must ensure during the order process that the price does not deviate from the current market price beyond a reasonable range and that the vendor guarantees price stability. The agreed-upon conditions are guaranteed by the vendor at the order confirmation. Thus, a correction to payment can occur during the verification of the invoice.

The invoice verification checks the correctness of the invoice total. It is possible that the vendor made a calculation error or an item was invoiced multiple times. In addition, the invoice payment terms must be compared to the order. For example, on the order, a 30-day time of allowed payment may be indicated, while on the invoice it is specified to be 10 days net. The invoice verification also includes the proper allocation of material and freight costs. The proportional freight costs must be extracted from the material positions, in order to allow them to be posted properly. After the postings, the accounting balance between the order and invoice postings is settled.

SAP Business One: Specific Description

An incoming invoice in SAP Business One occurs in reference to an order. This procedure is integrally connected to Accounting. Quantity variance, price variance, and schedule deviation are verified against the order or the incoming goods; this creates an open post after posting in the Accounts Payable account (A/P), which is balanced by Accounting with the payment. Account determination can take place automatically in the background during incoming invoice verification because the system creates an accounting document in which the appropriate accounts are specified.

New terms of payment can be entered when you are recording an invoice, or the agreements from the order are simply accepted. The discount (cash discount amount) can be posted with (net) or without (gross) tax. In the real world, the incoming invoice is processed by a different person, so someone else triggers the payment run for the invoice in the bank transaction later. An incoming invoice captured into SAP Business One can no longer be modified.

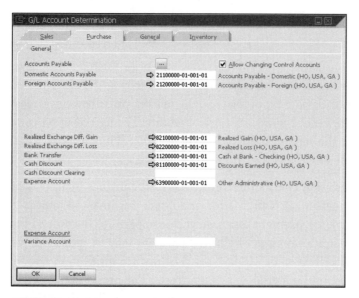

FIGURE 5.40 *Account determination in SAP Business One*

The following questions should be asked in your analysis of the incoming invoice process:

◆ Do you use automatic number allocation with sequential numbers, or do you allocate numbers manually?

◆ Do you use different numbers ranges for different invoices?

Application of the Process

In the Purchasing application, you must call the A/P Invoice function, which is displayed in a new window. The first step—the entry of the vendor into the input field—is necessary in order to create a reference to a purchase order. You can accomplish this by using the various search functions available in SAP Business One. All known and needed data from the selected vendor are entered into the fields, including the terms of payment created during the definition of the master data.

Clicking the Purchase Order or Goods Receipt PO button brings up the document to which a reference should be created. In the Model Company, an A/P invoice is to be created for a delivery. When the Goods Receipt PO button is chosen, a selection window is displayed with all available deliveries. Clicking the Choose button opens the Draw Document Wizard, which shows the delivery positions in a selection table. If not all positions appear in the invoice, then you can choose a selection here using the Customize indicator and confirming with Next, which brings up a selection table, Clicking on Finish transfers all positions into the current A/P invoice window. In the Remarks field, a note gives the reference to the purchase order and the goods receipt.

If you have entered all positions of the invoice and checked or adjusted all other details, you can submit the invoice to SAP Business One by clicking on Add. If all positions of the delivery receipt are transferred to the invoice, the delivery document is removed from the list of deliveries. The procedure for recording an invoice with reference to a purchase order is the same as recording an invoice with reference to a goods receipt.

Navigation Information

- **Menu Path:** Purchasing > A/P Invoice
- **Tables:** OPCH, PCH1, PCH2, PCH3
- **Incoming Trigger:** A/P Invoice
- **Outgoing Trigger:** Vendor Payables after Due Date, Outgoing Payment, Open Items List, Clear Unsolved Variance with Vendor

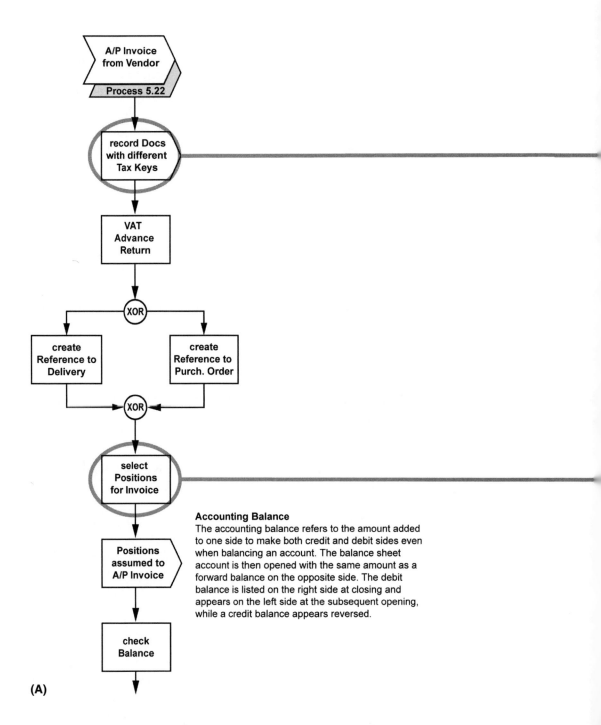

Accounting Balance

The accounting balance refers to the amount added to one side to make both credit and debit sides even when balancing an account. The balance sheet account is then opened with the same amount as a forward balance on the opposite side. The debit balance is listed on the right side at closing and appears on the left side at the subsequent opening, while a credit balance appears reversed.

(A)

FIGURE 5.41 *(a) Tax group table, (b) Selections for the delivery receipt*

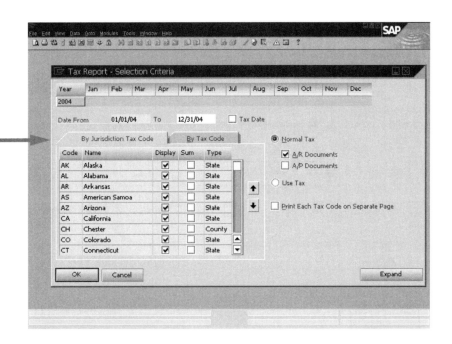

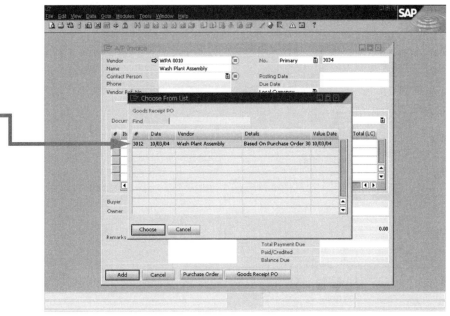

(B)

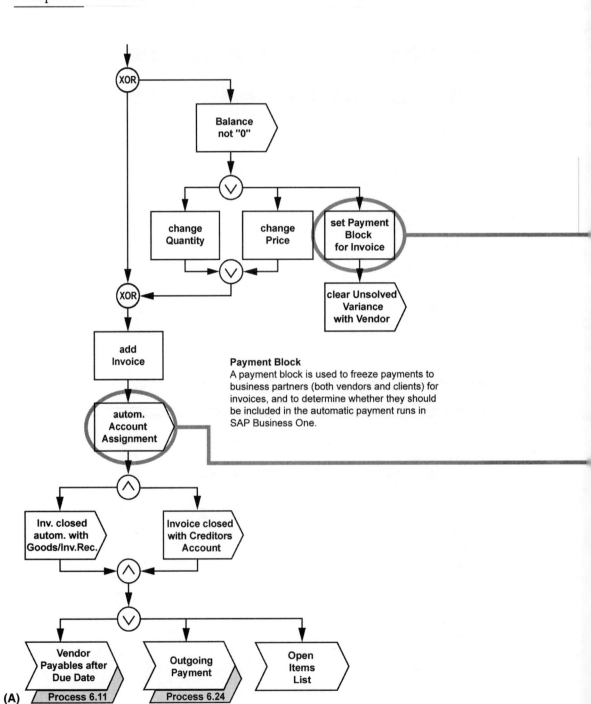

Payment Block
A payment block is used to freeze payments to business partners (both vendors and clients) for invoices, and to determine whether they should be included in the automatic payment runs in SAP Business One.

FIGURE 5.42 *(a) Determine payment block for the invoice, (b) Account locating for vendor accounts*

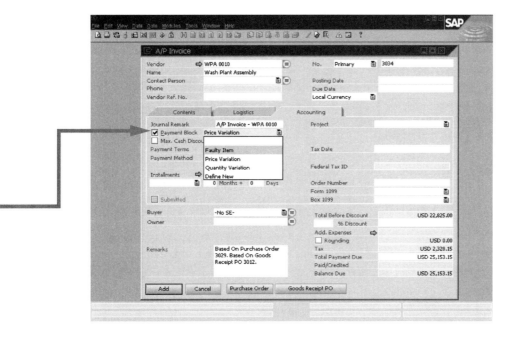

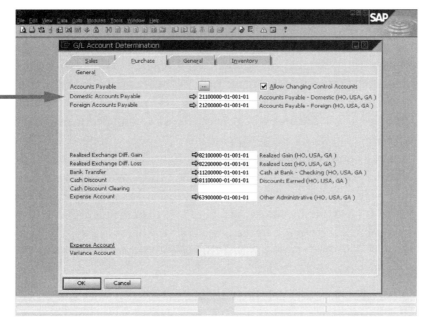

(B)

Delivery Processing

The central form of dispatch handling is the delivery note. All other shipping activities, such as commissioning, packing, goods issue processing, and transportation logistics use the delivery note document as a base.

Business Description

A shipment is usually put together for an outstanding customer order in a shipping facility. The basic data is transferred from the order and does not need to be entered again. Shipping triggers further functions, such as the printing of shipping documents and invoicing. In addition, a shipment sends products to an external company, but can also mean a transfer between two facilities belonging to different divisions of the enterprise. Delivery handling, also called *dispatch handling*, can represent a cash sale or include a more extensive handling process, with activities such as creating the delivery note, quality control, commissioning the goods, packing, and transportation logistics.

SAP Business One: Specific Description

A delivery note is generated after a customer order with items is present as a trigger document. The shipping-related data regarding customers and item positions are automatically transferred from the order, which makes a repeat entry of the information from the delivery note unnecessary. If a delivery is made without reference to an order, all data from the delivery have to be entered manually. If a service was rendered in the order, the delivery note process is dropped. SAP Business One permits the creation and sending of an outgoing invoice before a delivery note. Medium-sized businesses must often be flexible and send out an invoice before a delivery is completed. In that case, a value-based posting will be executed at the same time as the inventory posting. It is recommended that you create a sales document with reference to the preceding voucher in the system in order to show the complete sales process in SAP Business One (see *SAP Business One User Manual—Sales version 6.2 2003*).

During the creation of the delivery note, the underlying order is updated automatically. Furthermore, complete and partial deliveries can be carried out.

NOTE

In the SAP R/3 system, different document numbering can be defined; however, in SAP Business One, this is not the case.

Series - Purchase Order

		Number			String						
#	Name	First	Next	Last	Prefix	Suffix	Remarks	Group	Period Ind.		Lock
1	Primary	3000	3032					1	Default		
2	Metal	1030000	1030999					2	Default		
3	Plastic	2030000	2030999					3	Default		
4	Tools	3030000	3030999					4	Default		

☐ Display Series Linked to the Current Period Indicator

[Update] [Cancel]   [Set as Default]

FIGURE 5.43 *Number range for delivery*

Document Numbering

Document	Subdocument	Series	First	Next
Sales Quotation		Primary	1000	103
Sales Order		Primary	1000	105
Delivery		Primary	1000	102
Returns		Primary	1000	100
A/R Invoice		Primary	1000	102
A/R Credit Memo		Primary	1	
Incoming Payment		Primary	1000	100
Outgoing Payments		Primary	3000	300
Deposit		Primary	100	10
Purchase Order		Primary	3000	303
Goods Receipt PO		Primary	3000	301
Goods Returns		Primary	1	
A/P Invoice		Primary	3000	303

[OK] [Cancel]   [Original Names] [Name Change]

FIGURE 5.44 *Receipt range for delivery*

To cover different business requirements, delivery processing can be customized by designing different queries.

The following questions should be asked to analyze dispatch handling:

◆ From what set of numbers (see selection windows) does the document number originate when using either manual or automatic number allocation?

◆ Can deliveries only be entered if they are based on an order?

◆ Are deliveries allowed to have positions which are not referenced in any customer order?

◆ Can delivery data be included that does not refer to a customer order?

◆ Is a route determination needed and is it the result of a query?

◆ Should a query examine whether the delivery quantity falls below the stock level?

◆ Is stock location determined automatically by the item input?

Restrictions for delivery in SAP Business One are as follows:

◆ Delivery quantity of zero is not permitted.

◆ For each customer order, a separate delivery note must be recorded. Of course, the goods can be delivered physically together; however, the delivery then must have multiple delivery notes.

Application of the Process

If an order contains items meant to be shipped to a customer, then a delivery note must be created for those items in SAP Business One. This processing takes place in the Delivery function in the Sales application. When selecting the function, a new window is opened with a delivery input form.

Using the standard search functions, define a customer for which the delivery is recorded, or manually enter the customer data into the fields.

At the lower edge of the screen are the buttons for selecting a reference document. You can select Sales Quote Sales Order, or—if available—Returns and Invoices. If you want to record delivery of an order as we did in the model company, you may do so with reference to either the sales quote or the order. Click on the Sales Order button to get a separate window with a list of orders for the selected customer. Double-click to transfer the order from this list to the delivery work form. The individual entries on the order are shown in case delivery does not contain all items from the order. You can also select several complete orders. Confirm the selection to transfer the positions. In the lower area of the window, the Remarks field will appear with a notice that the delivery references the particular order.

If different payment terms were negotiated than were stored in the customer's master data, then they can be changed. Also, an agreed-upon discount can be entered in the Discount field. The amounts are adjusted automatically. Finally, confirm with the Add button and the document is submitted to the system.

Navigation Information

- ◆ **Menu Path:** Administration > System Initialization > Document Settings, Sales > Delivery > Order
- ◆ **Tables:** ODLN, OGSP, DLN1
- ◆ **Incoming Trigger:** Production Order Processing
- ◆ **Outgoing Trigger:** Credit Control, Picking, Invoice

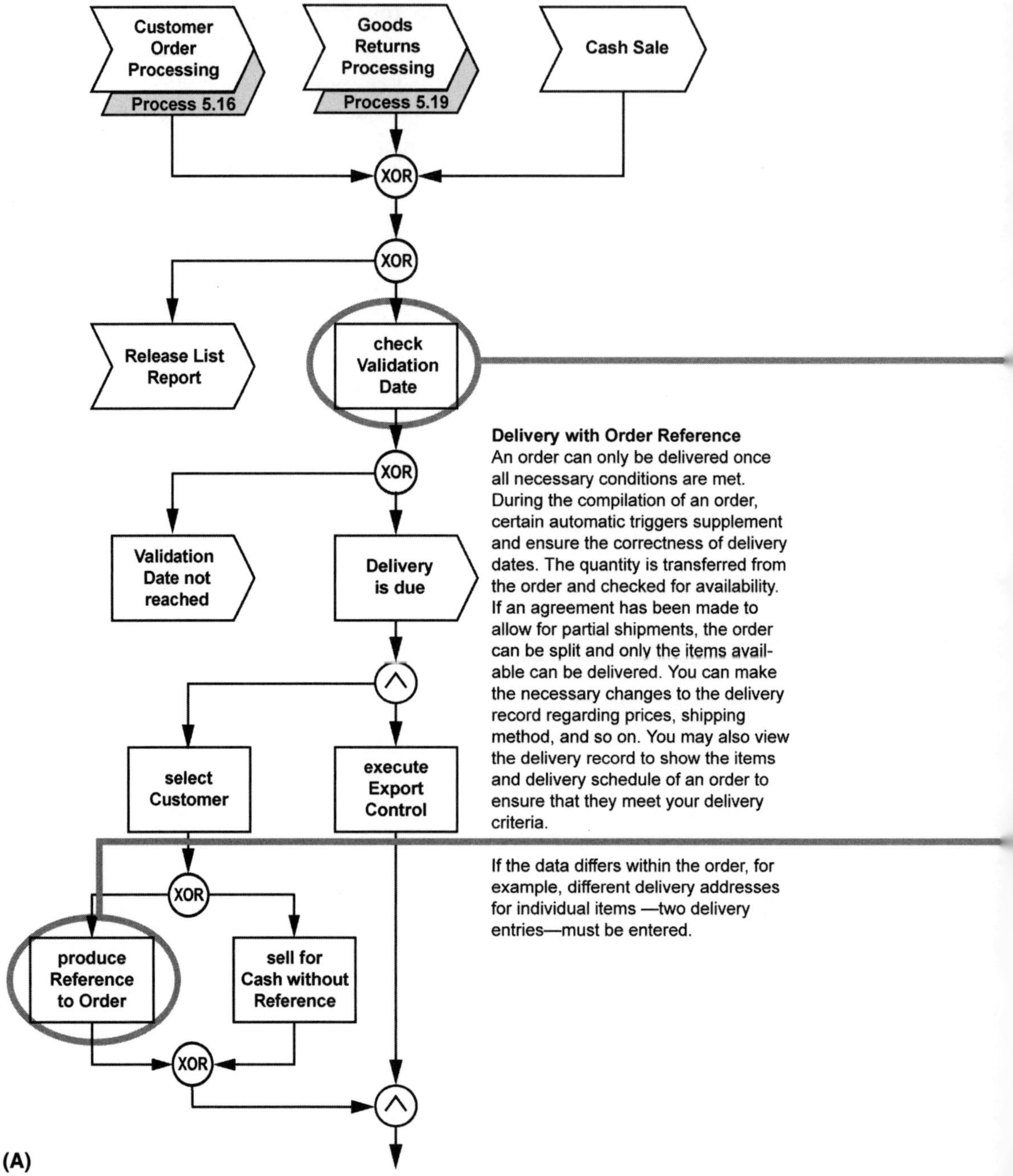
Customer Order Processing
Process 5.16
Goods Returns Processing
Process 5.19
Cash Sale
XOR
XOR
Release List Report
check Validation Date
XOR
Validation Date not reached
Delivery is due
select Customer
execute Export Control
XOR
produce Reference to Order
sell for Cash without Reference
XOR
(A)

Delivery with Order Reference
An order can only be delivered once all necessary conditions are met. During the compilation of an order, certain automatic triggers supplement and ensure the correctness of delivery dates. The quantity is transferred from the order and checked for availability. If an agreement has been made to allow for partial shipments, the order can be split and only the items available can be delivered. You can make the necessary changes to the delivery record regarding prices, shipping method, and so on. You may also view the delivery record to show the items and delivery schedule of an order to ensure that they meet your delivery criteria.

If the data differs within the order, for example, different delivery addresses for individual items —two delivery entries—must be entered.

FIGURE 5.45 *(a) List of current orders, (b) Detail description in connection to the order*

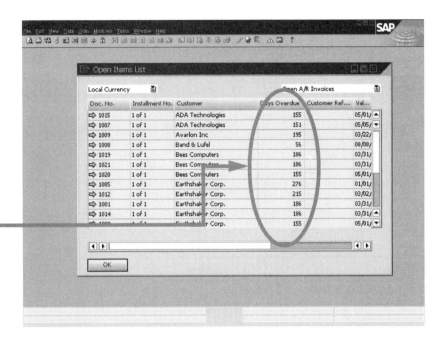

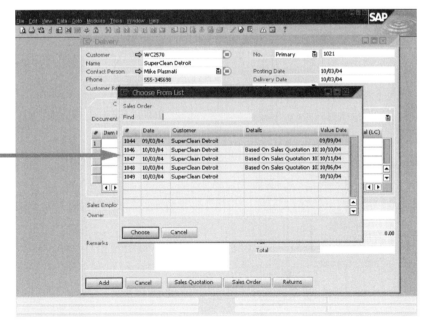

(B)

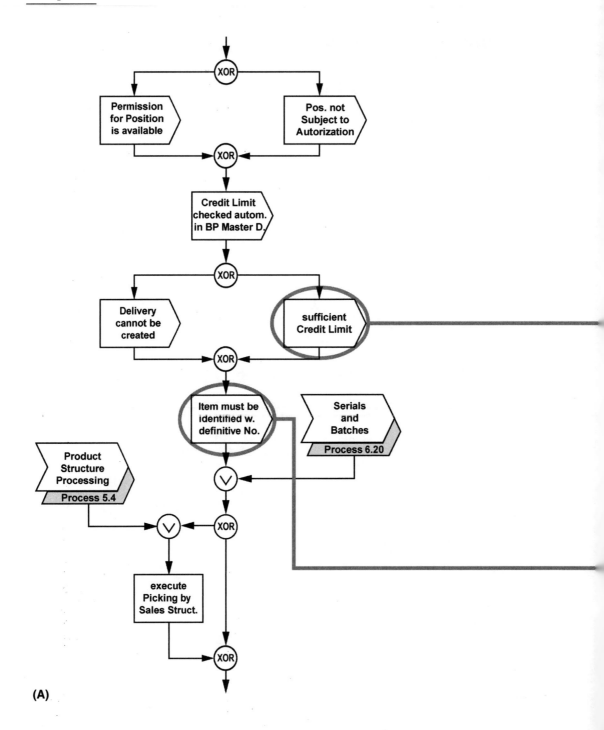

(A)

FIGURE 5.46 *(a) Credit limit in the payment terms, (b) Serial number administration*

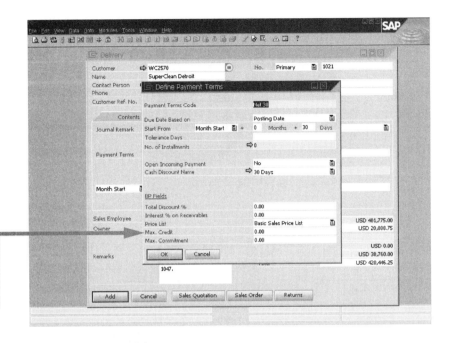

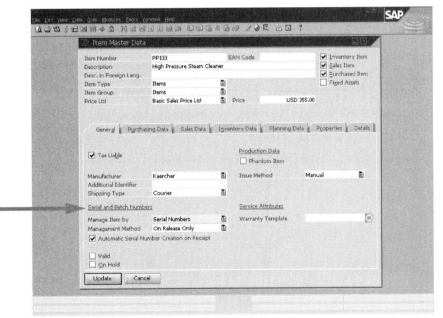

(B)

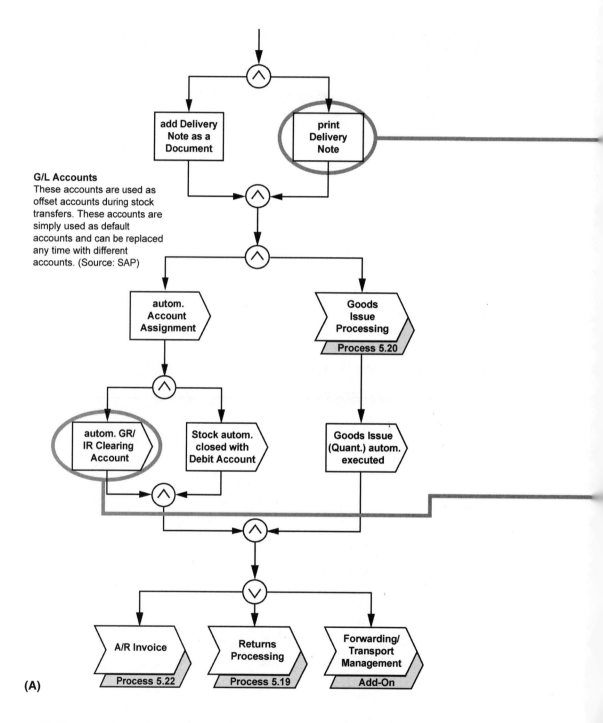

G/L Accounts
These accounts are used as offset accounts during stock transfers. These accounts are simply used as default accounts and can be replaced any time with different accounts. (Source: SAP)

FIGURE 5.47 *(a) Printer formatted image of a delivery receipt, (b) Detailed chart of accounts*

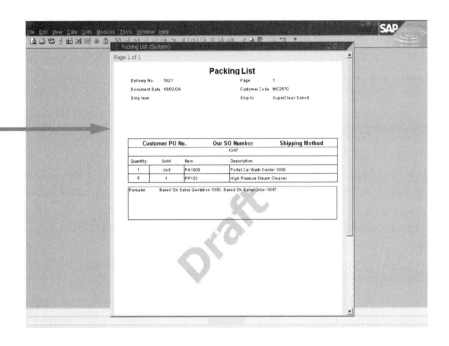

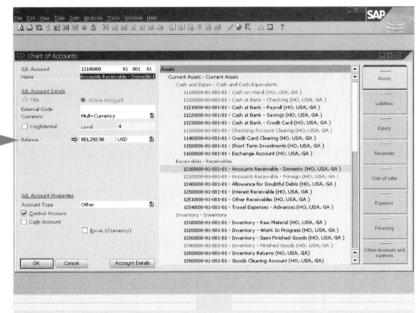

(B)

Returns Processing

A return is arranged, for example, when a customer complains about part or all of the shipment and therefore returns it.

Business Description

Sometimes, the customer only returns a part of the shipment as proof of the problem or if only part was not acceptable, the acceptable items are used so that production is not delayed. Once the return is received, the goods can be booked back into inventory in order to inspect them. After the goods have been inspected, a credit can be issued or a new shipment can be sent, most likely at no charge.

SAP Business One: Specific Description

The customer may complain about a delivery of goods because they were received already damaged or the quality criteria was not fulfilled—for example, with respect to tolerance limits on a precision machine part. A complaint may be received after the delivery has been made and the outgoing invoice was issued. In this case, delivery notes or outgoing invoices can no longer legally be changed or deleted in the system.

If a sales process is to be partially or totally cancelled, then returns with the goods receipt of the damaged goods must be included so that stock quantities can be reconciled with the appropriate values of the damaged goods. A Returned Goods document is the clearing document for the delivery note. If the outgoing invoice was already sent to the customer, then a value-based correction in the form of a credit must be issued to the customer In Accounting, the amount is credit to the customer account and the revenue account is adjusted by the same amount. The sales tax is also corrected automatically.

In Model Company A, the goods were delivered but no outgoing invoice was created. In order to establish a connection in the system between the two procedures, you must include the returns to be corrected with reference to the delivery note. As long as no invoice was generated for the procedure, the values do not need to be corrected; only an adjustment to the quantity is necessary.

The following questions should be asked when analyzing goods return processing:

♦ Is a return accepted only when the goods are returned?

♦ Do you generally include a goods receipt with a return?

♦ Do you repair damaged goods or do you send new ones?

Application of the Process

Items sent back due to defects or other reasons must be recorded in SAP Business One as returns. The recording of returns must take place with reference to the delivery note needing to be corrected, so that the connection between these two procedures is defined in the system.

Call the Returns function in the Sales application of the main menu. It is necessary to select the customer that arranged the returns in order to create a reference. You can note this either manually or with the search functions integrated in SAP Business One. Call up the selection list of deliveries with the Delivery button. Select the delivery with the returns and mark all entries by holding the Control key and confirming the selection. The item data is transferred to the Returns window. If all returns entries have been made, click the Add button to transfer the data into the system.

Navigation Information

♦ **Menu Path:** Sales > Returns > Delivery, Sales > Returns> Manual Entry, Purchasing > Goods Returns > Goods Receipt PO, Purchasing > Goods Returns > Manual Entry

♦ **Tables:** ORDN, RDN1, RDN2, RDN3

♦ **Incoming Trigger:** Invoice, Quality Protection, Delivery Processing

♦ **Outgoing Trigger:** Invoice, Credit Memo Declined, Customer Order Processing

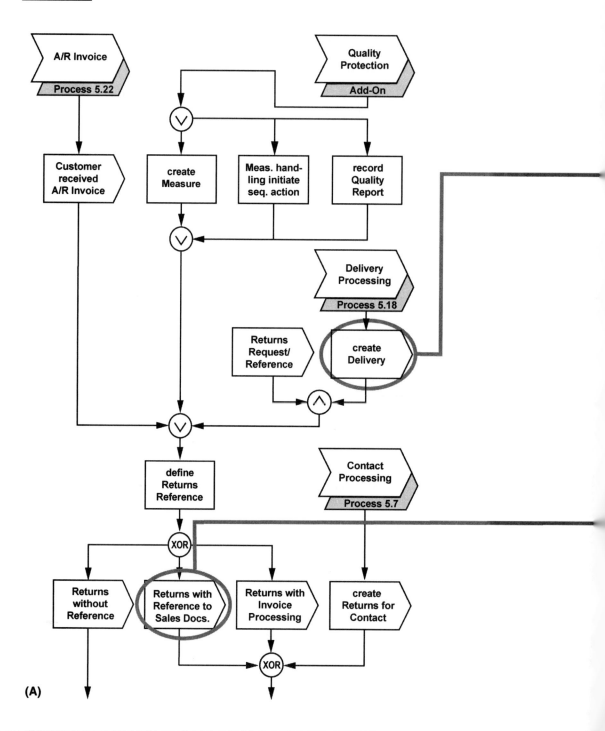

FIGURE 5.48 *(a) Initial screen for delivery, (b) Detail description of reference voucher to the delivery*

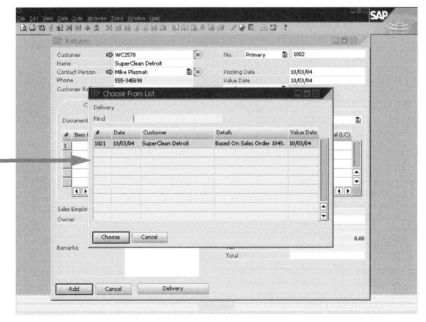

(B)

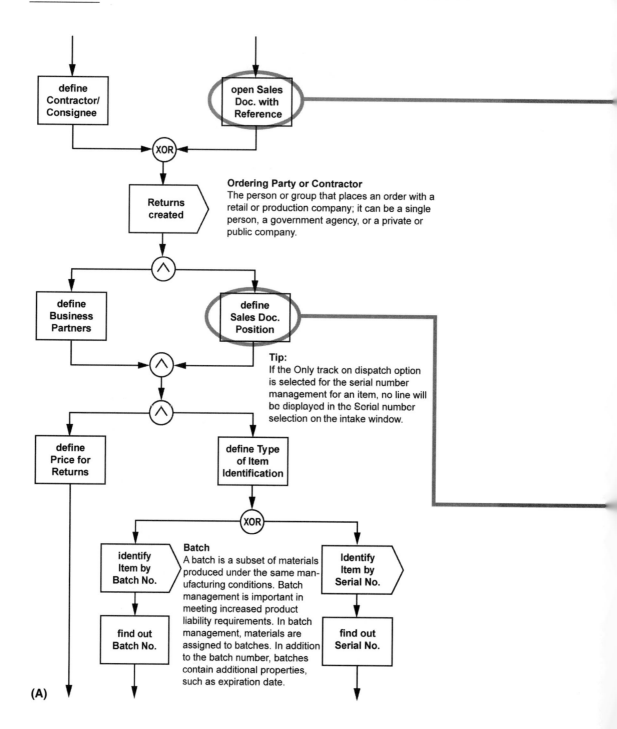

Ordering Party or Contractor
The person or group that places an order with a retail or production company; it can be a single person, a government agency, or a private or public company.

Tip:
If the Only track on dispatch option is selected for the serial number management for an item, no line will be displayed in the Serial number selection on the intake window.

Batch
A batch is a subset of materials produced under the same manufacturing conditions. Batch management is important in meeting increased product liability requirements. In batch management, materials are assigned to batches. In addition to the batch number, batches contain additional properties, such as expiration date.

(A)

FIGURE 5.49 *(a) Selection of the item to be copied, (b) Initial screen for a return*

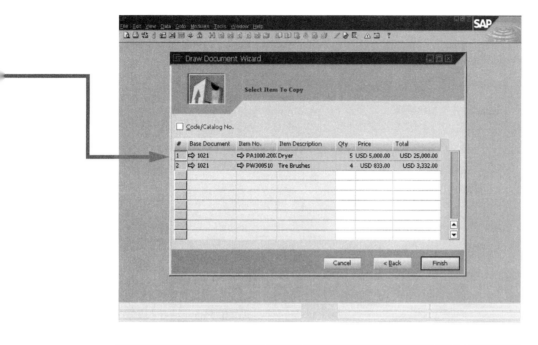

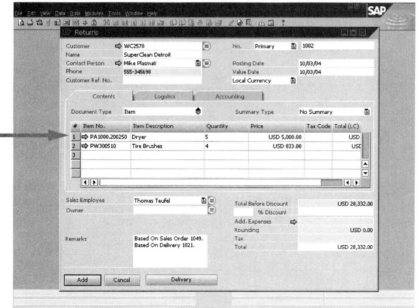

(B)

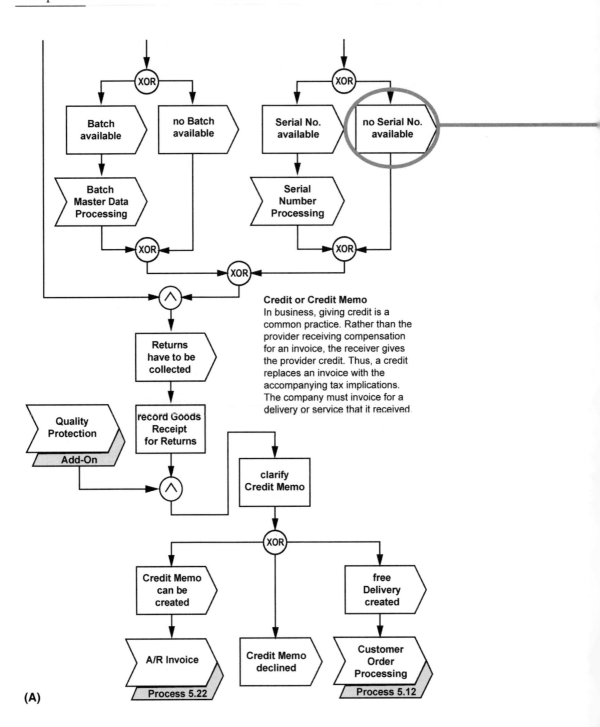

Credit or Credit Memo

In business, giving credit is a common practice. Rather than the provider receiving compensation for an invoice, the receiver gives the provider credit. Thus, a credit replaces an invoice with the accompanying tax implications. The company must invoice for a delivery or service that it received.

(A)

FIGURE 5.50 *(a) Indicator determination of the serial number administration!, (b) Return receipt*

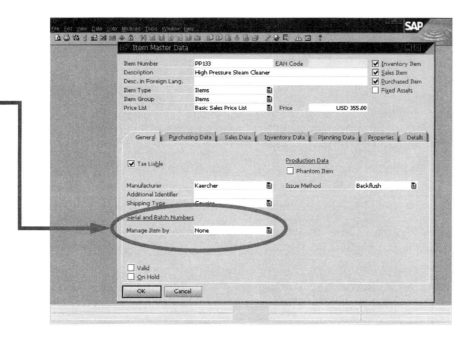

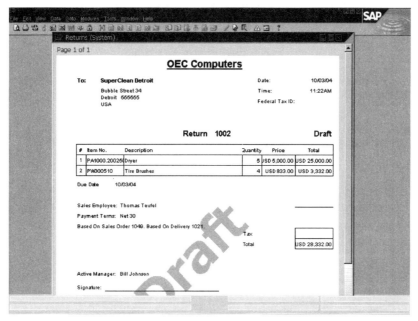

(B)

Goods Issue Processing

A goods issue, also called a *material dispatch*, represents a decrease in inventory, through a physical movement of a quantity of goods and the subsequent posting to inventory.

Business Description

Goods issue processing represents a decrease in warehouse stock as a result of goods being moved and booked. This can be initiated internally by a production order or externally by a delivery to a customer.

Material dispatch follows the request from different company divisions to the warehouse, which then are charged with preparing the goods for dispatch and making the shipment. If a goods issue is made in the context of delivery processing, the shipping documents, and if necessary, an outgoing invoice must be prepared. The shipping office is responsible for ensuring that the indicated quantity of goods is available in the designated transport containers (lattice boxes, pallets, cartons, and so on) at the loading dock. In addition, special shipping documents may have to be printed and included—such as special tariff and disclosure documents for exports, freight company shipping letters, or a hazardous material designation document. In manufacturing, it is possible that goods are stolen now and then. If this is the case, then a "closed warehouse" should be used. This will prevent the unplanned and illicit removal of goods.

SAP Business One: Specific Description

In SAP Business One, a goods issue, which is almost always a result of a delivery as part of a sale, leads to a quantity and value reduction of inventory. In the Inventory menu, goods issues can be processed even if they were unplanned and therefore detached from preceding processes. Most goods issues are however connected with other business processes:

◆ **Delivery to Customer:** The necessary data for the goods issue posting is transferred from the goods receipt. After the posting of the goods issue, SAP Business One automatically reduces the inventory level (warehouse and available stock) and the assessed value of the inventory accounts are adjusted. The quantity assigned to the customer order in the inventory status is also automatically reduced by the shipment.

- **Redelivery to Customer:** In the case of a redelivery, the connection to the order is re-established. A new delivery note is generated, which triggers the booking of another goods issue in the background. In order to execute a redelivery, it must first be determined whether the goods are available in a warehouse. In most organizations, the return goods are first booked into blocked stock. Only after the parts are repaired will they be booked to an available warehouse.

- **Scrapping:** If it is determined that parts in a warehouse are damaged beyond repair (for example, through water damage), they are removed from the inventory using a special goods issue. If the customer initiates a return and the goods cannot be repaired, then the same special goods issue is used for scrapping. These items can no longer be sold and therefore become unusable.

- **Material Dispatch for Production Order.** On the allocation date in a production order, materials must be taken out of the warehouse. By performing a quantity control of the production order, the controller can determine the availability of the needed material for the production. A *retrograde material dispatch* means that the material is already at the production site. These materials are then used as needed in the production process. The exact quantity used in production is only known at the time of completion, and only then is a goods issue executed to update the inventory.

- **Other Goods Issue:** Quality control, maintenance, due to inventory, and so on.

 TIP

If you post a goods receipt (for example, Goods Issue) for items with a price of 0.00 or 0.01, errors can occur during the inventory valuation. Your valuations in reporting will then be incorrect.

 TIP

The journal entry in the goods issue represents special information for Accounting. The expense account is automatically placed at the time of execution of the goods issue.

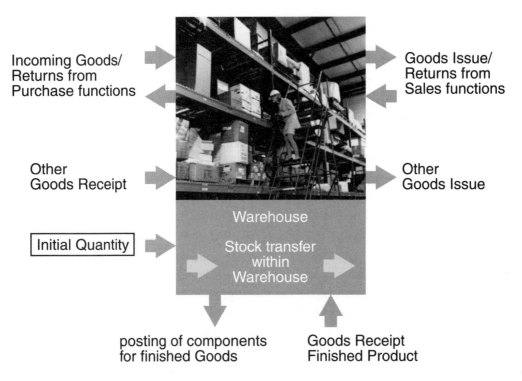

FIGURE 5.51 *Other product movement (Source: SAP AG)*

The following questions should be asked when analyzing goods issue processing:

- ◆ Which expense account is used for goods issue in Accounting?
- ◆ Do you have a closed warehouse location?
- ◆ Which warehouse structure do you define: available stock locations (raw, half-finished, finished goods), laboratory, and so on?
- ◆ Does the warehouse conduct another credit check before finishing dispatch (goods issue of the commodity)?

Application of the Process

When using the goods issue process, you first must determine whether it took place automatically, resulting from a system process, or whether it was done manually. You cannot directly influence an automatically running goods issue, such as one resulting from a delivery. You can only view the journals of the process in SAP Business One.

Choose the Goods Issue function in the Inventory Administration to create a manual goods issue. This opens a new window containing default values in the upper area, which can be changed if needed. These include the number range and the date. You can specify the price list in the Price list for the Goods Issue selection field; these are needed to determine the prices for items.

In the table area of the window, you may select the items to be taken from inventory using the Search function. The item information is transferred to the current window. In the lower part of the window, there is a Total field, which shows the total amount of all table entries. Click the Go To function in the toolbar, then click Line Details to get a detailed view of the individual table entries.

Below the table, you can insert other information in the Remarks field, such as the detailed reason for the goods issue. The pre-filled Journal entry field can also be changed. Finally click on Add to add the manual good issue to SAP Business One. Afterwards, you can recall the document and print it by using the Print function in SAP Business One.

Navigation Information

- **Menu Path:** Inventory > Inventory Transaction > Goods Issue, Sales > Delivery
- **Tables:** OIGE, IGE1, IGE2, IGE3
- **Incoming Trigger:** Delivery Processing, Returns Processing, Inventory Adjustment Processing, Stock Transfer, Scrapping, Goods Issue for Quality Protection, Goods Issue for Production to Operation
- **Outgoing Trigger:** Inventory Posting, Production Order Processing, Inventory Status Analysis, A/R Invoice

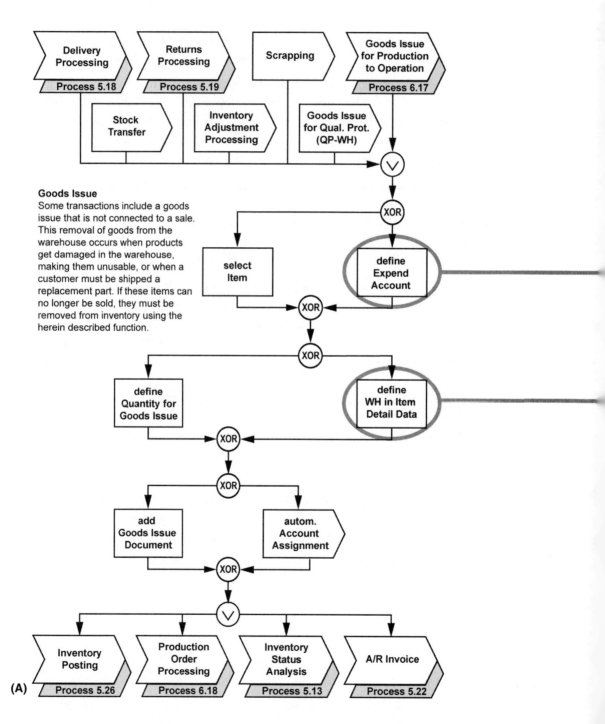

Goods Issue
Some transactions include a goods issue that is not connected to a sale. This removal of goods from the warehouse occurs when products get damaged in the warehouse, making them unusable, or when a customer must be shipped a replacement part. If these items can no longer be sold, they must be removed from inventory using the herein described function.

FIGURE 5.52 *(a) Initial screen for inventory control, (b) Inventory levels in the item master data*

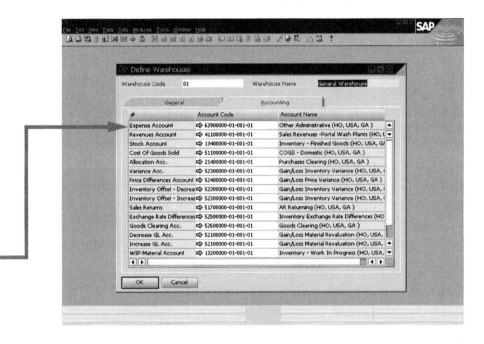

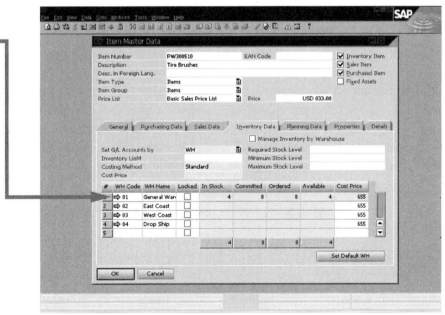

(B)

Customer Master Data Processing

A company's balance sheet is comprised of general ledger and sub-ledger accounts. Each sub-ledger account is specific to either a creditor or debtor, and they are kept in subsidiary books. A debtor sub-ledger account is a customer account and contains the audit trail about the obligations in detail.

Business Description

Multiple customer accounts can be grouped together for different reporting needs and are used within the different departments for financial and cost accounting, as well for logistical purposes. The customer master data must serve all of these purposes to ensure that the data accessed is consistent throughout the company.

SAP Business One: Specific Description

Customer master data is maintained in the Business Partners module and contains all of the relevant data from business dealings with the customer. Well-maintained customer master data allows a seamless expansion of the use of this data within the company.

The Accounting and Sales modules can be used to access the customer master data. The main purpose of customer master data is to clearly identify the customer. Functionalities are assigned by defining parameters to the customer account in the customer master data. Each customer master data contains general data needed by all departments within the company that access that data. The customer is identified primarily by the customer name and customer code. In addition, there is division-specific data, some examples of which are:

◆ **For Accounting:** Reconciliation account, sales tax-relevant data, and payment terms and data for trading partners (for example centralized billing).

◆ **For the Sales Division:** Delivery data, contact partners, price lists, and credit information.

Coding describes the sub-ledger account. Once a coding has been assigned and something has been posted to the sub-ledger account, it can no longer be changed or deleted from SAP Business One, because it is what creates the uniqueness of an account.

A special sub-ledger account is the One-Time Customer account. The associated customer master data is assigned only the code, designation, and associated price list. This customer master record is almost exclusively used for cash transactions; it is not recommended for use with infrequent customers, who will nonetheless be invoiced for later payment.

Application of the Process

The Business Partners Master Data function is in the Business Partners application, which you select in order to process debtor master data. The next window allows you to first define the general data for a business partner. If this is to be a debtor master data, you have to choose Customer as a Business Partner type. In the lower part of the window are the registers for the individual input areas. The number of registers depends on whether you are in Find or Add mode. Change to the Accounting register, which in the upper area has the Consolidation Business Partner, Payments Consolidation, and Delivery Consolidation fields. Here you can assign several debtors to a super ordinate master record, which is used for business partners with several locations and a central payment office. In the lower area of the register, you enter the business partner's customer account and sales tax status. Each field's data can be changed using a selection list. A change to the account is only allowed if you permit the reconciliation account to be changed.

Navigation Information

- ◆ **Menu Path:** Business Partners > Business Partner Master Data > Accounting
- ◆ **Tables:** ACRD, ACPR, ACR1, CRD1, OCRD
- ◆ **Incoming Trigger:** Create Debtor
- ◆ **Outgoing Trigger:** Sales Quotation Processing, Customer Order Processing, Delivery Processing, A/R Invoice

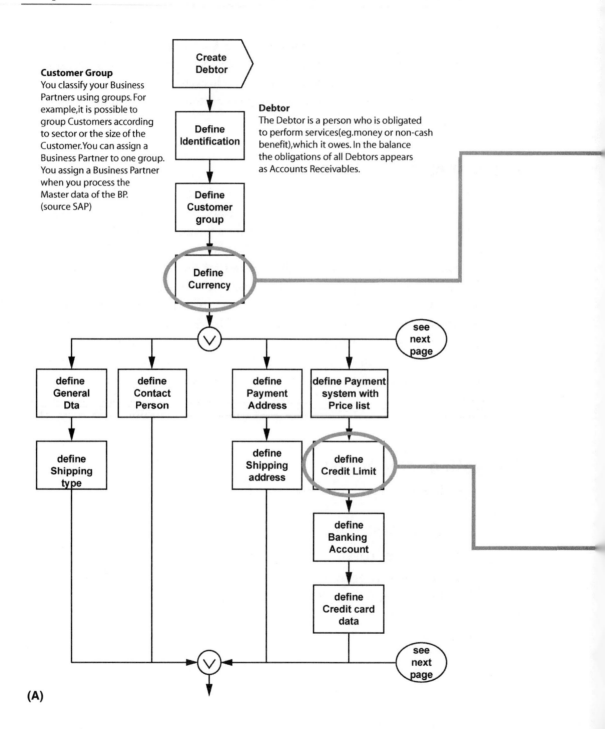

Customer Group
You classify your Business Partners using groups. For example, it is possible to group Customers according to sector or the size of the Customer. You can assign a Business Partner to one group. You assign a Business Partner when you process the Master data of the BP. (source SAP)

Debtor
The Debtor is a person who is obligated to perform services(eg.money or non-cash benefit),which it owes. In the balance the obligations of all Debtors appears as Accounts Receivables.

(A)

FIGURE 5.53 *(a) Currency selections, (b) Credit limit in the payment terms*

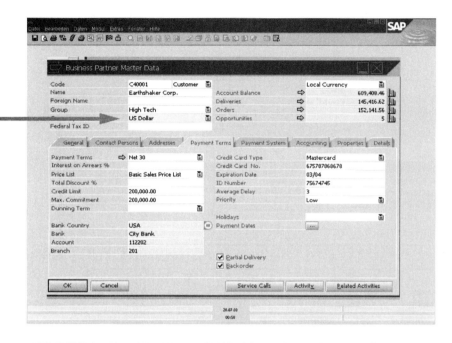

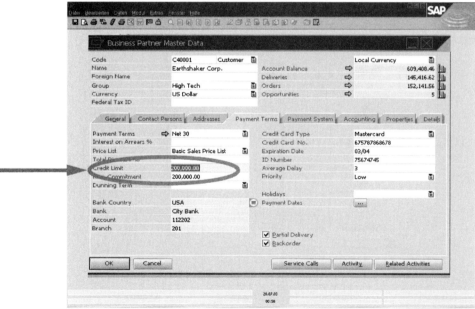

(B)

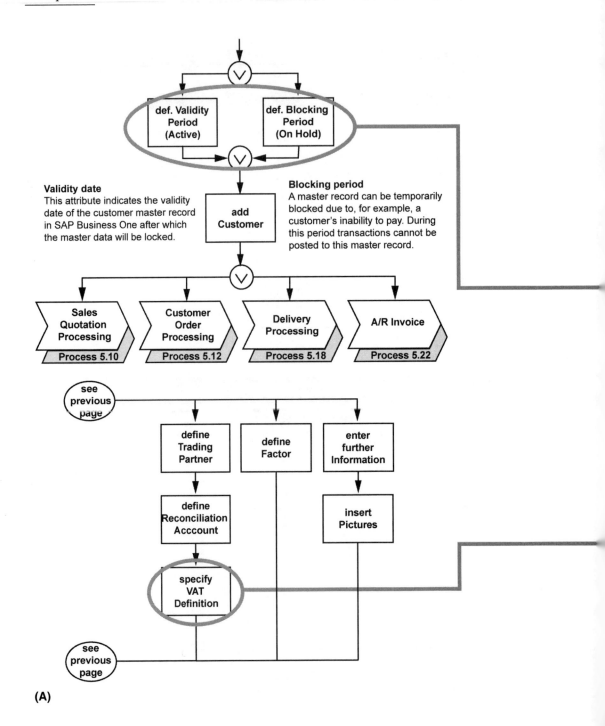

Validity date
This attribute indicates the validity date of the customer master record in SAP Business One after which the master data will be locked.

Blocking period
A master record can be temporarily blocked due to, for example, a customer's inability to pay. During this period transactions cannot be posted to this master record.

(A)

FIGURE 5.54 *(a) Detail description of the debtor/customer, (b) Accounting details of the debtor/customer*

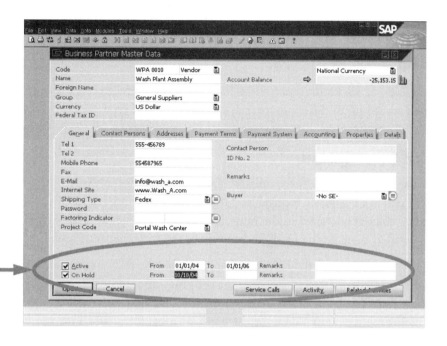

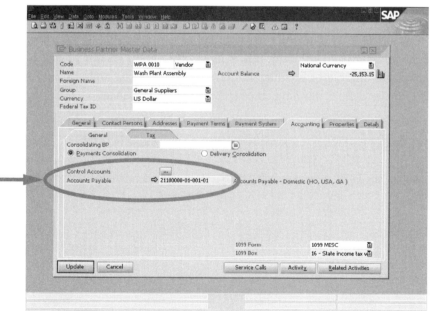

(B)

Processing of Receivable by Due Date

Receivables of all kinds represent a balance sheet item. Receivable entries are divided according to different criteria, such as time and type.

Business Description

The discussion here will focus only on short-term receivable. A delivery to a customer creates a customer receivable. The nature, type, and extent of the individual receivables are detailed in the outgoing invoice. The negotiated payment date, also specified there, is the basis for processing the customer receivable.

If the vendor allows for the invoice to be paid after the delivery of goods, the customer is granted an interest-free loan for the gross amount of the invoice from the delivery date. The term of the loan is limited by the date specified in the invoice, at which time payment is due in the form of a bank transfer into the vendor's account or a cash payment.

If a customer does not fulfill his payment obligation, then a dunning occurs, which means that the customer is reminded of his receivable. It is customary to redefine an exact payment date; this is most often upon receipt of the dunning. Also, the dunning might include an interest charge for the amount due. A company normally defines dunning steps to be taken in sequence.

 TIP

Reminders should be in written form, so that you will have reference documents in case further steps need to be taken to secure payment.

Some companies sell all or part of their dunning to a third party, which is common as part of outside financing for an enterprise. This special form of outside financing is referred to as *factoring*, where a factoring business, the so-called factor, buys the receivables resulting from deliveries and services.

Factoring has the following advantages for an enterprise:

- The company immediately receives the money it is owed.

- In true factoring, the factor assumes the risk that the debtor will not pay. In pseudo factoring, the company can be responsible for sold receivables if the customer does not meet their obligations.

- The factor takes over other administrative tasks associated with receivable.

The charges for factoring are usually 10–15 percent of the receivable, so this is a fairly expensive form of external financing.

Depending on the contract, the company which sells its receivables might only have one total receivable, which is the one against the factor.

Independently of the agreed-upon payment date in the invoice or the business with the factor, the supplier must fulfill his financial obligations. For example, the state demands payment of the sales tax and the supplier demands the settlement of their invoices.

SAP Business One: Specific Description

The open receivables can be listed in the Open Demands column. A filter can be added to restrict by range of receivable value, characteristic, or group of debtor accounts.

The individual customer accounts can be accessed from the displayed summary. The yellow arrows in SAP Business One should be reiterated; they provide access to the detailed information on the particular item.

The Generated Summary view of the individual customer accounts can be used efficiently for manual dunning. From this view, an appropriate inquiry can be used to produce a payment reminder to all customers currently in default. The Automatic Dunning function is part of the next SAP Business One release.

The view of customer receivables by due date is a good information source for company liquidity planning, as it exactly lists the dates and amounts of expected payments.

The following questions should be asked when analyzing receivables and dunning:

- How are the stages of dunning performed in your company?
- Who is responsible for dunning in your company?

Application of the Process

If you call the Receivable History Report function from the main menu of the Business Partner application of SAP Business One, the system opens a selection window. At the top of this window, you can filter the customer and receivables to be included in the report. You can select the following criteria ranges:

- Code number range of business partners
- Customer groups
- Properties of customers
- Date range of dunning run
- Range of due date
- Invoice number
- Down payment number

You can display dunning letters and invoices per customer and specify a dunning level to display only invoices and letters related to it. Select the All option to view all invoices and letters. To include invoices that are in the dunning run but not included in the dunning letters, activate the Include Unselected Invoices indicator.

Clicking on OK displays the report in a new window.

Navigation Information

- ◆ **Menu Path:** Business Partners > Business Partner Reports > Dunning History Report
- ◆ **Tables:** OCDT
- ◆ **Incoming Trigger:** Dunning Process, A/R Invoice
- ◆ **Outgoing Trigger:** None

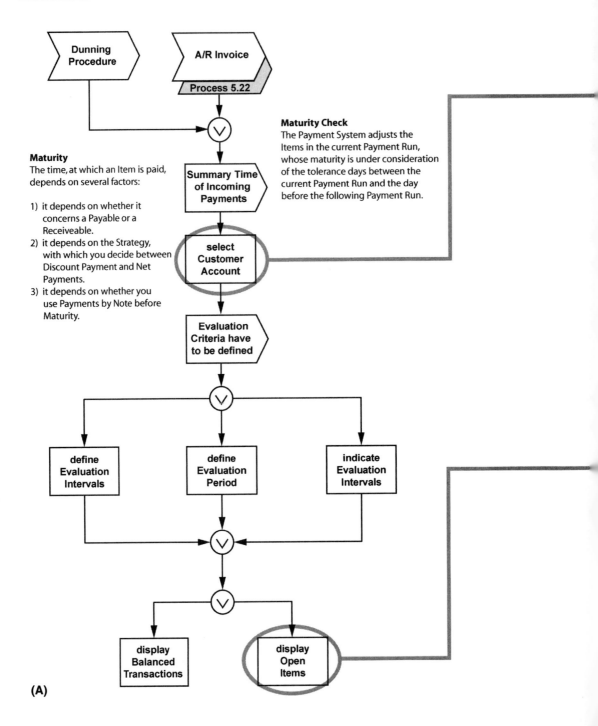

Maturity Check
The Payment System adjusts the Items in the current Payment Run, whose maturity is under consideration of the tolerance days between the current Payment Run and the day before the following Payment Run.

Maturity
The time, at which an Item is paid, depends on several factors:

1) it depends on whether it concerns a Payable or a Receiveable.
2) it depends on the Strategy, with which you decide between Discount Payment and Net Payments.
3) it depends on whether you use Payments by Note before Maturity.

(A)

FIGURE 5.55 *(a) Customer requirements selection, (b) Customer requirements by due date*

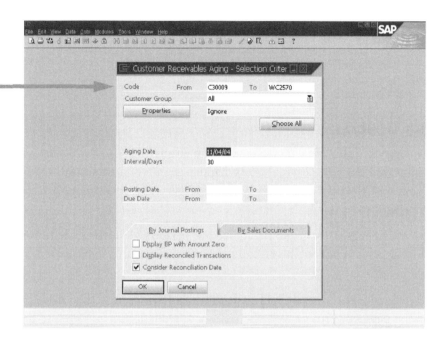

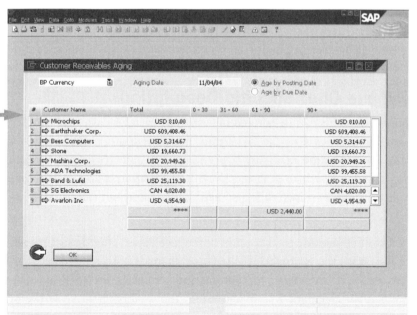

(B)

Incoming Payment

Financial management views operational payment streams in connection with the controlling of a company.

Business Description

The main goal of financial management is to ensure the liquidity of the company. Incoming and outgoing payments can happen at different times; this requires the availability of financial means to bridge that gap. The investment process is an ongoing process.

Incoming payments are made for deliveries, performed services, share financing (such as deposits), outside investment capital (for example, bank loan or venture capital investments).

Types of payments are cash, half cash, and cashless deposits. The most frequent incoming payment procedure is the receivable reduction; it is therefore based on an outgoing invoice. The payments are the basis for the liquidity of the business and should be paid particular attention by the company. Granting discounts for early payment is encourages settlement of the receivable within the due date. The scheduling also makes it possible to plan the incoming payment stream.

SAP Business One: Specific Description

Incoming payments can be entered in cash, half-cash, or cashless form. Customer deposits are processed in the Bank and Treasury function. When you are performing the procedure manually, every made payment triggers the creation of a posting document, which is noted in both the customer and cash account. It is possible to capture an incoming payment with or without reference to an outgoing invoice.

If the customer pays the total amount of the receivable (after deducting the appropriate discount), the posting of the payment is made with reference to the outgoing invoice. SAP Business One automatically reduces the total amount by the discount, if the payment was made within the qualifying time. If the outgoing invoice is reference, the postings are balanced. After the posting, the customer's OI (Open Item) list does not show either the outgoing invoice or the incoming payment.

If the customer makes partial payments, the deposits are posted without reference to the outgoing invoice expect for the final payment. However, you should include a reference to the outgoing invoice with each deposit using the document notes or another suitable method in SAP Business One. In order to have a full view of the business case, the partial payments and the outgoing invoice need to be listed on the OI list of the customer account until the full amount has been received for the outgoing invoice.

When you are entering the final payment, the reference is established between the outgoing invoice and all partial payments by marking the lines (the related customer account lines are marked in yellow). The posting of the final payment also clears the receivable with all of the corresponding documents. If a reference would be established to the outgoing invoice when posting the first or any future partial payment, then the documents would not be balanced. SAP Business One then generates an adjustment voucher, which would appear in the customer's OI list, and it would leave out the original outgoing invoice and partial payment. This adjustment voucher has the characteristics of a separate outgoing invoice, but without an associated outgoing invoice document. This method of representing payment of receivables is not recommended, as in proper accounting, a posting is not allowed without a corresponding document.

After entering the incoming payment in SAP Business One, the next step is to capture the bank statement in the system. This procedure is basically copying of the individual account transactions from the bank statement.

Once all incoming payments and the corresponding bank statements are recorded, the included bank statements can be reconciled with the incoming and outgoing payments. It is recommended, for the sake of simplicity and clarity, that you create a separate reconciliation document for each bank statement. If necessary, each reconciliation in SAP Business One can be reversed and the corresponding documents can be reconciled again.

Application of the Process

All customer payments are recorded with the Incoming Payments function. Payments can be in the form of bank transfers, checks, cash, or credit card payment. This process connects the incoming payment with the invoices sent to customers. An incoming payment is recorded using Incoming Payments function in the Banking application.

In the window for incoming payment processing, specify first whether the payment source is a customer or an account. In the model company, a customer makes a payment that should be entered into the system. Bring up and transfer the customer master data using the Selection icon to the right of the Code field or by using the search functions in SAP Business One. The document number is generated automatically using the defined number range, but it can be changed by altering the number range or by selecting the Manual field. The additional data and settings can be made according to your needs.

After selecting the customer, you will see all their open invoices listed in the table. Choose the document for which the payment was received. Of course, you can select multiple invoices at the same time. If the customer made only a partial payment of an invoice, mark the line and change the amount in the Total Payment field accordingly. Now, switch to the Payment Means function by choosing Payment Means Function from the Incoming Payment menu. Next, specify the form of payment by choosing from bank transfer, cash, check, or credit card. You can also specify a combination of payment forms. Define the amounts and the further necessary data in the window.

If payment is by check, indicate a G/L account for the payment; select a bank and an account and enter the check number. If the date differs from the default value, you can change the date. If the check can be endorsed, select the appropriate value and then enter the amount of the check.

If you receive payment by bank transfer, select a G/L account and enter the transfer date, the amount, and possibly a reference.

If payment is made with a credit card, specify the card information in the register and an amount in the Amount Due field. Next, define the credit documents for the payment in the Voucher list.

If the customer pays cash, specify a G/L account in the Cash register and enter the amount paid into the Total field.

In the lower area of the window, the total amount, the current balance due, and the partial payments are shown. Select Add, and the system creates an Accounting document for the incoming payment. This enters the cash payment into the G/L account indicated and credits the customer account.

Navigation Information

- **Menu Path:** Banking > Incoming Payments > Incoming Payments
- **Tables:** OCRP, ODPS
- **Incoming Trigger:** Customer Dunning after Due Date
- **Outgoing Trigger:** Bank Statement Coordinated, Display Reports

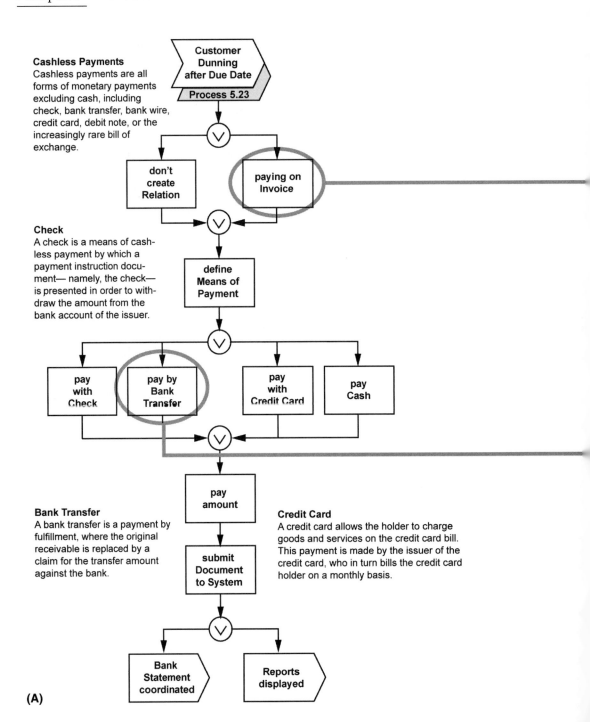

Cashless Payments
Cashless payments are all forms of monetary payments excluding cash, including check, bank transfer, bank wire, credit card, debit note, or the increasingly rare bill of exchange.

Check
A check is a means of cashless payment by which a payment instruction document— namely, the check— is presented in order to withdraw the amount from the bank account of the issuer.

Bank Transfer
A bank transfer is a payment by fulfillment, where the original receivable is replaced by a claim for the transfer amount against the bank.

Credit Card
A credit card allows the holder to charge goods and services on the credit card bill. This payment is made by the issuer of the credit card, who in turn bills the credit card holder on a monthly basis.

Customer Dunning after Due Date
Process 5.23

don't create Relation

paying on Invoice

define Means of Payment

pay with Check

pay by Bank Transfer

pay with Credit Card

pay Cash

pay amount

submit Document to System

Bank Statement coordinated

Reports displayed

(A)

FIGURE 5.56 *(a) Initial screen for payment processing, (b) Selection screen for payment method*

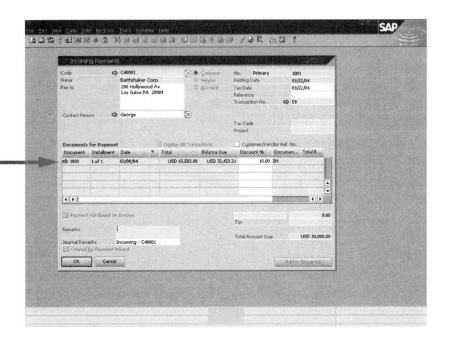

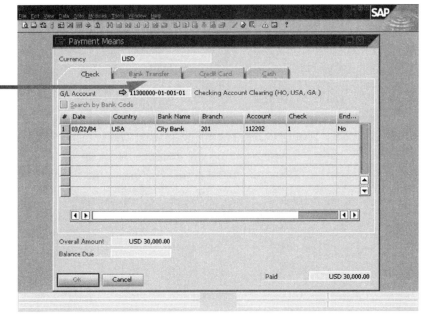

(B)

Inventory Posting Process

Taking of inventory (stock taking/material count) can be done in a variety of ways and is classified as either an annual or permanent inventory. The items recorded during inventory include available, special, and quality assurance stock.

Business Description

The annual inventory is the physical act of taking inventory by counting, measuring, and weighing. Often it is done near the fiscal year closing date, for example on December 31. Inventory deviations are corrected as either value adjustments or retroactive charges. Two material lists are printed to provide two inventory counts, which minimizes the chance of errors. During inventory, you can detect not only the differences in quantity, but also incorrect part numbers and the storage of materials in the wrong warehouse.

Another form allowed is the permanent inventory. The physical inventory can be carried out at any time during the year. However, proper inventory management calls for a system for keeping a continuous journal of transactions of received and issued goods. Depending on the value of the items, a physical inventory can be taken more often during the year. By classifying items in different levels, such as A, B, and C, you can give an indication as to which items need to be checked more often and which only need to be collected only quarterly or half-yearly.

Inventory management determines stock value by collecting the goods issued from the calculation of requirements and evaluating them in the accounting. This allows the creation of lists proofing the changes in inventory of the materials tracked. The inventory management provides Purchasing with the net and gross requirements for production by also indicating waste, unplanned usage, and missing stock levels. A good ERP system pays off especially in inventory management, by showing the relationship between the quantity and value of an inventory.

SAP Business One: Specific Description

The Inventory process in SAP Business One is divided into the following:

- ◆ Initial quantity
- ◆ Inventory tracking
- ◆ Stock posting

The initial quantity serves to enter the initial balance for items per warehouse location. In order to enter an initial balance of zero, the Allow Opening Balance without Price indicator must be checked.

In order to track inventory, you can print out the stock lists of the items to be counted and record the results in the system afterwards. However, the entry of an inventory does not post any goods movements.

Posting stock is initiated by item selection after the inventory. The stock levels are updated and the value of the items is adjusted according to the pre-defined price lists or the most recent cost calculations. Thus, inflow and outflow postings are executed in the warehouse and accounting system. The source of the item prices needs to be specified at the beginning of the batch-run.

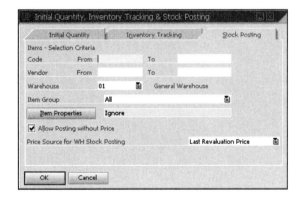

FIGURE 5.57 *Selection for the inventory control with specified criteria*

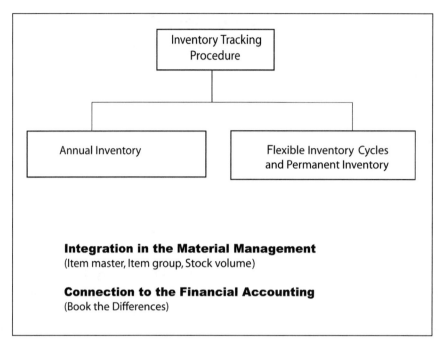

FIGURE 5.58 *Physical inventory management in Business One*

The following question should be asked when analyzing the inventory posting process:

◆ Which inventory procedure do you use (annual inventory, permanent inventory)?

Application of the Process

If you bring up the Inventory Tracking and Stock Posting functions from the Inventory application in SAP Business One, the window will display the following registers:

◆ Initial Quantity
◆ Inventory Tracking
◆ Stock Posting

In the Initial Quantity register, you select the items for which you want to set initial balances. Specify an item number range and a primary vendor number for the selection. Another method of selection is by item groups or properties. If you would like to post opening balances of zero, then you need to set the Allow Initial Quantities Without Price indicator. Once you have provided all specifications, you can confirm by selecting OK. SAP Business One opens a new window with the list of selected items so that you can enter the balances and prices into the provided fields. Transfer the values into the system after entering the balances by clicking on Add.

The Stock Tracking register is used to prepare and enter the results of a physical inventory. Select the items to be inventoried. If you don't specify a selection, all items are listed. The list is displayed again in a separate window when you click OK. You can print the list by clicking the Print icon; to record the results after the inventory, enter them into the input fields.

In the Stock Posting register, you can choose the selection criteria for items that need stock corrections after an inventory. You can also specify whether you would like to allow a posting without price and which source you would like to use for item prices. If you would like to use the most recently calculated prices, the inventory value is necessary to have the cost in the system. Make your corrections in the item list and transfer them by clicking on Add.

Navigation Information

- ◆ **Menu Path:** Inventory > Inventory Transactions > Initial Quantity, Inventory Tracking, Stock Posting
- ◆ **Tables:** O1TW, O1TM
- ◆ **Incoming Trigger:** Periodic Inventory, Perpetual Inventory, Sales Item, Purchasing Item
- ◆ **Outgoing Trigger:** Price Strategy, Cycle Count Recommendation, Inventory Status Analysis, Inventory Status Report, Inventory Valuation Report

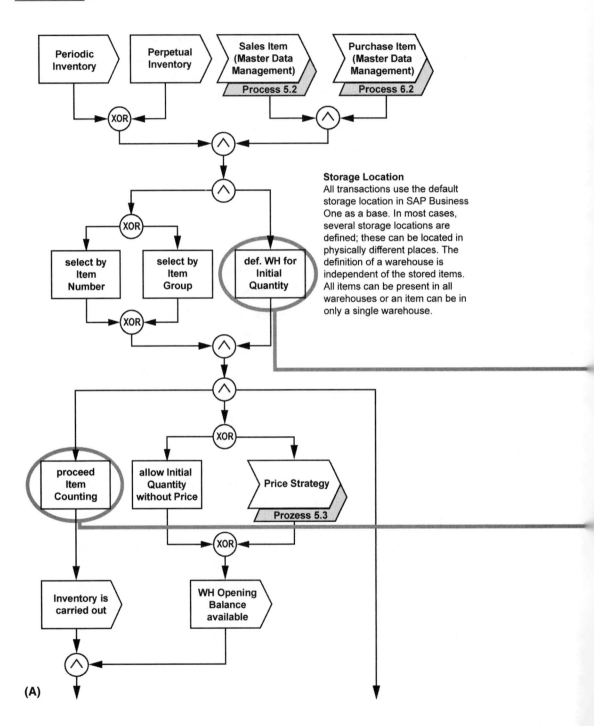

Storage Location
All transactions use the default storage location in SAP Business One as a base. In most cases, several storage locations are defined; these can be located in physically different places. The definition of a warehouse is independent of the stored items. All items can be present in all warehouses or an item can be in only a single warehouse.

(A)

FIGURE 5.59 *(a) Product category selection, (b) Master inventory list*

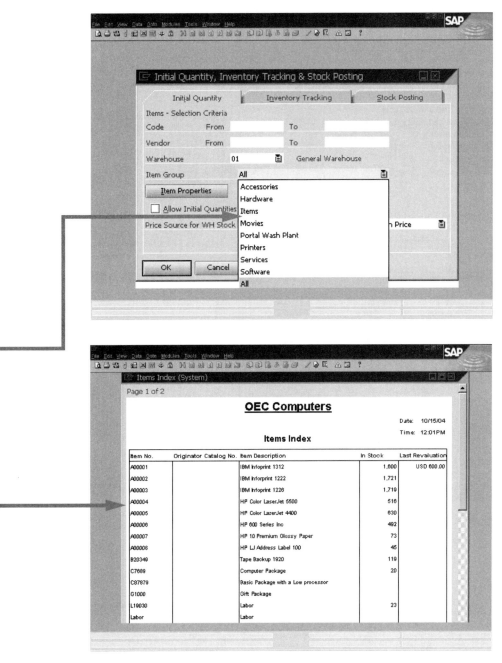

(B)

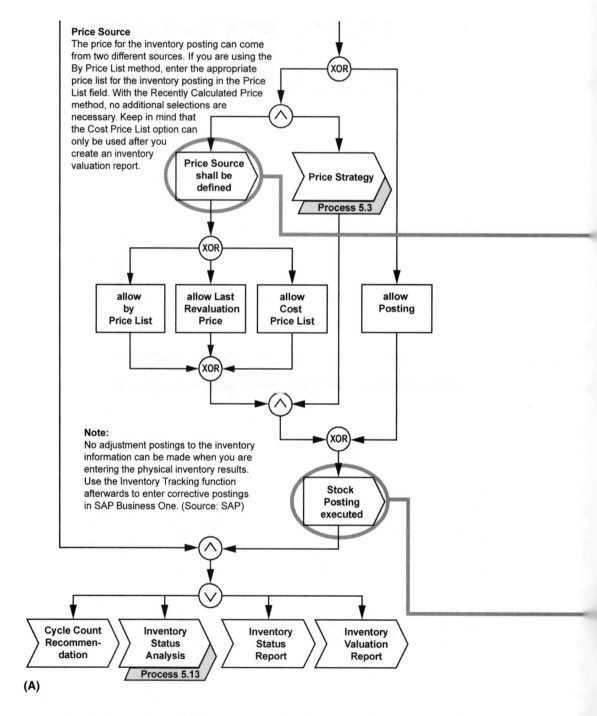

Price Source
The price for the inventory posting can come from two different sources. If you are using the By Price List method, enter the appropriate price list for the inventory posting in the Price List field. With the Recently Calculated Price method, no additional selections are necessary. Keep in mind that the Cost Price List option can only be used after you create an inventory valuation report.

Note:
No adjustment postings to the inventory information can be made when you are entering the physical inventory results. Use the Inventory Tracking function afterwards to enter corrective postings in SAP Business One. (Source: SAP)

(A)

FIGURE 5.60 *(a) Selection template for inventory posting, (b) Update table after physical inventory*

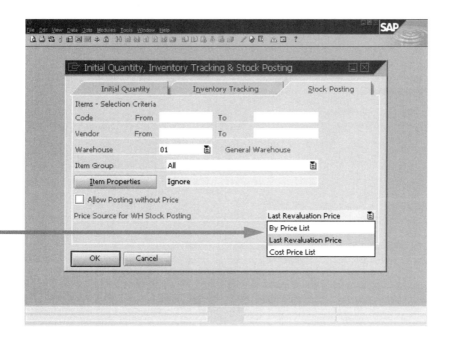

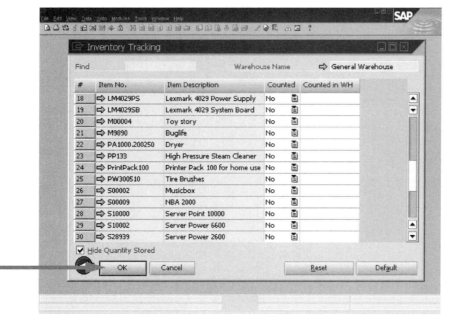

(B)

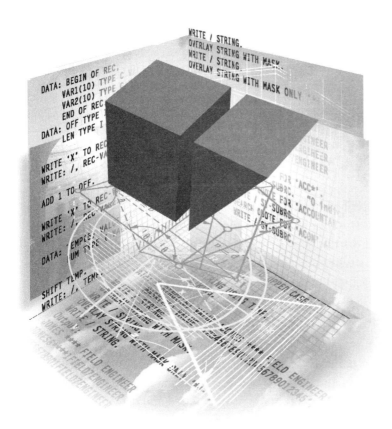

Chapter 6

Custom-Order Assembly Manufacturer

In Model Company A, described in Chapter 5, the primary concern was with the sales activities of a car wash, in which customer influence manifests itself mainly in order handling and distribution of inventory. Model Company B, the order-driven assembly plant, is responsible for accepting the orders of the distribution company and planning, producing, assembling, and preparing orders for delivery. Depending on an order accepted by Model Company A, Model Company B must alter assembly production and in special cases provide installation.

In Model Company B, an offer is usually prepared by the distribution company prior to an order. The starting point of this offer is a customer inquiry, which is handled by a sales employee. Some information and parameters are added by the sales employee so that the required product can be manufactured and delivered to the customer. This frequently necessitates that the salesman work with the customer on the requirements to complete the offer. If there are customized needs to be put into place, a drawing is developed in conjunction with the Construction department and then checked for technical feasibility.

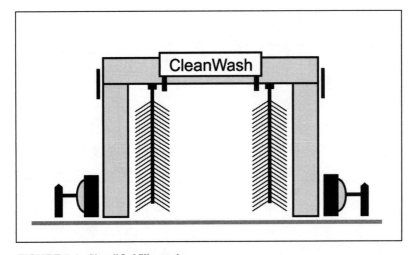

FIGURE 6.1 *Simplified Illustration*

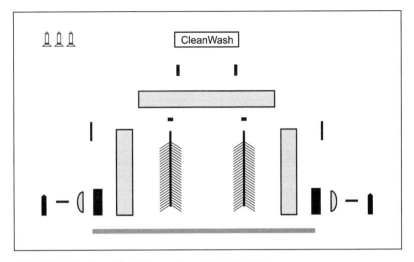

FIGURE 6.2 *Simplified Illustration of the individual parts*

Development includes defining and specifying the raw materials required. Once the materials are chosen, procurement is the next step. At the same time, the information is passed on to the work scheduling department. The work scheduling department determines if the order's deadlines are technically realistic. When the work schedule is developed and forwarded to the work areas, a production order can be opened.

The work order is released for production and assembly according to the availability of existing equipment and staff capacities. The individual work processes defined in the plan are executed and confirmed after completion. As soon as the last step of the order has been completed, the work order is acknowledged as complete so that subsequent steps can be arranged. One of these steps is to ensure that the produced plant is commissioned, packaged, and delivered according to instructions. Depending on the agreement with the Sales department, the product can be delivered directly to the customer or stored temporarily until distribution. Following delivery, the invoice is prepared for the two companies, using actual costs. Model Company B invoices Model Company A because it has placed the order for the production of the product.

Figures 6.3 and 6.4 illustrate the interaction of the two model enterprises on the basis of value-added chains with the existing connections.

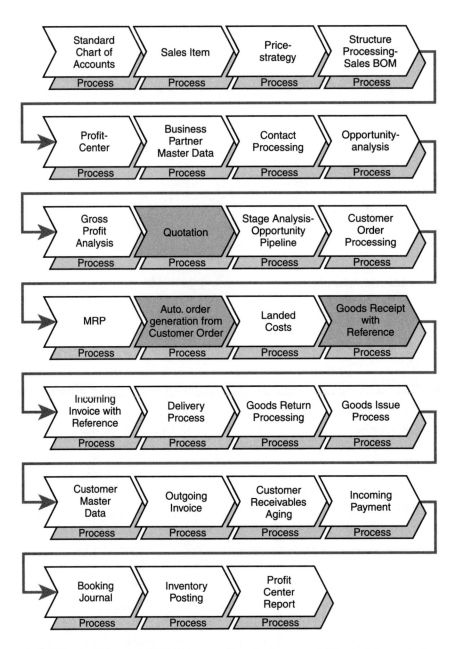

FIGURE 6.3 *Value chain Model/Example/Sample Company A. The shaded areas indicate the transition from Company A to Company B and the reverse later.*

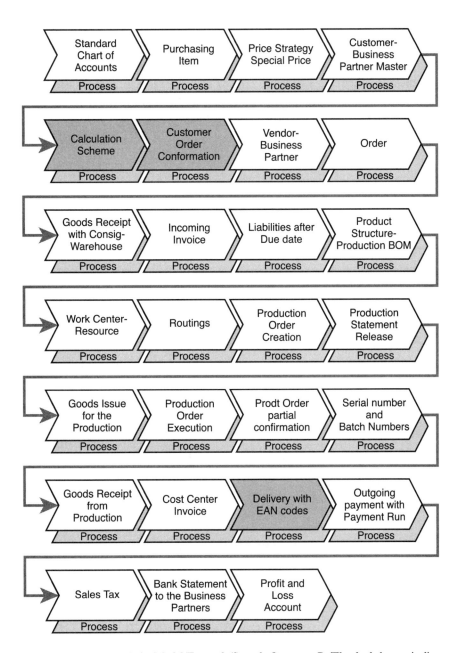

FIGURE 6.4 *Value chain Model/Example/Sample Company B. The shaded areas indicate the transition from Company B to Company B and the reverse later.*

Purchasing Item

Raw materials, semi-finished goods, products, and services are generally called materials or items. In nearly every area of an enterprise, materials affect the production process (see Figure 6.5). Materials (purchase items) increase in value during the production process so that the resulting products exceed the value of the materials used in production.

Economic Description

The information required for this process is stored in a materials master record, in order to prevent duplication. An important identifier for the material is the type of material. A material type identifies whether it is a purchase item, a plant, a commodity (trading goods), or exclusively a sales item. The identifying number of an item is called its *ID number*. This number is assigned to the purchase item by the supplier. The Purchasing department must make the necessary materials (purchase items) available for the manufacturing process. Purchase items must be procured in the necessary quantity, type, and quality and at the right time. Purchase items must be delivered as late as possible, so that procurement stock can be managed at optimal costs.

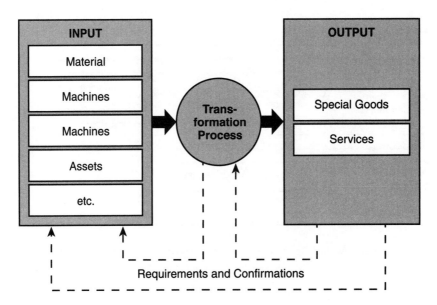

FIGURE 6.5 *The production process*

Material requirements for purchase items are determined from a BOM to the sales items ("Product Structure Processing," later in this chapter). If items are purchased in batches, then it is important to determine the most economical batch size to optimize production costs. A batch document features properties of an item, such as the production day (date of the extraction of the raw material), production length of the semi-finished goods of a supplier, and so on. Batch numbers are assigned to a group of items having the same characteristics. Batches are required for purchased items if the customer requires a proof by batch numbers for items produced.

SAP Business One: Specific Description

The required data for the purchase item are specified in SAP Business One inventory management under the Procurement Data tab. For new purchase items, inquiries normally are made to several prospective suppliers. The main supplier's catalog number for the item can be stored for frequently used raw materials. Other data, such as sales unit, packing unit quantity, and weight measures may be stored for each purchase item. Length, volume, and weight measures are stored centrally as a base in the inventory.

Customs numbers are important when importing materials. Customs groups can be created and sales tax requirements can be adjusted accordingly. The cost of import taxes is determined when recording import data at the time of purchase. Customs groups define and describe the import and sales tax, as well as other taxes, in percentages.

Import charges are calculated with the following formula:

$$Import\ charges = Purchase\ price \times (A + (A + 1) \times B \times (C + 1))$$

The calculation rate of the sales tax is specified under the procurement data in the item master data of SAP Business One. Select one of the tax groups defined under Administration (see Figure 6.6). The sales tax or value added tax (VAT) is the taxation of deliveries and is based on the fee.

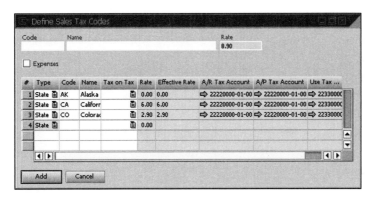

FIGURE 6.6 *Defining sales tax codes in SAP Business One.*

In the context of inventory management, the following questions should be asked:

◆ Which custom groups are defined?

◆ Which weights, volumes, and linear measures are specified as a base?

◆ Are materials procures from foreign countries, and is foreign trade data needed for it?

◆ During a new product development cycle, are similar existing purchase items reused (for example, microchips), so as to minimize item varieties and if necessary reach volume discounts for larger purchase quantities (which has an effect on volume discount groups)?

◆ Which tax groups do you need?

Application of the Process

Purchase items can be created with the Item Master Data function in the Inventory application. The creation of a new item in the initial window is not possible because the application opens in Find mode. Select the Add option in the symbol toolbar to switch to Add mode.

Next, you must specify regulation markings for the type of item. To do so, you have to set the characteristics of the purchased item. These are located in the active window on the top right. You can specify further characteristics, such as inventory item or fixed asset, after your guidelines.

In the lower area of the window, the fields are arranged for defining the item. In the Purchasing Data field, you can specify the dimensions, volume, and weight of the item. You can also set parameters for procurement-related data for your enterprise, such as purchasing quantities and packaging units for the item. If it is a sales item as well, you can duplicate the data for it in the Sales Data field (see Chapter 5).

In the General field, you'll find information about whether the item is on hold or available. You can define whether the item belongs to a certain batch or whether serial number management is necessary. During the recording of the item data, you can also specify which warehouse is to be used for this item. The item is saved in the system by clicking on Add.

Navigation Information

- ◆ **Menu Path:** Inventory > Definition > Determination of Customs Group, Inventory > Item Management
- ◆ **Tables:** AITM, AIT1, CUMI, OITG, OITM
- ◆ **Incoming Triggers:** Decision-Making Process for the Creation of a New Item, Creation of Trading Goods with Catalog Numbers
- ◆ **Outgoing Triggers:** Pricing Strategy, Sales Item, Warehouse Item, Chart of Accounts Processing, Product Structure Processing

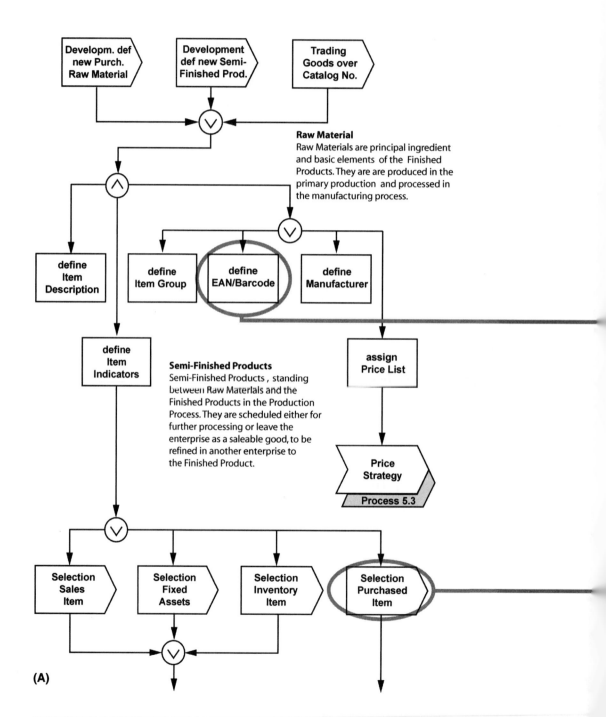

Raw Material
Raw Materials are principal ingredient and basic elements of the Finished Products. They are are produced in the primary production and processed in the manufacturing process.

Semi-Finished Products
Semi-Finished Products, standing between Raw Materials and the Finished Products in the Production Process. They are scheduled either for further processing or leave the enterprise as a saleable good, to be refined in another enterprise to the Finished Product.

(A)

FIGURE 6.7 *(a) EAN Code in the product master record, (b) Type selection in the product master record*

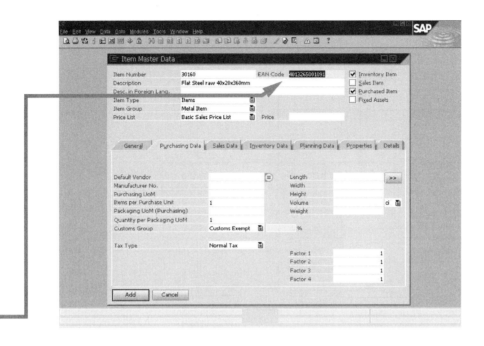

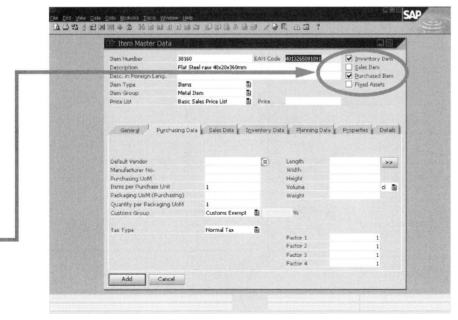

(B)

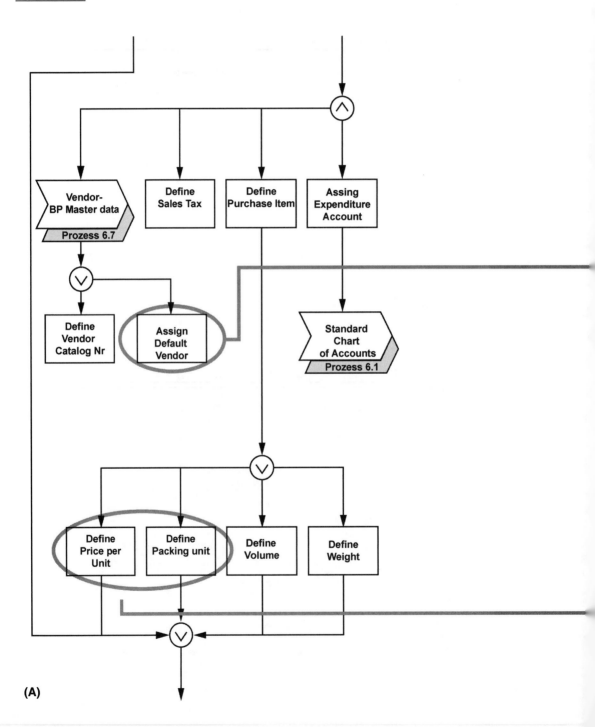

(A)

FIGURE 6.8 *(a) Main vendor selection, (b) Purchase data for products*

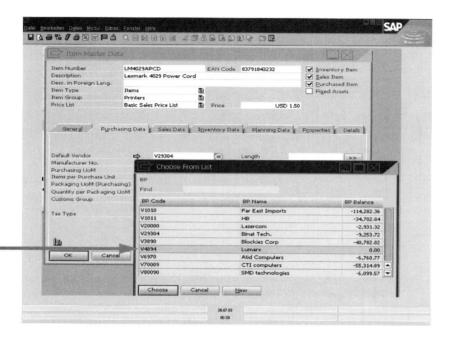

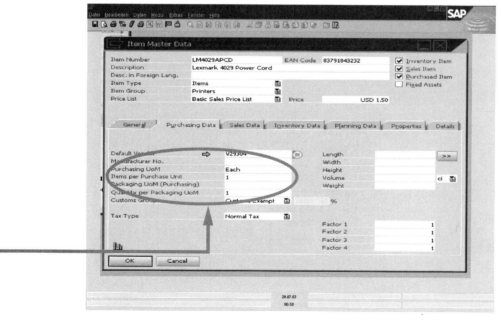

(B)

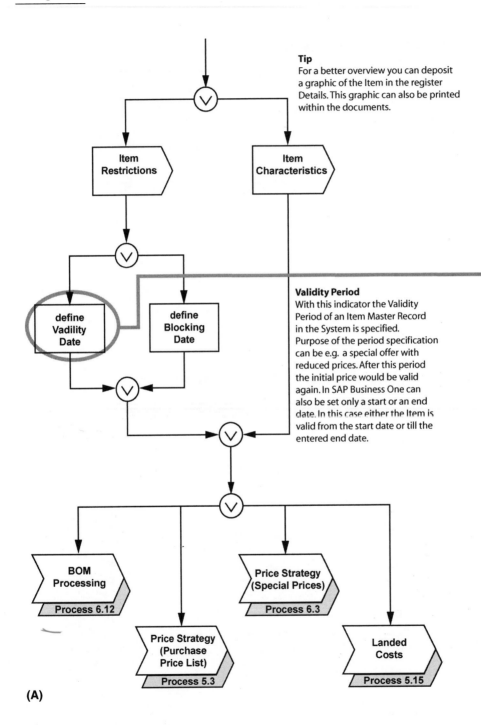

Tip
For a better overview you can deposit
a graphic of the Item in the register
Details. This graphic can also be printed
within the documents.

Validity Period
With this indicator the Validity
Period of an Item Master Record
in the System is specified.
Purpose of the period specification
can be e.g. a special offer with
reduced prices. After this period
the initial price would be valid
again. In SAP Business One can
also be set only a start or an end
date. In this case either the Item is
valid from the start date or till the
entered end date.

(A)

FIGURE 6.9 *Detailed view of inventory control, (b) Product details with image*

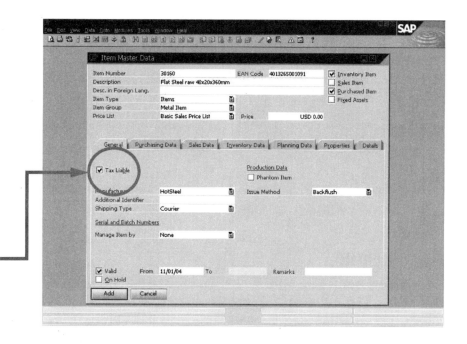

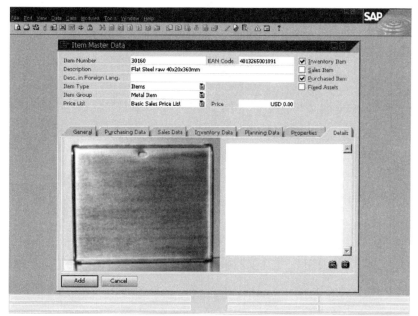

(B)

Pricing Strategy: Special Pricing

Price strategy, also called price policy, specifies measures that influence prices. The price of a product is set by the law of supply and demand, in which the seller sets a price that will attract a number of potential buyers. The price is specified when:

- A price is set for a new product.
- Current trading conditions require changes in demand and cost structures.
- It is necessary to match competitors' adjustments to their pricing.
- It is necessary to match prices of similar products.

Business Description

The classic theory assumes the price to be determined by the quantity in demand. To determine the optimal price under this theory, price must be defined to maximize profit. The company must know the sales price formula and the cost formula, which describe the functional relationship between the quantity produced and the resulting cost. The sales price formula describes the functional relationship between the sales price p and the achievable sales volume x within a planning period as follows:

$$x = f(p)$$

Normally, the higher the sales volume, the lower the price. Figure 6.10 shows two common sales price functions.

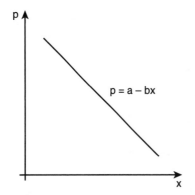
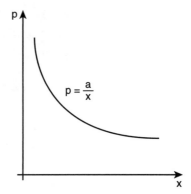

FIGURE 6.10 *Price–Sale function*

Different sales-price formulas can be characterized by an elasticity in demand caused by a reaction to price changes. Price elasticity is the relationship of the percentage of change in demand for a product after a price change.

The rising sales-price curve describes the "snob effect" of prestige products. Products that have high prestige value are preferred to cheaper products, despite a higher price. In setting a price strategy, it is important that a company know its market. In price theory, the following aspects are foremost:

◆ Relevant aspect

◆ Spatial aspect

◆ Personal aspect

The relevant aspect views products offered on the market through formulas and characteristics. The spatial aspect describes market regions, and the personal aspect describes the product's target buyer group.

The market can be divided into the following facets:

◆ Perfect market

◆ Number and size of participants

◆ Intensity of competitive relationships

◆ Behavior of market participants

A perfect market is present if all market participants strive to achieve the maximum target—the supplier for profit maximization, the buyer for usage maximization. Based on market share, the size of the market can be determined. The number of participants reflects the market structure, which might consist of many small or a few large participants. The intensity of competition is determined by the relationship between changing demand for an item and changes in the price of competitors' product. The behavior of market participants is determined at the entry of a new product into the market and the reaction of competitive suppliers and consumers.

SAP Business One: Specific Description

Prices, which are determined according to a certain price strategy for new items, must be entered in SAP Business One in a price list. As goods are sold mostly to different customer groups (market participants), such as large customers and small customers, different price lists can be associated with an item. Customer groups are defined centrally as business partners and then can be used later for the assignment of price lists. Different price lists in SAP Business One are process related and thus produce different item prices.

Since several prices can be stored in the system for the same item, *sales price calculation* determines the right price for a given process and business partner. It is necessary to look through various price lists, beginning with the most special price (special price, group discount, and so on). Figure 6.11 shows the sequence in which the price is determined in SAP Business One.

When creating a business partner (a customer or supplier), a price list is assigned in the master record. The item price is determined by consulting the assigned price list when an item is sold to a customer. If price adjustments take place, then only the main price list is revised. All other prices that are based on the main price list are automatically updated. Figure 6.12 shows how other price lists use the main price list as a basis.

FIGURE 6.11 *Pricing decision tree (Source: SAP AG)*

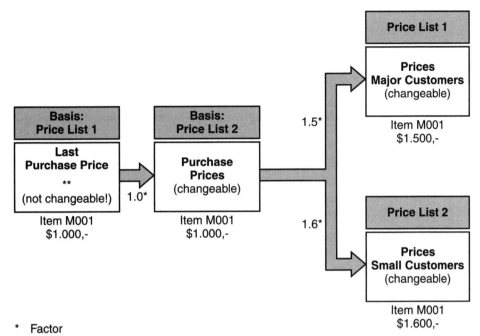

* Factor
** The last Purchase Price is updated by the System through:
A/P Invoice, Goods Receipt, Inventory Tracking & Stock Posting, with the production by
the Sum of the Purchase Prices of the Components

FIGURE 6.12 *Price lists*

To change the relationship between two price lists, you need only change the factor.
Of course, a price can also be altered manually at the time of purchase or sale of an
item. The price list *last purchase price* is updated after the following transactions:

- Opening with a positive balance for an item
- An incoming invoice
- A product shipment
- A positive inventory result that leads to incoming goods
- The manufacture of a product whose structure is that the price results
  from the last purchase prices of its components
- The receipt of data with new prices for an item

As long as none of these processes takes place for an item, the price list last purchase price will not be created.

By default, SAP Business One has 10 predefined price lists to make the structure easier to create at the beginning of system setup. You can amend or add to these lists to show their pricing logic, or you can delete them. Users can maintain price lists only if they belong to a group with privileges to do so. Authorization to maintain a price list is controlled by allocating a price list to a group. A user can amend price lists only if authorized to maintain a particular group of price lists.

Beyond that, special prices can be defined in the business partner master data to lower the price beyond the normal discount. If a discount was assigned to a business partner, it is computed on the sum of the item prices in the receipt. Special prices are for an item group or limited to a single item. Special prices also can apply to a certain time period, such as for a special sale, a trade show prices, and so on. The following price scenarios are possible:

Table 6.1 Special Pricing Possibilities

Scenario	Characteristics of Special Prices	Scenario
1	Business Partner-Dependent	Specify from special prices, which require the input of a GP number and specify the special prices for the appropriate articles.
2	Business Partner-Dependent group	If you defined the special prices for a certain business partner in scenario 1, then you can copy these for other business partners or groups according to different rules.
3	Date dependent	For the definition of scenario 1, double-click on the item number and a temporal delimitation of the special price can be indicated.
4	Quantity dependent	For an order, by double clicking on the item number you can indicate a quantity discount given to you by the supplier.
5	Item groups/Discount groups related	If you want to assign the business partner discounts independently on certain item groups, then you can specify Discount groups.
6	Business Partner-Independent	The special prices are specified to a price list, and apply if no other special prices were already defined for a business partner.

Special prices can be updated globally with a Special Prices Global Update transaction, by which you determine a proportional discount from the special price list.

Regarding pricing strategy, the following questions should be considered:

- ◆ Do you have several price lists for the same item and for what reason do you differentiate? What factor determines a reduction from the base price list?
- ◆ Which predefined system price lists can you use?
- ◆ Which customers get special prices?
- ◆ Are there item-related special prices?
- ◆ Which special price scenarios do you pursue?
- ◆ Do you define customer group discounts?

Application Process

Special prices in SAP Business One are administered by items and by customers. After setting individual prices for items in the price lists, special prices can be defined for those items and for various business partners. This is done by selecting the Inventory application and then the Special Prices folder and choosing the Special Prices for Customers function. In the first step, special prices are defined for a business partner. Enter the business partner for which you want to apply the new special price into the BP Code and BP Name fields. You can use the search functions provided by SAP Business One to enter the Business Partner fields. Select a base price list for calculating special prices from the selection list. If you do not want your special prices to be based on an existing price list, select the Without Price List option and enter the prices manually.

If several items are provided with the same proportional discount, a value can be defined in the Discount field, which is consulted for all the following items. Enter the items into the table for which you would like to apply the special prices, as described above.

Use the previously described search and selection functions. In the lower area of the window is the Add Items button, which you can use to select several items at the same time. You can arrange your window in such a way as to filter item codes, supplier, item characteristics, or item groups. Combinations of selections also are allowed.

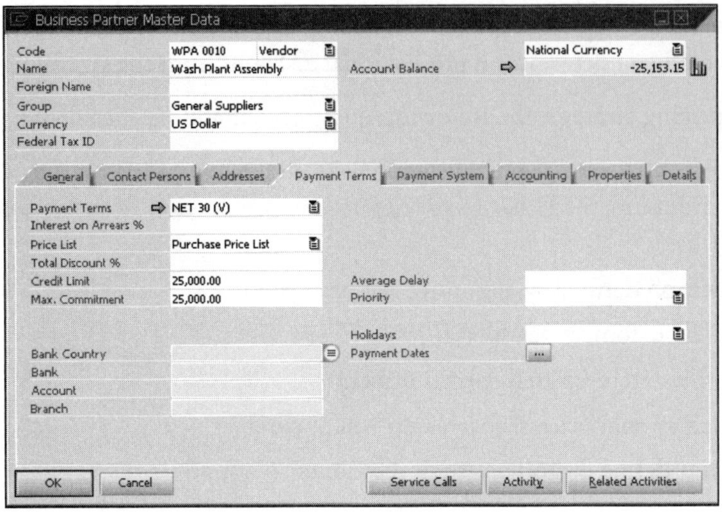

FIGURE 6.13 *Filter template for the product selection*

After you have assigned special prices to all desired items for a business, you can confirm your inputs with OK and add the inputs to the system.

If special prices for certain items are valid only for a limited time, you can specify date-dependent special prices. If such an item is sold within this specified time period, the special price applies. As soon as the time period ends, the regular price specified in the price list will automatically apply for the item. After specifying special prices, a time-limited special price can be added by double-clicking on an item line in the table. An additional window opens with the line extensions and offers the option to define a valid date. Press Update to be returned to the previous window. Those lines that are defined as time-limited special prices are displayed in blue.

The third option in assigning special prices is quantity-dependent discounts. To use this kind of special price, the item line in the window with the line extensions must be double-clicked. A new input window appears with the fields for quantity-dependent special prices. Even if you did not assign date-dependent special prices, you can specify quantity-dependent special prices. After finishing the assignment, return to the base window by clicking on Update.

If you do not want to specify special prices for each individual item for a business partner, you can define more general discounts in discounts groups. These groups can be dependent on individual item groups, item characteristic combinations, or item brands. To establish a discount group, call up the Special Prices function. After selecting the business partner, you can specify discount groups in the fields. Click on Add to store your input.

Navigation Information

- ◆ **Menu Path:** Business Partner > Definition > Determine Customer Group > Administration > Authorizations

    Inventory > Price Lists > Price List

    Inventory > Price List > Special Price

- ◆ **Tables:** OPLN, OSPP, OSPG

- ◆ **Incoming Triggers:** Customer-Business Partner, Vendor-Business Partner, Price Strategy, Item Master Processing

- ◆ **Outgoing Triggers:** Quotation Processing, Customer Order Processing, Precalculation Customer Order, Order Processing

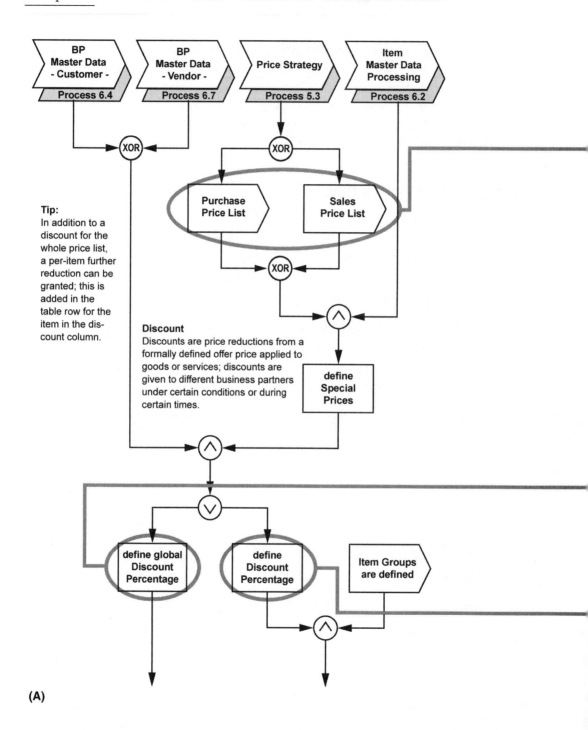

Tip:
In addition to a discount for the whole price list, a per-item further reduction can be granted; this is added in the table row for the item in the discount column.

Discount
Discounts are price reductions from a formally defined offer price applied to goods or services; discounts are given to different business partners under certain conditions or during certain times.

(A)

FIGURE 6.15 *(a) Price list selection for special pricing, (b) Special pricing rebates*

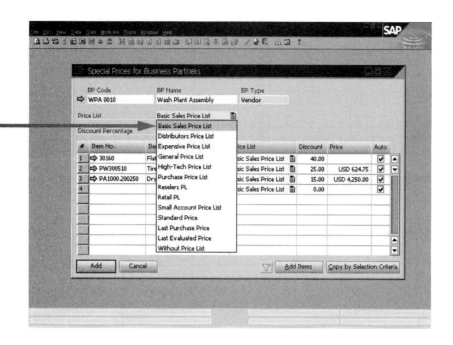

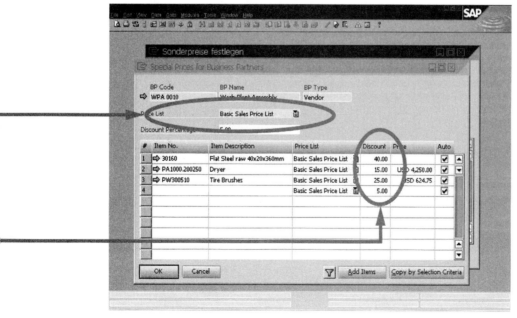

(B)

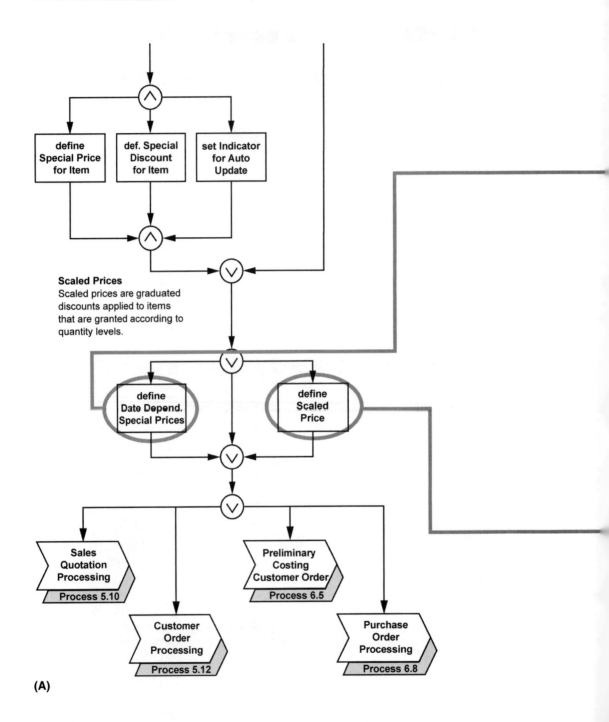

Scaled Prices
Scaled prices are graduated discounts applied to items that are granted according to quantity levels.

(A)

FIGURE 6.15 *(a) Line extension for rebates, (b) Graduated/Scaled pricing*

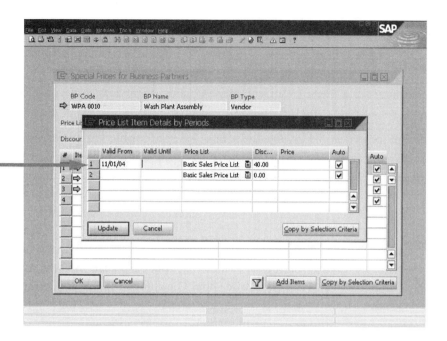

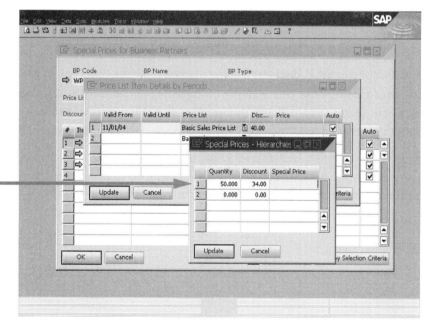

(B)

Customer Business Partner Master Data

The customer is a buyer of an enterprise's goods or services. If a contract exists between the customer and the enterprise, then the buyer is referred to as a customer.

Several processes can be involved in a business relationship with a customer during different stages. A relationship with a customer might take place on only one occasion, on an irregular but repeated basis, or over the course of a number of years.

Business Description

Access to customer data is essential to an enterprise, particularly in sales and marketing. Any employee of the enterprise should be able to call up all relevant information about a customer quickly and easily. This is the only way for employees of an enterprise with different areas of responsibility to work with a customer in a uniform manner.

SAP Business One: Specific Description

The philosophy of SAP Business One is to update all data relevant to a customer in a master record. This is called the *customer master record* or the *debtor master record*, and it is intended to serve the needs of both Accounting and Sales. It can be either generated from the lead master record or created independently.

During the creation of lead master data, all existing contacts are incorporated. When creating the master data record for a customer account, it is necessary to adapt the naming conventions of the debtor master data.

Different roles can be included in a customer master record:

- ◆ Ordering party
- ◆ Payer
- ◆ Goods recipient
- ◆ Invoice recipient

In most customer accounts, these will be provided by a master record. In master data management, for example, it is possible to assign several goods recipients to a payer. To do so, it is necessary to activate the Summarizing Payment option and enter the customer master records of the goods recipient in the customer account of the payer in the Accounting main menu.

In the master record of a customer account, several delivery addresses can be recorded, apart from a billing address. The necessary addresses are entered on the Address tab field. If more than one delivery address is maintained in a customer master record, then a clear designation in the Name field is recommended because this entry is used in the application, such as when recording a delivery.

The following questions apply to customer business master record analysis:

- Is the company master data already captured as a lead?
- Are the billing and delivery addresses the same?

Application Process

A master record for a customer as a business partner can be defined in two ways. One is to change a lead into a customer by changing the Lead indicator to Customer in the upper-right area of the window in the Business Partner Master Data function.

If the master data is to be newly entered, you can proceed in the same way as during the recording of master data for a lead (see Chapter 5). When selecting whether the record is that of a customer, vendor, or lead, be sure that Customer is chosen.

Navigation Information

- **Menu Path:** Business Partner > Business Partner Master Data > Customer Selection by BP Code
- **Tables:** ACRD, ACPR, ACR1, CRD1, OCRD
- **Incoming Triggers:** Lead-Business Partner, Customer Master Data
- **Outgoing Triggers:** Contact Processing, Opportunity Analysis, Pricing Strategy–Special Prices, Quote Processing, Customer Order Confirmation, Production Order Creation

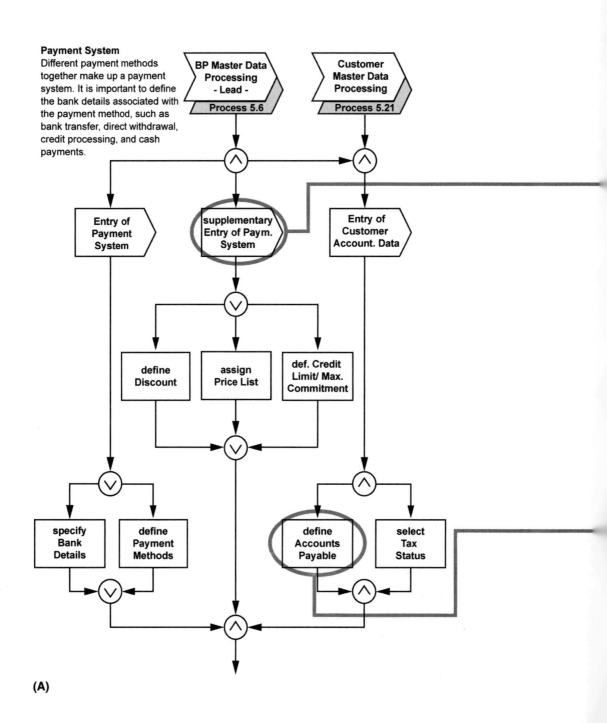

FIGURE 6.16 *(a) GP-Payment terms, (b) Account assignment for the GP*

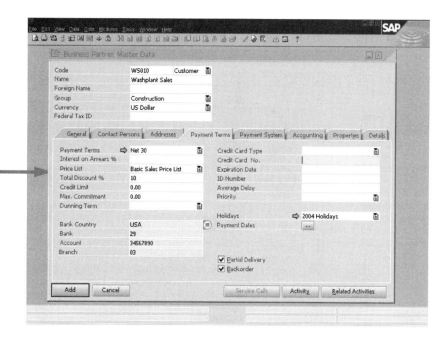

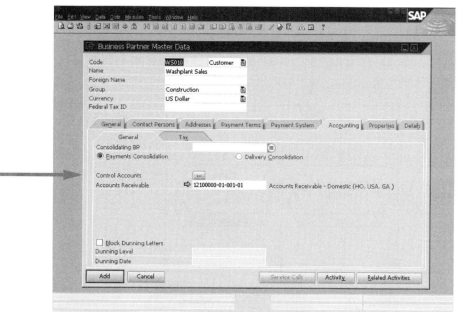

(B)

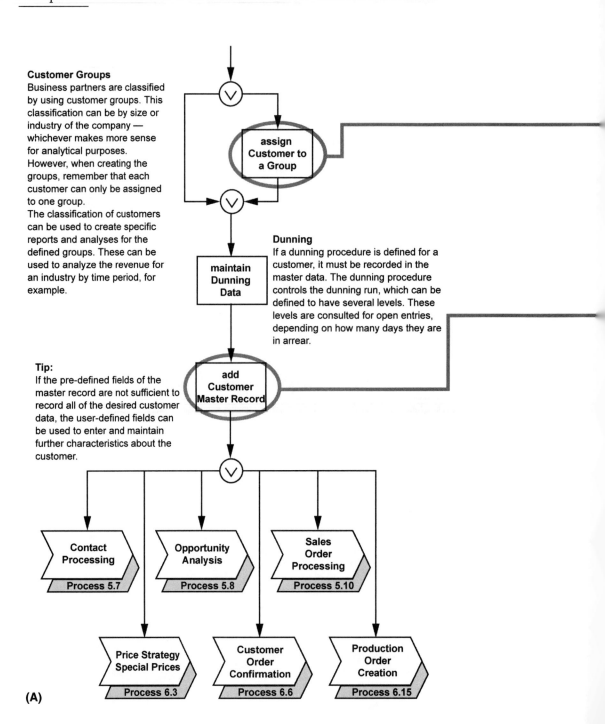

Customer Groups
Business partners are classified by using customer groups. This classification can be by size or industry of the company — whichever makes more sense for analytical purposes. However, when creating the groups, remember that each customer can only be assigned to one group.
The classification of customers can be used to create specific reports and analyses for the defined groups. These can be used to analyze the revenue for an industry by time period, for example.

assign Customer to a Group

maintain Dunning Data

Dunning
If a dunning procedure is defined for a customer, it must be recorded in the master data. The dunning procedure controls the dunning run, which can be defined to have several levels. These levels are consulted for open entries, depending on how many days they are in arrear.

Tip:
If the pre-defined fields of the master record are not sufficient to record all of the desired customer data, the user-defined fields can be used to enter and maintain further characteristics about the customer.

add Customer Master Record

Contact Processing
Process 5.7

Opportunity Analysis
Process 5.8

Sales Order Processing
Process 5.10

Price Strategy Special Prices
Process 6.3

Customer Order Confirmation
Process 6.6

Production Order Creation
Process 6.15

(A)

FIGURE 6.17 *(a) GP group assignments, (b) Business partner attributes*

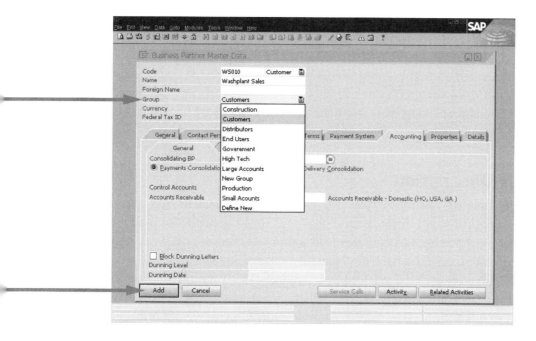

(B)

Preliminary Costing of Customer Order

Preliminary costing is used to determine manufacturing costs and make an immediate statement of total costs possible. Costing is based on the quantity structure of the BOM for the item to be calculated. A costing document for manufacturing and total production costs is different in every enterprise because the costing sheet is usually adjusted individually.

Business Description

Direct costs and overhead costs are based on cost element and cost center accounting. Although direct costs are assigned to the goods to be produced, the calculation of overhead costs is an added amount. If overhead costs (indirect costs such as current consumption, administrative costs of an enterprise, and so on) are included in costing, this is referred to as a full cost calculation. Direct costs, however, can be assigned directly to a cost objective such as a customer order. The allocation of direct costs takes place according to the Cost-by-Cause principle (cost objective accounting). Material costs and manufacturing wages are typical direct costs. The direct costing method (marginal costing) developed by Riebel is designed to illustrate real cost accumulation as accurately as possible.

The type of costing procedures used depends heavily on the type of services rendered. At a manufacturing facility with the same or similar products, division costing is suitable. Overhead costing or a scale basis calculation is meaningful with similar manufacturing products. Overhead costing is common in practice. In the first section, overhead costing assigns direct costs included in the cost element calculation to the cost objectives. As a result, manufacturing costs are stated. In the second section, overhead costs are added proportionally. Table 6.2 shows the basic formula for overhead costing.

Table 6.2 Basic Scheme for Overhead Costs Calculation

Calculation Components	Overhead	Overhead Basis
Direct Material Costs		
+ Material Overhead Costs	Overhead Costs of the Material Cost Center	Direct Material Costs
+ Direct Production Costs		
+ Manufacturing Overhead Costs	Overhead Costs of the Production Cost Center	Direct Production Costs
+ External Service		
+ Miscellaneous Costs		
= Cost of Goods Manufactured		
+ Overhead Rates Administration	Overhead Costs of the Administration Cost Centers	Cost of Goods Manufactured
+ Overhead Rates Sales and Distribution	Overhead Costs of the Sales and Distribution Cost Center	Cost of Goods Manufactured
= Total Production Costs		

SAP Business One: Specific Description

Preliminary costing is an important step in executing a customer order because without it a customer order cannot be confirmed (see the following section, "Customer Order Confirmation"). In preliminary component costing, product calculation uses Microsoft Excel. Most product calculations, particularly in a business of medium size, also use Excel. SAP Business One offers a familiar Excel interface for this task. For a firm order, costing is carried out before the product is even manufactured. It is the basis of prices and adjusted prices for customer order confirmation.

In preliminary costing, the following questions should be analyzed:

◆ What cost calculation procedure is used in your enterprise?

◆ What degree of detail does your calculation plan exhibit?

◆ What workstations are available in your enterprise and what work processes can be done on them?

- How do you want to evaluate external services?

- How are materials needed for the production of a product and consequently used for pricing calculation evaluated?

- How do you want to calculate surcharges for the overhead costs?

- How do you want to account for waste, special direct costs, summary costs, and setup costs?

Application Process

Prices can be entered into SAP Business One after calculating them in MS Excel with the Import function over article data. All master records can be overwritten, or you can update only those that have changed. Data is copied from the MS Excel table to the associated fields in SAP Business One. However, first it is necessary to configure the necessary data mappings for the import. To be imported to SAP, the data in MS Excel must be in the A to BT column range. Also, the number of characters in an Excel field may not be higher than the defined length of the associated field in SAP Business One. You can check the permitted size of the import fields in the tables in Appendix A, Hardware and System Requirements for SAP Business One. Also, some fields are mandatory for data transfer; this information is in Appendix A as well.

In addition to the mandatory Item Number field for price information, you must define three other columns to import a price list from MS Excel: Number of the Price List, Price in the Price List, and Currency of the Price List, which enables you to import calculations with different currencies in SAP Business One. If no currency is explicitly indicated in the import file, the local currency is used by the system. When arranging columns for import, you must make sure that the column with the price list number is to the left of the column for the currency.

Before import, some further rules must be considered to ensure a smooth transfer:

- The tables may not contain blank lines or titles.

- The field lengths of SAP Business One may not be exceeded.

- The mandatory fields (business partner number/item number) may not contain special characters (!, *, ?, %, {,}, or =).

- The MS Excel file to be imported must be closed before transferring.
- The MS Excel file must be stored in a text format.

When these conditions are met, the actual import procedure can be started. For safety reasons, it is recommended that you make a backup of the SAP Business One database. It is also recommended that you make sure all users are signed onto the system during the import. Call the Import from Excel function in the Data Import menu in Administration. Item must be selected in the Data Type to Import field. In the Import window list, each line equates to a column of the MS Excel table to be imported. Select Item Code in line A and Price List Code in line B. Two lines with additional price information are automatically transferred with the Price List Code. You can then select other lines to be transferred into SAP Business One as needed. Just select the appropriate entries from the lists offered.

In the lower area of the window you can set whether existing data records should be updated with the import and whether account data for the item should be updated during an item import. When you click OK, Windows Explorer is opened, where you select the file to be imported. The import starts following confirmation of the selected files. When the process is complete, you receive a report of all information relevant to the import. It is a good idea to store this report to track possible errors.

Navigation Information

- **Menu Path:** Administration > Data Import/Export > Data Import > Import from Excel
- **Tables:** AIT1, OITM, IPF1, OPLN
- **Incoming Triggers:** Customer Queries, MS Excel Calculation Sheet
- **Outgoing Triggers:** Quote Processing, Customer Order Processing, Pricing Strategy

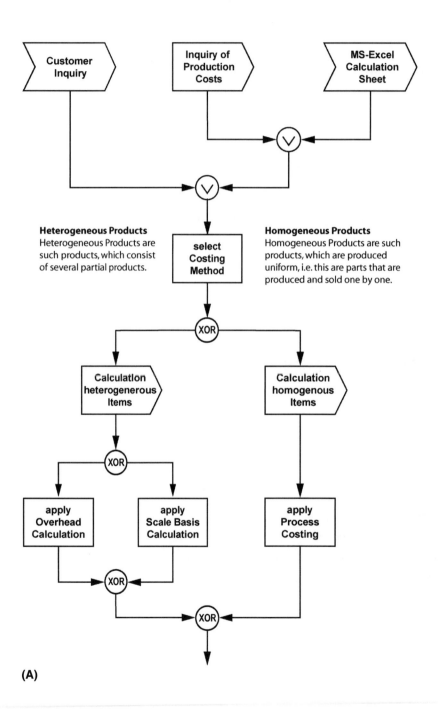

Heterogeneous Products
Heterogeneous Products are such products, which consist of several partial products.

Homogeneous Products
Homogeneous Products are such products, which are produced uniform, i.e. this are parts that are produced and sold one by one.

(A)

FIGURE 6.18 *(a) Price lists detailed view, (b) Export function in SAP Business One*

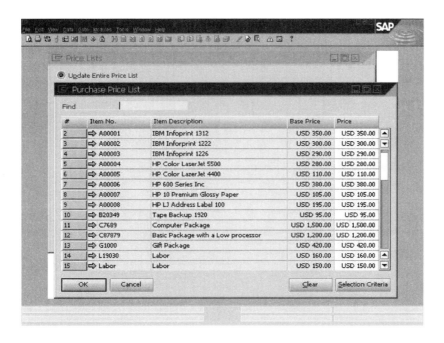

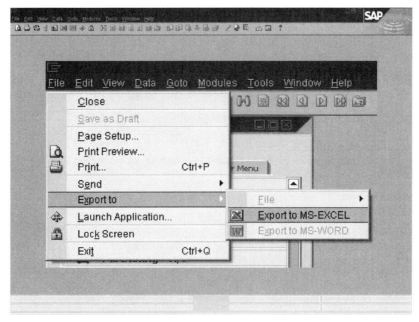

(B)

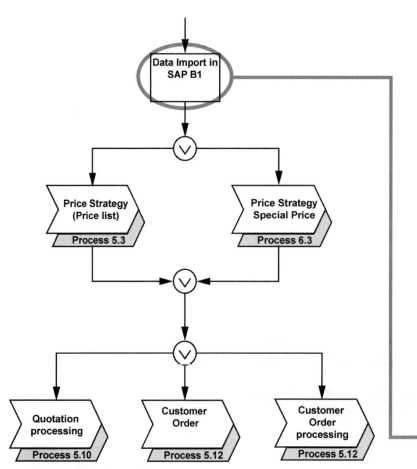

Preparing Import data for Price lists
Lay out the following three columns in the Microsoft Excel table for the Price information.
A. Price list number
B . Price into Price list
C . Currency of the Price list
You can import Prices in a Price list in different Currencies.
If no currency is defined in the import file, the system organizes the prices automatically
the Local currency.Make sure that the column for these
Price list number stands on the left of the column for the Price list currency.

Tip
You can import several Item Price lists at the same time. Insert additional columns for these Price lists
in the MS Excel-Table. You must define three columns for every Item price: one for the Price list number, one
the Item price in the Price list and one for the Price list currency. These three Price list columns
you must always import together.

(A)

FIGURE 6.19 *(a)Excel costing/price calculation example, (b) Import preparation in SAP Business One*

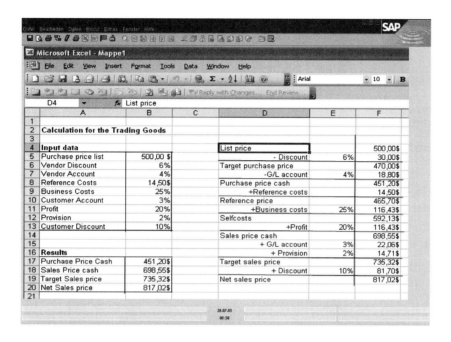

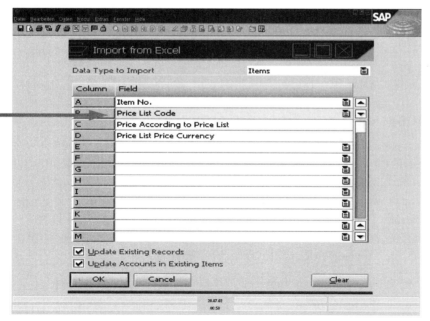

(B)

Customer Order Confirmation

Customer order confirmation is a customary form of proof in business of final agreement. The supplier confirms to the customer that he can deliver the goods at an agreed-upon price and date.

Business Description

If there are difficulties with the goods delivery, the customer must be informed immediately. In extreme cases, customers can refer to the order confirmation to demand compensation. For example, the customer might have a detailed manufacturing plan that has little margin for delay in receiving supply shipments. If a delivery delay leads to a loss of production, this might cause a loss. A lack of response to a customer order confirmation is considered acceptance of the terms specified in the customer order confirmation. Even if the customer order deviates and contains new conditions from previous discussions, the agreement is valid. Any disagreement must take place within a short amount of time. Therefore, the customer order confirmation should be examined carefully by the customer and compared with the preceding customer order. If necessary, the customer can create a new order confirmation. If two contradicting order confirmations are sent, then neither supplier nor customer must react. In this case, renewed contract negotiation is necessary.

SAP Business One: Specific Description

If a customer order is confirmed, it can be entered into SAP Business One. After the order is checked, it can be printed and confirmed. The order confirmation is included in the printed document. In our example, Model Company B confirms the customer order document to Model Company A with the Automatic Order Generation from Customer Order process. Model Company B enters the customer order and prints the customer order confirmation. Verification by the seller is necessary before order confirmation can take place:

- Is the sold item authorized and can the delivery date be kept?
- Is the given price correct? (See the "Preliminary Costing of Customer Order" section earlier in this chapter.)
- Was a credit check run on the business partner?

If an item was offered to the customer but was discontinued (for example, an item might be discontinued for quality reasons) before the customer order was assigned, then no order confirmation can take place for that item. The Disable flag is found in the Restriction field in the article source set. The item can be temporarily or permanently discontinued. After verification of delivery dates, the date can be specified both on the order header level and on the item position level. The exact shipping date of a certain item can be calculated using a work plan add-on program which allows the sequencing of workstations with their corresponding manufacturing times. (See Chapter 3).

The type of credit limit check (see Figure 6.20) varies as a function of the order quantity (see Figure 6.21), the customer position, and the type of financing. When including a sales document, the system also verifies the credit limit of the customer and compares it with open orders already placed. Normally, a company does not perform an extensive credit limit check with products on the consumer market. If the order is for expensive consumer goods (such as machinery, industrial plants, and so on), then a financing option is agreed upon between the business partners, and no credit check is performed. For products on the producer market, a credit limit is assigned to the customer in the business partner master data. If during the credit check it is found that the maximum limit has been exceeded, then an order or a delivery block is set until clarification of the payments.

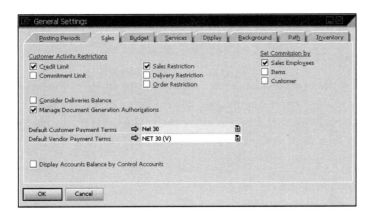

FIGURE 6.20 *Customizing of the credit limit within the Administration menu*

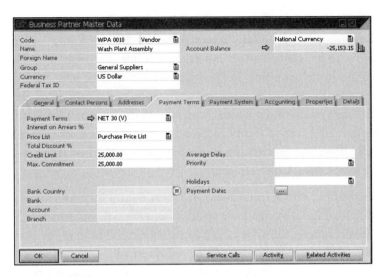

FIGURE 6.21 *Setting credit limits in business partner master data*

From a sales perspective, the following questions should be asked regarding order confirmation:

- Do you work with credit limits?
- For which business partners do you enter credit limits in the master record?

Application of the Process

As described in the previous section, order confirmations in SAP Business One are in the form of printed order documents. That is significant because an order confirmation is normally sent to the client by mail. With SAP Business One's integrated Layout Designer, you can design the order confirmation document simply and according to your own needs.

To open the Layout Designer, call an order with the Sales Order function in the Sales application and select the Print Layout Designer icon, or select the same function in the Tools menu. In the opening window, you can select an existing template for your documents. The document templates are displayed in the editor in full size, as they will appear on paper. They are displayed in different colors and contain the objects necessary for the area, such as text fields, system fields, and pictures. Contents and characteristics of individual areas as well as the entire template can be changed with Layout Designer.

A document template is normally divided into five independent sections: Page Header, Start of Report, Repetitive Area, End of Report, and Page Footer. These contain objects necessary for the data in the document. The objects within these areas can be rearranged, added, or deleted.

The upper-right area of the screen displays a Field Index window with all objects allowed in the template. The index is divided into the different areas to allow simple navigation within the template. The associated object in the template is selected by double-clicking on a line in the index window. The following options are available:

- Select fields and areas
- Change position of a field
- Change size of a field
- Insert data, text, diagram, calculation, or extension fields

In addition to the processing options, template, area, and object properties can be modified by calling the Document Properties function in the Print Layout Designer menu or by double-clicking into the area whose properties you would like to change.

Once you are finished editing the order confirmation, select the Save As function in the Print Layout Designer menu to store the template using your own document name. The stored document then appears in the selection list.

Navigation Information

- **Menu Path:** Administration > System Initialization > General Settings > Sales

    Sales > Order > Order Confirmation Printout
- **Tables:** ORDR, RDR1, RDR2, RDR3
- **Incoming Triggers:** Customer Business Partner Master Data, Customer Order Processing, Quote Processing
- **Outgoing Triggers:** Automatic Order Generation, Order Processing, Production Order Creation

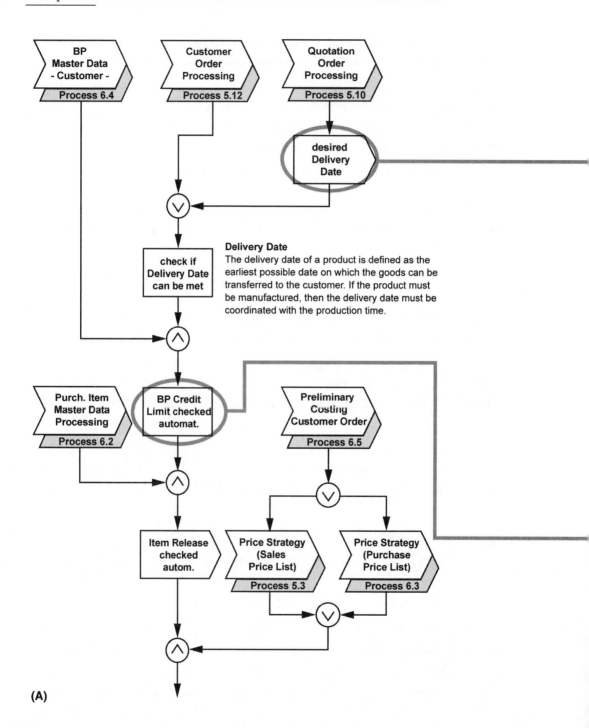

FIGURE 6.22 *(a) Order window with delivery date, (b) GP credit limit master data*

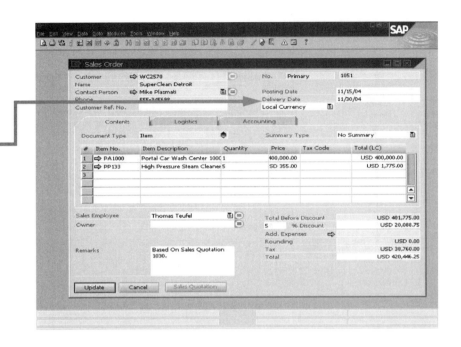

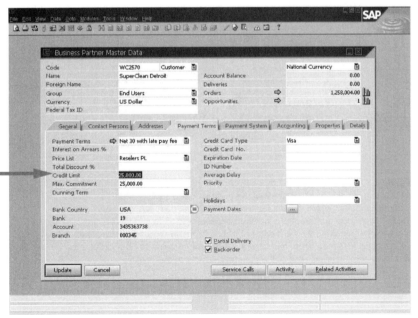

(B)

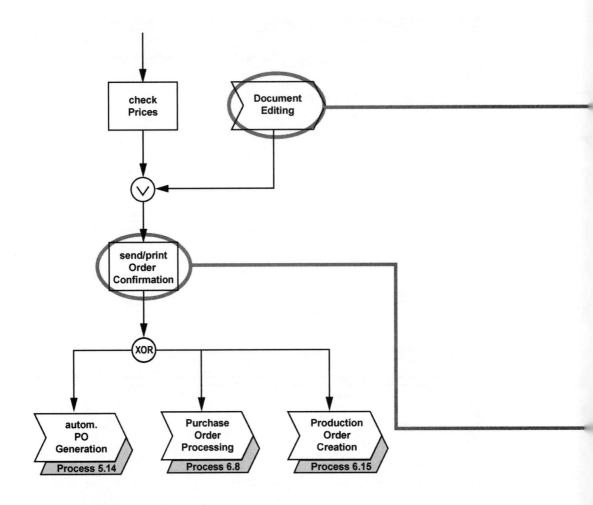

Order Confirmation
The order confirmation is the written acceptance of the contract offer. Usually, the confirmation is done using a confirmation letter, which constitutes the closing of the contract. The confirmation letter can also be the contextual summary of a contract between the parties. If the context differs from the previous verbal agreement, then a prompt objection from the recipient is necessary. Failing to reply constitutes an acceptance, except when the disparity between the confirmation letter and the verbal agreement is extreme or the confirmer is acting maliciously.

(A)

FIGURE 6.23 *(a) Receipt editor, (b) Print preview order receipt*

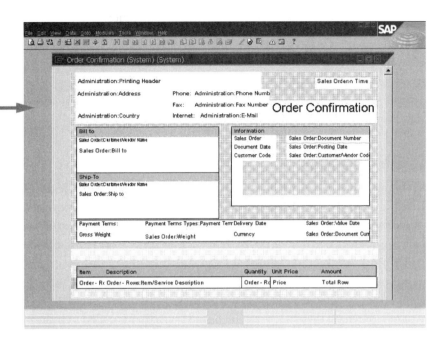

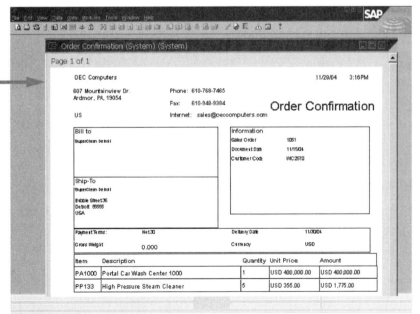

(B)

Vendor–Business Partner

Suitable vendors are identified for external procurement and selected as business partners. The role of the vendor is to provide adequate quantity and quality supplies of materials (raw materials, semi-finished goods, or finished goods for trading/merchandising).

Business Description

If a vendor is a continuous business partner, he is called an *In-Supplier*. In-Suppliers have a main vendor-offer position. There is a close business relationship with the customer that is called *vendor loyalty*. A vendor of a commodity can be an invoicing party as well as a payee at the same time. Therefore, the business partner is both a vendor and creditor at the same time, depending on quantity and value aspects. If logistic aspects are regarded within a business process, then the business partner is called a vendor. If it is a financial business transaction (such as payment of a purchase invoice), then the business partner is called a creditor. Business partners for procurement are selected according to two main criteria:

According to economic capabilities

- ◆ Price
- ◆ Delivery Terms
- ◆ Payment Terms
- ◆ Reliability/Delivery Reliability
- ◆ Image

According to technical capabilities

- ◆ Product Quality
- ◆ Standard or Technical Integration Options
- ◆ Warranty/Service
- ◆ Recycling Options

Point models are used for rating vendors. The individual values are weighed against different target criteria. When selecting criteria, it is important to avoid duplication and cover only one circumstance without any overlaps. The result could be a list of vendors with an A-B-C ranking, for example, in which an A vendor is the main vendor. If the A vendor is not available for a project for some reason, then a B or C vendor is used. Furthermore, subjective variables (perhaps a personal connection between a buyer and a seller) also play a role in the selection of suitable vendors. A justifiable decision can be made only after all objective and subjective criteria are considered.

SAP Business One: Specific Description

The vendor business partner master record in SAP Business One uses the same structure as the customer and lead business partner records. Therefore, the vendor business partner type must be specified before the code (vendor number) is determined. In turn, the code is a unique characteristic for the identification of the master record. In general, the name, vendor group, telephone number, partner, and address for each vendor or creditor are maintained. Procurement-relevant data is arranged into further detailed field tabs. It concerns the following data:

♦ Terms of payment and payment system

♦ Accounting data

♦ Detail data (figures and text modules)

Terms of payment are agreed upon with the business partner regarding the time of payment of liabilities (calculations). The calculation of the due date is based on the posting date of the purchase document. Proportional terms (discount payments) are a discount related to the agreed-upon payment schedule. The payment terms entered in the master record are set; however, they can be amended in the purchase document at the time of the business transaction (such as the order).

SAP Business One also allows the capturing of proportional interest rates on arrears if historically the vendor charges them (entered for information purposes only). Additional payment terms agreed to with the vendor, such as a proportional overall discount or a credit limit, are to be maintained as part of the payment terms. When an item is purchased, it must be assigned to the price list of the vendor, which is consulted for price calculation. If checks are accepted from a business partner, the Maximum Liability data field can be maintained. This represents the total of open invoices plus any open checks. Finally, in the captured payment terms, you will find banking information for the vendor, which is extracted from an automatic payment run.

Accounts receivable, tax status, and tax group for a business partner are to be maintained as part of the accounting data. Chart of accounts and business partner accounts are administered together in SAP Business One and use the same key field. Therefore, the account keys of the chart of accounts and the business partner must not overlap, so that no business partner can use a key number that is already assigned to another account. The payables account in the vendor master record is the reconciliation account (there is a connection from accounts payable to the general ledger). When postings (automatic account identification with business transactions) with vendor business partners are transacted, these postings are recorded directly on the registered G/L account. In this way the general ledger is up to date at any time (see Figure 6.24).

A special account can be created for foreign liabilities resulting from creditors outside the country of business. When creating a master record in which the invoice address is in a foreign country, a special account is suggested as a reconciliation account.

If needed, a note can be attached to a creditor within the accounting data, pointing to the master record of another business partner that serves as the main office of the vendor business partner. You find this form of decentralized vendors with a central invoice statement repeatedly when dealing with large conglomerates.

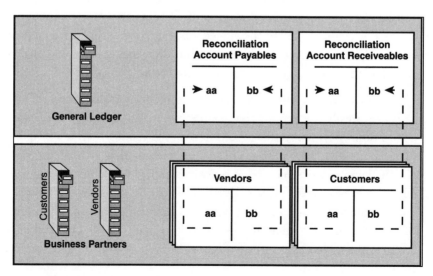

FIGURE 6.24 _Creditor account in general ledger_

It is best to create a dummy vendor for vendors from whom you buy materials only once or quite seldom. A dummy vendor master record is used for several vendors in order to avoid creating an unnecessarily large number of master records.

During vendor master record administration, the following questions should be asked:

◆ What payment and delivery terms have you agreed to with your vendors?

◆ What type of accounts payable do you use for vendor accounting?

◆ Do you classify your vendors? If so, by what characteristics?

Application of the Process

Vendor master data is entered at the same time as lead and a customer master data collection (see the sections "Business Partner Master Data" in Chapter 5 and "Customer Business Partner Master Data," earlier in this chapter). However, make sure that Vendor was specified as the business partner type. Detailed information on the vendor can be entered in the different fields of the lower area of the input window. These can deviate from customer or lead master data. In the Payment Terms field, you can choose the payment terms for this business partner from the selection list, after which you define a price list that is valid for the vendor. Next, you can enter the information for the vendor's bank account. If a vendor has different payment methods, such as transfers or credit card payments, these can be entered in the Payment System field in the payment forms table according to the previous definition in the Define Payment Terms menu. Characteristics for payment means can be set as required.

Navigation Information

◆ **Menu Path:** Business partner > Business Partner Master Data

◆ **Tables:** ACR1, ACRD, ACPR, OCPR, OCQP, OCRD

◆ **Incoming Triggers:** Sales Contact Processing, Purchasing Analysis

◆ **Outgoing Triggers:** Contact Processing, Ordering

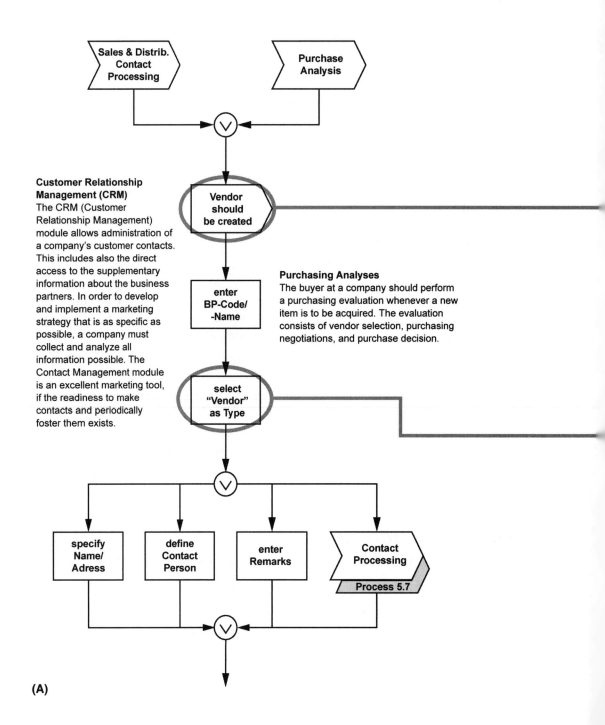

Customer Relationship Management (CRM)
The CRM (Customer Relationship Management) module allows administration of a company's customer contacts. This includes also the direct access to the supplementary information about the business partners. In order to develop and implement a marketing strategy that is as specific as possible, a company must collect and analyze all information possible. The Contact Management module is an excellent marketing tool, if the readiness to make contacts and periodically foster them exists.

Purchasing Analyses
The buyer at a company should perform a purchasing evaluation whenever a new item is to be acquired. The evaluation consists of vendor selection, purchasing negotiations, and purchase decision.

FIGURE 6.25 *(a) Main navigation area, (b) Business partner type selection*

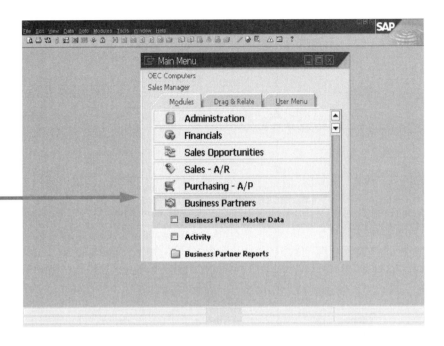

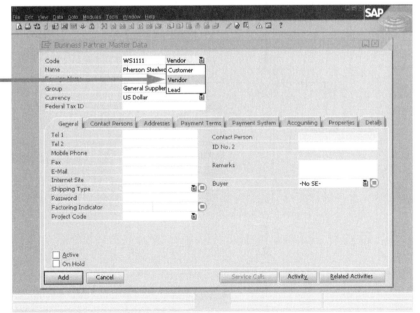

(B)

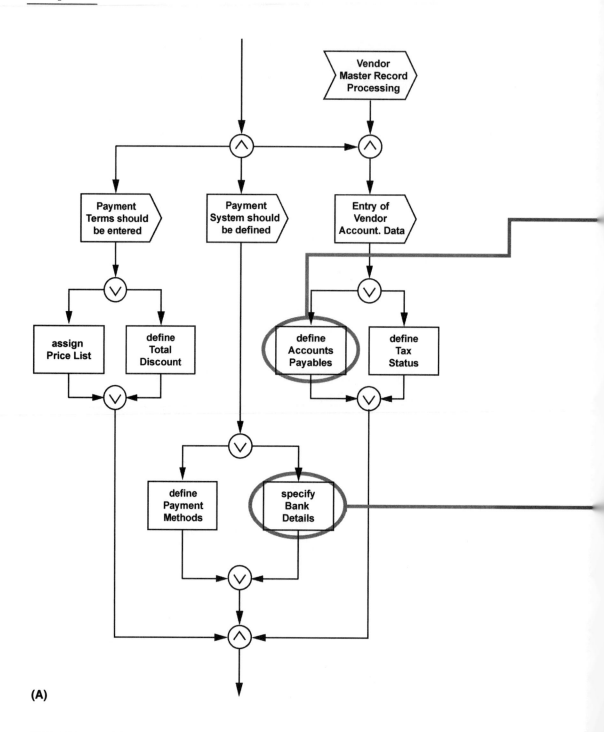

(A)

FIGURE 6.26 *(a) Assignment of primary vendor in the item master data, (b) Vendor groups*

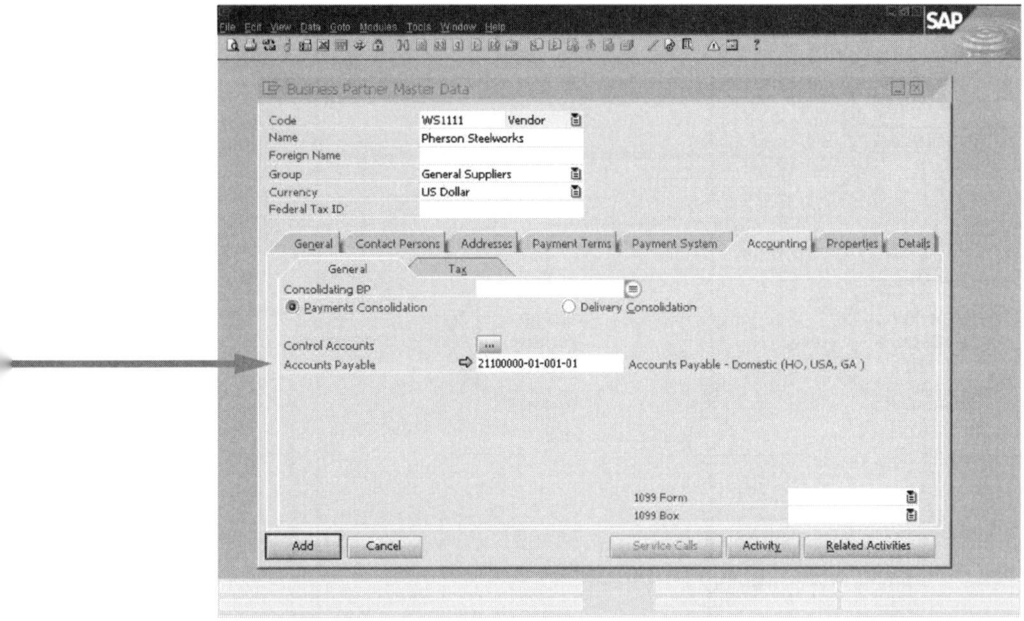
File Edit View Data Goto Modules Tools Window Help
SAP
Business Partner Master Data
Code
WS1111
Vendor
Name
Pherson Steelworks
Foreign Name
Group
General Suppliers
Currency
US Dollar
Federal Tax ID
General
Contact Persons
Addresses
Payment Terms
Payment System
Accounting
Properties
Details
General
Tax
Consolidating BP
Payments Consolidation
Delivery Consolidation
Control Accounts
Accounts Payable
21100000-01-001-01
Accounts Payable - Domestic (HO, USA, GA)
1099 Form
1099 Box
Add
Cancel
Service Calls
Activity
Related Activities

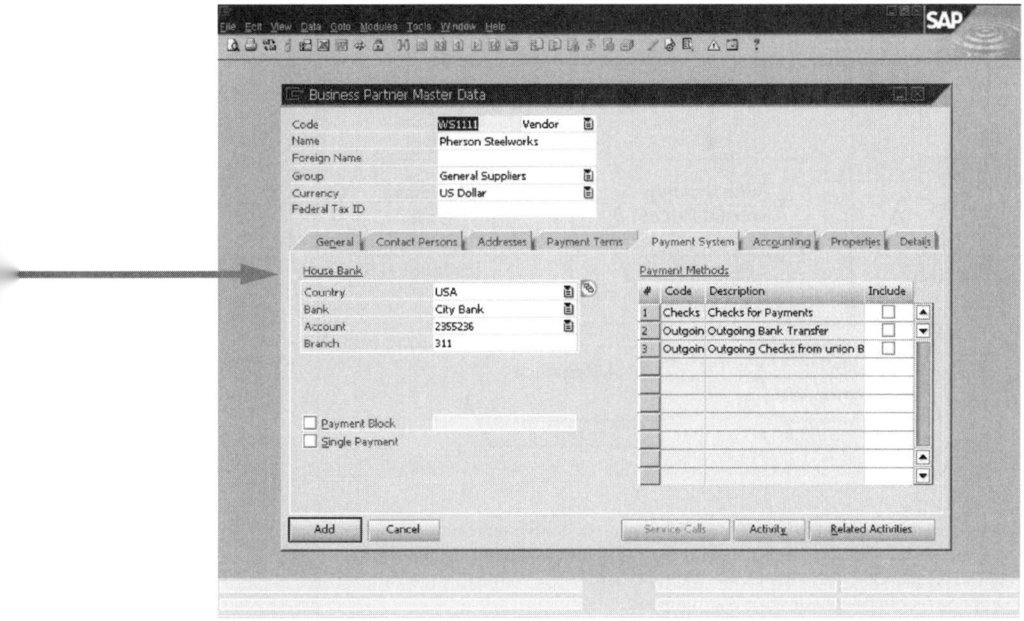
File Edit View Data Goto Modules Tools Window Help
SAP
Business Partner Master Data
Code
WS1111
Vendor
Name
Pherson Steelworks
Foreign Name
Group
General Suppliers
Currency
US Dollar
Federal Tax ID
General
Contact Persons
Addresses
Payment Terms
Payment System
Accounting
Properties
Details
House Bank
Country
USA
Bank
City Bank
Account
2355236
Branch
311
Payment Block
Single Payment
Payment Methods
Code Description Include
1 Checks Checks for Payments
2 Outgoin Outgoing Bank Transfer
3 Outgoin Outgoing Checks from union B
Add
Cancel
Service Calls
Activity
Related Activities

(B)

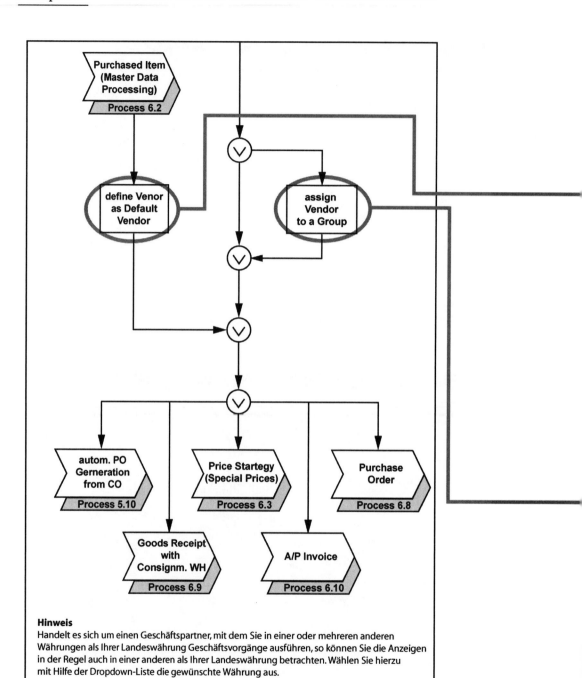

FIGURE 6.27 *(a) Account assignment in GP, (b) GP Payment systems*

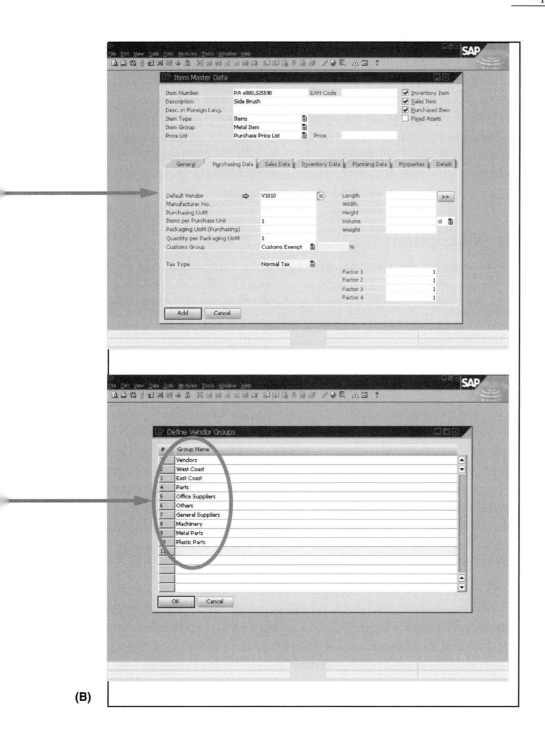

(B)

Order Processing

The order can be used for different procurement processes. Materials can be ordered for direct consumption, for storage in a warehouse, and for services. Raw material orders are usually carried out for a pre-defined quantity that is made in fixed time intervals. The quantity is usually determined by past values and is described as continuous consumption. For more valuable raw materials, the time intervals between orders are shortened. Shorter time intervals result in a lower average duration of the storage time and capital lockup.

Business Description

Every company must determine the optimal order quantity of valuable raw materials needed for production. Determining an optimal order is more difficult for areas in which market prices for raw materials fluctuate daily. The company should attempt to minimize the overall procurement costs, which are made up of a combination of procurement, storage, and shortfall costs.

SAP Business One: Specific Description

Orders are used to cover demand via external, meaning a vendor supplies a service or delivers a raw material. Likewise, an order can be used to ensure that a material needed in one factory is made available internally from another factory— meaning it is transferred. The activities that follow orders, such as goods receipt and incoming invoices, are recorded in the system in order track the procurement process. If you are going to buy material from a vendor only once, then you create an order. If you are considering initiating a long-term business relationship with this vendor, it is recommended that you enter into a framework agreement, which usually allows more favorable conditions with vendors.

The item master data contains descriptions of all articles and parts that the company purchases, produces, and stores. The item master data represents the central source of material-specific information for a company. Raw materials for procurement are labelled Purchase Item and Warehouse Item in the item master data. Thus, the procurement and warehouse data is stored for the item. The integration of all the item data into one master data record avoids duplication problems. Also, the item data can be used not only in procurement, but also in other areas, such as inventory management and invoice verification.

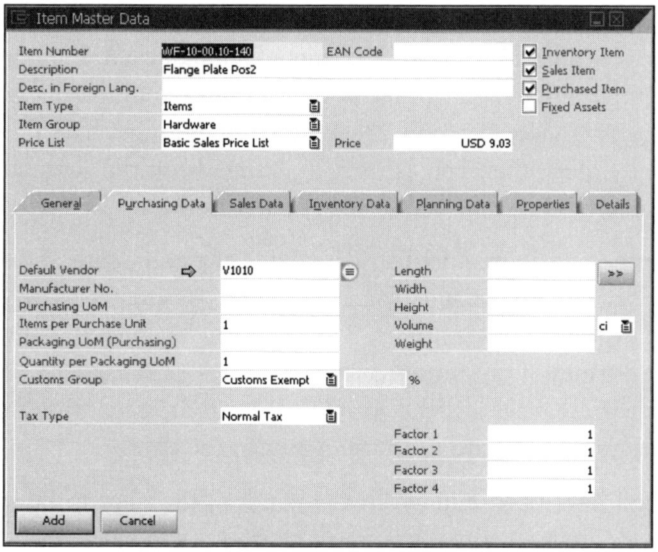

FIGURE 6.28 *Definition of a raw material*

During the raw material order processing, the following questions should be answered:

◆ How do you determine the optimal order size for valuable raw materials?

◆ Do you use information such as minimum stocks and open purchase order quantity in your warehouse management?

Application of the Process

In contrast to the automatic order generation for parts of a customer order as described in Chapter 5, here a process involves a manual order of raw materials necessary for the refinement or subsequent treatment in this process.

Open the order mask in the Purchase module in the main navigation field. Open the selection list of vendors by clicking the symbol on the right, next to the Vendor Input field. Select the vendor from whom you would like to order the items from the vendor list. If a contact was defined in the business partner's master data, then it is automatically transferred to the Input field.

As soon as all data for the vendor is entered and examined for correctness, then the rest of the order's header data must be examined and adjusted. Each number is assigned a sequential number according to the document numbering convention defined during system initialization. If several number ranges have been predefined for purchase orders, then you can select a range from the suggested list. The document number is then adjusted to the specifications.

In the posting date and the desired delivery date fields, the entry date of the order is entered automatically as the default. You can change these dates based on the validation date and expected delivery times. The dates can be entered without any punctuation. SAP Business One interprets the numbers as dates and puts the punctuation in the correct places. If the current year is to be used, then you can omit it as well. The system will add the current year to the date.

Once all header data have been entered in the window, the item to be ordered must be entered in the table. A distinction must be made as to whether the items have been defined in the system already or whether this is a new item to be added. If the item or items have been defined already, then you can make your selection from an item list by using the SAP Business One Search function. You can mark a single or several items from this list and then transfer them to the table. To select several items from the list, press and hold the Ctrl key and click on the desired lines in the selection list with the mouse, and then release the Ctrl key. Click on the Choose field in order to transfer the marked items to the order table. All items in the table default to a quantity of a single unit in SAP Business One. If you would like to order more than one unit of an item, then the number in the Quantity column must be changed for the appropriate item. The total price is automatically adjusted afterwards.

If this is a new item, the procedure is exactly the same—except that you must add a new master record for the item in the inventory.

If you have negotiated price conditions with your vendor that are not shown in the price list for the ordered items, then you can also change the item prices.

In the Logistics register, you can view the ship-to address in exactly the way the vendor will display it later on the purchase order. In this register, you can also indicate the permission to split the order, the need to approve the order, and the permission for partial deliveries.

In SAP Business One, you can assign an order to an already existing project. If you want do this, you must assign an existing project in the Accounting register or define a new project for which this order is designated.

There are additional input fields for general order information below the different register data. It is possible, for example, to assign a company's purchasing agent to the order. The payment terms negotiated with the vendor are included in this section of the form. Special arrangements, which might be limited to this order only and recorded in the system, can be entered in the Notes field.

The totalled prices of the individual lines in the table are listed on the right side. If you negotiated with your vendor an additional discount on the total order, you can specify it in the Input field either proportionally or as an amount.

After checking all inputs, quantities, prices, and miscellaneous conditions, you can save the document by clicking the Add button. SAP Business One offers several functions with which to send the order. Recall the document and choose from the Print, E-mail, or Fax options. These options can be accessed via SAP Business One title bar.

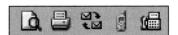

FIGURE 6.29 *Part of a symbol toolbar*

Navigation Information

- ◆ **Menu path:** Business Partner > Business Partner Master Data
- ◆ **Tables:** ACR1, ACRD
- ◆ **Incoming Triggers:** Vendor—Business Partner Master, Purchase Item, Unreferenced Order
- ◆ **Ougoing Triggers:** Price Strategy—Special Pricing, Incoming Goods Processing with Order Reference, Customer Order Confirmation, Vendor- Business Partner Master

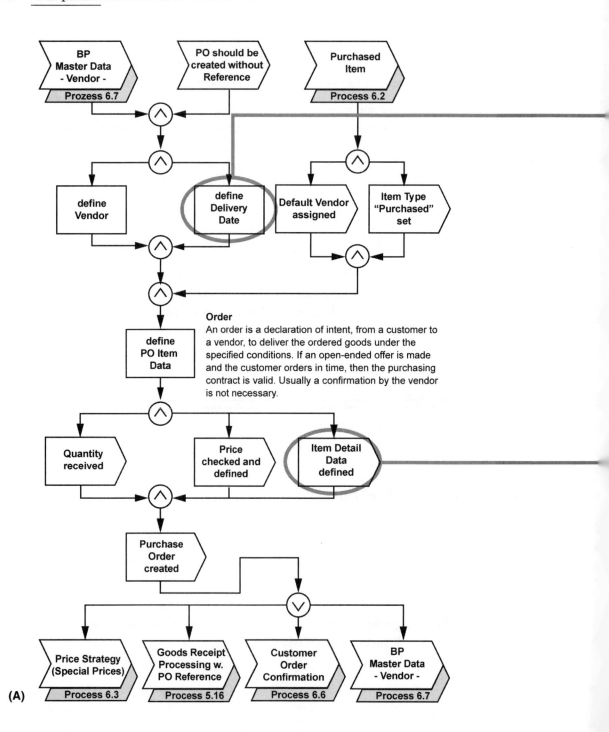

FIGURE 6.30 *(a) Order delivery date, (b) Order line details*

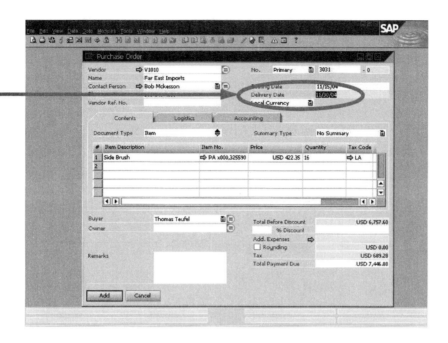

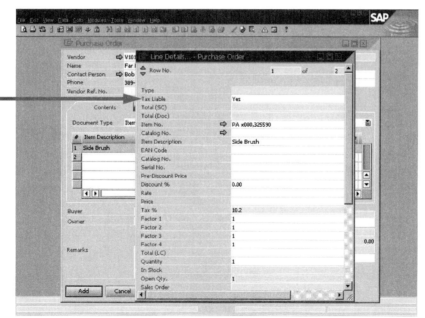

(B)

Goods Receipt with Warehouse Consignment

Receiving materials, also known as goods receipt, is a planned activity in most cases. The planning of goods receipt assumes that the following information is known ahead of time:

- What material?
- How much (quantity)?
- When (delivery date)?
- Where from (from what vendor)?
- Where to (what destination or delivery address)?

Business Description

Planning makes the receiving process easier and faster. If goods receipt is expected, then inventory of goods ordered or manufactured internally can be monitored.

Goods receipt is part of the procurement process and is based on the delivery receipt from a vendor. A discrepancy between the quantity ordered and the quantity delivered is resolved by accepting the difference in the case of an over-delivery or requiring a subsequent delivery to complete an under-delivery. A quality discrepancy is resolved by returning part or all of the material.

Goods receipt and quality control often are performed together, and the goods are booked into a storage area for locked stock. Goods receipt is complete once it is documented where the material was received (in which warehouse). For example, the goods received might be booked just-in-time directly into a temporary area in the production area.

During goods delivery, close coordination of the purchasing, warehousing, and planning areas is important in order to carry out a rapid transfer of the materials to manufacturing. Of particular importance during goods receipt are cases that involve collaboration with an external service provider, such as a freight company, or the use of transportation aids such as lattice boxes or pallets. These transportation aids are usually administered and calculated separately.

Normally, delivered goods are stored in the company's inventory. Until they are used in production, raw materials and semi-finished goods have value and tie up the company's capital. An alternative is to use a consignment warehouse (also called a *distribution center*), at which the goods are made available at the vendor's expense. This decreases the customer's capital exposure for its own stock levels while at the same time guaranteeing a smooth production run. For billing, the vendor is usually notified monthly of materials withdrawn. If withdrawals are made through consignment stores, then goods received are booked quantitatively.

SAP Business One: Specific Description

If a commodity is delivered as the result of an existing order, then goods receipt is tracked in reference to the order, which provides the following advantages: The SAP Business One system provides data from the order when entering the incoming goods (item, quantities ordered, and so on), which is advantageous for both tracking and control (over- and under-deliveries) of the incoming goods. The incoming invoice is checked against the quantities ordered and supplied (as a basis for an audit). The evaluation of the incoming goods takes place according to the purchase price list. If the delivery is found to be below or above the quantity ordered, then it can be reduced for a partial delivery or increased for an excessive quantity. If you do not expect further goods receipt after a partial delivery, it is advisable to close the order by reducing the quantity.

 NOTE

If goods receipt takes place without reference to an order, it can nevertheless be posted in SAP Business One without the corresponding documents. This flexibility is often needed in small to medium-sized businesses.

When the goods receipt document is processed, the system automatically finds the G/L accounts in the background. These accounts are predefined during system initialization in the chart of accounts, the warehouse definition, and account allocation in the vendor master record. Figure 6.31 shows the posting of the goods receipt.

If a commodity exhibits inferior quality and is to be returned, you can arrange this during goods receipt with the Delivery button in the returns document but only if the goods receipt has not yet been calculated. You also can add entries to the goods returns document that do not refer to the corresponding delivery receipt.

Goods receipt into consignment stock is booked only when the material is withdrawn. Consignment materials are still the property of the vendor, so to the company, their value = 0. When the material is withdrawn (for manufacturing, for

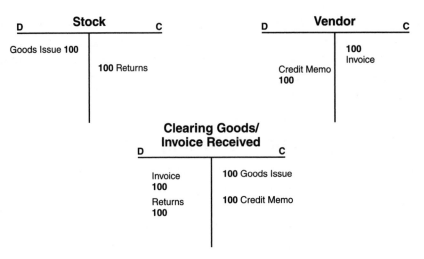

FIGURE 6.31 *Automated reversals*

example), the value is transferred into inventory (Inventory transfer). Only then is the material evaluated. The vendor is informed about the withdrawal so that he can invoice for the material. Materials that are not taken can be sent back (Return). Consignment material can be tracked using the same material number in the item master data used for inventory. Inventory quantities in the storage location are tracked by vendors, and prices are administered according to vendor-specific price lists. The valuation of the inventory is assessed by using a sliding average price, which is recalculated after each delivery. Figure 6.32 shows the individual steps in a consignment transaction.

The following questions should be asked regarding goods receipt:

- Do you book goods receipt with a corresponding order, or is unplanned goods receipt allowed?
- What accounts for automatic account determination serve as account reconciliations?
- How do you define material assessment (last purchase price, sliding price, and so on)?
- What warehouse structures do you use for receiving goods (QA-blocked stock area, main warehouse, consignment stock, provision warehouse)?
- How do you handle deliveries with quantities below or above the quantity ordered?

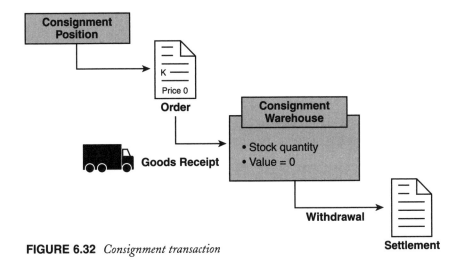

FIGURE 6.32 *Consignment transaction*

Application of the Process

Following an order, the vendor arranges for the goods ordered to be delivered to the customer. When the goods are delivered, they must be recorded. This is done by calling up the function for the goods receipt per purchase order. After you select and bring up the vendor, you can choose the shipping invoice for this delivery. This is done by clicking on the Purchase Order selection in the lower area of the window and selecting the order that contains the supplied goods. If the delivery consists of several orders, you can select multiple documents by holding down the Control key and clicking on those for which goods were delivered. If all positions correspond, press OK to transfer the data to the goods receipt form. Now the delivery quantities must be examined and possibly corrected. After verification of the delivery, save the document by clicking the Add button.

Navigation Information

- ◆ **Menu Path:** Purchase > Goods Receipt (PO)
- ◆ **Tables:** IGN1, IGN2, IGN3, OGSP, OIGN, OPDN
- ◆ **Incoming Triggers:** Order Processing, Automatic Order Generation from Customer Order, Business Partner–Vendor, Import Data
- ◆ **Outgoing Triggers:** Goods Return Processing, Current Inventory Analysis, Inventory Transfer, Vendor Processing, Goods Issue for Production, Quality Check

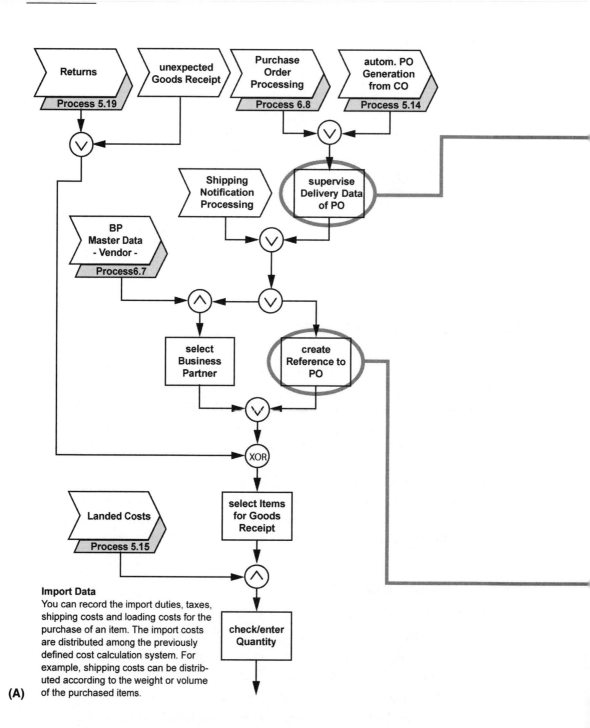

Import Data
You can record the import duties, taxes, shipping costs and loading costs for the purchase of an item. The import costs are distributed among the previously defined cost calculation system. For example, shipping costs can be distributed according to the weight or volume of the purchased items.

(A)

FIGURE 33 *(a) List of open orders, (b) Delivery receipt for the received items*

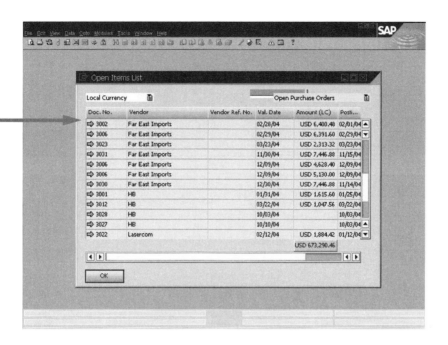

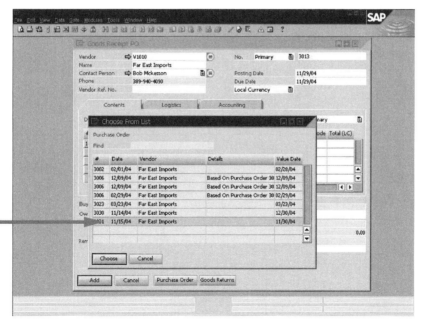

(B)

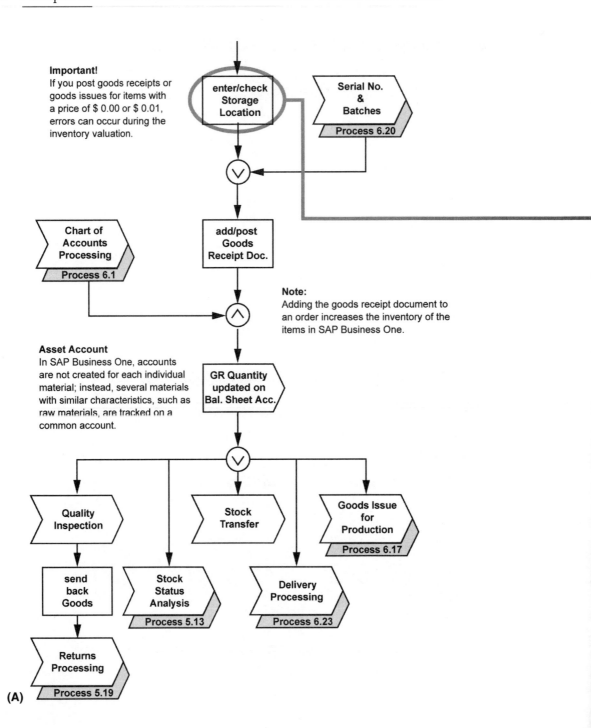

Important!
If you post goods receipts or goods issues for items with a price of $ 0.00 or $ 0.01, errors can occur during the inventory valuation.

enter/check Storage Location

Serial No. & Batches
Process 6.20

Chart of Accounts Processing
Process 6.1

add/post Goods Receipt Doc.

Note:
Adding the goods receipt document to an order increases the inventory of the items in SAP Business One.

Asset Account
In SAP Business One, accounts are not created for each individual material; instead, several materials with similar characteristics, such as raw materials, are tracked on a common account.

GR Quantity updated on Bal. Sheet Acc.

Quality Inspection

Stock Transfer

Goods Issue for Production
Process 6.17

send back Goods

Stock Status Analysis
Process 5.13

Delivery Processing
Process 6.23

Returns Processing
Process 5.19

(A)

FIGURE 34 *(a) List of available inventory, (b) List of inventory postings*

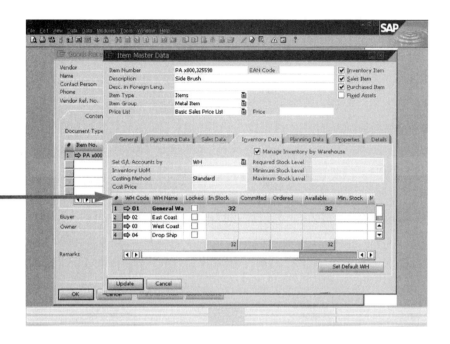

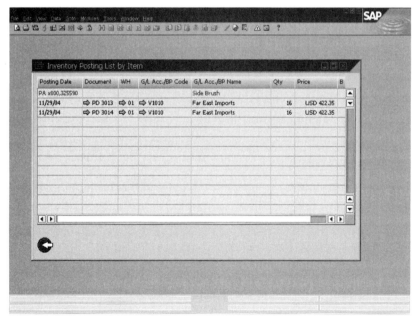

(B)

Incoming Invoice

A purchasing invoice describes a liability of the company according to type and scope and must correspond to certain legal requirements.

Business Description

Besides the layout criteria for an invoice, commerce law plays an important role. All statements in the law can be summarized as follows:

- Every invoice has to be individually entered.
- Demands and liabilities may not be balanced.
- The assessment of invoices on the date of balancing the books takes place individually and considering the evaluation rules. Liabilities have to be considering their repayment amount.

An incoming invoice reports the net value of the related delivery or other service, as well as the sales tax due.

SAP Business One: Specific Description

Incoming invoices are tracked in the Purchase category. An incoming invoice might be entered into SAP Business One as a result of the following:

- An order maintained in the system.
- A delivery maintained in the system.
- A delivery without reference to a preliminary administrative stage carried out in the system.

Since Model Company B, the assembly company, has continuous inventory management, incoming invoices from acquisitions may trigger inventory updates under certain circumstances.

In principle, the following applies to a defined continuous inventory management:

- If a reference to an order or a delivery exists, then this reference must be produced. If an incoming invoice is included without reference to an order or a delivery, then the corresponding inventory updates will be captured both in value and quantity with this posting.

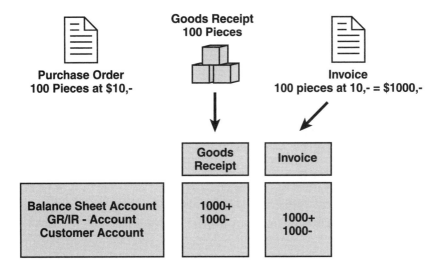

FIGURE 6.35 *Inventory postings*

- If an incoming invoice is included with reference to a delivery, then the price per position of the incoming invoice can be adjusted accordingly if necessary. The quantitative inventory update was already captured during the processing of the delivery.

- If an incoming invoice is included with reference to an order, then the order quantity of the item is reduced by the number specified. The inventory increases by the quantity and value based on the incoming invoice.

The special posting information of the invoice publisher is populated in advance by selecting the vendor from the master data records. All orders and deliveries currently in the system from that vendor are available for selection.

The assembly company captures most of its input invoices from deliveries already booked. The respective delivery is tagged to the corresponding incoming invoice in the selection window, and its contents are transferred to the entry form for the incoming invoice. All target/line positions can still be edited if necessary.

If an incoming invoice is to be entered without reference to an existing receipt, then it is necessary to use the input mask for items and services. Afterward, the vendor master data is transferred into the input form, and a description of the delivered items with their quantities or the rendered services is added. Once the items are selected, the price list is chosen according to the payment terms. These prices will then appear in the form for acquisition of incoming invoices. These appear as suggested values, and all individual prices can still be adjusted in this view if necessary for this and subsequent receipts of this vendor. The service price is independent of a price list defined in the payment terms and needs to be entered individually in each instance.

If discounts were granted, they are to be maintained either on the planning level or for the entire document.

An incoming invoice created and saved is immediately added to the respective A/P account. Consequently, the open liability appears instantly on the reconciliation account.

Incoming invoices can be retrieved in read-only mode at any time after being created. A document change later is obviously not possible.

While creating an incoming invoice, the following questions can be asked:

◆ Is the item number series defined during system initialization as an internal number allocation (automatic allocation of numbers) with continuous sequential numbers?

◆ Do you use external (manual) allocation of item numbers?

◆ Do you use different sets of numbers for different invoices?

Application of the Process

After a vendor delivers the goods ordered, he provides an invoice for the supplied items. The invoice might be provided at delivery. The invoice can also be furnished through other means such as mail or monthly summary invoices. It is necessary, however, for the invoice to be delivered to enter the data into the SAP Business One system. Start by opening the A/P Invoice function in the Purchase application. Transfer the vendor's data from the selection list to the bill header. You can list all deliveries from this vendor not yet entered by clicking on the Goods Receipt PO button. Select one or several entries from this list, which contains the invoice entry dates. After confirming the reference document selection with the Choose key, you can select all displayed entries to be transferred into the calculation form. From this listing you can choose to select one, several, or all positions to be transferred to the invoice form. To choose several positions, press and hold the Control key. The selection is confirmed by pressing OK and is transferred to the table in the A/P Invoice window.

If you would like to make further adjustments to the purchase invoice, you need to transfer to the Accounting index. Here you can define a temporary payment block, for example, specify payment terms, or assign the invoice to a project. If you would like to prepare the document for an automatic payment run, the date of payment must be defined. This is done by setting the installment number and entering the appropriate numbers in the fields. If you would like to send the invoice at the end of the month in which the project was entered, set this attribute and enter 1 in the Month field. If you want to send the invoice on the fifteenth of the subsequent month, set the attribute and enter 15 in the Day field.

It is also prudent to re-examine the totals of the invoice and make changes if there are any discrepancies. Finally, you can pass the document to the system by clicking on the Add button.

Navigation Information

- ◆ **Menu Path:** Purchase > A\P Invoice
- ◆ **Tables:** OPCH, PCH1, PCH2, PCH3
- ◆ **Incoming Triggers:** Order Processing, Automatic Order Generation from Customer Order, Business Partner[nd]Vendor, Import Data
- ◆ **Outgoing Triggers:** Goods Return Processing, Stock Situation Analysis, Stock Transfer, Vendor Processing, Goods Issue for Production, Quality Check

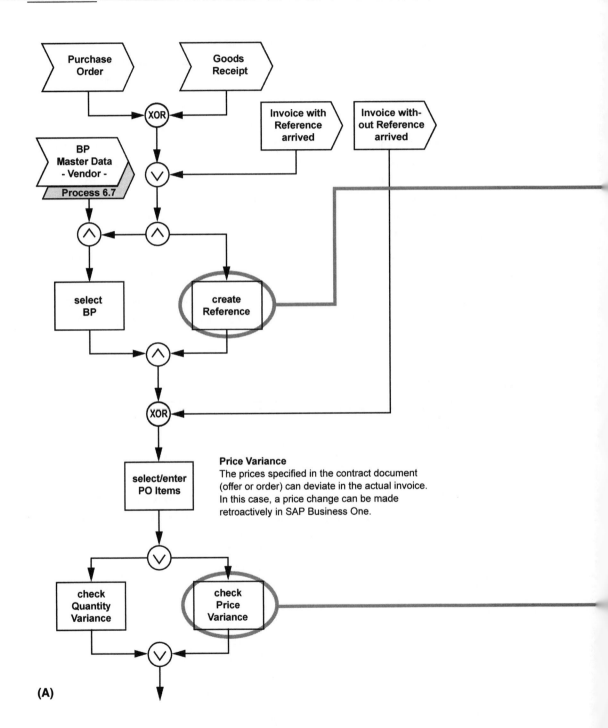

FIGURE 6.36 *(a) Purchase invoice with order reference, (b) Purchase invoice window – Price check*

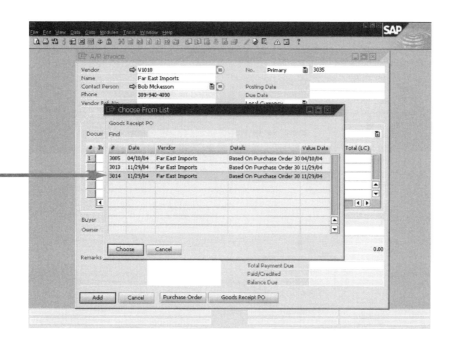

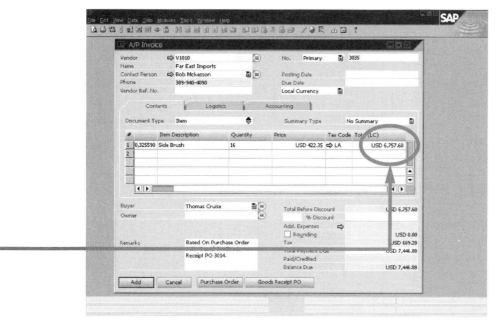

(B)

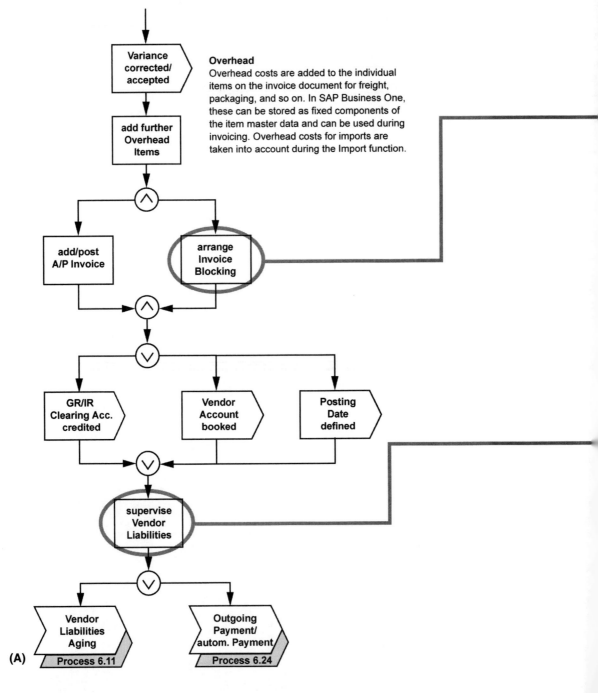

Overhead
Overhead costs are added to the individual items on the invoice document for freight, packaging, and so on. In SAP Business One, these can be stored as fixed components of the item master data and can be used during invoicing. Overhead costs for imports are taken into account during the Import function.

FIGURE 6.37 *(a) Payment block for invoices, (b) Vendor accounts payable*

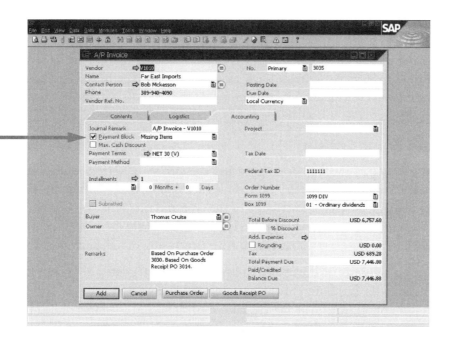

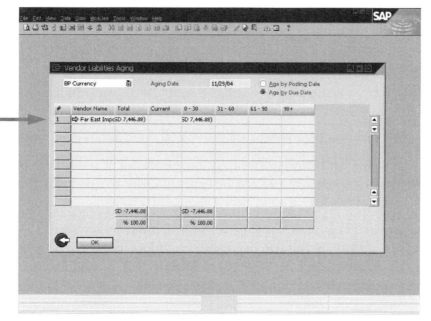

(B)

Processing Liabilities by Due Date

All types of liabilities represent items on the balance sheet. They are arranged according to different criteria, such as maturity and type of liability. Liabilities represent outside capital and are recorded on the debit side of the balance sheet.

Business Description

In this section, we will be dealing exclusively with short-term liabilities. The liability is incurred with delivery from a supplier. The previous section provides the attributes and a detailed description of the type and extent of an individual liability. The date of payment agreed upon also is specifically defined there. The date of payment represents the basis for further processing of a liability to the vendor.

When a vendor grants the option to pay an invoice at a date after goods delivery, a vendor credit is granted to the customer for the gross amount of the invoice. This form of outside financing creates a credit line and is simple to be obtained. The term ends as stipulated in the invoice, at which time payment is due for the invoice, either as a receipt of transfer to the vendor account or as a cash payment.

To get early payment of his invoices, a vendor might offer discount rates to the buyer in the payment terms. Naturally, the vendor has already included a discount as part of the product cost.

Let's look at an example of the payment term "2% 10 days, 30 days net" on a $100.00 invoice:

$100.00 less 2% = $98.00

Up to the tenth day following invoicing, the invoice can be settled with payment of $98.00, which represents the required sales price for the product according to the seller's cost calculation.

After the tenth day, credit financing begins, and if the invoice amount is paid in full on the eleventh to thirtieth day, then a credit for a maximum of 20 days was used. This means that $.67 (67 cents) of interest must be paid for the supplier credit granted.

The following formula applies in our example:

$$30\ days - 10\ days = 20\ days\ (20\ days = 2\%)$$

$$360\ Days = x$$

$$x = (2\% \times 360\ Days) / 20\ Days$$

$$x = 36\%\ per\ Year$$

This suggests that it is a good idea to take advantage of any discounts offered or granted by vendors.

These considerations can also have a significant effect on cash flow planning (see the section "Receivable Processing Based on Due Date (Dunning)" in Chapter 5.

SAP Business One: Specific Description

In the Reporting category the outstanding liabilities can be listed. The list can be filtered by range of values, vendor account characteristics and group assignment.

The individual customer accounts can be assessed from the resulting list by using the yellow arrows. At this point, it is important to reiterate the importance of these yellow arrows in SAP Business One which provides the ability to view details of the associated record.

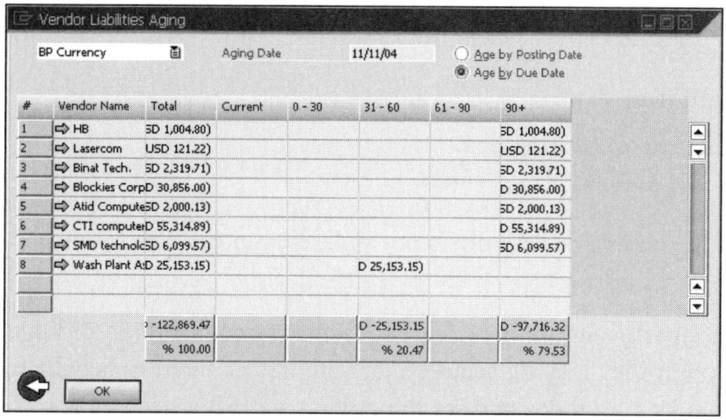

FIGURE 6.38 *List of payables with selection arrow*

The listing of the vendor liabilities by due date represents a good information source for the liquidity planning of the company, since it shows the details about due dates and amounts expected.

The following questions should be asked when dealing with liabilities:

- In what ways do you take advantage of discounts?
- Do you use discounts on payment terms or do you always pay the net amount at the invoice due date?
- Did you agree upon payment terms with your vendors?

Application of the Process

A liabilities overview report can be created in SAP Business One. This report can be viewed and printed out according to different criteria, which are adjustable in SAP Business One. This provides an instant view of what liabilities are outstanding for which deliveries. The selection form with all choices and adjustments can be found by selecting the Vendor Liabilities Aging function in the Reports application.

The following can be selected as criteria:

- Code number range of business partners
- Vendor group
- Properties of vendors
- Aging date
- Interval/days
- Date range for posting date
- Date range for due date

For the booking and value date filters possibilities, you can also select the adjustment date.

Based on the report, you can then create accounting documents according to vendor. At this point they may be balanced, but are not required to be. Change into the By Journal Posting index and set the criteria according to how you want the report to appear. If you choose the By Sales Document index and set one or both criteria, the report runs on the basis of sales documents to a vendor. When you have specified your data concerning selection and representation method of the report, click OK to confirm your selections. The system runs the report and then displays it in a separate window.

The listed positions in the table are sorted according to the maturity of the posting date. By changing the criteria in the right upper corner of the form, you can sort the table according to the maturity of the valid date.

To list the liabilities of business partners who use a different currency than the defined system currency, a foreign currency can be chosen. In the table that follows, all lines are displayed in the selected currency.

Reports can be printed. You have the option to forward the report to other employees internally, so that the subsequent steps can be carried out, such as payment of the liabilities. These functions are found in the toolbar with the respective icons.

Using the document editor in the Vendor Liabilities Aging menu, you can adjust the format of the printed report to your requirements. You can call up the Print Layout Designer function in the toolbar.

Navigation Information

- ◆ **Menu Path:** Reports > Financials > Accounting > Aging > Vendor Liabilities Aging
- ◆ **Tables:** OCDT, OCRD, OPCH, OVPM
- ◆ **Incoming Triggers:** Incoming Invoice
- ◆ **Outgoing Triggers:** Outgoing Payment

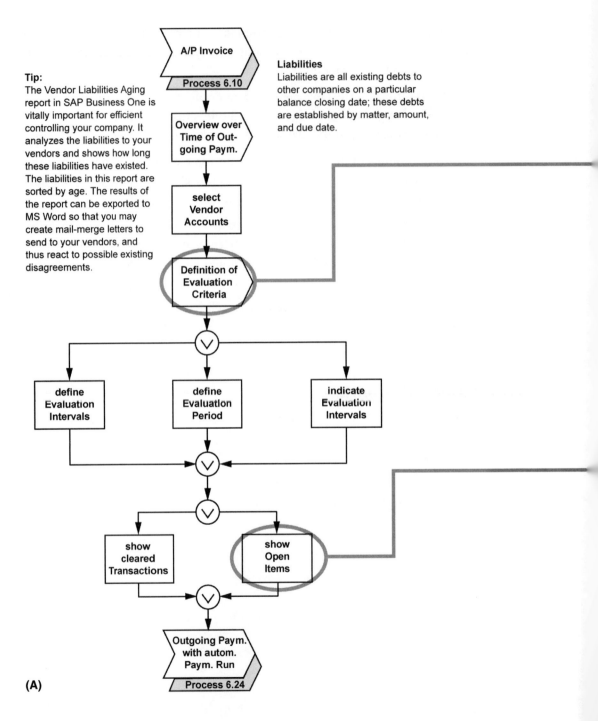

Tip:
The Vendor Liabilities Aging report in SAP Business One is vitally important for efficient controlling your company. It analyzes the liabilities to your vendors and shows how long these liabilities have existed. The liabilities in this report are sorted by age. The results of the report can be exported to MS Word so that you may create mail-merge letters to send to your vendors, and thus react to possible existing disagreements.

Liabilities
Liabilities are all existing debts to other companies on a particular balance closing date; these debts are established by matter, amount, and due date.

(A)

FIGURE 6.39 *(a) Selection field for payables, (b) Vendor accounts payables sorted by due dates*

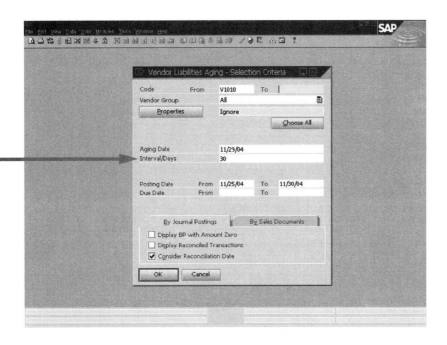

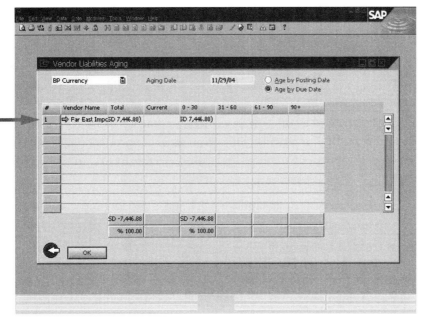

(B)

Product Structure Processing

A product structure for a new product most often is developed by the construction department, which then provides drawings and lists of materials for manufacturing.

Business Description

A bill of materials (BOM) is meant for end products and assemblies that consist of several parts or materials. The data in the BOM header includes the work or company affiliation, validity period, and status (such as approval), while the BOM structure can be illustrated by entries of different kinds. The parts list is significant not only of in production planning for manufacturing but also for pre- and post-calculation. The BOM itself normally contains only material numbers, designation of standard parts, and volume specifications.

SAP Business One: Specific Description

A product structure describes the different components that make up a product. For example, a product structure for a bicycle contains the frame, the saddle, the wheels, and so on. The listing of assemblies or individual materials is done in the BOM. A single-level BOM is available in SAP Business One as a BOM type. In the single-level BOM, the items and the quantities that are part of the final product or assemblies are entered. The information is used for the production planning of the assembly, as well as for ordering corresponding components and raw materials. SAP Business One provides bills of material for production, assembly, sales (see the section "Product Structure Processing—Sales BOM" in Chapter 5), and operations.

The difference between an assembly BOM and a production BOM is that the product is put together briefly before the sale in assembly. The production BOM, however, describes which components change during the production process into an end product. This can also be an assembly process or a packing process if certain production steps are included. Usually, there are manufacturing processes with a production order. In SAP Business One, a corresponding production order must be created to correspond to a production BOM.

On the basis of the production papers (production order and production work instructions), components are taken in accordance with the BOM from the warehouse. The inventory and value postings are executed for the stock movements. After the end product is finished, it is listed as warehouse material, in contrast to an assembly list, where the final product is not listed as warehouse material. It is often customary to list not only physical parts in the BOM but also working hours (performances/services) as separate components. A BOM in a proposal list is a sales list that suggests the components for a sales document (such as a quote) in such a way that they can be amended if necessary. For example, the quantity of components from a sales set can be adjusted for a particular customer.

The following question should be asked regarding a production or assembly BOM:

◆ Would you like to keep your end products as warehouse material—and therefore need a production BOM—or are assembly and sales BOMs sufficient?

 NOTE

If the end product is created with a production BOM, then it must have an item master record as both a store material and a sales material. If the end product is created with an assembly BOM, then the item master record may contain it only as a sales item.

Application of the Process

A BOM is created in the Production Under Product Structure application. The steps correspond to the creation of a sales BOM, as described in the "Product Structure Processing—Sales BOM" section of Chapter 5. You only have to choose the product type selection Production or Assembly Structure.

Navigation Information

◆ **Menu Path:** Production > Define Product Structure
◆ **Tables:** ITT1
◆ **Incoming Triggers:** Sales Item, Warehouse Item, Price Strategy
◆ **Outgoing Triggers:** Product Structure, Production Order Creation, Quotation Processing, Customer Order Processing, Vendor Processing, Outgoing Invoice Processing

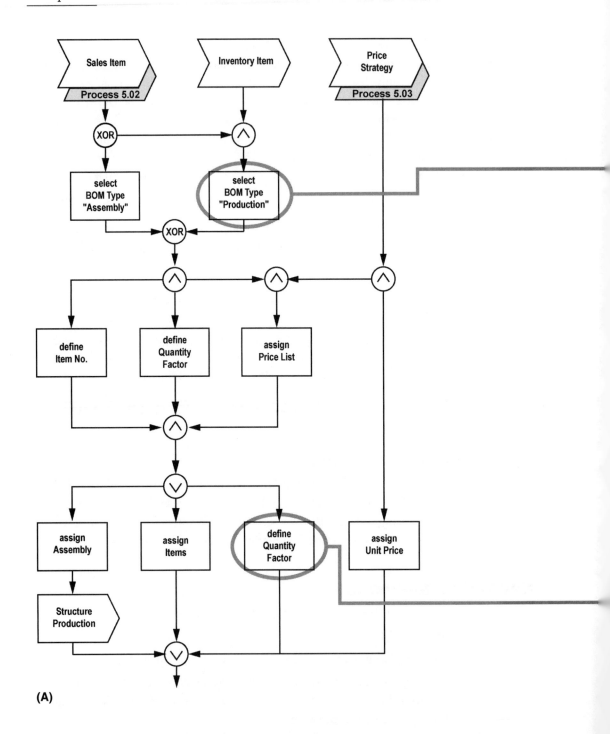

(A)

FIGURE 6.40 *(a) Product structure types, (b) Quantity amounts/factor in the item list*

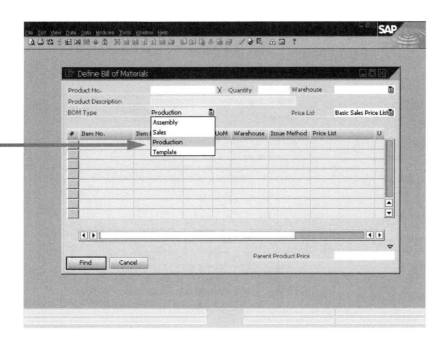

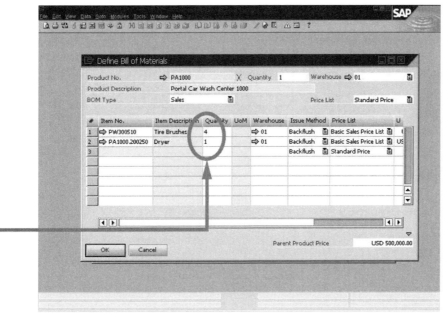

(B)

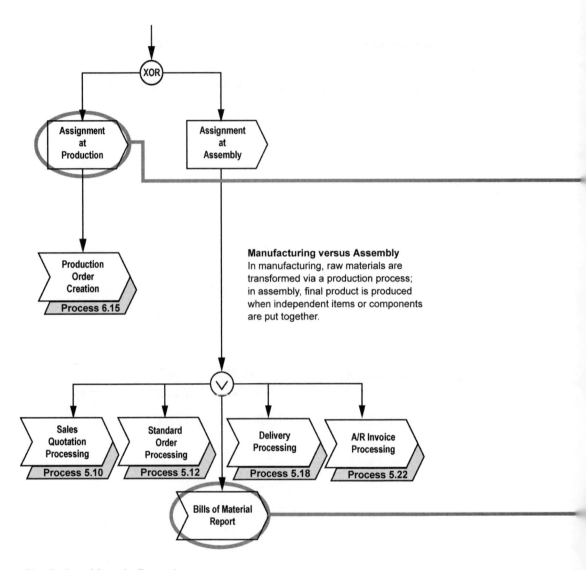

Manufacturing versus Assembly
In manufacturing, raw materials are transformed via a production process; in assembly, final product is produced when independent items or components are put together.

Distribution of Capacity Demand
The distribution of capacity demand over the duration of the production depends, in the real world, on the capacity type. While the labor demand on a machine setter is needed only at the beginning of the production process, the machine operator must inspect every 30 minutes. However, the machine capacity is used continuously over the whole production period. These different types of capacity distribution are controlled as part of the capacity planning by the allocation formula.

(A)

FIGURE 6.41 *(a) Item selection list for the production order, (b) Product structure report*

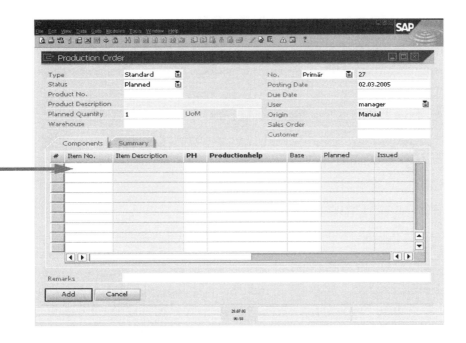

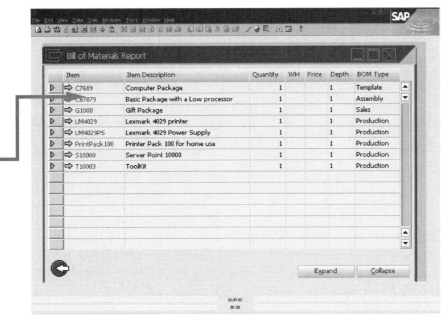

(B)

Work Station Resources

In business administration theory, a work station is defined as one available capacity (manufacturing ability within a time period). Work stations are categorized as follows:

- ◆ **Type 1:** Robots, machines, and plants
- ◆ **Type 2:** Machines with human operation
- ◆ **Type 3:** Manual work stations using human strength

Business Description

During the collection of operational work stations, it is also possible to define work station groups (departments or workgroups at teamwork organizations). Each work station is assigned to a cost center and usually contains a location key (work affiliation). If it is a type 2 and 3 work station, then a connection is made to HR (Human Resources) with the personnel number in the work station master. The determination of the capacity of a work station is based on the normally available operating time. Work stations are therefore assigned to an operating calendar that describes shift models and capacity-reducing dates, such as vacations, public holidays, and so on. The normal available capacity usually deviates from the actual available (effective) capacity.

In practice, this deviation results from worker illnesses, machine malfunctions, and so on. Therefore, a factor (labor utilization rate) of the effective capacity that relates more to company real-life experiences is considered instead of the normal capacity.

The following formula is used to compute the normal capacity and the capital need:

Normal capacity = number of shifts × shift duration × capacity reductions
Capacity need = (order quantity × job time × setup time) × labor utilization rate

Capacity need in the manufacturing process itself is determined by assignment of the work stations to the work plans in the scheduling of production orders. Work stations are also used in individual work plan operations. With the help of the data maintained in the work stations, you can specify which machines or persons should be employed or determine costs, capacities, and appointments. The terms *work station* and *resources* often deviate from each other in manufacturing companies: A work station is found in discrete manufacturing, while the term *resources* has a more global meaning and covers not only work stations but also production

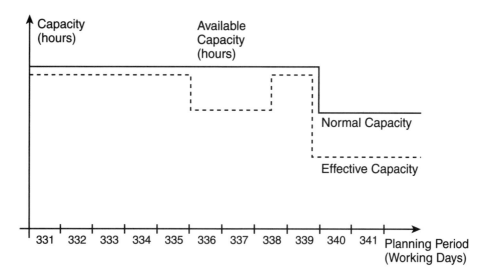

Work center group 1830

FIGURE 6.42 *Relationship between normal and Effective capacities (Source: Steinbuch, Olfert)*

plants, process units, and all other manufacturing-associated means of production (tanker, filling container, means of transport, and so on).

SAP Business One: Specific Description

Under SAP Business One, the extended functionality work station is an add-on that was developed by Teufel Software with the Software Development Kit (SDK). It is completely integrated into SAP Business One with the same look and feel and fits in the menu tree for navigation under the Production/Assembly category. The work station master record under SAP Business One mimics the structure of the work station master record of the big SAP Systems R/3. This is done in order to achieve optimal integration between subsidiaries who use SAP Business One and want to take advantage of SAP R/3 or mySAP used by the main office.

A work station type is selected in the work station master record first. The work station type determines what data will be maintained in the work station master record. This specifies the functions the Work station will be used for (such as scheduling or cost calculation). The most typical work station types are people, machines, production lines, and process units, just to name a few. Every work station type can be specified as to what master data must be maintained (mandatory entry fields) and in which work plan it can be used. Every work station is assigned to an organizational unit and a responsible person. The work station details contain the available capacity types, such as machine capacity, people capacity, and pool capacity keys, that are tracked by date.

A pool capacity can be used by several work stations. It must be created before assignment to the work station and is shown by a key in the work station. The whole capacity can be divided between different operational steps such as setup time, working time, and tear down time. Certain master data can be entered into the work station for scheduling a production order (for example, following a control post add-on). The scheduling base specifies which capacity determines the basis for scheduling. Further formulas can be stored to calculate execution time. This means that the time for each individual process step is calculated via formulas.

If you use a human resource system (such as mySAP-HR) with SAP Business One, you can link the logistics work station with the HR work station. This allows connecting to an organizational unit from HR. This relationship allows the potential for further linkages to other HR objects, such as people, positions, requirement profiles, and qualifications.

Another link of the work station is the connection to controlling the cost center to track rendered services.

The work stations themselves are assigned in the work schedule (see the next section) on the process level. This link indicates which work stations carry out a work process (an operation) or a sub-process. To calculate execution time, the formulas for each process step (setup, working, and tear down) are considered from the work station.

During work station processing, the following questions should be answered:

- Do you track your work stations?
- Is integration with HR management necessary?
- How do you structure your work stations?
- Which work stations types do you define?
- Do you work with normal capacities, or do you also consider the effective capacity?
- What formulas do you use to compute capacity?

◆ Do you use your own operating calendar/shift plan?

◆ What cost centers do you define for work stations in accounting?

Application of the Process

After you integrate the SAP Business One Work Station add-on into your system, it can be accessed under the Production/Assembly application. In the initial form, you must assign a factory for the work place and enter a work station number. If work stations already exist in the system, then these can be used for the selection.

To create a new work station, the next step is to define the type of work station and the person responsible. The location of the work station also must be indicated.

The default value keys can be used to preset values of a procedure into specific fields. Alternatively, you may define your own values.

After entering the values, you can call up a window to display an overview of the capacities. These capacities are divided into machine and people capacities. Different types of capacities can be assigned to the work station.

The time limitation key opens another window, in which the time for production execution is collected. The execution time of a procedure consists of the three processes—setup, work, and tear down—and is computed accordingly. Define either a time limitation or assign your own capacities according to your defaults. The transition period can be entered into the specified areas and denote the time between the end of use of this center and the first procedure at the next work station.

Navigation Information

◆ **Menu Path:** Production–Work Station Add-On > Work Station

◆ **Tables:** Depends on the SAP Business One Add-On Used

◆ **Incoming Triggers:** Product Structure Processing–Production BOM, Precalculation Customer Order, Wages and Salary Add-On

◆ **Outgoing Triggers:** Work Plan Processing

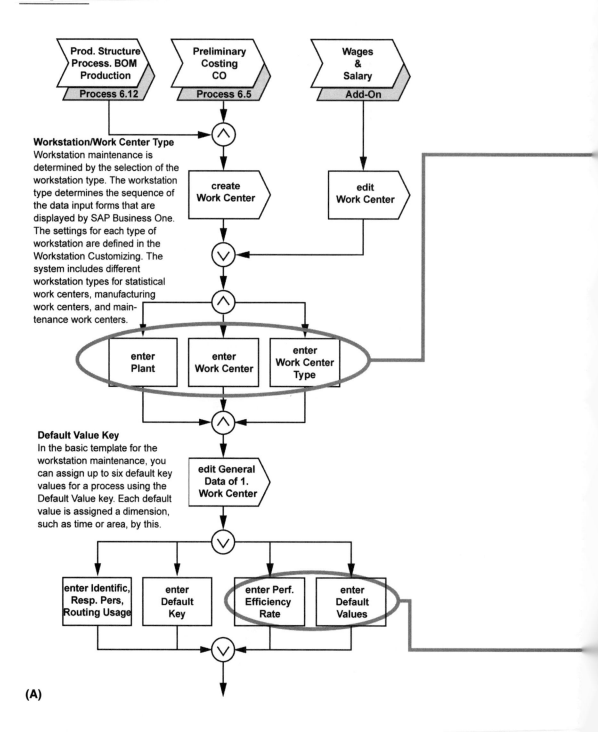

FIGURE 6.43 *(a) Work station type selection, (b) Labor rate utilization–determination*

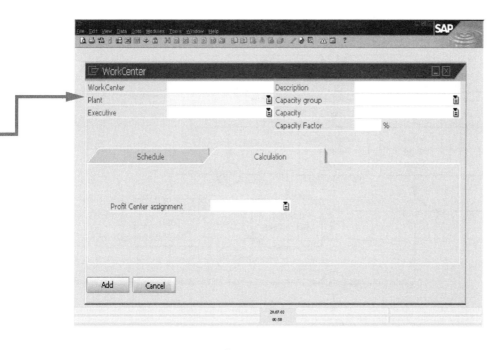

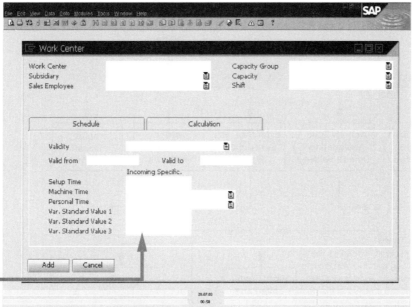

(B)

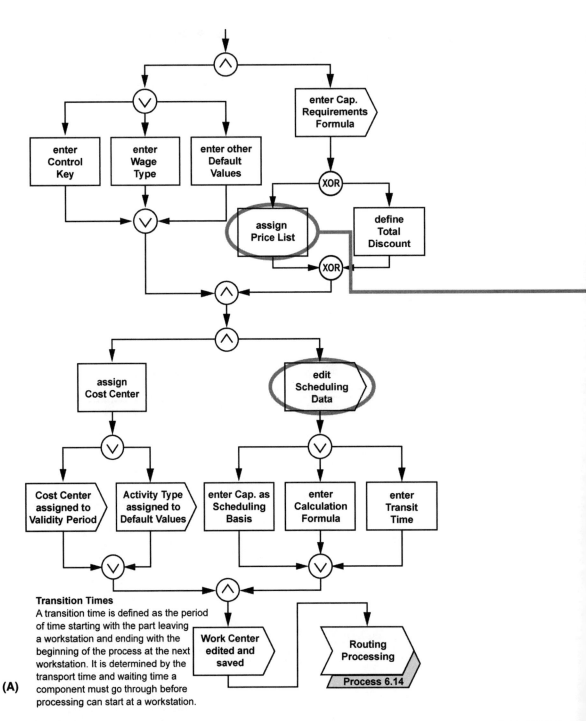

Transition Times
A transition time is defined as the period of time starting with the part leaving a workstation and ending with the beginning of the process at the next workstation. It is determined by the transport time and waiting time a component must go through before processing can start at a workstation.

(A)

FIGURE 6.44 *(a) Price lists assignments, (b) Scheduling data for the work station*

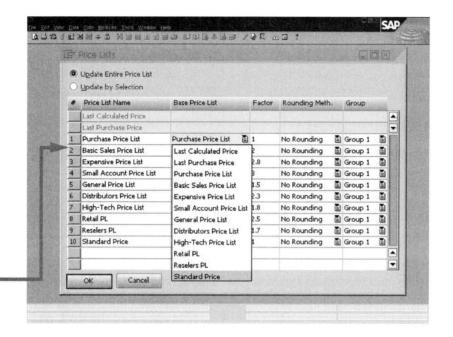

(B)

Work Plan Processing

Together with the production order and the BOM, the work plan forms the production process of an item.

Business Description

The attributes of the work plan are its status, its validity period, an alternate plan, and the data of the work processes with the work times through their assignments to work stations. The operations describe the individual work procedures needed for the manufacturing of products. The individual operations in the work plan can refer to different work stations (see the previous section, "Work Station Resources"). Likewise, information such as the operation number (predecessor, successor), description, and resources (production resources) is captured. The work plan always refers to a product that can be produced (BOM with parts) for a production order. The work plan is order neutral, and so it can be consulted for different production orders. The defined dates (duration of the work procedure) in the work plan serve as preset values for a later run time limitation of a production order (for example, in connection with a control post for forward and backward scheduling).

The corresponding cost rate can be available at the time of the process. The more time shares and cost rates there are available for the allocated work processes, the more exact the costs can be calculated for a work step. In controlling, the operating costs are allocated to the cost object (such as a production order).

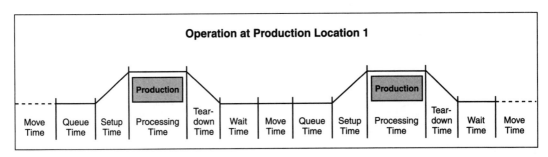

FIGURE 6.45 *Possible time slices for a production transaction/process*

SAP Business One: Specific Description

The extended work plan functionality under SAP Business One is an add-on developed by Teufel Software with the Software Development Kit (SDK) of SAP. It is completely integrated into SAP Business One by using the same look and feel and fits in the navigation menu under the Production/Assembly category. The work plan under SAP Business One mimics the structure of the work plan of the big SAP Systems R/3. This is done in order to achieve optimal integration between subsidiaries that use SAP Business One and want to take advantage of SAP R/3 or mySAP used by the main office.

Several work plan types exist:

◆ The Normal work plan describes material-related production.

◆ The Standard work plan is largely material independent and can be used as a reference and model for Normal work plans. Standard work plans can be created with either internal or external number allocation.

◆ The Rate work plan describes material-related manufacturing output relative to time with a production line.

◆ The Standard Rate work plan assists in developing a Rate work plan.

A work plan is meant for a production order (integration into the production order opening process) or a serial production order. It describes the manufacturing steps (procedures) to be taken, their sequence, and the work station at which they will take place by integration to the work station and resource processes. If a product calculation is needed before manufacturing, the work plan is passed on to product pre-costing. In the work plan, planned times are listed for the execution of individual operations (pre-set values). A work plan specifies the order of the individual operations necessary to manufacture the finished product. If the operations are linear by operation number, this is referred to as a sequence. Sequences are used to design the fundamental features of the production run.

To create more complex production runs, several sequences may be put together. If a work plan consists of only one sequence, it is called a standard sequence. Each additional sequence is either alternative or parallel to the standard sequence. It must therefore be decided which structure will be used to construct the work plan. Operation design in the work plan provides a high potential for optimization, which later can result in improved run time.

After defining the operations, the procedures can have further objects subordinated if necessary. The following subordinated work plan objects are available:

- Suboperation
- Parts
- Production resources and tools
- Quality Assurance (QA) checkpoints

Suboperations are needed if several machines or workers are used for the same operation. Suboperations cannot be scheduled individually, and it is important whether the suboperation is accomplished internally or with outside processing (workbench extended). This entry contains the control key that is also used to publish whether costs are calculated and a confirmation is completed per production step. The allocation of parts can be assigned only to the operation, not to the suboperation. In operations with subcontracting, parts are automatically defined as submitted materials. The assignment of production tooling aids (operational resources) to the operation requires the existence of a production tooling aid master record in the form of an item master in SAP Business One.

During work plan processing, the following questions should be asked:

- Which work plan types do you use?
- Do you assign work plan master record numbers internally or externally?
- Do your work plans use estimated time values as a basis for product calculation (integration interface necessary)?
- What types of sequencing are used for your operations?
- Are alternative sequences to be used? Which sequences can be done in parallel?
- Do you use subprocesses?
- Do you generally assign parts to the production order when opening or at the work plan level?
- Do you assign production resources to operations or are they generally available in the production area?
- Do you use a Quality Assurance (QA) system and do you need QA checkpoints during operations?

♦ If you use external operations (extended work bench), how do you control their completion?

Application of the Process

When the Work Plan function is called in the Production application, the general data for the work plan is captured in an entry form. In this window, you need to assign a number to the work plan, specify the item for which the work plan is made, and provide a work plan group and type. The revision number and the deadline date indicate whether the work plan is up to date. By pressing Add, you change into the next window, in which you define heading data for the work plan regarding the use, the status, the lot sizes, and information concerning initial creation and responsible person. The previous work plan called also can be viewed here.

The work plan's partial operations entry window can be reached by clicking on Operation. Enter the fields with the data specified in the column headings. Fill out the steps of the work plan and indicate any existing suboperations, predecessors, and successors. If you click on the arrow at the beginning of a line, you get the respective detail views of the operation, which contain the data for the operation and the default values that are defined for the operation, such as Set-Up Time, Machine Time, and Labor Time. The work plan's Activity category and Performance Efficiency Rate are defined here.

Navigation Information

♦ **Menu Path:** Production/Assembly> Work Plan Add-On

♦ **Tables:** Depends on the use of SAP Business One

♦ **Incoming Trigger:** Work Station Processing

♦ **Outgoing Trigger:** Production Order Creation

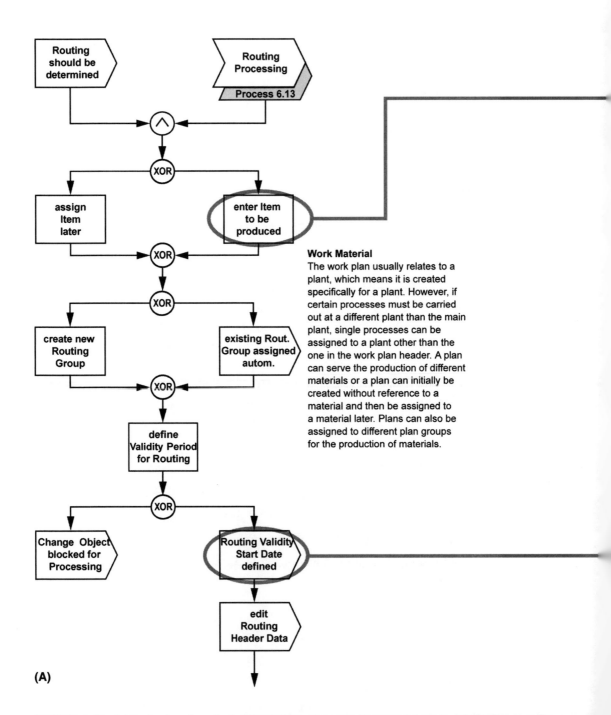

(A)

FIGURE 6.46 *(a) Production plan selection, (b) Validity of a production plan*

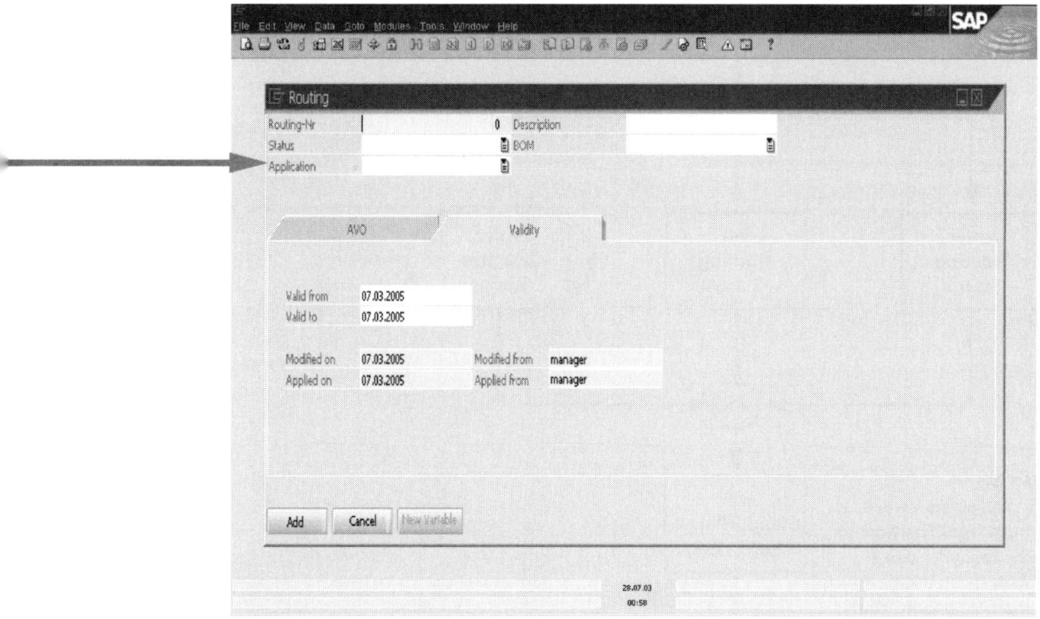

(B)

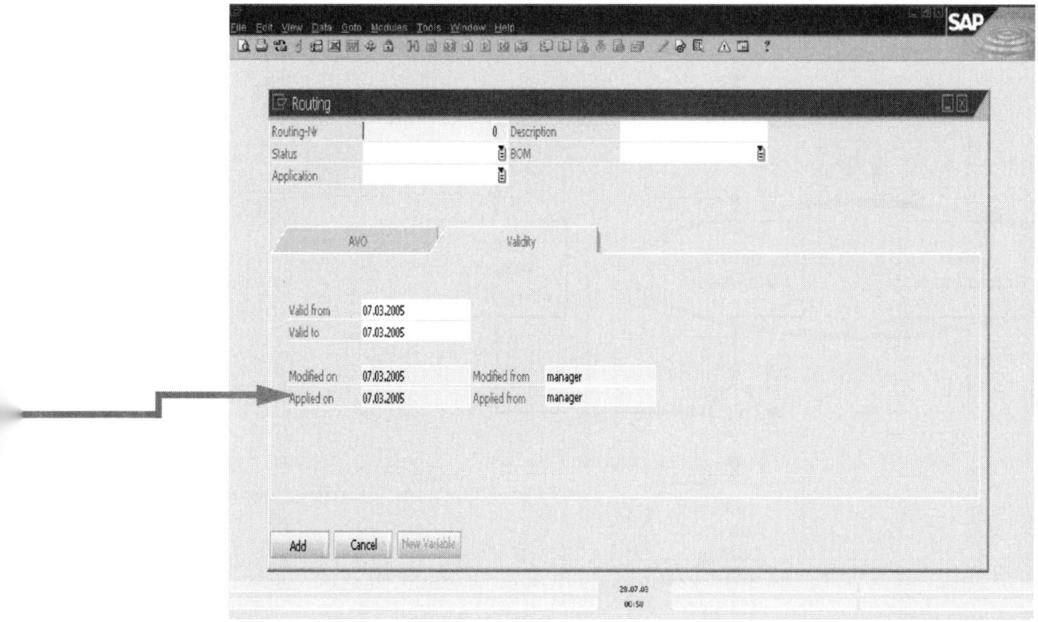

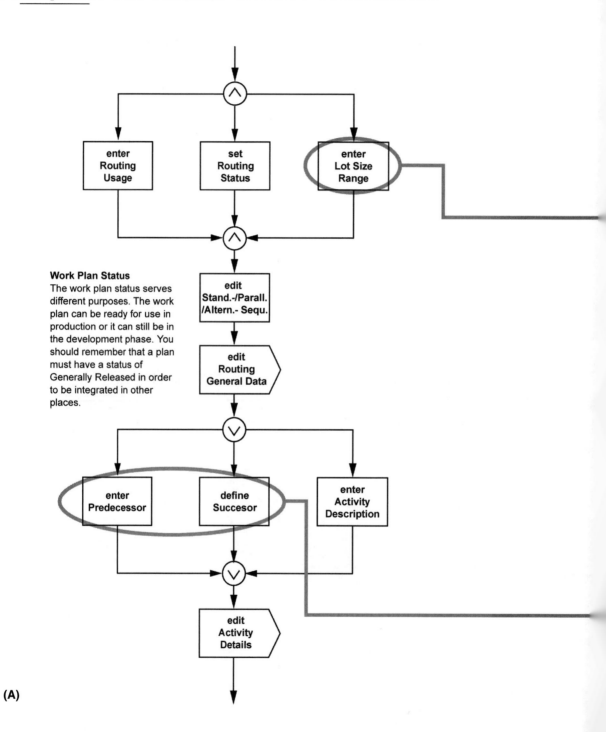

Work Plan Status
The work plan status serves different purposes. The work plan can be ready for use in production or it can still be in the development phase. You should remember that a plan must have a status of Generally Released in order to be integrated in other places.

(A)

FIGURE 6.47 *(a) Production lot determination, (b) Predecessor and successor production steps*

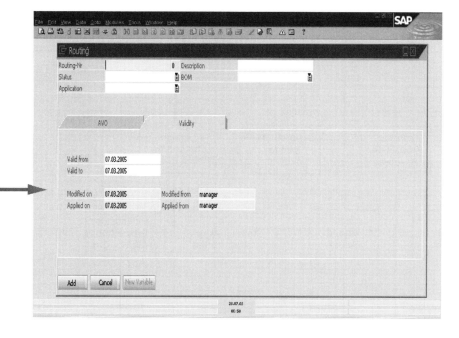

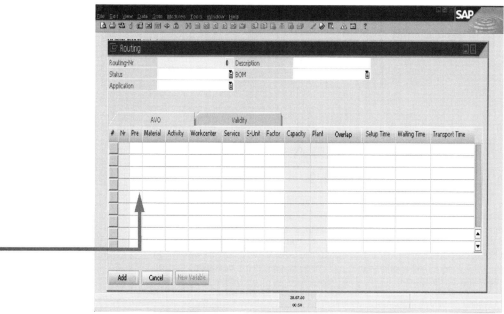

(B)

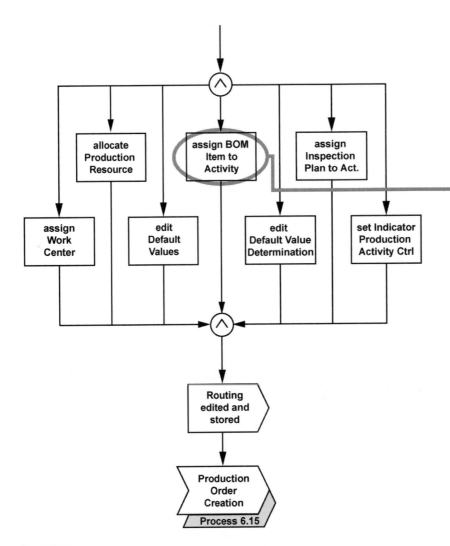

Operations

The tasks that make up a production flow are described by something called operations. An operation determines at which workstation or work center and with which default values the task is executed. You can describe how an operation is to be carried out in the accompanying note. The order of the operation numbers determines the sequence in which the steps of the work plan are to be done. How the operation is processed is set with the operations control key, which manages the calculation, scheduling, capacity planning, and confirmation or production document printing. Specific data for the operation, such as splitting or overlapping of processes, is defined in the Detail window. You can also assign material components, production resources, and different inspection characteristics to an operation.

(A)

FIGURE 6.48 *(a) Production's structure assignments, (b) Preview production's plan papers*

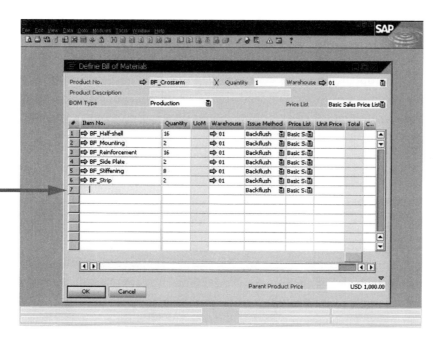

Creating Production Orders

The creation of the production order starts the planning of manufacturing orders with the appropriate planning intervals. Planning tools such as the use of control stations provide load overviews, lead-time scheduling, and lead-time shortening for production orders. The beginning and ending dates of individual operations are specified without consideration of capacity restrictions. This allows verification of whether the ending date for the production order is feasible.

Business Description

The available methods for creating production orders are backward scheduling, forward scheduling, bottleneck scheduling, and lead-time scheduling. Backward scheduling tries to find the latest possible beginning date for a given ending date. The forward scheduling method computes the earliest finishing date based on the starting date given. However, forward scheduling assumes that all needed parts are available at the beginning date; otherwise the plan time is not realistic. Bottleneck scheduling uses an approach of building high-quality schedules by first optimizing the schedule of bottleneck resources. The lead-time scheduling method is used for every production order. If dates cannot be kept, then several work stations can be overlapped or divided (such as using the same machines to divide partial lots) to reduce lead time.

The tasks of lead-time scheduling and lead-time shortening are usually carried out by a materials requirement planner or workshop master in a company. In the context of a control station, capacity scheduling is presented in a load overview either graphically or tabular. The individual operations or sequences are assigned to different work stations in production run-time. The task of the MRP controller in production order creation is to correct variations of supply and demand in order to accomplish as uniform a utilization of manufacturing resources as possible. How individual tasks are executed depends on the production method and the organization.

A manufacturer of custom or single items needs to schedule based on both lead times and the work plan, but at the start of planning he does not have a complete BOM or work plan available. Nonetheless, he is expected to give rough completion dates when quoting a project. Product structures (BOM) and work plans are completed in detail during the course of the order. The planning data then is reviewed regarding the completion date and corrected if necessary.

A serial manufacturer usually has all the details needed for an exact production order. Time scheduling can therefore be completely carried out according to work plans. If a company uses production lines in its manufacturing, then time limitation is not necessary because operational resources are linked technically.

SAP Business One: Specific Description

A production order in SAP Business One always must refer to a BP number (the customer) in the system because production is usually the result of an order. If production is carried out without a customer order, then a dummy customer is created to serve as a placeholder. In our Model Company, the item is produced for Model Company A, and the BP number is indexed to A.

The item positions (items that contain a production structure/BOM) are captured for the production order. Manufacturing cost (MC) is stored in its own price list in the production order header. The calculation can be performed using the BOM in which the service sets are provided with the materials. Otherwise, the Work Station and Work Plan add-on programs can be used. If a work plan is used, then the times for the calculation are stored in the work stations. The order scheduling operations for the individual items are transferred from the Work Station add-on. For every operation there is an operation number, possibly a suboperation number, details of the work station, and the parts and production tooling aids. The parts are available at the creation of the production order (see the section "Goods Issue for Production," later in this chapter).

If a control station is used as an add-on, then the starting and completion dates and the parts can be carried over to the procedural level of the individual operation. Self-defined user fields, such as order map, machine name, and so on can be included in the production order for better execution. For example, an order map can be individualized in the document editor.

In the production order, the following questions should be asked:

♦ Do you use Work Station and Work Plan add-ons in production or do you create a complete description of the necessary components using the available production software?

♦ How do you calculate manufacturing costs?

♦ What price list do you use for this?

◆ Do you need a Control Station add-on in production for forward and backward scheduling of production orders on an operational level?

Application of the Process

By creating a new production order in SAP Business One, you specify that a product consisting of several individual items and arranged in a BOM shall be produced either for a customer or for subsequent processing in another operation. The initial window for the creation of a production order is accessed via the Production Order function in the Production application.

In SAP Business One, there are three types of production orders:

◆ **Standard:** Produce a regular production BOM item.

◆ **Special:** Produce or repair a regular production BOM item.

◆ **Disassembly:** Dismantle a production BOM item into its components.

If the production order is manufactured for a customer, the associated customer number must be entered into the first field. You can use the Search function of SAP Business One for this task. If the final product is for internal use within the company, there is no need to enter a customer number. The Customer Number, Name, and Partner, fields remain empty. Alternatively, a dummy customer master record can be created in the business partner master data if it is for internal use.

The current system date is suggested as a posting date, but you can enter an alternate date if necessary. The Status field (order and completion) can be changed only after the operation is carried out; field values are Released, Completed, and Cancelled. Planned is the default value for a new production order. You can enter a date at your discretion in the Planned Due Date field.

The sequential production order number is assigned automatically by the system. You have to pay attention to the numbering only if it is necessary to specify a different number series. This is done by changing the selection in the Series field.

You can enter an employee into the User field if you know who will carry out the order.

After the data and properties are entered in the top part of the window, you can start transferring items into the table. Open the Choose from List window by positioning the cursor in the first column of a table row and pressing the Tab key.

You can also use the other SAP Business One search functions for this. This selection lists only those items for which BOMs are already defined in the system. If you enter the number of an item or a final product directly into the field, the system will display its description.

After completing all the fields in the table, you should make sure all entries are correct. For example, if you want to specify another warehouse to which the finished units should be posted after production, you can change it in the Warehouse column.

To avoid a production order that cannot be accomplished on time and properly because of missing material, you can check whether the necessary materials are in sufficient quantity in the warehouse by right-clicking and selecting Issue for Production. The items with inadequate inventory to fill the production order are listed. After the entry is confirmed, a system message informs you of the items with insufficient quantities for processing the production order. If missing material is listed, you must order the missing items from your vendors as early as possible (see the section "Purchase Order Processing," earlier in this chapter). It may be that sufficient raw material is in the warehouse but has already been reserved for another production order and therefore is unavailable.

Clicking the Add button stores the production order in the system. This is how you record the production of an item in the SAP Business One system.

Navigation Information

- **Menu Paths:** Production > Work Order

    Production > Work Order > Quantity Check

- **Tables:** OWKO, WKO1, OITT
- **Incoming Triggers:** Production Structure Processing–Production BOM, Customer Order Confirmation, Goods Issue for Production, Control Station
- **Outgoing Triggers:** Production Instructions, Production Release

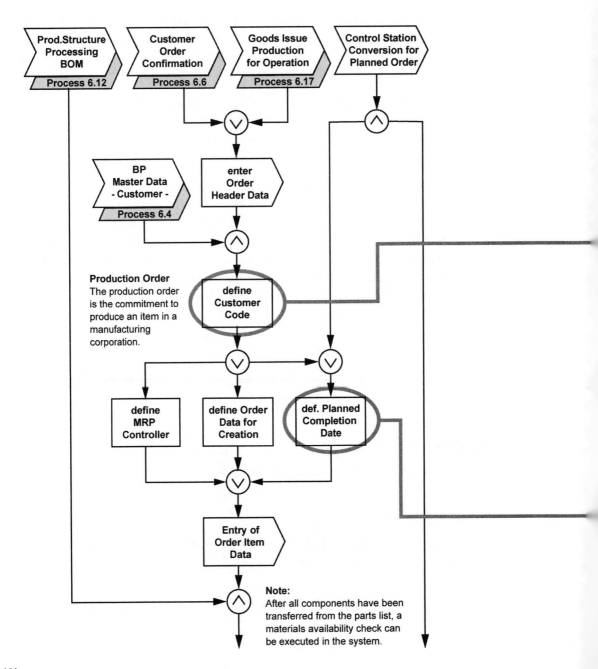

(A)

FIGURE 6.49 *(a) Customer assignments for the production order, (b) Detail information – Completion date*

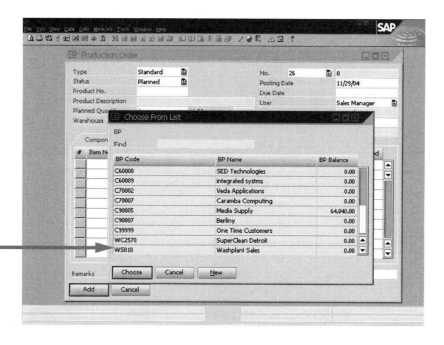

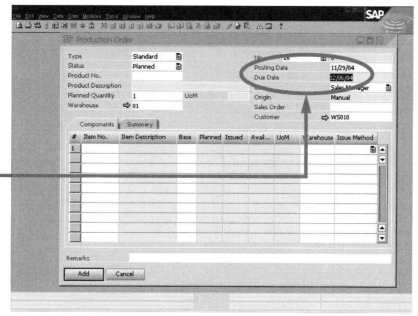

(B)

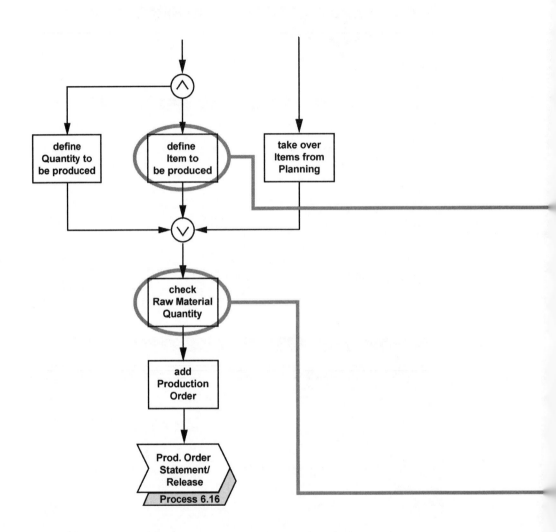

Note
When you add or release a Production Order the system carries out an automatic quantity check. If the system diagnoses that one or several components are not available in sufficent quantity, you will get a specific system message. You can change directly from the message to the list of missing Items.

(A)

FIGURE 6.50 *(a) Production order positions, (b) Display notice about missing parts*

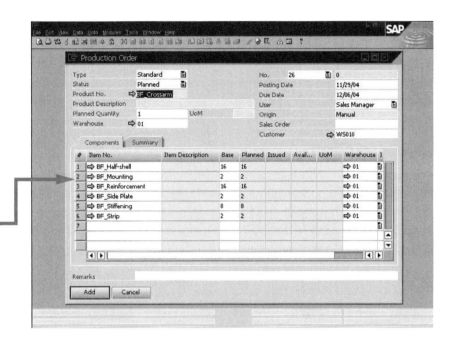

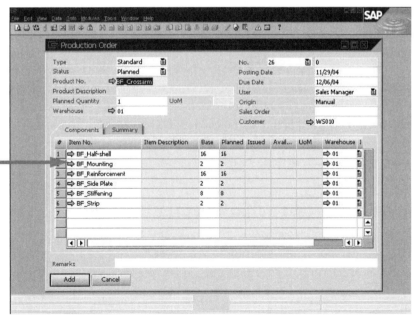

Production Instructions Release

Before a production order is carried out, you must make sure that all materials needed are available. The necessary components can be locked at release time, but they must be ready at the time needed.

Business Description

The part check is used to guarantee that the manufacturing process is not unnecessarily interrupted due to missing materials. If a parts shortage occurs unexpectedly before production instructions, the amount of the shortage and the duration of the interruption need to be determined, so as to consider if it is possible to delay or change the order of the planned production flow.

In order to avoid a stop in manufacturing, the company can find an alternate supplier to close the supply gap. The higher costs resulting from procuring via an alternate vendor are passed on to the original supplier in the form of conventional penalties. Shortfall costs might include the price difference, profits missed because of the production delay, penalty costs due to non-delivery, and goodwill losses reflected in reduced incoming orders.

If all parts are available at the instructions date, then the order can be released. In addition, the personnel policy and the production technical process aspects can be relevant at the order release date. The personnel policy includes everything from the manpower planning through to the payroll processing after production order confirmation. The production technical process covers the preparation of the technical production instructions such as work plan, inspection plan, and if necessary computerized numerical control (CNC) programs.

SAP Business One: Specific Description

The parts availability check can take place at any time during the creation of a production order. For the production instructions, lists are created for those parts not available in the quantity needed. The list of missing parts shows the quantity available, the quantity ordered from the supplier, and the quantity needed for the customer request. Using these numbers, available stock is calculated in SAP Business One.

NOTE

Definition: Available stock *equals* stock quantity *plus* order quantity *minus* customer order quantity.

If no quantity check takes place at the time of the production order, the system runs a check automatically. The system creates a report of any missing parts for the materials requirement planner.

The production instruction is either new or created from a production order. If production orders are present, they should be converted. The planned completion date is suggested at the starting date, and it can be modified manually. The system does not post any inventory modification at the time of the production order statement.

From a manufacturing viewpoint, the following questions should be asked regarding a production order statement:

- Which processes do you apply when dealing with shortfalls to minimize production delays ?
- Do you pass on shortfall costs to your supplier?

Application of the Process

The entry of a new production instructions happens at the same time as the recording of a production order (see the previous section in this chapter, "Creating Production Orders"). The only change is to open the order with the SAP Business One search function and set the status to Released. You can also change the date of instruction, if necessary. Pressing Update stores the production instruction in the system.

Navigation Information

- **Menu Path:** Production > Work order > Production Instructions
- **Tables:** OWKO, WKO1, OITT
- **Incoming Triggers:** Production Order Creation, Open Production Orders
- **Outgoing Triggers:** Goods Issue to Operations for Production, Production Order Execution

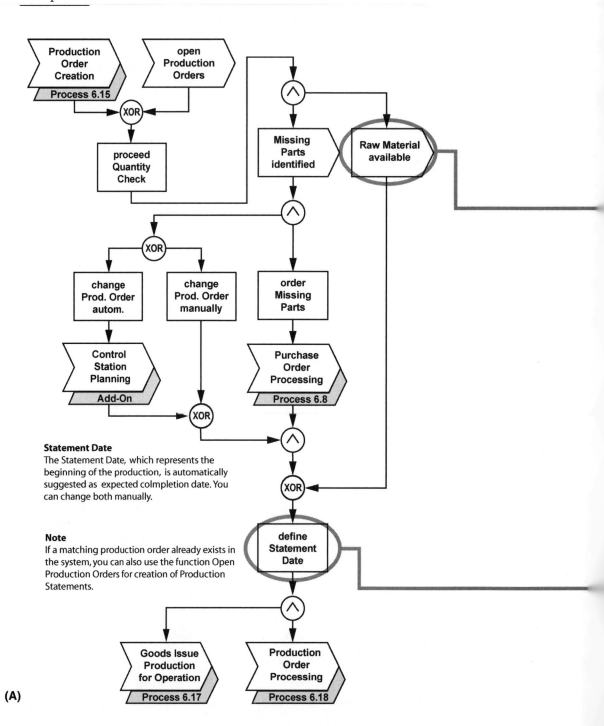

Statement Date
The Statement Date, which represents the beginning of the production, is automatically suggested as expected colmpletion date. You can change both manually.

Note
If a matching production order already exists in the system, you can also use the function Open Production Orders for creation of Production Statements.

(A)

FIGURE 6.51 *(a) Notice about availability of materials, (b) Order assignments with date*

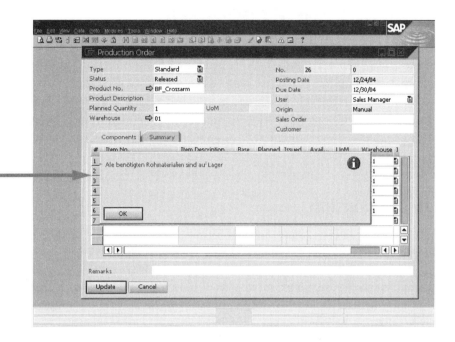

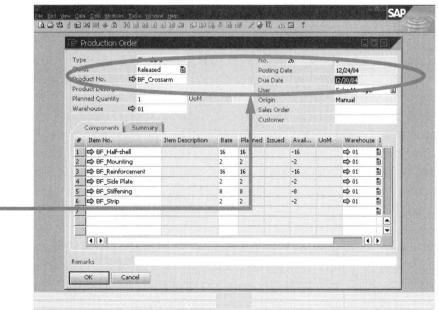

(B)

Goods Issue for Production

When a part or a material is physically withdrawn from inventory, it is referred to as a *goods issue*. When a goods issue is generated for production, normally you assume that the required goods are reserved in inventory. Reserved parts reduce the available stock in the warehouse and are made available at a certain date in the necessary quantity. Goods issue leads to an inventory reduction in both quantity and value and triggers an update of warehouse lists and inventory accounts in accounting.

Business Description

In some cases, a material transfer is carried out from the main warehouse into a temporary manufacturing warehouse before the goods issue is created. Depending on the organization, goods are stored in different ways until used in production. A buffer warehouse, for example, is a short-term warehouse that is frequently used for intermediate storage. A provisional warehouse or distribution warehouse can store materials before they are distributed to different productions plants.

A special form of supply material management for production is the *Kanban system*, which uses a card system to organize production control. (Kanban is Japanese for "card signal.") Kanban manufacturing is very closely connected to material requirement planning. The system's purpose is to optimize material replenishment with an automatic control system to enable efficient production. The methodology is based on a system of *consumers* and *sources* in which manufacturing processes are the consumers. The automatic control system specifies the replenishment strategy and controls the number of storage locations in use and the design of the Kanban cards. The status of a location changes; if it is empty, then a signal is released in the automatic control system for replenishment. A Kanban card is used for each material location to communicate between consumers and sources. The manufacturing manager can retrieve clear information about consumers and sources from the Kanban card and check the availability of materials. Kanban does not require an acknowledgment because the status changes automatically if a location is empty. The Kanban board enables manufacturing to be controlled to avoid such problems as bottlenecks and production interruptions. Kanban systems are ideal for use in assembly productions.

SAP Business One: Specific Description

To begin manufacturing, the necessary parts must be available. This takes place through a physical goods issue from the warehouse to reserve the materials. Withdrawal of the parts triggers an update in the values in accounting. Materials withdrawal can be both planned and unplanned. Material issue slips are necessary for the withdrawal to be used in production orders. Planned material withdrawals can be performed only on goods in stock that were reserved.

At every inventory movement, two procedures are created:

- ◆ Quantity posting in the form of a materials voucher
- ◆ Value posting in the form of a posting to stock

The materials voucher documents the quantity posting for inventory update. Value postings are shown using the List the Stock Postings transaction from the Account view. The posting voucher display can be set in the Goods Issue selection criteria. You can branch out to the Inventory view from the posting voucher and see the expense and revenue accounts under the Accounting tab.

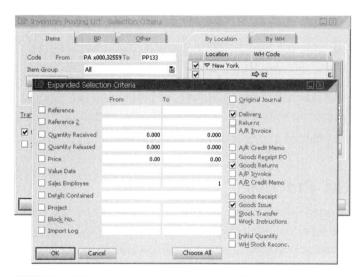

FIGURE 6.52 *A look at the inventory posting for incoming items for the list of inventory postings*

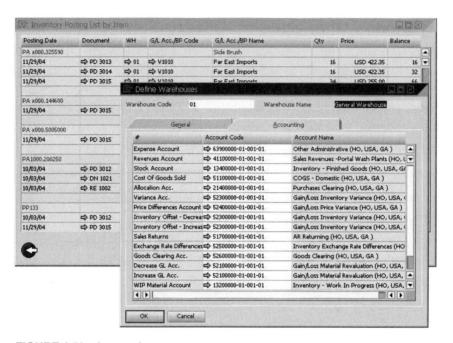

FIGURE 6.53 *Account view*

The following questions should be considered with regard to a goods issue for production from a manufacturing viewpoint:

◆ Which warehouse types do you define for production (provisional warehouse, distribution warehouse, buffer warehouse, and so on)?

◆ Do you use planned goods issue or a Kanban system?

Application of the Process

For a production order to be carried out, the materials necessary for processing must be available at a designated location. This can be accomplished in an enterprise through the use of provisional warehouses. An inventory transfer is necessary from the warehouse where the material is located to the provisional warehouse so that the system can track where a material is available. Stock quantities are already confirmed when a production order is created, so a separate goods issue needn't be booked. The stock of available materials in the warehouse is adjusted automatically when production is complete.

A stock transfer in Model Company B from a material warehouse to a provisional warehouse can be done with the Inventory function. When the Stock Transfer function is opened, the window has proposed values in the upper area that you can change if necessary. A customer is not necessary for an internal stock transfer, but a dummy customer can be used to make it easier to trace the stock transfer later. The number range or date can also be changed as required. Set the warehouse from which the goods are to be transferred in the From Stock field. Next, use the search functions to select those lines that contain items to be transferred into the warehouse indicated in the Warehouse column. Item information is transferred to the current window after confirmation. You can insert entries in the Remarks field below the table to add details, such as the reason for the stock transfer. Finally, click on Add and confirm the resulting message.

If you want a paper copy, recall the document after confirmation and use the Print function in SAP Business One.

Navigation Information

- ◆ **Menu Path:** Inventory > Inventory Transactions > Stock Transfer Inventory > Item Master Data > Register Warehouse Data
- ◆ **Tables:** OITW, OWTR
- ◆ **Incoming Triggers:** Production Statement, Production Order Execution, Stock Analysis
- ◆ **Outgoing Triggers:** Production Order Execution, List of Stock Posting

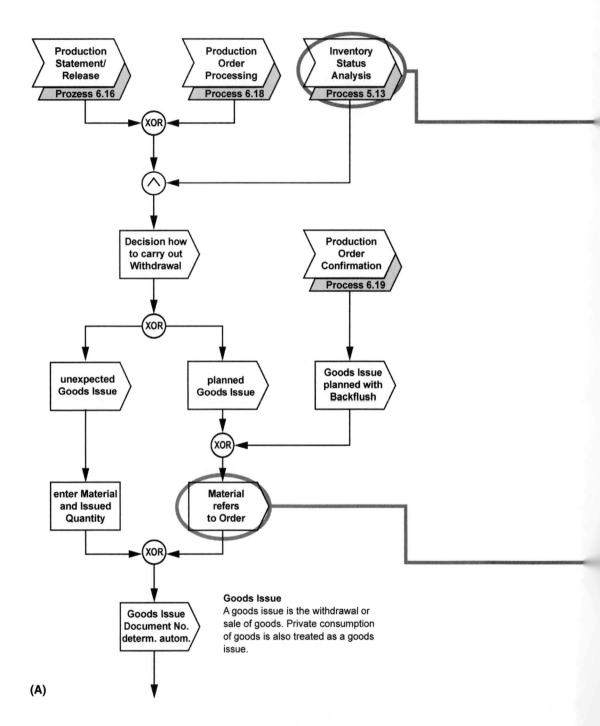

(A)

Goods Issue
A goods issue is the withdrawal or sale of goods. Private consumption of goods is also treated as a goods issue.

FIGURE 6.54 *(a) Current inventory view, (b) Assigned orders*

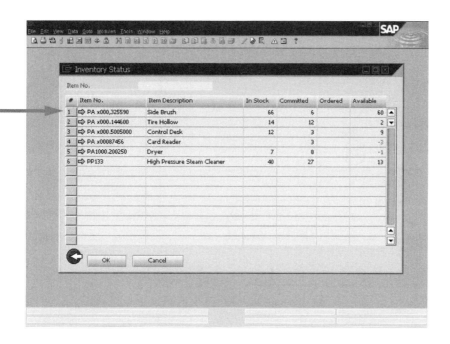

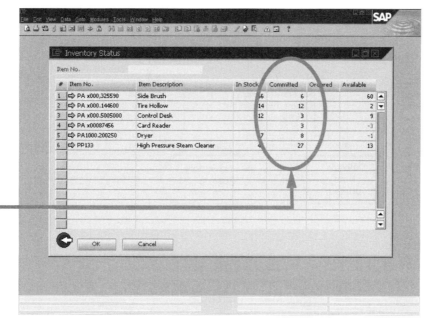

(B)

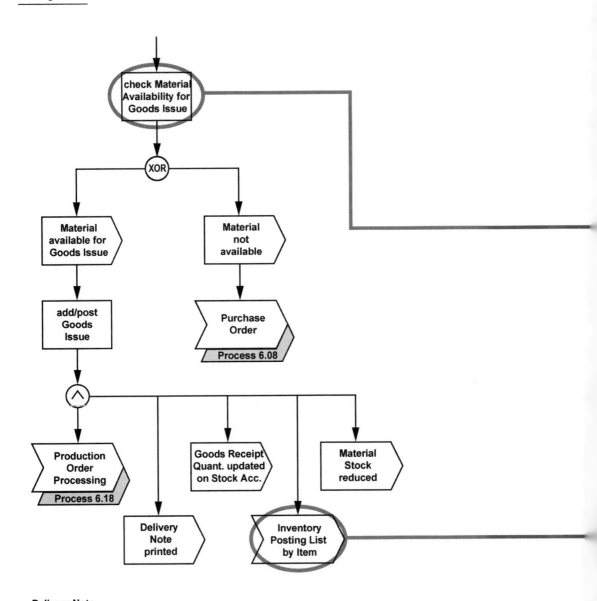

Delivery Note

If a goods issue is made from the warehouse, then the goods are accompanied by a so-called delivery note, which can be printed after the goods issue has been entered into SAP Business One and saved to the database. It can then be attached to the goods. The creation of a delivery note increases the transparency of goods movement

(A)

FIGURE 6.55 *(a) Inventory data in item master data, (b) List of inventory postings*

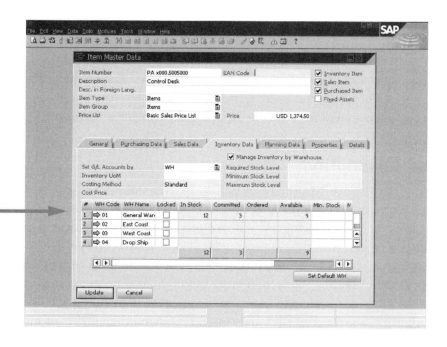

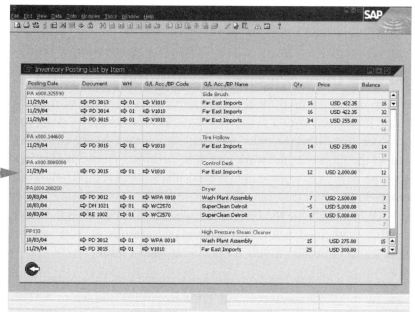

(B)

Production Order Execution

Coordinating and executing a production order involves all areas of the ordering process: Purchasing, Inventory, Production Planning, Requirement Planning, Personnel, Controlling, and so on. If it concerns an order-related production, then close coordination with the Sales or Shipping department is necessary.

Business Description

Much of the product data, such as materials, BOMs, and work schedules, is set at the time of production order execution and stored in the approved production order working folder. Tracing order-driven production requires the linkage of the production process with the customer order. It should always be possible to determine which customer order refers to a production order and its current acknowledgment status. During production order execution, it is necessary to employ an order monitoring procedure to supervise the progress of quantities and deadlines. It documents adherence to start and completion dates, the number of manufactured parts, good and bad parts, and resumption of interrupted manufacturing processes. Costs and types of execution are affected drastically by the degree of automation in the manufacturing organization.

SAP Business One: Specific Description

Production orders are used for the execution and monitoring of manufacturing. Execution is possible when a production order is released and working papers and parts are present. A unique order number is important during execution. Status tracking of the process at the work plan level permits accurate production control and documents current work status. A particular state of completion is reached by those who do the work (planning manager, industry master, worker, and so forth), and in SAP Business One the current status can be illustrated on the order header level with user-defined fields. For performance reasons, it is recommended to maintain status information only on the order header level.

When carrying out a production order, a determination of the operating time can be made by means of an Access and Time Recording add-on to SAP Business One. The operating time indicates when work was done. It is based on a calendar that lists work days and holidays. The work start and end times with associated breaks can be defined per work day. A calendar can be assigned to the work station master record, which is then taken into account during implementation of the production order. In practice, rather than using the complete operating time possible at a work station, a rate of capacity utilization is calculated. This rate of capacity utilization is the percentage calculation between the actual and the theoretically possible operating times. It is then possible during production to call up an exact date overview of the procedures with accurate wait, setup, processing, teardown, and idle times. If a control station is used, then a Gantt chart can be used to display the execution of the production order graphically.

The following questions should be asked at production order execution from a manufacturing viewpoint:

♦ Do you use a graphic control station for better production control?

♦ Do you need different status information during production?

♦ Do you need the Workplace and Work Plan add-on?

♦ Would you like to attach your access and time registration system to SAP Business One?

Application of the Process

Production order execution is independent of the SAP Business One system and is accomplished in the Production department. It is possible to use a Control Station add-on in SAP Business One to complete order execution. However, this is not necessary in all production branches. It is often sufficient to know the current status of production. This can be added to the SAP Business One system by using a user-defined field in the production order. How to add a user-defined field in SAP Business One to an existing form is described in Chapter 7.

Navigation Information

♦ **Menu Path:** Production > Work Order > User-Defined Field > Production Status

♦ **Tables:** CUFD, CUFV

♦ **Incoming Triggers:** Preliminary Costing Customer Order, Item Master Processing, Work Center, Routing, Goods Issue for Production

♦ **Outgoing Triggers:** Goods Receipt from Production, Serial Number and Batch, Production Order (Partial) Confirmation

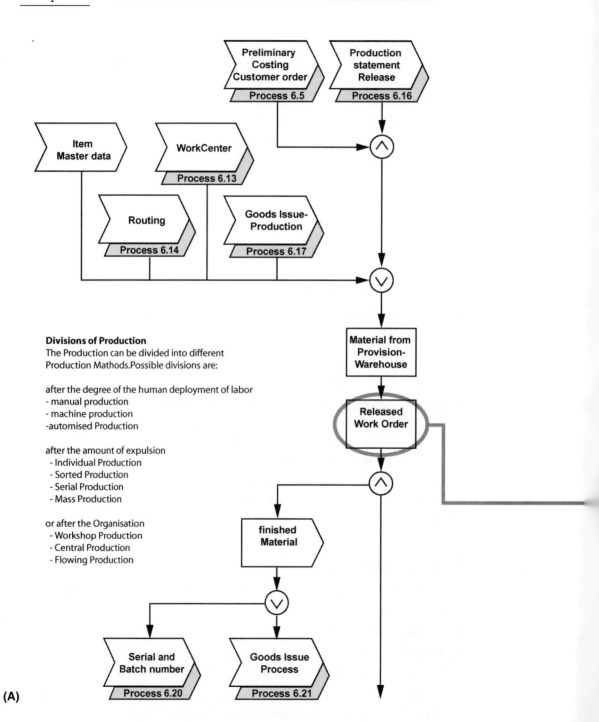

Divisions of Production
The Production can be divided into different
Production Mathods.Possible divisions are:

after the degree of the human deployment of labor
- manual production
- machine production
-automised Production

after the amount of expulsion
- Individual Production
- Sorted Production
- Serial Production
- Mass Production

or after the Organisation
- Workshop Production
- Central Production
- Flowing Production

(A)

FIGURE 6.56 *(a) Job order card, (b) Instructions for production form*

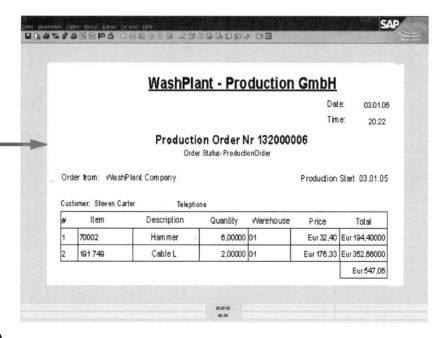

(B)

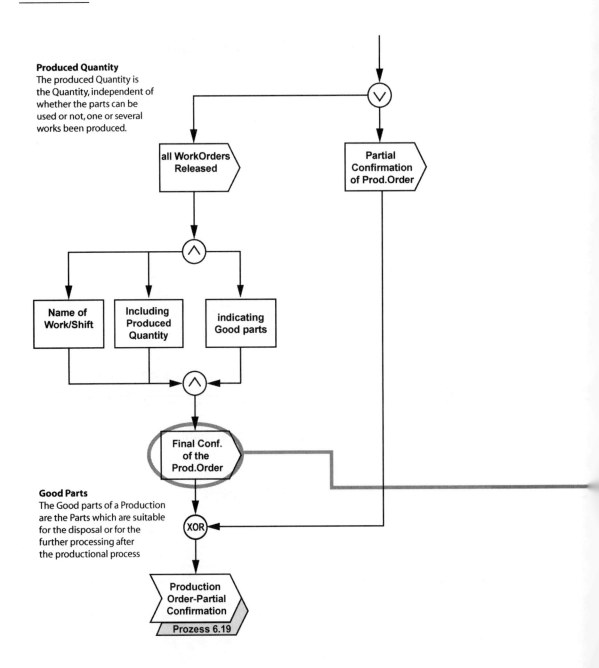

Produced Quantity
The produced Quantity is the Quantity, independent of whether the parts can be used or not, one or several works been produced.

Good Parts
The Good parts of a Production are the Parts which are suitable for the disposal or for the further processing after the productional process

(A)

FIGURE 6.57 *(a) Ready message window (or paper), (b) Production order in SAP Business One*

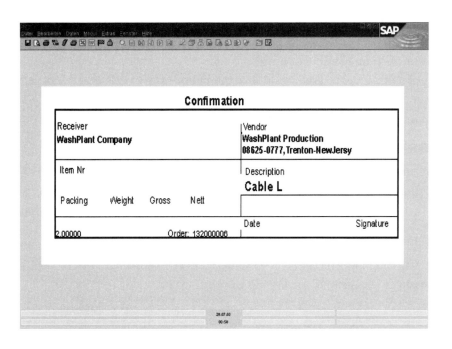

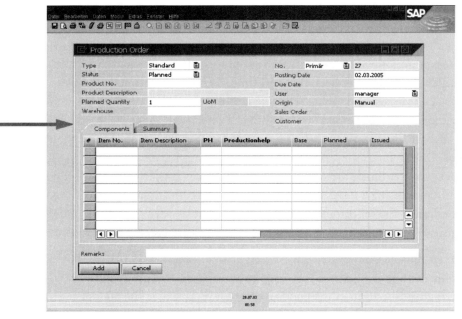

(B)

Production Order: Partial Confirmation

Confirmation of a production order is an internal service carried out during the execution of an order. You can follow and control the progress of the order using the confirmation as a base.

Business Description

Confirmations can refer to an entire order, a process or a subprocess, or capacity of a process. Usually, production is confirmed by indicating the quantity produced, the services needed (such as man-hours), the workplace at which the process was executed, and who accomplished the process. The confirmation also changes the order status to indicate Confirmed Completed. If only individual operations are confirmed, then the status stays at Confirmed Partial until the last procedure is completed.

SAP Business One: Specific Description

A confirmation identifies the quantity produced in a production order as Yield and Scrap Quantity. It is possible to capture confirmations for an order, a process (if you use the Work Schedule add-on), a subprocess, an individual capacity of a process, or an individual capacity of a subprocess. If a confirmation is tracked on the order header level in SAP Business One, then the Confirmed Completed date is added. If you use the Work Schedule add-on, then the processes are confirmed in relation to the confirmed total quantity. If confirmations are being tracked outside of SAP Business One (such as with a BDE system), then it is possible to import the data into the SAP Business One system. In practice, BDE production data capture terminals are often used, which makes simple confirmation possible (for instance, using a BDE terminal with barcode collection or with oil-protective plastic film at the machine). If confirmation errors are detected during BDE data acquisition and transmission, then BDE bug rates are created for re-dos.

Different business processes can be triggered automatically with the completion of confirmation. The actual costs can be updated in the production order. After receiving confirmation of the goods receipt for production, the appropriate inventory postings are booked using retrograde withdrawals.

The following questions should be asked regarding production order confirmation from a manufacturing viewpoint:

- Do you use a BDE system for confirmation?
- Do you report on the production order header level or on the process level?

Table 6.3 Advantages and Disadvantages of using BDE Systems

Advantages	Disadvantages
Real-time process control	Relatively high capital investments
Paperless manufacturing	Modification of workflow management (upon approval by worker representation)
Decentralization of decisions	Independent introduction project advisable
Barcode interface	
Transparency improvement in production	
Availability of manufacturing status	
Control of full and respectively partial automated machines	

Application of the Process

Confirmation of a production order takes place following the completion of the order. Open and release the (dependent) production order to be confirmed by calling up the Production Order function and using the search function to find the order. Select the Order Closed status button and confirm with Update. This action triggers inventory postings in SAP Business One. The stock of the raw materials is reduced and the stock of finished goods increased accordingly.

Navigation Information

- **Menu path:** Production > Work Order > Work Completed (Mark)
- **Tables:** OWKO, WKO1, OITT
- **Incoming Triggers:** BDE Add-On, Production Order Execution
- **Outgoing Triggers:** Goods Issue for Production to the Operation, Goods Receipt Processing from Production, Cost Center Accounting

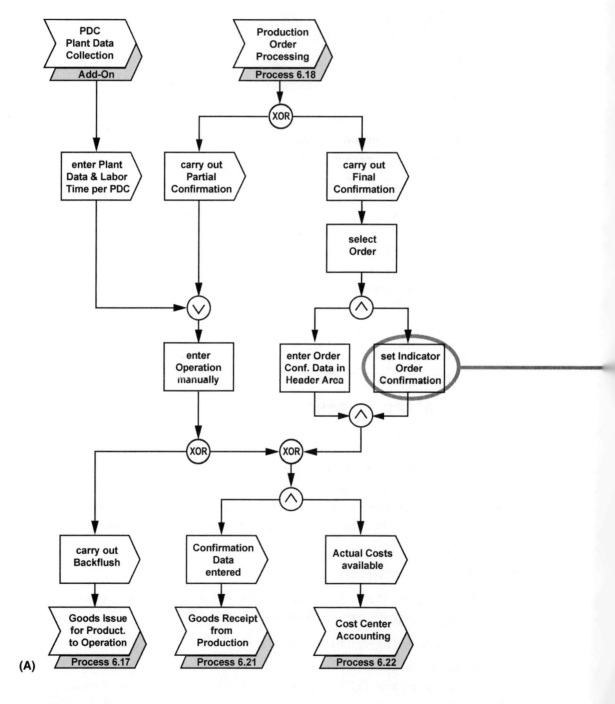

FIGURE 6.58 *(a) Production order acknowledgment with date, (b) Information notice regarding inventory situation*

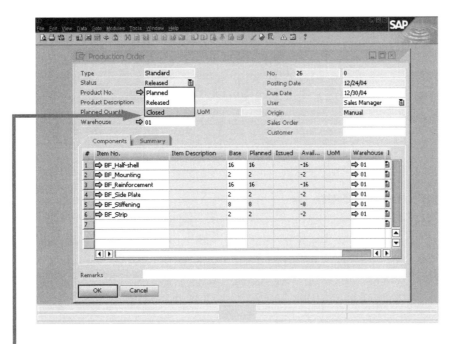

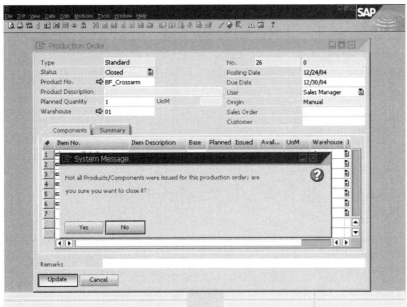

(B)

Serial Number and Batch Number

In business, serial and batch numbers often are mixed up. Serial numbers are used during execution of a serial production. A series is a defined number (lot) of manufactured products having the same structural characteristics. The serial number can be used for a small series (apparatus engineering) as well as for mass production of large series (home appliances, cars). If faulty products are shipped, serial numbers become very important for such actions as recalls.

Business Description

A special form of serial production is batch production. Batches are needed in companies involved in the creation of value-added products, where the tracing of responsibilities might be necessary for possible recourses under product liability laws. It is necessary to keep track of both supplier-provided batches of materials and a production batch. If a faulty product is discovered, the subprocess and process manager involved can be proven. A batch is a lot (subset) of an item developed under the same manufacturing conditions.

In batch administration, materials are assigned a batch number. A batch is tracked, along with all material movement, from production confirmation to shipping. Sometimes a batch assignment is necessary even for purchased parts such as raw materials and semi-finished goods. Besides the batch number, tracking information might include attributes for an expiration date, the goods receipt date, the country of origin, and the inventory level for its storage location. The key to batch production is to mark the parts so that the batch number remains identifiable at every step of the process.

SAP Business One: Specific Description

In SAP Business One, after activating serial number administration under Administration in System Initialization, you can track items by serial number. Serial number administration or batch number administration in item management is selected in the master record under the General setting. The system creates sequential serial numbers (according to a continuous counter in the system) that can be selected in the following documents: Delivery Note, Incoming

Invoice, Purchase Return, Purchase Credit Note, Goods Receipt, Work Instruction, and Goods Transfer (see the *SAP Business One User Manual*, Chapter 11). If you set the attributes in batch administration, batch numbers are used for items to allow clear identification of the manufacturing lots. (For example, pharmaceutical products are identified and listed in inventory not only by product number but also by batch number.) Batch processing makes it possible to identify and administer not only units from internal manufacturing, it also keeps a separate inventory of production or delivery lots from suppliers. If it is mandatory to assign a batch number to an item, then each partial inventory of the item must be assigned to a batch as well. The batch number must always be indicated with each goods movement.

Batch administration is connected to all logistics areas, including procurement, inventory management, and manufacturing. In SAP Business One, the attribute for batch administration under the Administration menu in the System Initialization submenu is essential for activation.

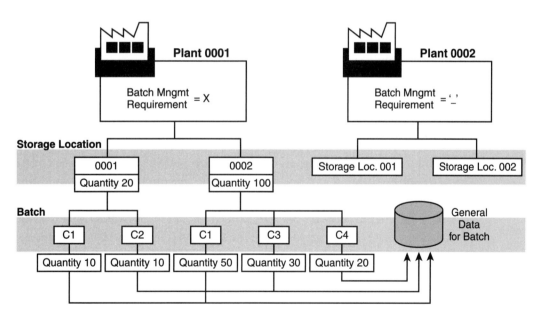

FIGURE 6.59 *Configuration of the load data*

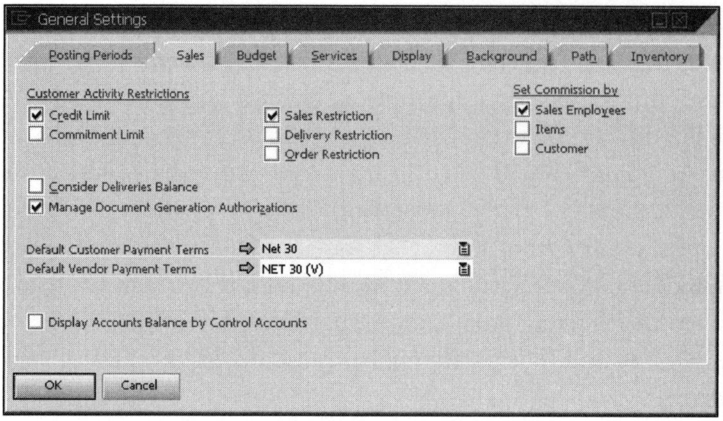

FIGURE 6.60 *General configuration in SAP Business One*

During serial and batch number administration, the following questions should be asked:

- ◆ Do you work with serial numbers and/or batch numbers for certain items?
- ◆ Do you always get batched materials from your suppliers?

Application of the Process

As previously indicated, a setting should be turned on during system initialization in the administration phase in order to use serial number and/or batch number administration. However, it is also possible to activate it later. Go to the Administration application and open System Initialization. Here you will find the General Settings function, which you must open. Switch to the Inventory index in the settings window shown. You will find the fields for activating number administration in this index. If you click the attributes for number administration and check the box, the selection menu for the type of numbering system is activated, where you can activate manual, internal, or batch number administration.

If you choose batch administration, then you can select if the batch status is to be distributed and if batch numbers are to be administered in customer orders.

Next you specify under Item Management in the General register of the Inventory menu whether an item will be managed in serial or batch number administration or is to be treated independently. When you select one of the buttons, additional attribute fields are displayed. In serial number administration, you can choose to have serial numbers shown On Release Only. You can also require the issue of serial or batch numbers in both types of number administration.

Navigation Information

- ◆ **Menu Paths:** Administration > System Initialization > General Settings > Register Items
  Inventory > Item Master Data > General Index
- ◆ **Tables:** NNM1, NNM2, OIBT, OSRD, OSRI, OSRL, SRI1
- ◆ **Incoming Triggers:** Purchase Item, Sales Item, Order Confirmation, Goods Receipt with Consignment Warehouse, Delivery Processing
- ◆ **Outgoing Triggers:** Goods Receipt with Consignment Warehouse, Goods Receipt from Production, Delivery Processing

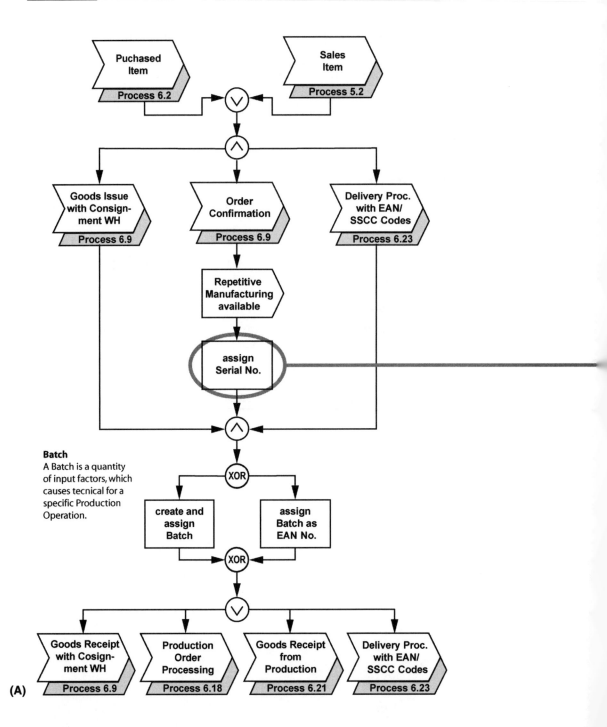

FIGURE 6.61 *(a) Serial and load numbers in item master data, (b) Load management window*

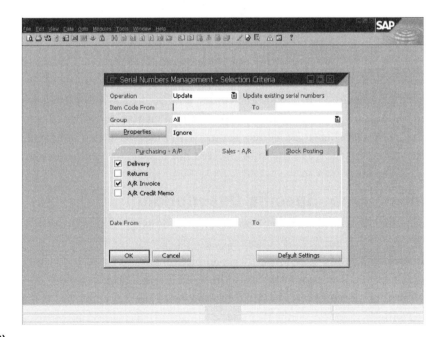

(B)

Goods Receipt Processing from Production

During the production process, material goes through different warehouse stages, such as from a raw material warehouse to a semi-finished goods warehouse or a finished items warehouse. Material logistics covers the procurement, production, and sales sections, where the material flow within production is described as internal logistics.

Business Description

The procurement of material influences all actions related to the supply of parts. Internal logistics, as a subsystem of the production system, controls the flow of material within the production plant. For example, the Kanban system, discussed previously, provides information as to whether a material storage location is full or empty. Suppliers fill the first source location (the just-in-time inventory), and at the end of the Kanban automatic control system is a finished goods storage location. At the end of production, the goods receipt is also acknowledged through input from production. Once the goods are delivered by manufacturing, they need to be stored as part of the internal logistics, and a goods receipt slip is issued as confirmation of the delivery. After quality inspection, the goods are stored in a finished goods warehouse, which can also be a distribution warehouse. The delivered goods are assigned to a customer order and booked as reserved stock. If a company produces goods that are not specific to a customer, then the goods are stored as freely available stock. When dealing with made-to-order and small batch production, it is best to store the units ordered in the warehouse as reserved stock.

SAP Business One: Specific Description

Confirmation of a partial production order or a by way of the Order Finished indicator is the trigger for execution of a goods receipt for the produced goods into the finished goods warehouse. The completion confirmation slip needs to be examined for the correct quantity. Since this is an internal goods receipt, any questions regarding a quantity or quality deviation from the customer order must be clarified with production. Since this check has already happened automatically in the system through the production order confirmation, any shortfalls in the goods receipt can be attributed to a loss by the internal transport system. If a special check of the goods receipt is performed, then a SAP Business One Quality Management System add-on has to be used.

In addition to the physical location of the goods (the warehouse to which the items were posted), it is also important to know when the stock was moved (the delivery date of the customer order). The delivery date determines if a product is posted into the finished goods warehouse or directly to the goods distribution ramp. In SAP Business One, the goods distribution ramp is listed as a separate warehouse location. If goods are delivered this way, then transport documents (pallet note, label, and such) are prepared and printed at the same time.

The following question should be asked during the processing of goods receipt from production:

♦ Are batches necessary during the processing of goods receipt?

Application of the Process

The confirmation of the production order constitutes goods receipt after production. When the order was opened, you specified a warehouse location for the finished products, and the stock is now posted to that warehouse. If the warehouse chosen is temporary, such as for quality assurance, then another stock transfer is necessary to the finished goods warehouse after the QA Check (see the "Goods Issue for Production" section, earlier in this chapter).

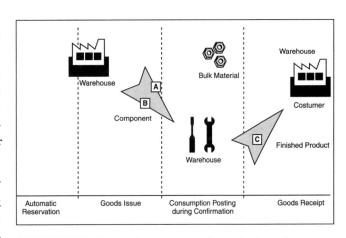

FIGURE 6.62 *Material movement in the production order*

Navigation Information

♦ **Menu Path:** Production > Work Order > Work Completed

♦ **Tables:** OITW, OWTR

♦ **Incoming Triggers:** Production Order (Partial) Confirmation

♦ **Outgoing Triggers:** Quality Check, Stock Analysis, Delivery Processing

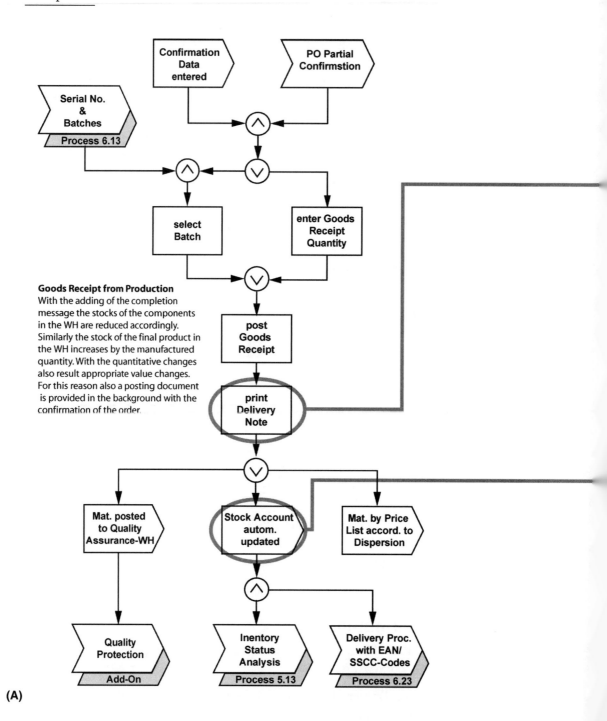

Goods Receipt from Production
With the adding of the completion message the stocks of the components in the WH are reduced accordingly. Similarly the stock of the final product in the WH increases by the manufactured quantity. With the quantitative changes also result appropriate value changes. For this reason also a posting document is provided in the background with the confirmation of the order.

(A)

FIGURE 6.63 *(a) Material supply note, (b) Booking account in chart of accounts*

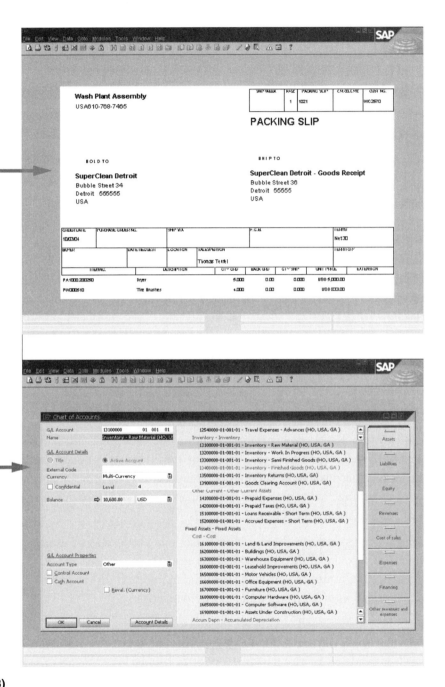

(B)

Delivery Processing with EAN Codes

The description of delivery for Model Company A is described in the "Delivery Processing" section in Chapter 5.

Business Description

It should be mentioned in this context that more and more companies are switching from logistics to supply chain management.

Supply chain management refers to a system of logistical processes spanning multiple companies to produce detailed information flow from the supplier to the customer (downstream) and back (upstream). This increases the efficiency of the transaction and thus provides a competitive advantage over other companies not logistically integrated with their customer networks. The Efficient Consumer Response (ECR) concept has become an IT infrastructure solution to control material flow. It defines the standards for an automatic numbering system for identifying logistic objects. A well-known base technology of the ECR concept is the European Article Number (EAN) numbering system; in the context of international standards it is referred to as the GTIN (Global Trade Item Number).

What Are EAN Codes?

Application of an EAN code is typically automated and used with barcodes for scanner-OCR technology. Barcodes represent EAN codes in machine-readable barcode format (narrow and broad lines in a sequence). They indicate numbers by displaying an arrangement of bars in different sizes and strengths and can nowadays be found on most products and materials.

In delivery, a transportation label with a barcode is produced and attached to a Lattice box or a pallet of the commodity for example. Nowadays the EAN code with a barcode has established itself as the primary method for the automatic and secure identification of logistical units during deliveries.

EAN numbers are assigned worldwide for every item object, thus providing identification that spans all countries and industries. The unique composition of the EAN code is regulated by a local issuing authority. In the United States this authority is the Uniform Code Council, Inc., which can be found at www.uc-council.org). Since January 1, 2001, the detailed composition of the EAN code has been regu-

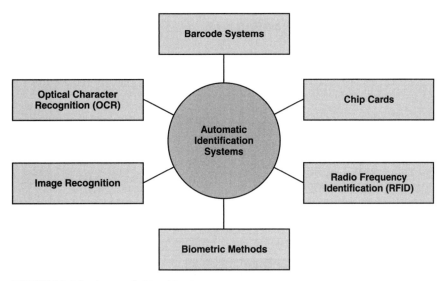

FIGURE 6.64 *Automatic identification system*

lated using ILN codes. ILN codes of Type 1 are intended for small companies not needing a large number range, whereas Type 2 codes are intended for larger companies. The last digit is a checksum calculated from the preceding digits in accordance with an internationally agreed-upon algorithm. The remaining 10 numbers are freely available.

A further base technology of ECR is the Electronics Data Interchange (EDI) system. This technology enables standardized data exchange for electronic records and can be defined to be specific to a given industry. EDI technology is used primarily for ordering, invoices, and dispatch notifications (notification before the delivery reaches the customer). EDI documents are translated into the general format for ERP (Enterprise Resource Planning) systems using converters for further processing.

SAP Business One: Specific Description

The item master data record in SAP Business One has a designation for the EAN code for the item number. In our example, if the creation of a delivery notice with EAN codes is planned, then a delivery notice with transport labels is generated. The document editor can print the barcodes for automatic capture via a scanner.

FIGURE 6.65 *EAN number as barcode*

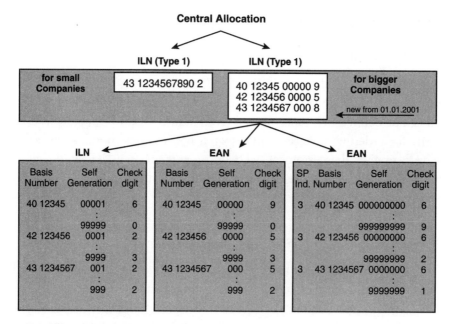

FIGURE 6.66 *EAN number system.*

The following questions should be asked during delivery processing with EAN codes from the view of sales:

- Do you use EAN codes?
- Do you use barcodes with your shipping labels?
- Do you use EDI for your dispatch notifications?

Application of the Process

Receipts resulting from a delivery can contain a barcode. This barcode simplifies the automation of goods identification because the information can be retrieved using a scanner to read the barcode. This saves a lot of time that otherwise would have to be spent entering the item codes manually. A prerequisite for using barcodes is EAN number administration in the item master. There is an input field in the Item Administration function to add an EAN number to an item. You also have the capability to structure your item numbers in such a way that you can capture them automatically using the barcodes.

The document editor in Document Processing allows the representation of numbers as barcodes. To simplify the delivery of goods in the model company, articles are accompanied by a transport bill. In order to accomplish this, open the Delivery function in the Sales application. Enter a new delivery with an order reference or call up an existing data record. In the Delivery menu, open Document Processing. All documents pertaining to the delivery are displayed in a list. Double-click on Transport Bill. Select the Supply Line Item Code field in the document window and double-click to open a properties window. By selecting the Print as Barcode attribute in the General tab, you can have barcodes on printed receipts. You can also display the content of the EAN Number field as a barcode.

Navigation Information

- **Menu Path:** Sales A/R > Delivery > Document Editing > Packing List (double-click) > Object Properties > General Index
- **Tables:** OITM, DLN1, DLN2, DLN3, ODLN, OGSP, RDOC
- **Incoming Triggers:** Goods Receipt from Production, Goods Return Processing, Cash Sales
- **Outgoing Triggers:** Outgoing Invoice, Returns

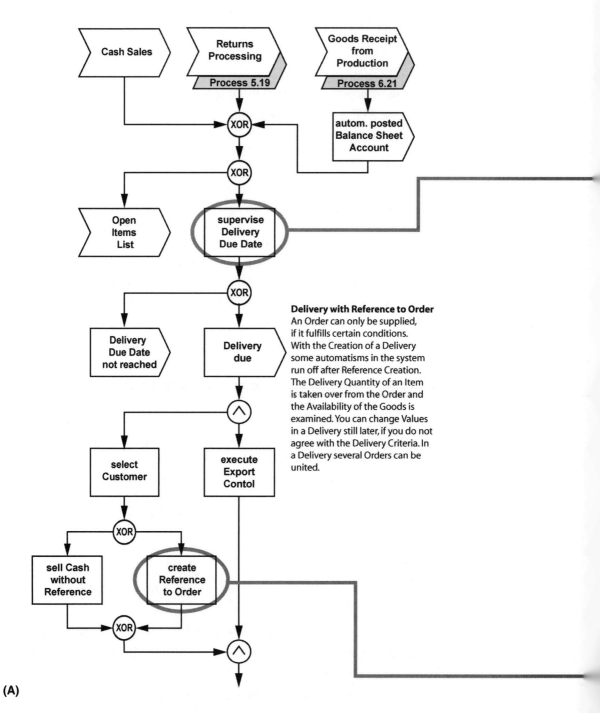

Delivery with Reference to Order
An Order can only be supplied, if it fulfills certain conditions. With the Creation of a Delivery some automatisms in the system run off after Reference Creation. The Delivery Quantity of an Item is taken over from the Order and the Availability of the Goods is examined. You can change Values in a Delivery still later, if you do not agree with the Delivery Criteria. In a Delivery several Orders can be united.

(A)

FIGURE 6.67 *(a) List of open delivery notes, (b) Delivery in SAP Business One*

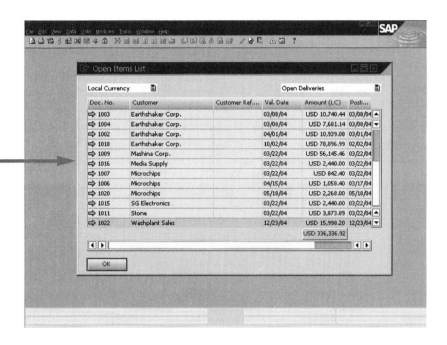

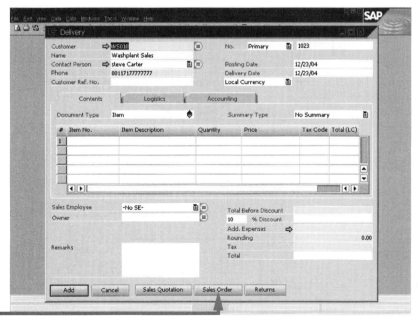

(B)

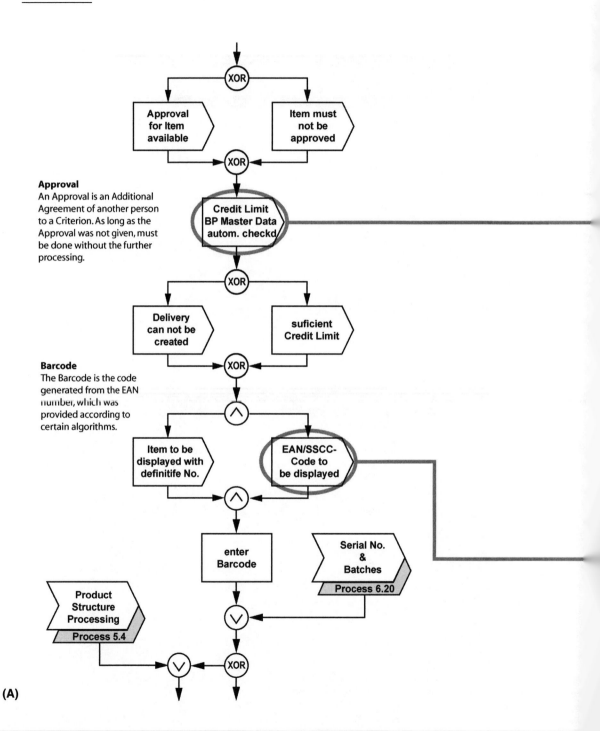

Approval
An Approval is an Additional Agreement of another person to a Criterion. As long as the Approval was not given, must be done without the further processing.

Barcode
The Barcode is the code generated from the EAN number, which was provided according to certain algorithms.

(A)

FIGURE 6.68 *(a) Credit limit check for delivery, (b) Delivery table details*

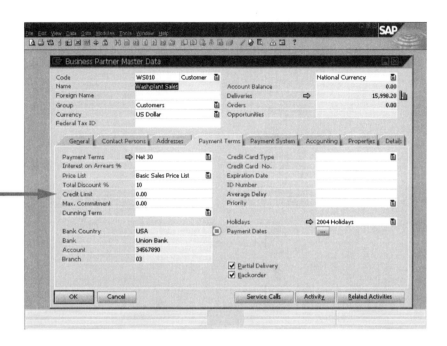

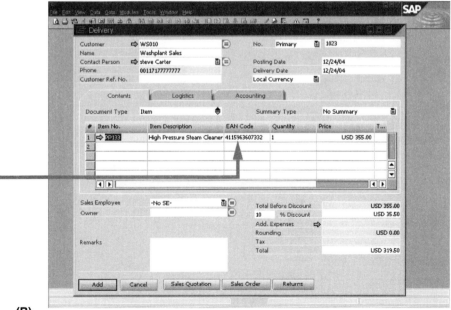

(B)

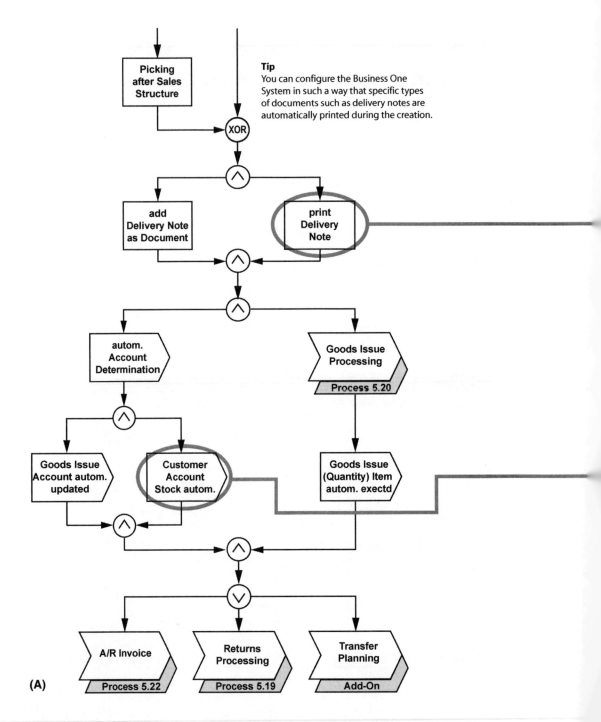

Tip
You can configure the Business One System in such a way that specific types of documents such as delivery notes are automatically printed during the creation.

FIGURE 6.69 *(a) Print preview for delivery including a barcode, (b) Allocation/Offset/Settlement account overview*

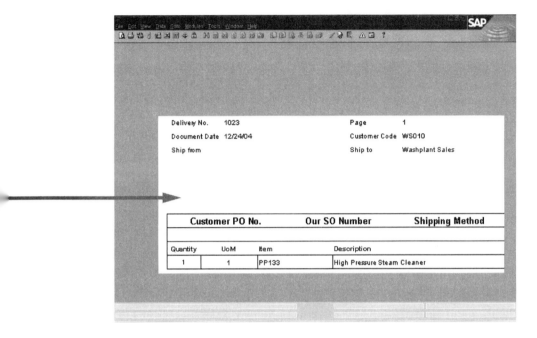

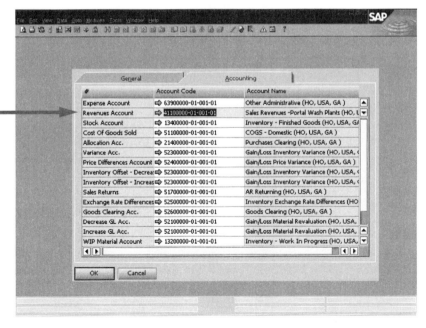

(B)

Outgoing Payment with Automatic Payment Run

Payments are used to purchase production needs and for repayment and investments. As a result, they lead to the reduction of liabilities.

Business Description

Settling liabilities can be accomplished in different ways:

- ◆ **Cash Payment:** Payment is made in actual real currency.

- ◆ **Half Cash or Cash-Saving Payment:** Part of the payment is made in cash and part in non-cash form such as a cashier's check or a payment bill.

- ◆ **Non-Cash Payment:** Payment is made through a credit institution. The typical form is a bank transfer.

- ◆ **Payment Instruction:** This form is neither cash nor a deposit. The typical form is a check. The obligation exists until the amount is credited to the account of the vendor, who is then able to use the money.

Payments are also differentiated with respect to whether they are made in a country's own or foreign currency. If payments are made in a foreign currency, then special attention has to be paid foreign exchange and its regulations.

Outgoing payment is usually based on a received invoice. The gross amount and the payment terms come from calculation of this purchase invoice. According to the payment terms, a discount might be deducted from the total invoice amount for payment within a certain time period (see the "Incoming Invoice" section, earlier in this chapter).

Also, partial payments or payments in different forms might be allowed for an invoice according to an agreement with the vendor

SAP Business One: Specific Description

Outgoing payments in SAP Business One can be illustrated for all payment methods. Thus cash, half-cash, non-cash, and mixed payments can all be used. Outgoing payments to vendors are processed in the Banking menu. In manual mode, each payment produces a voucher. In principle it is possible to include payments with reference to other procedures booked to an account payable. It is just also possible to include bookings without reference to another voucher for a vendor account.

If an invoice is paid in full (after subtracting an applicable discount if appropriate), then a payment receipt must be prepared with reference to the invoice. Just as when a receipt is created, the purchase invoice is cleared and the associated payment is made, so that data no longer appears on the OI list for the account. A discount is automatically booked by SAP Business One with the payment during the discount period if the necessary settings were put in general ledger configuration during system initialization.

If a purchase invoice is settled by several partial payments, then all vouchers except the final one are entered without reference to the invoice. When a voucher for a partial payment is created, a place should be provided within the voucher text or elsewhere to designate that the incoming invoice should have a fast allocation characteristic. When capturing the final payment as a voucher, the connection to the invoice and all partial payments is established by marking all individual receipt lines to be included in yellow. The receipt for the final payment allows the purchase invoice to be balanced with all previous payments by marking the associated lines. All single documents then disappear from the OI list. As long as a liability is not yet balanced, the original purchase invoice and all partial payments made to date should be left in the vendor's account as OI to provide a complete picture of the business case.

If a partial payment were to trigger a reference to the invoice and therefore clear the invoice and the partial payment, then a difference voucher would have to be created to be kept as an OI in the vendor's account. This posting then would have the characteristics of a purchase invoice. However, since there was no purchase corresponding to the partial payment, no invoice voucher would exist for the posting. Since there should be no posting without a voucher, this alternative should not be used in proper accounting within accounts payable.

Each output voucher produces an OI within the respective financial account in order to balance. When the outgoing payment voucher is created in SAP Business One, the transaction is posted to the appropriate financial account or accounts.

Statements of financial accounts need to be recorded independently of incoming and outgoing payment vouchers. Special attention has to be paid to the fact that you are in reality copying the physical account statements. The same process stages exist with automatic exchange.

The following questions should be asked in the context of outgoing payments with automatic payment:

- Do you use written receipts or online banking?
- How often do you issue payments?
- Are your payments automated?
- Can you use predefined standards for your payments?

Application of the Process

Automatic payment runs must be configured in advance. First, the means of payment must be configured. Go into the Banking application, open the Payment System selection, and select the Define Payment Methods function.

Next, define in the input form a code as well as a name for the means of payment. You can select one of two types for the means of payment:

- **Outgoing:** Payments to a vendor (Purchase)
- **Incoming:** Payments from a customer (Sales)

Next, you must specify the payment method to be either a check or a bank transfer. This setting can be specified only for an outgoing payment.

There are various validation options in the lower area, which can be marked to be checked during the payment run. You can combine several characteristics. The selection fields on the right side of the window are used to identify the bank. Only banks defined in the Define Banks function are included in the selection list. If checks are the payment method, additional restrictions such as minimum and maximum amounts can be added.

General information regarding your payment runs must be entered. In Banking, open the Define Payment Run Defaults function in the Payment System selection. In the new window, which includes several definition fields, you can set the leniency days for purchasing, the minimum discount for purchasing, and a minimum amount per payment. The Payment Methods selection enables you to specify the means of payment for the payment run.

The actual payment run is activated and processed with the Payment Wizard. Start the wizard and follow the instructions, which consist of eight steps. The first step allows you to recall a previously defined wizard or create a new one. Clicking on Next gets you to the next step. Provide the entries requested during each step to set up the payment run.

Navigation Information

- **Menu Paths:** Banking > Payment System > Define Payment Run Defaults

  Banking > Payment System > Payment Wizard
- **Tables:** DSC1, OCRP, OCTG, ODSC, OPDF, ORCR, PDF1, PDF2, PDF3, PDF4, PDF5, VPM1, VPM2, VPM3, VPM4, VPM5
- **Incoming Triggers:** Delivery Process with EAN
- **Outgoing Triggers:** Receivable Process by Due Date, Account Statement to the Business Partner, Sales Tax, Profit and Loss Accounting

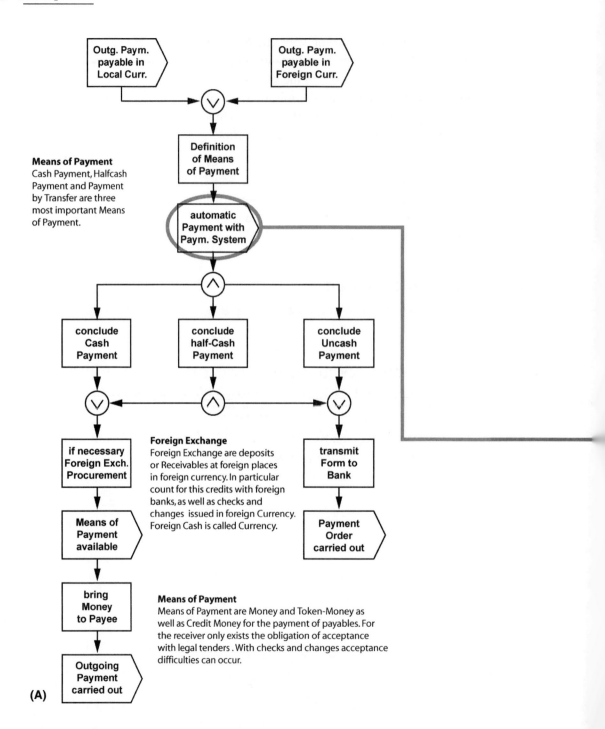

Means of Payment
Cash Payment, Halfcash Payment and Payment by Transfer are three most important Means of Payment.

Foreign Exchange
Foreign Exchange are deposits or Receivables at foreign places in foreign currency. In particular count for this credits with foreign banks, as well as checks and changes issued in foreign Currency. Foreign Cash is called Currency.

Means of Payment
Means of Payment are Money and Token-Money as well as Credit Money for the payment of payables. For the receiver only exists the obligation of acceptance with legal tenders. With checks and changes acceptance difficulties can occur.

FIGURE 6.70 *(a) Payments input form, (b) Payment processing assistant in SAP Business One*

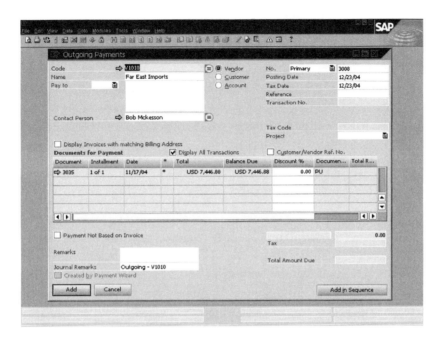

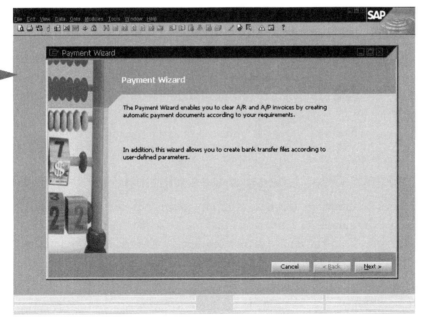

Bank Statement to the Business Partner

When creating a master data record for a business partner, an associated account is opened as well to serve as a repository for all documents concerning dealings with that business partner. It has the basic characteristics of a balance sheet account.

Business Description

If the account concerns a customer account (a debtor), then postings will flow into a summary account for receivables and to the assets side of the balance sheet. If the account concerns a vendor account (a creditor), postings will flow into a summary account for liabilities and to the debit side of the balance sheet. In either case, the account itself permits both debit and credit postings. If a business partner is or becomes both a customer and a supplier, then two separate accounts must be kept, so as to prevent a balancing of receivables and liabilities, which is illegal.

Certain circumstances can arise in which an account receivable shows a credit or an account payable shows a debit balance. This can happen if the customer has made full payment to the vendor and later a credit is given due to a return of goods.

These are normal business procedures and must be processed according to respective requirements when the balance sheet is closed. The account of a business partner reflects the individual financial activities of the business relationship. Depending on how detailed individual documents are, an account can give an overview of what has happened in the relationship and under what conditions.

SAP Business One: Specific Description

The system administers business partner account numbers together with general ledger account numbers. This means that the same key field is used. Therefore, the keys of the G/L and business partner account numbers must be unique. The use of a naming convention for assigning account numbers in the company is essential.

In its default configuration, SAP Business One uses external number allocation for the key field. This can easily be switched to internal number allocation with a query when creating accounts. The system always interprets account numbers alphanumerically. Because the SQL database would interpret mathematical operators falsely, these are not allowed as part of an account number.

Account numbers can be changed or deleted as long as no transaction is associated with the account. Once a transaction has been posted, the account number can no longer be altered or removed. The account can only be blocked in the system.

The link between the customer account and the chart of accounts is the reconciliation account, used during the master data record creation. The account of a business partner can be viewed in several places within SAP Business One.

In the master records view of a business partner, an account can be brought up quickly with the yellow arrow. Limitations for the selection such as the date and the number of transactions displayed can also be applied. The display can simply be translated to the OI by clicking on the check mark to carry over previous restrictions to the date and number of transactions. Other fields, such as due date, can be viewed with the appropriate settings.

Application of the Process

You must balance accounts from time to time. When receiving statements from the bank, you must verify that transactions are reflected according to your instructions. If deducted amounts are correct, then you have to reproduce the necessary debit and credit postings in the system. This process is called *account reconciliation*. You balance the accounts of business partners in the same manner. Compare the dates in your system with those kept by your business partner for the same action. Open the Process External Bank Statement window within the Banking menu and change the selection to BP.

Next you can choose a business partner and enter the associated dates in the table. As an alternative, you can import the dates from an external file. Confirm the entries by clicking on Add.

Navigation Information

- ◆ **Menu Path:** Banking > Bank Statements and Reconciliation > Process External Bank Statements
- ◆ **Tables:** DSC1, OCPR, OCTG, ODSC, OPDF, ORCR, PDF1, PDF2, PDF3, PDF4, PDF5, VPM1, VPM2, VPM3, VPM4, VPM5
- ◆ **Incoming Triggers:** Outgoing Payment
- ◆ **Outgoing Triggers:** None

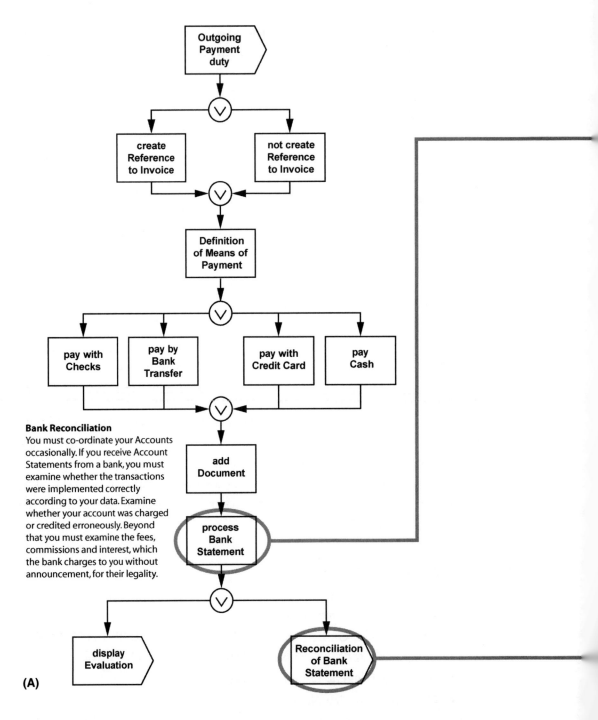

Bank Reconciliation
You must co-ordinate your Accounts occasionally. If you receive Account Statements from a bank, you must examine whether the transactions were implemented correctly according to your data. Examine whether your account was charged or credited erroneously. Beyond that you must examine the fees, commissions and interest, which the bank charges to you without announcement, for their legality.

(A)

FIGURE 6.71 *(a) Input field for external statement, (b) Selection field for account reconciliation*

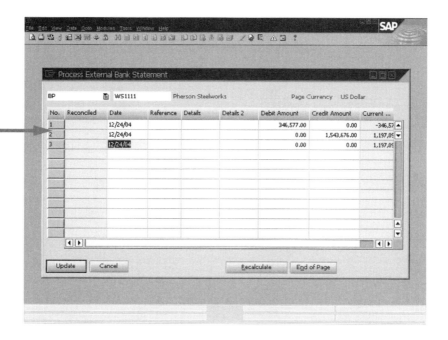

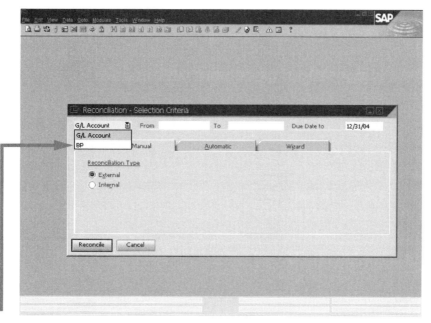

(B)

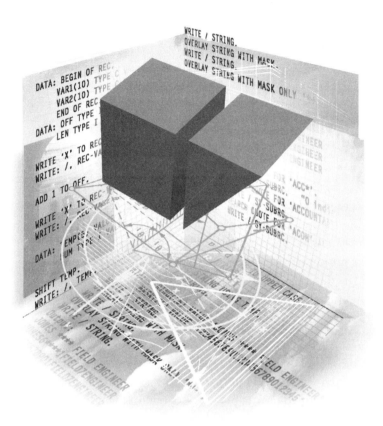

Chapter 7

**Project
Approach to SAP
Business One**

Mid-sized companies usually will not undergo extended implementation of ERP systems, as they have as their goal a quick implementation and, thus, a faster road to improving their efficiency. However, in order for implementation to be achieved as quickly as possible, a regimented project approach is an absolute necessity. Indeed, the project needs to be standardized to such a level that the resulting ERP software (in this case, of course, SAP Business One) can be brought online usually within one to three months. The more extensive the functional requirements defined in the project, the more steps will be required in the implementation process.

While project management on any scale can quickly become very complex, the complexity is more profound when you're trying to map an ERP system to larger, enterprise-level processes. A well-defined project plan is essential. In turn, a well-defined process analysis—the focus of this chapter—can help to streamline the entire Business One implementation.

The Analysis Phase (Process Analysis Workshop)

During the selection phase of new ERP software, a process "chain," or process map, of the organization's entire operation should be developed. Such a map should reflect the actual process flow and the target process flows of each area and highlights processes that can be improved on and made more efficient. The duration of a process analysis workshop for a small to mid-sized business is usually two days. Note that the duration of the workshop can vary, depending on the organizational complexity of the business.

The process map does not have to be complex (see Figure 7.1). It can be roughly sketched on a couple of pieces of $8^1/_2 \times 11$ paper. Individual process components can be generally defined. For example, a process analysis was undertaken for a beverage dealer. In this example, the customer requires mobile data input via a PDA. The process map can highlight specific customer requirements.

As the process map is developed, the process analyst must remember to consider the "high level" input of management in relation to that of the employees "in the trenches," who actually work through the company's processes. The consultant must not be afraid to ask specific questions about the processes in order to understand the exact organization of the enterprise. During this discussion, the central, or "core," processes are usually the first to be defined, and from these, prioritization of additional tasks can be derived. It is necessary to recognize the weak points of existing processes so that the analysis can achieve its (arguably) major goal: the elimination of inefficiencies and the maximization of productivity.

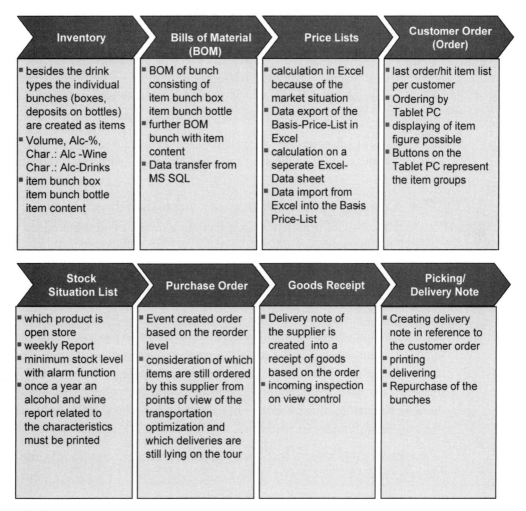

Inventory	Bills of Material (BOM)	Price Lists	Customer Order (Order)
• besides the drink types the individual bunches (boxes, deposits on bottles) are created as items • Volume, Alc-%, Char.: Alc -Wine Char.: Alc-Drinks • item bunch box item bunch bottle item content	• BOM of bunch consisting of item bunch box item bunch bottle • further BOM bunch with item content • Data transfer from MS SQL	• calculation in Excel because of the market situation • Data export of the Basis-Price-List in Excel • calculation on a seperate Excel-Data sheet • Data import from Excel into the Basis Price-List	• last order/hit item list per customer • Ordering by Tablet PC • displaying of item figure possible • Buttons on the Tablet PC represent the item groups

Stock Situation List	Purchase Order	Goods Receipt	Picking/ Delivery Note
• which product is open store • weekly Report • minimum stock level with alarm function • once a year an alcohol and wine report related to the characteristics must be printed	• Event created order based on the reorder level • consideration of which items are still ordered by this supplier from points of view of the transportation optimization and which deliveries are still lying on the tour	• Delivery note of the supplier is created into a receipt of goods based on the order • incoming inspection on view control	• Creating delivery note in reference to the customer order • printing • delivering • Repurchase of the bunches

FIGURE 7.1 *Result after a process analysis workshop (selection from a process chain for a beverage dealer)*

TIP

Identifying responsible persons—that is, those charged with completing/running/ managing processes and tasks—is important for the successful execution of all processes. To reiterate what was stated earlier, the input of management must always be weighed against that of the people who actually perform the production work. Moreover, if processes are changed, the process map must be updated accordingly—not only for record-keeping purposes but so that additional areas of improved efficiency can be identified and exploited.

The Implementation Phase (Customization)

For the small business customer, self-implementation is often necessary because of budget limitations. Mid-sized customers can be more demanding of a consultant, as they often require complete support through analysis and implementation (and beyond).

Generally speaking, the following tasks are associated with the implementation phase:

- Customization of the system according to the defined process.
- Execution of process training, including review of all value-added chains and process components.
- System training in a working environment.
- Ensuring accurate key data collection points.
- Process documentation.

ERP implementations often fail because the established process chains cannot be mapped to the function of the actual software. Too often, organizations don't want to undertake the time, effort, and expense of mapping out functional process map/process chain requirements. The result is that the project is usually a failure because this critical information—indeed, the most critical information required for a successful implementation—is missing!

A successful project starts with a strong project manager. Specifically, the project manager must

1. Establish clear project milestones.

2. Consistently monitor cost for specific components of the project and in relation to the entire project. A project is too often delayed when the specific components are not consistently reviewed in and of themselves and in relation to the entire implementation.

3. Petition for the authority and freedom of the project team to move forward as deemed necessary by the project plan. This includes allowing those involved in the project the necessary resources to continue their daily work as well as be involved as members of the project team.

Implementation Checklist

As with any major business purchase, an ERP solution must be carefully considered. Prior to the actual purchase, two central questions must be answered simultaneously: What does the new system offer, and what are the expectations of the users as to what the new system will bring? In this decision-making process, there are various checklists that can help determine the viability (and applicability) of SAP Business One to the mid-size enterprise.

NOTE

In addition to determining general applicability of SAP Business One, the questions in this chapter can also help you determine what specific adjustments to the standard application (adjustments made possible through the SDK described in earlier chapters) are needed.

The modules for which the questions in the following subsections were prepared are arranged according to how SAP Business One is usually first introduced into a company. If the majority of questions, specific to each module, can be answered so that increased proficiency can be seen, then you can say with confidence that Business One is suitable as an integrated solution for your enterprise.

TIP

The results of the following list of questions can also be used during the software implementation phase to help in customizing settings that are specific to your enterprise.

Administration Component

Analyze the Administration component based on the following criteria:

- How many PCs (clients) do you want to use with SAP Business One?
- Is the enterprise related to a parent group?
- Which software does the parent group utilize?
- Which draft of the accounts is used?
- In which (system) currency do you balance?
- How many production centers (and at which locations) does the enterprise have?
- How many branch offices belong to the enterprise (and at which locations)?
- In what languages must SAP Business One operate?
- In what national currencies must SAP Business One operate?
- Shall negative credit balances be shown?
- Is the financial year the same as the calendar year? If not, then how is the financial calendar determined?
- Will there be a central IT center for all locations?

Restricted Customer Processes

- Do you work with a flat/fixed guarantee limit? If yes, what is the amount?
- Do you work with flat/fixed credit limit? If yes, what is the amount?
- Do you work with flat/fixed sales restrictions? If yes, what are they?
- Do you work with flat/fixed delivering restrictions? If yes, what are they?
- Do you work with flat/fixed order restrictions? If yes, what are they?
- Shall delivery note balances be taken into consideration?
- Shall the document release method be activated?
- Please indicate the standard payment term for customers.
- Please indicate the standard payment term for suppliers.

Sales Commission

- Is turnover commission cashed as seller-related?
- Is turnover commission processed as article-related?
- Is turnover commission processed as customer-related?

Budget Initialization

- Will this be performed under larger budget administration? If yes, what are the restrictions?
- Which alarm functions shall be used (order, delivery note, accounting and so on)?

Services

- Shall the alarm functions make reference to the monthly or annual budget?
- If necessary, how will the change table governing exchanges be kept in good condition?

Articles

- Will a proxy server be utilized?
- Which standard unit of measurement will be utilized?
- Which standard unit of weight will be utilized?
- Will serial numbers be utilized?
- Will shelf life be recorded and tracked?
- Will rank numbers be recorded and tracked?

Receipt Calibration

- Are there forms with standard texts? If yes, please attach samples.
- Which piece of receipt number range shall be worked with?
  - Supply, order, delivery note
  - Exit invoice, credit note, return
  - Exportation data
  - Enquiry, order, delivery, initial invoice
  - Credit note entrance, return delivery
  - Import data
  - Receiving, shipping, inventory relocation, inventory receipt
  - Production order, production instruction (work schedules)
  - Deposit, payment, check submission
- Would you like single receipts to be named differently? If yes, which ones and how shall they be named?

◆ Shall the gross profit be calculated? If yes, with reference to the selling price or with reference to the cost price?

◆ Is a release below the minimum inventory level permitted when issuing a receipt?

◆ If yes, with or without warning?

Definitions

◆ How many users are there?

◆ Are there user groups? If yes, then what are they?

◆ Who becomes a super user? What are the requirements?

◆ Which terms of payment do you use? Please differentiate for both purchasing and sales.

◆ Are commission groups used? If yes, then what are they?

◆ Do you have a sales team? If yes, please list each salesman by name.

◆ Are release methods required for particular documents? If yes, for which ones?

Reports Component

You should determine which reports are needed based on the following list of examples:

◆ Open item list (purchasing documents/sales documents)

◆ Evaluation demands (for news, the date, and so on)

◆ Evaluations liabilities (after supplier, the date, and so on)

◆ Sales reports (sales analysis) quarterly, monthly, annual

◆ Version reports (purchase analysis) quarterly, monthly, annual

◆ Cash-flow/liquidity overview

◆ Contact overview (list of acquisitions)

◆ Factual account reports

◆ Project reports

◆ Sales tax report to the tax office

◆ Balance sheets

◆ Profit and loss account

◆ Controlling reports

◆ Comparison reports

- Stock reports, article lists
- Bill of materials lists (product structure lists)

Also ask

- Which reports are still missing?
- Which do you need today, and which will you also need in the future?

The Accounting Component

In the Accounting module, there are many questions that need to be considered prior to implementation. The following questions help clarify the need for customization within the Accounting module:

- Which draft of the accounts is used?
- Do bookings get pre-recorded?
- Shall recurring bookings be included? If yes, which ones?

The Controlling Component

The Controlling component should be analyzed based on the following criteria:

- Are you planning on using profit centers (cost accounting)? If yes, please include a compilation of centers.
- Is the work planned with cost centers? If yes, please list.
- Are there primary costs that are distributed following a particular example? If yes, please indicate what they are.
- Which enterprise reports are needed for what? Please enclose samples of the previous reports and define ideas for future reports.
- Is there a need to review last year's data/comparisons?

The Banking Transactions Component

Analyze the Banking Transactions component based on the following criteria:

- Shall initial/exit payments be run?
- Are checks allowed for initial payments? If yes, shall antedated checks be submitted?
- Are checks allowed for exit payments?
- How is the ledger organized?
- Is there a list of antedated checks?

- Are credit cards accepted?
- How is the credit card administration tracked and recorded?
- How are bank statements tracked and recorded?
- At which credit institutions are the accounts kept?
- What credit cards does the enterprise have at its disposal?
- Which groups within the company have the credit cards?
- Which modes of payment are allowed with the credit cards?
- Are there further lenders (shareholder loans, building loans, and so on)? If yes, what/who are they?
- Which documents must be printed? Please indicate number of copies.
- Do you work with profit centers? If yes, which ones and how many?

The Sales Documents Component

The Sales and Purchasing Modules must also be customized as necessary, depending on the specific requirements of the enterprise. The following questions should be answered to help clarify the Sales Document component:

- Which sales documents (supply, order, delivery note, return, exit invoice, credit note) must be printed? Please indicate number of copies.
- Do you work with drafts (copy templates)?
- Do you also sell services?
- Must the numbering of documents be done manually, or can this be automated?
- Do you use an article catalogue number for your products?
- Who are the sellers and to which groups are they assigned?
- How is the pricing organized?

The Purchasing Documents Component

The Purchasing Documents component should be analyzed based on the following criteria:

- Which purchasing documents (order, delivery note for the order, return delivery, initial invoice, credit note purchase) must be printed? Please indicate number of copies.
- Do you work with an invoice release?
- Which import data will be acquired (custom details, freight, and so on)?
- Do you work with provisions of material?

- ◆ Who are your buyers, and are they assigned to groups?
- ◆ Do you work with drafts (copy templates)?

The Business Partners Component

Without business partner contacts, no enterprise would be able to function. For this reason, it is important to plan in accordance with the requirements of your business partners, including—critically—the format in which critical business data is to be transmitted. The possible questions regarding business partners include the following (note that these questions form part of the Customer Relationship Management (CRM) module settings):

- ◆ Which business partner master data records do you want to keep?
  - Customer/vendor
  - Lead
  - Customers/supplier groups
  - Qualities Business Partners (region, etc.)
- ◆ Would you utilize stages in the sales process (for example, Lead, first meeting, second meeting, offer, meeting/sampling, order)?
- ◆ Would you like to track contact management information with customers and suppliers?
- ◆ Which contacts need to be made and are near closing (sales opportunity)?
- ◆ Would you like to perform an analyses per sales person (open or closed sales)?
- ◆ Would you want to analyze the sales pipeline?

The Inventory Component

After the questions to the business partners have been answered, the next concern should be to clarify how all of the items will be handled in a new inventory management system. The questions listed below hint at the extensive and varied methods of how article-specific master data can be tracked and recorded:

- ◆ Which items do you manage (purchase, sales, store)?
- ◆ Which sort of storage do you have (raw supplier, half and finished warehouse)?
- ◆ Are there item groups?
- ◆ Do you group by item qualities?

♦ Which items have different packing units between purchase and sale (for example, items bought in cartons and sold in pieces)? Please specify the item/item relations.

♦ Do modes of transport have to be taken into account? If yes, which ones?

♦ How are the price lists indicated?

♦ Do you accept special reduced prices and/or discounts? If yes, which ones?

♦ Are there price hierarchies (sliding prices)? If yes, what are they?

♦ Are there special feature transfers of the goods receipt, goods issue?

♦ Do inventories take place? If yes, how (ongoing, at the end of the year, and so on)?

♦ Are there customers/supplier catalogue numbers? If yes, in which area?

♦ Do you work with pre-orders? If yes, give examples.

♦ What must be taken into account for items not sold? For example, for lost or broken items?

The Production/Final Assembly Component

If your enterprise is not a purely commercial enterprise, you should answer some specific questions within the Production/Final Assembly module in order to simply the implementation of SAP Business One.

♦ Which kinds of bills of material (product structures) do you have?

♦ Do you work with production orders?

♦ What do the work schedules (production instructions) look like?

♦ How is the production feedback arranged?

♦ Who has access to the list of open production orders/instructions?

♦ How are issues regarding missing parts addressed? Is a production list of recommendations (list of orders) sufficient?

♦ How do reviews of the final assembly (bill of materials) take place?

Hardware and System Requirements for SAP Business One

Specific system requirements must be met for a successful SAP Business One implementation. These requirements are listed in Table 7.1.

Table 7.1 SAP Business One System Requirements

	Server	Workstation
Operating System:	Microsoft Windows 2000 Server/ Advanced Server	Microsoft Windows 2000 Professional
	Microsoft Windows 2003 Server Standard/Enterprise	Microsoft Windows XP SP1
Minimum CPU:	1× Intel Pentium III	1× Intel Pentium III
RAM Memory:	256 MB	128 MB
HD Free Space:	System partition: 500MB/Data partition: 2GB	500MB
CD-ROM drive:	24× or higher	24× or higher
Display:	640 × 480 with 256 colors or higher	800 × 600 with 256 colors or higher
Database:	Microsoft SQL Server 2000 SP3	Microsoft IE 6.0 SP1
Software:	Sybase Adaptive Server Enterprise 12.5.1 IBM DB2 Universal Database 8.1 SP3 Microsoft IE 6.0 SP1 Microsoft Data Access Components (MDAC) 2.6 / 2.8 for Windows 2003 Server	Microsoft Data Access Components 2.6 (MDAC) or higher
	For IBM DB2: Microsoft Visual C++ 6.0 – Windows 2000 Microsoft Visual C++ .NET – Windows 2003	
Recommended CPU:	3-20 Users: 1× Intel Pentium IV	1× Intel Pentium III
RAM Memory:	21-75 Users: 2× Intel Pentium IV	256 MB
HD Free Space:	75+ Users: 4× Intel Pentium IV	500MB
CD-ROM drive:	3-10 Users: 1024MB	24× or higher
Display:	More than 10 Users: 1024MB + 64MB × number of users above 10 System partition: 1GB/ Data partition: 5GB 24x or higher 640 × 480 with 256 colors or higher	1024 × 768 with 256 colors or higher Microsoft IE 6.0 SP1 Microsoft Data Access Components 2.6 (MDAC) or higher
Database:	Microsoft SQL Server 2000 SP3	
Software:	Sybase Adaptive Server Enterprise 12.5.1 IBM DB2 Universal Database 8.1 SP3 Microsoft IE 6.0 SP1 Microsoft Data Access Components (MDAC) 2.6 / 2.8 for Windows 2003 Server	
	For IBM DB2: Microsoft Visual C++ 6.0 – Windows 2000 Microsoft Visual C++ .NET – Windows 2003	

Data Migration (Data Import from Legacy Systems)

As an enterprise moves to a new ERP system, it will need to access and use data it has recorded with its previous software. It is, of course, critical that this legacy data not be lost during the implementation of the new system.

SAP Business One facilitates this data import/transfer via a special import interface. If the interface is used, you can be assured that all legacy data will be transferred to SAP Business One.

The following steps must taken to migrate data from legacy systems:

1. Specify the data transfer procedure in detail.
2. Accomplish/execute the manual data transfer.
3. Accomplish/execute tests.
4. Test and examine the data transfer plan.
5. Remove the test results.

NOTE

It is not mandatory that all data fields in SAP Business One be filled with legacy data in order to simply meet business partner requirements. Legacy data should be transferred in such a method as to work within the new system and to best facilitate new processes (as described in this chapter).

Different steps must be executed, depending on what data is exported from the legacy system. The master data of the individual business partners can be finalized at a later time, in conjunction with other data stored within Business One.

In order to avoid difficulties with the migration, you should ensure that the following data sets are properly exported:

- Chart of accounts
- Business partner
- Item management
- Production structure
- Journal entry

- ◆ Account statement
- ◆ Catalog number
- ◆ Special prices
- ◆ Opening warehouse stock
- ◆ Marketing and sales documents

The data sets that are to be migrated should be documented in the status report for the Business One implementation plan, so that said data can be reconstructed at any time. MS Excel data upload functions are used in conjunction with SAP Business One in order to complete this process.

 CAUTION

Note that to import data, no hyphens or minus signs can be used in the data fields of the customer code number, user number, and so on. If a space is required between two syllables, use an underscore. Data corruption within the SQL database can occur if hyphens or minus signs are used.

Another tip for easy data migration: If you want to use numbers and still want to be able to sort for reporting functions, then you should use leading zeros in the sorting. By doing so, you can avoid incorrectly recognized numbers. So if you choose to use three digit numbers, then use leading zeros for the numbers from 1 to 99 (for example, 7 would be listed as 007).

The following migration tools are available for use in the data transfer:

- ◆ Data migration services via the MS SQL Enterprise Manager (DTS)
- ◆ Uploads via MS Excel
- ◆ Uploads via an API interface

System Initialization

This section explains the fundamental and special settings of initial system initialization.

These initialization processes are of significant importance: You must ensure that the related initialization settings are carefully carried out from the beginning, as making changes later—that is, once the system is in production—can be complex and difficult.

Some corrections can be made by using the Annual Transfer function in SAP Business One. After this procedure has finished all changes (financial, purchasing, and sales documents) are removed from the system and the changes have to be applied again. If a lot of changes have already occurred and need to be entered again, it might not be worth the effort. After the Annual Transfer you have to reset the system date and year.

System Initialization: Chart of Accounts

The Chart of Accounts initialization is at the heart of Business One, as far as document bookings are concerned. It is essential that the initialization is well planned, as no changes are possible to the chart of accounts afterwards. A standard draft of accounts (in this example, SKR03) is acceptable. If the customer works with accounting via an external source (such as an accounting consultant), the selected chart of accounts must match with the external consultant's charts. The integrated DATEV interface to Business One facilitates simple and fast transfer of accounting data to your tax consultant.

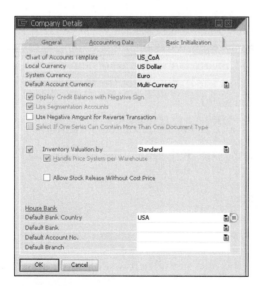

FIGURE 7.2 *Initialization of Chart of Accounts in SAP Business One*

System Initialization:
National Currency and System Currency

With the Currency settings, you can make clear whether you differentiate between national currency and system currency. These can be different if the company belongs to a larger operational organization and/or the system currency is defined, such as in $US. In this case, the reports and journals that are forwarded to the group would be issued in $US. The system then works in parallel to all accounting, according to the $US system currency as well as the national currency (such as EUR).

System Initialization:
Account Identification G/L Accounts

Probably the most important part of the system initialization is the account identification. It should be planned very carefully from the beginning, and executed with great care. As soon as the first bookings are processed on an account, the number of accounts for national debtors, foreign debtors, checks, cash, national creditors, and foreign creditors cannot be changed (although you can, at a later date, change the account name). If you don't define the continuous inventory valuation in the context of the base initialization, the register board stock level won't be at your disposal during the system initialization. (See Figure 7.3.)

The following listed accounts cannot be changed once you process the first booking:

- Turnover
- National and foreign debtors
- Check
- Bar
- Purchase
- Accounts payable inland/foreign country
- Stock
- Profit/loss account

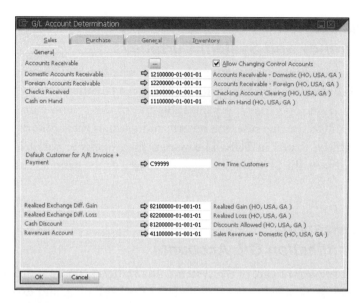

FIGURE 7.3 *Account Identification for General Ledgers "Debit" in SAP Business One*

System Initialization: Continuous Inventory Management

If the Continuous Inventory Management field is highlighted, then a permanent update takes place between stock value and the amount of stock. Then, the profit and/or loss account must be assigned in the account identification for general ledgers (see Figure 7.3). Furthermore, every stock account, an account for production costs, and a transfer account are assigned to the general ledger. (See Figure 7.4.)

System Initialization: Document Numbering

With document numbering, you assign a set of numbers to each document specific to the enterprise. You can create sub-serial numbers over the series field if your company has, for example, different divisions or subsidiary companies. In Figure 7.5, you can see that the Metal division is assigned with Series; General was assigned for the document input invoice. After the creation of the first document, the set of numbers that were created for the document cannot be deleted; instead, sets of numbers can be closed and a new set of numbers created.

G/L Account Determination

Sales | Purchase | General | Inventory

	Account Code	Account Name
Stock Account	13400000-01-001-01	Inventory - Finished Goods (HO, USA, GA
Cost Of Goods Sold	51100000-01-001-01	COGS - Domestic (HO, USA, GA)
Allocation Acc.	21400000-01-001-01	Purchases Clearing (HO, USA, GA)
Variance Acc.	52300000-01-001-01	Gain/Loss Inventory Variance (HO, USA, G
Price Difference Account	52400000-01-001-01	Gain/Loss Price Variance (HO, USA, GA)
Inventory Offset - Decrease	52300000-01-001-01	Gain/Loss Inventory Variance (HO, USA, G
Inventory Offset - Increase	52300000-01-001-01	Gain/Loss Inventory Variance (HO, USA, G
Sales Returns	51700000-01-001-01	AR Returning (HO, USA, GA)
Exchange Rate Differences Acc.	52500000-01-001-01	Inventory Exchange Rate Differences (HO,
Goods Clearing Acc.	52600000-01-001-01	Goods Clearing (HO, USA, GA)
Decrease GL Acc.		
Increase GL Acc.		
WIP Material Account		
WIP Material Variance Account		
Expenses Clearing Account		

OK Cancel

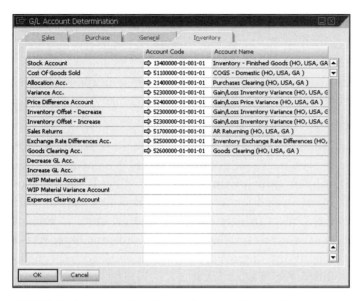

FIGURE 7.4 *Account identification for general ledgers "Inventory control" in SAP Business One*

Document Numbering

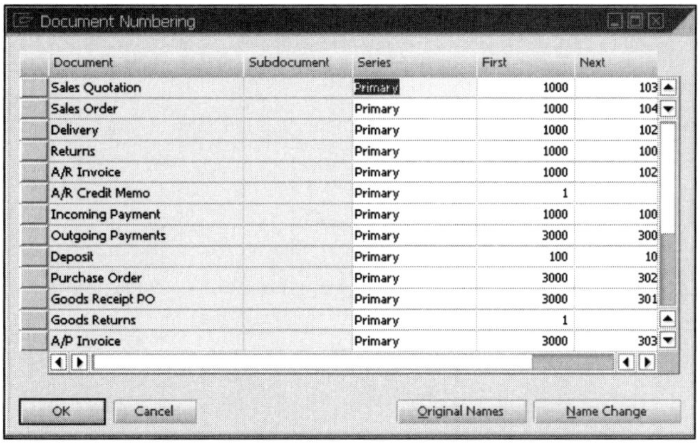

Document	Subdocument	Series	First	Next
Sales Quotation		Primary	1000	103
Sales Order		Primary	1000	104
Delivery		Primary	1000	102
Returns		Primary	1000	100
A/R Invoice		Primary	1000	102
A/R Credit Memo		Primary	1	
Incoming Payment		Primary	1000	100
Outgoing Payments		Primary	3000	300
Deposit		Primary	100	10
Purchase Order		Primary	3000	302
Goods Receipt PO		Primary	3000	301
Goods Returns		Primary	1	
A/P Invoice		Primary	3000	303

OK Cancel Original Names Name Change

FIGURE 7.5 *Receipt Numbering in SAP Business One*

System Initialization: Document Settings

For each document used in Business One, special settings can be carried out, depending on which document is selected under Per Document. These settings can also be modified later at any time. However, the modifications carried out in the settings affect only future documents. Existing documents are not affected by any setting changes.

One special issue to be aware of is how you can change the order of documents as they are listed in the system. If you decide to modify the document order, the Change of Existing Orders field is switched to Permitting: If you do allow this modification, then orders created for a customer can later be modified. Note that if Change of Existing Orders field is activated, and an order is subsequently placed, the activation cannot be cancelled. In other words, the order was created with the ability to modify the order—it can not be switched back so that the order cannot be modified. (See Figure 7.6.)

Another, part of the system initialization is the setting on which basis gross profit should be calculated. This setting is made in *General* register with the Gross Profit Calculation setting.

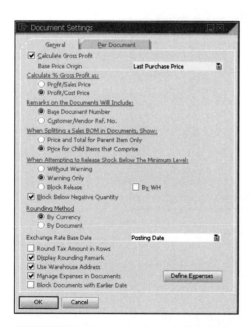

FIGURE 7.6 *Receipt Configurations in SAP Business One*

CAUTION

The settings for the sales or cost price can be modified. Modifying them, however, can have effects on the profit/loss report and result in the loss of data integrity within the system.

The Authorization Concept

SAP Business One's Authorization concept ensures that only selected users have authorization to read confidential information or execute transactions.

This authorization concept is carried out by the Authorizations function in the Administration menu. Using this function, SAP Business One directly defines the authorizations of users. Arbitrary graduations can be defined. For example, you can make one person a super user, having all authorizations, and another a user can be given restricted display and modification authorization. Yet another user may have no authorization at all. In addition, authorization for certain actions, such as changing prices, can be restricted so as to further limit user access to specified accounts.

User authorization can be individually assigned for individual functions. There are additional specific functions for accounting vouchers, such approving of a deviation/variation from the credit line. In short, all permitted actions can be specifically defined for an individual user.

In addition to the authorizations, approval procedures for the purchasing and sales transactions in the system can also be defined so that a user can override the standard permissions. For example, if a user is authorized to add an invoice even if it exceeds the customer's credit limit, then an additional release procedure can be activated whenever the credit limit is exceeded by a specific amount.

Before the allocation of authorizations, users must be defined in the system. When a user is defined in the system, a specific user type is also set. If the user is a super user, he or she automatically has full authorization for all functions in the system. Users who are not defined as super users cannot assign authorization to other users.

The Authorization Window

When the Authorization function is selected, the main Authorization window appears, as shown in Figure 7.7. All users of the system are listed on the left side frame of the window.

FIGURE 7.7 *Authorization Entries*

When a user is selected, the authorization defined to that user is displayed in the right column of the window; authorizations can be changed here. Authorizations can be assigned for entire applications or for individual sub-functions. Placing the cursor over the orange arrows allows you to view the sub-functions (where, in turn, you can define the associated authorizations for said sub-functions).

 NOTE

Authorizations for super users cannot be changed in this window.

The sub-functions can be made visible or can be hidden, respectively, with the Expand and Collapse buttons.

The following authorizations can be assigned for a user:

◆ **Full Authorization**. If this authorization is assigned, then the user has full view and modify rights to the program or function.

◆ **No Authorization**. If this authorization is assigned, the user does not possess any view and modify authorization in the program.

◆ **Read Only**. If this authorization is assigned, the user possesses only a view authorization in program or function, and cannot modify anything.

◆ **Different Authorizations**. If different authorizations are assigned to a user throughout the program, this option is specified automatically (it cannot be selected in the drop-down menu).

Individual Queries

The Query Wizard in SAP Business One allows for the creation of queries accessing a wide range of data, all of which is available in the system. With the Query Wizard, you can represent meaningful indicators and evaluations in a simple way according to your individual needs. The Query Wizard can be found in the Reporting application within the main navigation area.

When you start the Wizard, you navigate through several working windows in which you must define your query with system support. If you have defined a query with the Query Wizard, the results are graphically presented in a window;however, you can also view the results within the Query interface. You can also directly access the vouchers and master records found in the query. In addition, you can have your query results represented onscreen. (See Figure 7.8.)

Another way to create these individual queries, which are not in the base version of SAP Business One, is to create them yourself by using the *Queries Generator* function. This however requires some basic knowledge of the SQL language. The query can be created by using the available options in SAP Business One, such as selection of tables, fields, and variables or by direct input into the affected areas in the dialog window of the query interface.

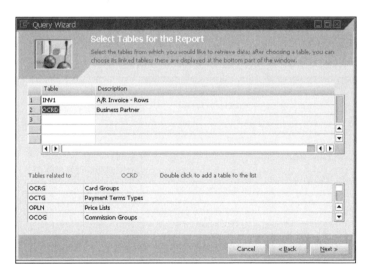

FIGURE 7.8 *Inquiry Assistant Display*

When you open the Query Wizard, a dialog window appears in which you specify the tables from which to base your queries. In addition, you have the following two options:

♦ Press and hold the Tab key while the cursor is on the marked field. A selection window with a list of all SAP Business One tables appears. Select a table on which you'd like to continue working by double-clicking on it. Contents of the marked table appear within the table range of the inquiry window. To select another table, click again on the header of the table range and press the Tab key

♦ Place the cursor in the title field of the table area and enter the desired table name, then press the Tab key. Repeat the process to select additional tables.

When you select a table, all fields contained in this table appear in the field area of the window. If the selected table contains fields that are linked with another table, these fields will be emphasized in bold. If you draw such a field into the table range, the table linked with it is added to the list of the selected tables. (See Figure 7.9.)

The right area of the main window contains the fields in which the corresponding field elements are displayed. The following options are available:

♦ **Select.** The table elements are registered, which are to be utilized in the query.

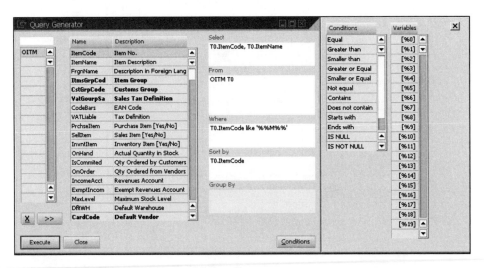

FIGURE 7.9 *Inquiry Entry Form with Details*

◆ **From.** This area contains the source table (with abbreviation) that is valid for further processing of the query. From this source table, the field elements are taken for result representation.

◆ **Where.** Within this area, certain selection criteria can be specified in order to receive a desired result.

With the Execute command, you start the SQL query. The result appears in a dialog window. All tables, fields, conditions, and other parameters that were selected in the window are displayed in the upper area of the window in SQL format. The lower area contains the results of the SQL query.

Consider the following example: The document number, the GP code, the complete document, and a 10 percent discount shall be queried for a document total price. (See Figure 7.10.) The following arithmetic expression is necessary to compute the answer:

```
T0.DocTotal-T0.DocTotal*10/100
```

The queries generated can now be saved in assorted categories and used in combination with user-defined fields to populate corresponding forms for particular SAP Business One functions.

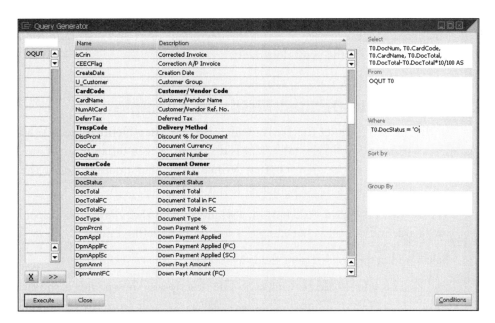

FIGURE 7.10 *Inquiry Creation: Example 1*

Appendix A, "Query Tables," includes all tables used in SAP business One that can be consulted for the generation of an query.

User-Defined Fields

Business One allows you to define additional fields in the system for the business management objects. These fields are available in addition to the standard fields and without limit to the number, which can be added to each function or object. You can store image files or links in the user-defined fields.

With these fields

◆ You can categorize customers and suppliers in different ways (this is in addition to the categorizations offered by the attributes of an object).

◆ You can show results from user-defined queries in the function fields.

◆ You can create links on customer or supplier web sites to access the particular web page directly from SAP Business One.

◆ You can display item images (in addition to the images which can be stored in the master record details area; the images which are stored in user-defined fields are shown on the screen right when the item is pulled up).

You can also include user fields in the document draft and distribute the values contained in it on the print document.

Creating a User-Defined Field: An Example

In the menu bar, under the Tools menu, open the User-Defined Fields – Manage User Fields option. In the table that is displayed, eleven different areas are listed, to which you can assign your user-defined fields. For example, select the Title entry under Marketing Documents. (See Figure 7.11.)

When you click on the Add button, a window opens that allows you to specify the various definitions and characteristics for the user-defined fields.

Select and complete different fields as follows:

1. The title should be *Customer*. The description shown later is the *Customer Group*. Choose *alphanumerical* as the type from the menu and set the structure to *regular*.

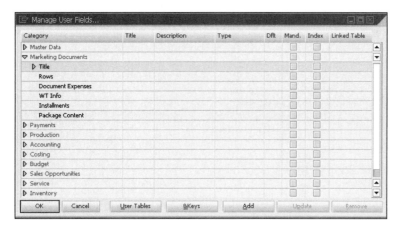

FIGURE 7.11 *Management of User-Definable Fields Table*

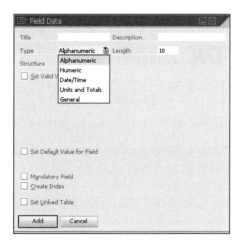

FIGURE 7.12 *User Definable Fields—Data*

2. Now you have to set the characteristic to allowed values to get the table (see Figure 7.13) displayed, which allows the entry of the values. At the same time the default values for the user-defined field are assigned. In our example this would be customers in Groups A and B.

3. At this point you can choose to make the field mandatory and to create an index for the field. Save the user-defined field with ADD.

4. After selecting the functions the fields are displayed to the right of the order window and can be activated at any time.

FIGURE 7.13 *Determine the Data Fields*

SAP Business One SDK 2004

Business One with SDK offers users the possibility of adapting their own needs and preferences to the standard functionality of SAP Business One. The SAP Business One SDK consists of two Application Programming Interfaces (APIs).

- ◆ **DI-API (Data-Interface Application Programming Interface).** The DI-API is a collection of COM objects (Component Object Model) called *business objects.* These objects describe various methods for updating, retrieving, and manipulating data in the SAP Business One database. For example, you can use the Data Interface API to connect an external data warehouse management system to Business One.

- ◆ **UI-API (User-Interface Application Programming Interface).** The UI-API is a collection of DCOM objects that provide access to forms, controls within these forms, and menus. DCOM (Distributed Component Object Model) is a standard interface for object communication in distributed applications. You can use the User Interface API to integrate customer-specific programming or third-party products into SAP Business One. In addition, helpful tools and important documentation (such as the *Standards and Guidelines* document) are included with the Business One SDK.

SAP Business One is implemented as a two-layer, client/server architecture. The client software consists of a graphical user interface and business object classes that connect to the database. The SDK business objects (DI-API) connect to the database directly using the ODBC-protocol. They do not communicate with any of the SAP Business One client components.

The server software consists of a fax, mailing, and dialing service, as well as the database itself.

A modified Business One installation is called *Partner Package*. Such a package consists of two components: the standard SAP Business One installation and the add-on program, which must be equipped with a suitable installation routine as well as suitable user documentation. The partner is responsible for the upgrade consistency of the add-on components delivered to the customer. The SAP Business One runtime SDK is part of the standard SAP Business One installation.

In general, modifications to standard SAP Business One objects are not allowed. However, each object has specific attributes that can be modified to some degree via the user-defined fields (UserFields) with which most customer requirements for adjustments can be realized.

There are two types of SAP Business One SDK object:

♦ **Business objects**. These grant access to different business data.
♦ **Raw data access objects**. These can be used to access data on a generic level.

Authorization checks are done for all SAP Business One business objects. If a user does not have permission to view objects in SAP Business One, he or she will not have permission to access the data belonging to the business objects using the Data Interface API. For example, the Items object has the same authorization as the material master data form in SAP Business One. (See Figure 7.15.)

With DI-API, you can access additional database tables, user-defined database tables, and user-defined fields.

If you create additional database tables, follow the naming conventions. There is no tool support for creating new database tables. Additional database tables are not visible within the SAP Business One data dictionary. The standard business objects in the Data Interface API cannot access additional database tables. If you need to access additional database tables, use the RecordSet object instead.

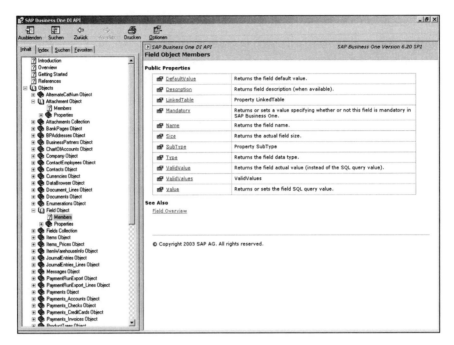

FIGURE 7.15 *SDK development platform*

User-defined database tables can be created and maintained differently from the additional tables directly in SAP Business One. User-defined database tables are also visible in the SAP Business One data dictionary. The advantage of user-defined tables is that they are fully integrated into SAP Business One. For this reason, you should use user-defined tables instead of solution-specific database tables.

You can use user-defined fields to expand the SAP Business One data model without defining new database tables. As user-defined fields can be accessed by standard business objects in the data interface API, you should create user-defined fields instead of new database tables. It is not possible to deliver user-defined fields automatically to the customer site in the current version of SAP Business One. You must create user-defined fields manually on the customer's system. You can create user-defined fields using the Data Interface API or using the BC Sets add-on.

Application of Data Interface API

If you implement an external client application with the help of the DI API, then there are different databases that must be considered during the implementation.

The Company object represents a company database for Business One and is the highest object in the object hierarchy. This means that the Company object controls access to SAP Business One and logon takes place using this object. The Company object is an instance of the class SAPbobsCOM.Company. The client program has created a Company object with which to log on to SAP Business One for the first time. You must then set the following Company object properties (connection parameters): Server, Username, Password, language, and CompanyDB. Set the Server property to the name of the MS SQL database server. Set the CompanyDB property to the name of the company you want to work with. The UserName, Password, and language properties must contain the name of the SAP Business One user, the user's password, and the language in order for the session to be opened.

Logical constants exist to specify the logon language. They are members of the BoSuppLangs enumeration and are described in the language property documentation for the Company object. To connect to the company database, you call the Company object Connect() method.

```
Public XYZ_Company as SAPbobsCOM.Company
Set XYZ_Company = New SAPbobsCOM.Company ( )
XYZ_Company.Server = "local" 'Name of the MS SQL DB Server
XYZ_Company.CompanyDB = "My_Company" Enter the name of your company
XYZ_Company.UserName = "Manager"
XYZ_Company.Password = "Manager"
XYZ_Company.language = SAPbobsCOM.ln_English
XYZ_Company.conncet ()
```

Once you've established a connection to a Business One Company database, you can access the data using the business objects contained within the SAPBobsCOM component. To create a business object and to get a reference to it, you use one of the Company object methods GetBusinessObject (object as SAPBobsCOM.BoObjectTypes) or GetBusinessObjectFromXML (filename as string, index as long).

```
WorkOrders lWorkOrders;
lWorkOrders =(WorkOrders)XYZ_Company.GetBusinessObject
(SAPbobsCOM.BoObjectTypes.oWorkOrders);
```

GetBusinessObject always creates a new, empty business object. Before any business data can be retrieved or manipulated using this object, you need to set appropriate object properties. You must set the parameter objtype to the type of business object to be created (for the values defined, see the documentation; they are defined as members of the enumeration SAPBobsCOM.BoObjectTypes).

In contrast, GetBusinessObjectFromXML creates a new business object with predefined properties from the contents of an XML file. The document structure of the file must be the same as for the concrete business object saved using the SaveXML method. Business objects have methods for creating (Add), changing (Update), deleting (Remove), and reading a data object of this kind (GetByKey).

When a data operation is performed on a business object, a transaction is started. If the operation is successful, then a commit is issued and the data is saved. If the operation fails, then a rollback is issued and the data is discarded. This kind of transaction handling is sufficient as long as only one business object is being modified.

If you want to perform a consistent transaction that contains changes to more than one business object, you must specify the start and end of the transaction using the company object methods StartTransaction() and EndTransaction (endType as SAPBobsCom.BoWfTransOpt). Use this start transaction method to start a "global" transaction that can contain multiple changes to several business objects. When you call StartTransaction, all business object changes that are issued after this call and before a following call to the method EndTransaction belong to one logical unit of work. If one of the business-object changes fails during any process, the transaction ends and a rollback is issued. If the changes are successful, you *must* use EndTransaction to run the commit in order to de-queue the locked records and to allow other users to access them. Use this end transaction method to mark the end of a global transaction opened by StartTransaction. You must pass a parameter to EndTransaction to indicate whether the changes contained within this transaction are to be committed or rolled back.

SAP Business One allows you to define additional fields, such as user-defined fields, for the business data categories. You can access the contents of user-defined fields using the UserFields object. This object is read-only, and contains a reference to a UserFields object that grants access to the contents of the user-defined fields for that business object.

Application of User Interface API

The Application instance represents the surface of the SAP Business One application. Use the Application instance for its containers (menus and forms), event manipulation, and property settings. In order to connect to COM UI, you must supply a connection string to the add-on. The connection string provides the add-on with essential information.

```
Dim oSboGuiApi As New SAPbouiCOM.SboGuiApi
Dim oApp As New SAPbouiCOM.Application
Dim sConnectionString As String
#If Release = True Then
SConnectionString = Split (Command)(0)
#Else
SConnectionString = "String supplied from SAP"
#End If
```

The Form object represents a form window in SAP Business One. It is uniquely identified by its InstId field (form pointer address in the application in current life cycle). The Form object holds all data of the referenced form that is open to manipulations through the API (except the identifier). The Business One SDK UI API Item object represents an item in Business One forms. It is uniquely identified by its item number and holds all data of the referenced form (except for the identifier and type).

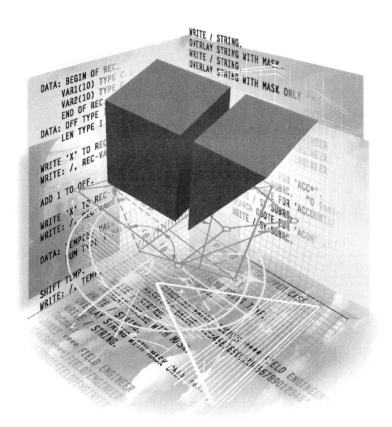

Appendix A

Query Tables

Following are listed all tables used in SAP business One that can be consulted for the generation of a query.

Object	Name	Object	Name
AACT	G/L Account - History	TNN1	1099 Boxes
ACH1	Checks for Payment - Rows - History	OTNN	1099 Forms
ACHO	Checks for Payment - History	OTOB	1099 Opening Balance
ACPR	Contact Persons	E874	835874 Report - Final Record
ACR1	Business Partners - Addresses - History	R874	835874 Report - Import Log Record
ACR3	BP Control Account - History	I874	835874 Report - Invoices Record
ACR4	Allowed WT Codes for BP	H874	835874 Report - Opening Record
ACRB	Business Partner - Bank Accounts	K874	835874 Report - Petty Cash/VAR
ACRD	Business Partner - History	F874	835874 Report - Selection Criteria
ADM1	Administration Extension	L856	856 Report - Record 60
ADO1	A/R Invoice (Rows) - History	FLT1	856 Report - Selection Criteria
ADO2	A/R Invoice (Rows) - Expenses - History	H856	857 Report - Record 70
ADO3	A/R Invoice - Expenses - History	CPI3	A/P Correction Invoice - Expenses
ADO4	Document Tax Info. - History	CPI1	A/P Correction Invoice - Rows
ADO5	Withholding Tax Data	CPI2	A/P Correction Invoice Rows - Expenses
ADO6	Documents History - Installments	ORPC	A/P Credit Memo
ADO7	Delivery Packages	RPC9	A/P Credit Memo - Base Docs Details
ADO8	Items in Package	RPC4	A/P Credit Memo - Document Tax Info.
ADO9	A/R Invoice (Rows) - History	RPC3	A/P Credit Memo - Expenses
ADOC	Invoice - History	RPC6	A/P Credit Memo - Installments
ADP1	Object Settings - History	RPC10	A/P Credit Memo - Row Structure
AINS	Install Base - History	RPC1	A/P Credit Memo - Rows
AIT1	Item - Prices - History	RPC2	A/P Credit Memo Rows - Expenses
AITB	Item Groups - History	OPCH	A/P Invoice
AITM	Items - History	PCH9	A/P Invoice - Base Docs Details
AITT	Product Tree - History	PCH4	A/P Invoice - Document Tax Info.
AITW	Items - Warehouse - History	PCH3	A/P Invoice - Expenses
AIWZ	Summary Wizard	PCH6	A/P Invoice - Installments

Object	Name	Object	Name
AJD1	Journal Transactions - Rows - History	PCH1	A/P Invoice - Rows
AJDT	Journal Entry - History	OCSI	A/R Correction Invoice
ALR1	Queue of messages to be sent	CSI2	A/R Correction Invoice - Expenses
ALT1	Alerts - Users	ORIN	A/R Credit Memo
AMR1	AMR1	RIN9	A/R Credit Memo - Base Docs Details
AMRV	AMRV	RIN4	A/R Credit Memo - Document Tax Info.
AOB1	Sent Messages - User History	RIN3	A/R Credit Memo - Expenses
ARC1	Incoming Payment - Checks - History	RIN6	A/R Credit Memo - Installments
ARC2	Incoming Payment - Invoices - History		RIN10 A/R Credit Memo - Row Structure
ARC3	Credit Vouchers History	RIN1	A/R Credit Memo - Rows
ARC4	Incoming Payment - Account List - History	RIN2	A/R Credit Memo Rows - Expenses
ARC6	Payments - WT Rows	INV9	A/R Invoice - Base Documents
ARC7	Payments - Document Tax Info.	INV4	A/R Invoice - Document Tax Info.
ARCT	Incoming Payment - History	INV3	A/R Invoice - Expenses
ARI1	User Add-on Table	ADO3	A/R Invoice - Expenses - History
ASC1	Service Call Solutions - History	INV6	A/R Invoice - Installments
ASC2	Service Call Inventory Expenses - History	ADO10	A/R Invoice - Row structure
ASC3	Service Call Travel/Labor Expenses - History	INV10	A/R Invoice - Row structure
ASC4	Service Call Travel/Labor Expenses - History	PCH10	A/R Invoice - Row structure
ASC5	Service Call Activities	INV1	A/R Invoice - Rows
ASCL	History	ADO2	A/R Invoice (Rows) - Expenses - History
ATT1	Bill of Materials - Child Items	ADO1	A/R Invoice (Rows) - History
ATX1	ATX1	ADO9	A/R Invoice (Rows) - History
ATXI	ATXI	INV2	A/R Invoice Rows - Expenses
AUSR	Archive Users - History	HEM1	Absence Info
AWHS	Warehouses - History	OASG	Account Segmentation
BGT1	Budget - Rows	OASC	Account Segmentation Categories
BOE1	Bill of Exchange for Payment - Rows	IWZ1	Accounts Revaluation History
BOT1	Bill of Exchange Transactions	OCLG	Activities
BOX1	Box Definition - Rows	OCLA	Activity Status
BTF1	Open Journal Voucher Pool	OCLS	Activity Subjects
CCPD	Period-End Closing	OCLT	Activity Types
CCRC	Create New Company	OARI	Add-on - Company definitions
CDC1	Confirmation Level - Row	OADM	Administration
CDRO	Drag & Relate - Output Fields	ADM1	Administration Extension
CDRU	Drag & Relate User Settings	OMRL	Advanced Inventory Revaluation

Object	Name	Object	Name
CFH1	Desc CFH1	OAGP	Agent Name
CHD1	Check for Payment Draft - Rows	OALR	Alerts
CHEN	Caching Update Notification	ALT1	Alerts - Users
CHFL	Choose From List Format	OALT	Alerts Template
CHO1	Checks for Payment - Rows	ACR4	Allowed WT Codes for BP
CIN1	Correction Invoice - Rows	CRD4	Allowed WT Codes for BP
CIN2	Correction Invoice Rows - Expenses	ORFL	Already displayed 347, 349 and WT reports
CIN3	Correction Invoice - Expenses	OALI	Alternative Items 2
CIN4	Correction Invoice - Document Tax Info.	AMR1	AMR1
CIN5	Withholding Tax Data	AMRV	AMRV
CIN6	Correction Invoice - Installments	SPRG	Application Start
CIN7	Delivery Packages	WTM5	Approval Templates - Queries
CIN8	Items in Package	AUSR	Archive Users - History
CIN9	Correction Invoice - Rows	ATX1	ATX1
CINF	Company Info	ATXI	ATXI
CLND	Journal Settings	OPRM	Authorization Tree
CLNU	Display Definitions - Journal	OUHD	Authorization Tree
CPI1	A/P Correction Invoice - Rows	DSC1	Bank Branches
CPI2	A/P Correction Invoice Rows - Expenses	ODSC	Bank Codes
CPI3	A/P Correction Invoice - Expenses	OIBT	Batch No. for Item
CPI4	Correction Document Tax Info	IBT1	Batch Number Transactions
CPI5	Withholding Tax Data	OSRD	Batches and Serial Numbers
CPI6	Documents History - Installments	OIBW	Batches in Warehouses
CPRF	Column Preferences	OBOE	Bill of Exchange for Payment
CPV1	Correction A/P Invoice Reversal - Rows	BOE1	Bill of Exchange for Payment - Rows
CPV2	Correction A/P Invoice Reversal - Expenses	BOT1	Bill of Exchange Transactions
CPV3	Correction A/P Invoice Reversal - Expenses	ATT1	Bill of Materials - Child Items
CPV4	Document Tax Info	ITT1	Bill of Materials - Child Items
CPV5	Withholding Tax Data	OBOX	Box Definition
CPV6	Documents History - Installments	BOX1	Box Definition - Rows
CRD1	Business Partners - Addresses	CRD3	BP Control Account
CRD3	BP Control Account	ACR3	BP Control Account - History
CRD4	Allowed WT Codes for BP	OBPP	BP Priorities
CRD6	Desc CRD6	OUBR	Branches
CSHS	Search Function	OBGT	Budget
CSI1	Correction A/R Invoice Reversal - Rows	BGT1	Budget - Rows

Object	Name	Object	Name
CSI2	A/R Correction Invoice - Expenses	OBGD	Budget Cost Assess. Mthd
CSI3	Correction A/R Invoice - Expenses	OBGS	Budget Scenario
CSI4	Document Tax Info	OCRD	Business Partner
CSI5	Withholding Tax Data	ACRB	Business Partner - Bank Accounts
CSI6	Documents History - Installments	OCRB	Business Partner - Bank Accounts
CSTN	Workstation ID	ACRD	Business Partner - History
CSV1	Correction A/R Invoice Reversal - Rows	CRD1	Business Partners - Addresses
CSV2	Correction A/R Invoice Reversal - Expenses	ACR1	Business Partners - Addresses - History
CSV3	Correction A/R Invoice Reversal - Expenses	CHEN	Caching Update Notification
CSV4	Document Tax Info	OCRG	Card Groups
CSV5	Withholding Tax Data	OCQG	Card Properties
CSV6	Documents History - Installments	OCFL	Cash Flow Additional Trans.
CTBR	Toolbars	OCFW	Cash Flow Line Item
CTG1	Installment Layout	OCBI	Central Bank Ind.
CTR1	Service Contract - Items	OCHO	Check for Payment
CUDC	User Display Cat.	OCHD	Check for Payment Draft
CUFD	User Fields - Descr.	CHD1	Check for Payment Draft - Rows
CULG	Company Upgrade Log	ACHO	Checks for Payment - History
CUMF	Folder	CHO1	Checks for Payment - Rows
CUMI	User Menu Items	ACH1	Checks for Payment - Rows - History
CUPC	Upgrade Control	OCHH	Checks Fund
CUVV	User Validations	OCRH	Checks Fund
DDT1	W/holding Tax Ded. - Hierarchy	CHFL	Choose From List Format
DLN1	Delivery - Rows	CPRF	Column Preferences
DLN2	Delivery Note Rows - Expenses	OCOG	Commission Groups
DLN3	Delivery Note - Expenses	CINF	Company Info
DLN4	Delivery - Document Tax Info.	CULG	Company Upgrade Log
DLN5	Withholding Tax Data	OCMT	Competitors
DLN6	Delivery - Installments	OWST	Confirmation Level
DLN7	Delivery Packages	CDC1	Confirmation Level - Row
DLN8	Items in Package	WST1	Confirmation Level - Rows
DLN9	Delivery - Base documents	OWTM	Confirmation Templates
DMW1	Query List	WTM3	Confirmation Templates - Documents
DPI1	Down Payment In - Rows	WTM1	Confirmation Templates - Producers
DPI2	Down Payment In - Expenses	WTM2	Confirmation Templates - Stages
DPI3	Down Payment In - Expenses	WTM4	Confirmation Templates - Terms

Object	Name	Object	Name
DPI4	Down Payment In - Document Tax Info.	ACPR	Contact Persons
DPI5	Withholding Tax Data	OCPR	Contact Persons
DPI6	Down Payment In - Installments	OCTT	Contract Template
DPI7	Delivery Packages	OCPI	Correction A/P Invoice
DPI8	Items in Package	OCPV	Correction A/P Invoice Reversal
DPI9	Down Payment In - Base Docs Details	CPV2	Correction A/P Invoice Reversal - Expenses
DPO1	Down Payment Out - Rows	CPV3	Correction A/P Invoice Reversal - Expenses
DPO2	Down Payment Out - Expenses	CPV1	Correction A/P Invoice Reversal - Rows
DPO3	Down Payment Out - Expenses	PCH2	Correction A/P Invoice Reversal - Rows - Expenses
DPO4	Down Payment Out - Document Tax Info.	CSI3	Correction A/R Invoice - Expenses
DPO5	Withholding Tax Data	OCSV	Correction A/R Invoice Reversal
DPO6	Down Payment Out - Installments	CSV2	Correction A/R Invoice Reversal - Expenses
DPO7	Delivery Packages	CSV3	Correction A/R Invoice Reversal - Expenses
DPO8	Items in Package	CSI1	Correction A/R Invoice Reversal - Rows
DPO9	Down Payment Out - Base Docs Details	CSV1	Correction A/R Invoice Reversal - Rows
DPS1	Deposit - Rows	CPI4	Correction Document Tax Info
DRF1	Draft - Rows	OCIN	Correction Invoice
DRF2	Draft Rows - Expenses	CIN4	Correction Invoice - Document Tax Info.
DRF3	Draft - Expenses	CIN3	Correction Invoice - Expenses
DRF4	Draft - Document Tax Info.	CIN6	Correction Invoice - Installments
DRF5	Withholding Tax Data	CIN1	Correction Invoice - Rows
DRF6	Document Drafts - Installments	CIN9	Correction Invoice - Rows
DRF7	Delivery Packages	CIN10	Correction Invoice - Rows structure
DRF8	Items in Package	CIN2	Correction Invoice Rows - Expenses
DRF9	Document Drafts - Base Docs Details	OCRY	Countries
DSC1	Bank Branches	ORTT	CPI and FC Rates
DWZ1	Dunning Wizard Array1 - BP Filter	OIDX	CPI Codes
E874	835874 Report - Final Record	CCRC	Create New Company
ENT1	Entry - Lines	OCRC	Credit Cards
F874	835874 Report - Selection Criteria	OCRV	Credit Payments
FCT1	Sales Forecast - Rows	PDF3	Credit Vouchers
FLT1	856 Report - Selection Criteria	RCT3	Credit Vouchers
FRC1	Extend Cat. f. Financial Rep.	VPM3	Credit Vouchers
H856	857 Report - Record 70	ARC3	Credit Vouchers History
H874	835874 Report - Opening Record	OCRN	Currency Codes

Object	Name	Object	Name
HEM1	Absence Info	PYM1	Currency Restriction
HEM2	Education	OINS	Customer Equipment Card
HEM3	Reviews	OSCN	Customer/Vendor Cat. No.
HEM4	Previous Employment	OARG	Customs Groups
HEM5	Employee Data Ownership Authorization	OCYC	Cycle
HEM6	Employee Roles	ODMW	Data Migration
HLD1	Holiday Dates	ODOX	Data Ownership - Exceptions
HTM1	Team Members	ODOW	Data Ownership - Objects
I874	835874 Report - Invoices Record	UDG2	Defaults - Credit Cards
IBT1	Batch Number Transactions	UDG1	Defaults - Documents
IGE1	Goods Issue - Rows	OOFR	Defect Cause
IGE2	Goods Issue Rows - Expenses	OEXD	Define Expenses
IGE3	Goods Issue - Expenses	OCDC	Define OCDC
IGE4	Goods Issue - Document Tax Info.	ODLN	Delivery
IGE5	Withholding Tax Data	DLN9	Delivery - Base documents
IGE6	Goods Issue - Installments	DLN4	Delivery - Document Tax Info.
IGE7	Delivery Packages	DLN6	Delivery - Installments
IGE8	Items in Package	DLN1	Delivery - Rows
IGE9	Goods Issue - Base Docs Details	DLN10	Delivery - Rows structure
IGN1	Goods Receipt - Rows	DLN3	Delivery Note - Expenses
IGN2	Goods Receipt Rows - Expenses	DLN2	Delivery Note Rows - Expenses
IGN3	Goods Receipt - Expenses	ADO7	Delivery Packages
IGN4	Goods Receipt - Document Tax Info.	CIN7	Delivery Packages
IGN5	Withholding Tax Data	DLN7	Delivery Packages
IGN6	Goods Receipt- Installments	DPI7	Delivery Packages
IGN7	Delivery Packages	DPO7	Delivery Packages
IGN8	Items in Package	DRF7	Delivery Packages
IGN9	Goods Receipt - Base Docs Details	IGE7	Delivery Packages
INV1	A/R Invoice - Rows	IGN7	Delivery Packages
INV2	A/R Invoice Rows - Expenses	INV7	Delivery Packages
INV3	A/R Invoice - Expenses	PCH7	Delivery Packages
INV4	A/R Invoice - Document Tax Info.	PDN7	Delivery Packages
INV5	Withholding Tax Data	POR7	Delivery Packages
INV6	A/R Invoice - Installments	QUT7	Delivery Packages
INV7	Delivery Packages	RDN7	Delivery Packages
INV8	Items in Package	RDR7	Delivery Packages

Object	Name	Object	Name
INV9	A/R Invoice - Base Documents	RIN7	Delivery Packages
IPF1	Landed Costs - Rows	RPC7	Delivery Packages
IPF2	Landed Costs - Costs	RPD7	Delivery Packages
ITM1	Items - Prices	WTR7	Delivery Packages
ITT1	Bill of Materials - Child Items	OSHP	Delivery Types
ITW1	Item Count Alert	OUDP	Departments
IWZ1	Accounts Revaluation History	ODPS	Deposit
IWZ2	Inflation Warehouse Filter	DPS1	Deposit - Rows
IWZ3	Items Last Revaluation Data	CFH1	Desc CFH1
JDT1	Journal Transaction - Rows	CRD6	Desc Crd6
K874	835874 Report - Petty Cash/VAR	OBCG	Desc OBCG
L856	856 Report - Record 60	OBPL	Desc OBPL
LOGN	System Login	CLNU	Display Definitions - Journal
MLS1	Distribution Lists - Recipients	OMLS	Distribution List
MRV1	Material Revaluation Information Array	MLS1	Distribution Lists - Recipients
MSN1	MRP Scenario Whs Array	OWDD	Docs. for Confirmation
MSN2	MRP Run Results	RDOC	Document
MSN3	MRP Pegging Information	DRF9	Document Drafts - Base Docs Details
NNM1	Documents Numbering - Series	DRF6	Document Drafts - Installments
NNM2	Series Default	ONNM	Document Numbering
OACT	G/L Accounts	RDFL	Document Standards
OADM	Administration	CPV4	Document Tax Info
OADP	Print Preferences	CSI4	Document Tax Info
OAGP	Agent Name	CSV4	Document Tax Info
OAIB	Received Alerts	ADO4	Document Tax Info. - History
OALC	Loading Expenses	RTYP	Document Type List
OALI	Alternative Items 2	WDD1	Documents for Approval - Authorizers
OALR	Alerts	WDD2	Documents for Approval - Terms
OALT	Alerts Template	ADO6	Documents History - Installments
OAOB	Message Sent	CPI6	Documents History - Installments
OARG	Customs Groups	CPV6	Documents History - Installments
OARI	Add-on - Company definitions	CSI6	Documents History - Installments
OASC	Account Segmentation Categories	CSV6	Documents History - Installments
OASG	Account Segmentation	NNM1	Documents Numbering - Series
OBCG	Desc OBCG	ODOR	Doubtful Debts
OBGD	Budget Cost Assess. Mthd	ODPI	Down Payment In

Object	Name	Object	Name
OBGS	Budget Scenario	DPI9	Down Payment In - Base Docs Details
OBGT	Budget	DPI4	Down Payment In - Document Tax Info.
OBNK	External Bank Statement Received	DPI2	Down Payment In - Expenses
OBOE	Bill of Exchange for Payment	DPI3	Down Payment In - Expenses
OBOX	Box Definition	DPI6	Down Payment In - Installments
OBPL	Desc OBPL	DPI1	Down Payment In - Rows
OBPP	BP Priorities	DPI10	Down Payment In - Rows structure
OBTD	Journal Vouchers List	ODPO	Down Payment Out
OBTF	Journal Voucher	DPO9	Down Payment Out - Base Docs Details
OCBI	Central Bank Ind.	DPO4	Down Payment Out - Document Tax Info.
OCCD	OCCD	DPO2	Down Payment Out - Expenses
OCDC	Define OCDC	DPO3	Down Payment Out - Expenses
OCDT	Due Dates	DPO6	Down Payment Out - Installments
OCFH	OCFH	DPO1	Down Payment Out - Rows
OCFL	Cash Flow Additional Trans.	DPO10	Down Payment Out - Rows structure
OCFT	OCFT	DRF4	Draft - Document Tax Info.
OCFW	Cash Flow Line Item	DRF3	Draft - Expenses
OCHD	Check for Payment Draft	DRF1	Draft - Rows
OCHH	Checks Fund	DRF10	Draft - Rows structure
OCHO	Check for Payment	DRF2	Draft Rows - Expenses
OCIN	Correction Invoice	ODRF	Drafts
OCLA	Activity Status	CDRO	Drag & Relate - Output Fields
OCLG	Activities	CDRU	Drag & Relate User Settings
OCLO	Meetings Location	OCDT	Due Dates
OCLS	Activity Subjects	ORIT	Dunning Interest Rate
OCLT	Activity Types	ODUN	Dunning Letters
OCMT	Competitors	ODUT	Dunning Terms
OCOG	Commission Groups	ODWZ	Dunning Wizard
OCPI	Correction A/P Invoice	DWZ1	Dunning Wizard Array1 - BP Filter
OCPR	Contact Persons	SDEX	Dynamic Extensions
OCPV	Correction A/P Invoice Reversal	SDIS	Dynamic Interface (Strings)
OCQG	Card Properties	HEM2	Education
OCR1	Profit Center - Load Factor	OHED	Education Types
OCRB	Business Partner - Bank Accounts	HEM5	Employee Data Ownership Authorization
OCRC	Credit Cards	OHPS	Employee Position
OCRD	Business Partner	HEM6	Employee Roles

Object	Name	Object	Name
OCRG	Card Groups	OHST	Employee Status
OCRH	Checks Fund	OHTM	Employee Teams
OCRN	Currency Codes	OHTY	Employee Types
OCRP	Payment Methods	OHEM	Employees
OCRV	Credit Payments	OEOY	End-of-Year Transfer
OCRY	Countries	ENT1	Entry - Lines
OCSI	A/R Correction Invoice	SCL4	Expense Documents
OCST	States	FRC1	Extend Cat. f. Financial Rep.
OCSV	Correction A/R Invoice Reversal	UPT1	Extend User Perm. Tree
OCTG	Payment Terms Types	OBNK	External Bank Statement Received
OCTR	Service Contracts	OFRM	File Format
OCTT	Contract Template	OFRC	Financial Report Categories
OCYC	Cycle	OFRT	Financial Report Templates
ODDG	W/holding Tax Ded. - Groups	CUMF	Folder
ODDT	W/holding Tax Ded. - Hierarchy	PSAR	Frame for Sales Analysis Report
ODLN	Delivery	AACT	G/L Account - History
ODMW	Data Migration	OACT	G/L Accounts
ODOR	Doubtful Debts	OIGE	Goods Issue
ODOW	Data Ownership - Objects	IGE9	Goods Issue - Base Docs Details
ODOX	Data Ownership - Exceptions	IGE4	Goods Issue - Document Tax Info.
ODPI	Down Payment In	IGE3	Goods Issue - Expenses
ODPO	Down Payment Out	IGE6	Goods Issue - Installments
ODPS	Deposit	IGE10	Goods Issue - Row structure
ODPT	Postdated Deposit	IGE1	Goods Issue - Rows
ODRF	Drafts	IGE2	Goods Issue Rows - Expenses
ODSC	Bank Codes	OIGN	Goods Receipt
ODUN	Dunning Letters	IGN9	Goods Receipt - Base Docs Details
ODUT	Dunning Terms	IGN4	Goods Receipt - Document Tax Info.
ODWZ	Dunning Wizard	IGN3	Goods Receipt - Expenses
OENC	OENC	IGN10	Goods Receipt - Row structure
OENT	Shipping Types	IGN1	Goods Receipt - Rows
OEOY	End-of-Year Transfer	IGN6	Goods Receipt- Installments
OEXD	Define Expenses	OPDN	Goods Receipt PO
OFCT	Sales Forecast	PDN9	Goods Receipt PO - Base Docs Details
OFLT	Report - Selection Criteria	PDN4	Goods Receipt PO - Document Tax Info.
OFPR	Posting Period	PDN3	Goods Receipt PO - Expenses

Object	Name	Object	Name
OFRC	Financial Report Categories	PDN6	Goods Receipt PO - Installments
OFRM	File Format	PDN1	Goods Receipt PO - Row
OFRT	Financial Report Templates	PDN10	Goods Receipt PO - Row Structure
OGSP	Goods Shipment	PDN2	Goods Receipt PO Rows - Expenses
OHED	Education Types	IGN2	Goods Receipt Rows - Expenses
OHEM	Employees	RPD4	Goods Return - Document Tax Info.
OHLD	Holiday Table	RPD3	Goods Return - Expenses
OHPS	Employee Position	RPD2	Goods Return Rows - Expenses
OHST	Employee Status	ORPD	Goods Returns
OHTM	Employee Teams	RPD9	Goods Returns - Base Docs Details
OHTR	Termination Reason	RPD6	Goods Returns - Installments
OHTY	Employee Types	RPD10	Goods Returns - Row Structure
OIBT	Batch No. for Item	RPD1	Goods Returns - Rows
OIBW	Batches in Warehouses	OGSP	Goods Shipment
OIDC	Indicator	ASCL	History
OIDX	CPI Codes	HLD1	Holiday Dates
OIGE	Goods Issue	OHLD	Holiday Table
OIGN	Goods Receipt	ARC4	Incoming Payment - Account List - History
OIND	Triangular Deal	ARC1	Incoming Payment - Checks - History
OINM	WH Journal	RCC4	Incoming Payment - Credit Vouchers
OINS	Customer Equipment Card	ARCT	Incoming Payment - History
OINV	Invoice	ARC2	Incoming Payment - Invoices - History
OIPF	Landed Costs	OIDC	Indicator
OIRT	Interest Prices	OOND	Industries
OISR	Service Calls	IWZ2	Inflation Warehouse Filter
OITB	Item Groups	OIWZ	Inflation Wizard
OITG	Item Properties	OOSR	Information Source
OITM	Items	AINS	Install Base - History
OITT	Product Tree	CTG1	Installment Layout
OITW	Items - Warehouse	OOIN	Interest
OIWZ	Inflation Wizard	OOIR	Interest Level
OJDT	Journal Posting	OIRT	Interest Prices
OJPE	OJPE	RIT1	Interest Rates
OLCT	Location	OMRV	Inventory Revaluation
OLGT	Length Units	OINV	Invoice
OMLS	Distribution List	ADOC	Invoice - History

Object	Name	Object	Name
OMRC	Manufacturers	AIT1	Item - Prices - History
OMRL	Advanced Inventory Revaluation	ITW1	Item Count Alert
OMRV	Inventory Revaluation	OITB	Item Groups
OMSN	MRP Scenario	AITB	Item Groups - History
OMTH	Reconciliation History	OITG	Item Properties
ONNM	Document Numbering	OITM	Items
OOCR	Loading Factors	AITM	Items - History
OOFR	Defect Cause	ITM1	Items - Prices
OOIN	Interest	OITW	Items - Warehouse
OOIR	Interest Level	AITW	Items - Warehouse - History
OOND	Industries	ADO8	Items in Package
OOPR	Opportunity	CIN8	Items in Package
OORL	Relationships	DLN8	Items in Package
OOSR	Information Source	DPI8	Items in Package
OOST	Sales Stage	DPO8	Items in Package
OPCH	A/P Invoice	DRF8	Items in Package
OPDF	Payment Draft	IGE8	Items in Package
OPDN	Goods Receipt PO	IGN8	Items in Package
OPDT	Predefined Text	INV8	Items in Package
OPEX	Payment Results Table	PCH8	Items in Package
OPID	Period Indicator	PDN8	Items in Package
OPKG	Package Types	POR8	Items in Package
OPKL	Pick List	QUT8	Items in Package
OPLN	Price Lists	RDN8	Items in Package
OPOR	Purchase Order	RDR8	Items in Package
OPR1	Opportunity - Rows	RIN8	Items in Package
OPR2	Opportunity - Partners	RPC8	Items in Package
OPR3	Opportunity - Competitors	RPD8	Items in Package
OPR4	Sales Opportunity - Interests	WTR8	Items in Package
OPR5	Opportunity - Reasons	IWZ3	Items Last Revaluation Data
OPRC	Profit Center	AJDT	Journal Entry - History
OPRF	Preferences	OTRC	Journal Entry Codes
OPRJ	Project Codes	OJDT	Journal Posting
OPRM	Authorization Tree	CLND	Journal Settings
OPRT	Partners	JDT1	Journal Transaction - Rows
OPVL	Lender - Pelecard	AJD1	Journal Transactions - Rows - History

Object	Name	Object	Name
OPWZ	Payment Wizard	OBTF	Journal Voucher
OPYD	Payment Run	OBTD	Journal Vouchers List
OPYM	Payment Method	OIPF	Landed Costs
OQCN	Query Catagories	IPF2	Landed Costs - Costs
OQUE	Queue	IPF1	Landed Costs - Rows
OQUT	Sales Quotation	OPVL	Lender - Pelecard
OQWZ	Query Wizard	OLGT	Length Units
ORCM	Recommendation Data	OALC	Loading Expenses
ORCN	Retail Chains	OOCR	Loading Factors
ORCR	Recurring Postings	OLCT	Location
ORCT	Receipt	OMRC	Manufacturers
ORDN	Returns	MRV1	Material Revaluation Information Array
ORDR	Sales Order	OCLO	Meetings Location
ORFL	Already displayed 347, 349 and WT reports	OAOB	Message Sent
ORIN	A/R Credit Memo	MSN3	MRP Pegging Information
ORIT	Dunning Interest Rate	MSN2	MRP Run Results
ORPC	A/P Credit Memo	OMSN	MRP Scenario
ORPD	Goods Returns	MSN1	MRP Scenario Whs Array
ORTM	Rate Differences	ADP1	Object Settings - History
ORTT	CPI and FC Rates	OCCD	OCCD
OSAL	Outgoing	OCFH	OCFH
OSCL	Service Call	OCFT	OCFT
OSCN	Customer/Vendor Cat. No.	OENC	OENC
OSCO	Service Call Origin	OJPE	OJPE
OSCP	Service Call Problem Type	BTF1	Open Journal Voucher Pool
OSCS	Service Call Status	OOPR	Opportunity
OSCT	Service Call Type	OPR3	Opportunity - Competitors
OSHP	Delivery Types	OPR2	Opportunity - Partners
OSLP	Sales Employee	OPR5	Opportunity - Reasons
OSLT	Service Call Solutions	OPR1	Opportunity - Rows
OSPG	Special Prices for Groups	RDR9	Order - Base Docs Details
OSPP	Special Prices	RDR4	Order - Document Tax Info.
OSQR	Standard Queries	RDR3	Order - Expenses
OSRD	Batches and Serial Numbers	RDR6	Order - Installments
OSRI	Serial Numbers for Items	RDR10	Order - Row Structure
OSRL	Serial Numbers	RDR1	Order - Rows

Object	Name	Object	Name
OSRT	OSRT	RDR2	Order Rows - Expenses
OSST	Service Call Solution Status	OSRT	OSRT
OSTA	Sales Tax Authorities	OTPI	OTPI
OSTC	Sales Tax Codes	OTSI	OTSI
OSTT	Sales Tax Authorities Type	OTXD	OTXD
OTER	Territories	OSAL	Outgoing
OTNN	1099 Forms	OVNM	OVNM
OTOB	1099 Opening Balance	OVRT	OVRT
OTPI	OTPI	OPKG	Package Types
OTRA	Transition	OPRT	Partners
OTRC	Journal Entry Codes	OPDF	Payment Draft
OTRT	Posting Templates	PDF4	Payment Draft - Account List
OTSI	OTSI	PDF1	Payment Draft - Checks
OTXD	OTXD	PDF7	Payment Draft - Document Tax Info.
OUBR	Branches	PDF2	Payment Draft - Invoices
OUDG	User Defaults	OPYM	Payment Method
OUDO	User-Defined Object	OCRP	Payment Methods
OUDP	Departments	OPEX	Payment Results Table
OUHD	Authorization Tree	PEX1	Payment Results Table - Rows
OUKD	User Key Description	OPYD	Payment Run
OUPT	User Autorization Tree	PYD1	Payment Terms Allowed in Payment Run
OUQR	Queries	OCTG	Payment Terms Types
OUSR	Users	OPWZ	Payment Wizard
OUTB	User Tables	PWZ1	Payment Wizard - Rows 1
OVNM	OVNM	PWZ2	Payment Wizard - Rows 2
OVPM	Vendor Payment	PWZ3	Payment Wizard - Rows 3
OVRT	OVRT	PWZ5	Payment Wizard - Rows 5
OVTG	Tax Definition	VPM1	Payments - Check Rows
OVTR	Tax Report	ARC7	Payments - Document Tax Info.
OWDD	Docs. for Confirmation	RCT7	Payments - Document Tax Info.
OWGT	Weight Units	VPM7	Payments - Document Tax Info.
OWHS	Warehouses	RCT2	Payments - Invoices
OWHT	Withholding Tax	VPM2	Payments - Invoices
OWKO	Work Instructions	VPM4	Payments - List of Accounts
OWOR	Production Order Header	ARC6	Payments - WT Rows
OWST	Confirmation Level	PDF6	Payments - WT Rows

Object	Name	Object	Name
OWTM	Confirmation Templates	RCT6	Payments - WT Rows
OWTR	Stock Transfers	VPM6	Payments - WT Rows
PCH1	A/P Invoice - Rows	OPID	Period Indicator
PCH2	Correction A/P Invoice Reversal - Rows - Expenses	CCPD	Period-End Closing
PCH3	A/P Invoice - Expenses	OPKL	Pick List
PCH4	A/P Invoice - Document Tax Info.	PKL1	Pick List Rows
PCH5	Withholding Tax Data	ODPT	Postdated Deposit
PCH6	A/P Invoice - Installments	OFPR	Posting Period
PCH7	Delivery Packages	OTRT	Posting Templates
PCH8	Items in Package	TRT1	Posting Templates - Rows
PCH9	A/P Invoice - Base Docs Details	OPDT	Predefined Text
PDF1	Payment Draft - Checks	OPRF	Preferences
PDF2	Payment Draft - Invoices	HEM4	Previous Employment
PDF3	Credit Vouchers	OPLN	Price Lists
PDF4	Payment Draft - Account List	OADP	Print Preferences
PDF6	Payments - WT Rows	OITT	Product Tree
PDF7	Payment Draft - Document Tax Info.	AITT	Product Tree - History
PDN1	Goods Receipt PO - Row	OWOR	Production Order Header
PDN2	Goods Receipt PO Rows - Expenses	WOR1	Production Order Lines
PDN3	Goods Receipt PO - Expenses	OPRC	Profit Center
PDN4	Goods Receipt PO - Document Tax Info.	OCR1	Profit Center - Load Factor
PDN5	Withholding Tax Data	OPRJ	Project Codes
PDN6	Goods Receipt PO - Installments	OPOR	Purchase Order
PDN7	Delivery Packages	POR9	Purchase Order - Base Docs Details
PDN8	Items in Package	POR4	Purchase Order - Document Tax Info.
PDN9	Goods Receipt PO - Base Docs Details	POR3	Purchase Order - Expenses
PEX1	Payment Results Table - Rows	POR6	Purchase Order - Installments
PKL1	Pick List Rows	POR10	Purchase Order - Row structure
POR1	Purchase Order - Rows	POR1	Purchase Order - Rows
POR2	Purchase Order Rows - Expenses	POR2	Purchase Order Rows - Expenses
POR3	Purchase Order - Expenses	PWZ4	PWZ4 - Rows 4
POR4	Purchase Order - Document Tax Info.	OUQR	Queries
POR5	Withholding Tax Data	OQCN	Query Catagories
POR6	Purchase Order - Installments	QWZ2	Query Fields
POR7	Delivery Packages	QWZ3	Query Fields

Object	Name	Object	Name
POR8	Items in Package	DMW1	Query List
POR9	Purchase Order - Base Docs Details	QWZ1	Query Tables
PSAR	Frame for Sales Analysis Report	OQWZ	Query Wizard
PWZ1	Payment Wizard - Rows 1	OQUE	Queue
PWZ2	Payment Wizard - Rows 2	QUE2	Queue Elements
PWZ3	Payment Wizard - Rows 3	QUE1	Queue Members
PWZ4	PWZ4 - Rows 4	ALR1	Queue of messages to be sent
PWZ5	Payment Wizard - Rows 5	QUT9	Quotation - Base Docs Details
PYD1	Payment Terms Allowed in Payment Run	QUT10	Quotation - Row Structure
PYM1	Currency Restriction	ORTM	Rate Differences
QUE1	Queue Members	RTM1	Rate Differences
QUE2	Queue Elements	ORCT	Receipt
QUT1	Sales Quotation - Rows	RCT4	Receipt - Account List
QUT2	Sales Quotation Rows - Expenses	RCT1	Receipts - Checks
QUT3	Sales Quotation - Expenses	OAIB	Received Alerts
QUT4	Sales Quotation - Document Tax Info.	ORCM	Recommendation Data
QUT5	Withholding Tax Data	OMTH	Reconciliation History
QUT6	Sales Quotation - Installments	ORCR	Recurring Postings
QUT7	Delivery Packages	RCR1	Recurring Postings - Rows
QUT8	Items in Package	OORL	Relationships
QUT9	Quotation - Base Docs Details	OFLT	Report - Selection Criteria
QWZ1	Query Tables	RITM	Reporting Element
QWZ2	Query Fields	ORCN	Retail Chains
QWZ3	Query Fields	RDN2	Return Rows - Expenses
R874	835874 Report - Import Log Record	ORDN	Returns
RCC4	Incoming Payment - Credit Vouchers	RDN9	Returns - Base Docs Details
RCR1	Recurring Postings - Rows	RDN4	Returns - Document Tax Info.
RCT1	Receipts - Checks	RDN3	Returns - Expenses
RCT2	Payments - Invoices	RDN6	Returns - Installments
RCT3	Credit Vouchers	RDN10	Returns - Row Structure
RCT4	Receipt - Account List	RDN1	Returns - Rows
RCT6	Payments - WT Rows	HEM3	Reviews
RCT7	Payments - Document Tax Info.	USR2	Run External Application
RDFL	Document Standards	OSLP	Sales Employee
RDN1	Returns - Rows	OFCT	Sales Forecast
RDN2	Return Rows - Expenses	FCT1	Sales Forecast - Rows

Object	Name	Object	Name
RDN3	Returns - Expenses	OPR4	Sales Opportunity - Interests
RDN4	Returns - Document Tax Info.	ORDR	Sales Order
RDN5	Withholding Tax Data	OQUT	Sales Quotation
RDN6	Returns - Installments	QUT4	Sales Quotation - Document Tax Info.
RDN7	Delivery Packages	QUT3	Sales Quotation - Expenses
RDN8	Items in Package	QUT6	Sales Quotation - Installments
RDN9	Returns - Base Docs Details	QUT1	Sales Quotation - Rows
RDOC	Document	QUT2	Sales Quotation Rows - Expenses
RDR1	Order - Rows	OOST	Sales Stage
RDR2	Order Rows - Expenses	OSTA	Sales Tax Authorities
RDR3	Order - Expenses	OSTT	Sales Tax Authorities Type
RDR4	Order - Document Tax Info.	OSTC	Sales Tax Codes
RDR5	Withholding Tax Data	STC1	Sales Tax Codes - Rows
RDR6	Order - Installments	SAL1	Salida - Rows
RDR7	Delivery Packages	CSHS	Search Function
RDR8	Items in Package	AOB1	Sent Messages - User History
RDR9	Order - Base Docs Details	SRI1	Serial No. Trans. for Item
RIN1	A/R Credit Memo - Rows	OSRL	Serial Numbers
RIN2	A/R Credit Memo Rows - Expenses	OSRI	Serial Numbers for Items
RIN3	A/R Credit Memo - Expenses	NNM2	Series Default
RIN4	A/R Credit Memo - Document Tax Info.	OSCL	Service Call
RIN5	Withholding Tax Data	ASC5	Service Call Activities
RIN6	A/R Credit Memo - Installments	SCL5	Service Call Activities
RIN7	Delivery Packages	SCL2	Service Call Inventory Expenses
RIN8	Items in Package	ASC2	Service Call Inventory Expenses - History
RIN9	A/R Credit Memo - Base Docs Details	OSCO	Service Call Origin
RIT1	Interest Rates	OSCP	Service Call Problem Type
RITM	Reporting Element	OSST	Service Call Solution Status
RPC1	A/P Credit Memo - Rows	OSLT	Service Call Solutions
RPC2	A/P Credit Memo Rows - Expenses	SCL1	Service Call Solutions
RPC3	A/P Credit Memo - Expenses	ASC1	Service Call Solutions - History
RPC4	A/P Credit Memo - Document Tax Info.	OSCS	Service Call Status
RPC5	Withholding Tax Data	SCL3	Service Call Travel/Labor Expenses
RPC6	A/P Credit Memo - Installments	ASC3	Service Call Travel/Labor Expenses - History
RPC7	Delivery Packages	ASC4	Service Call Travel/Labor Expenses - History
RPC8	Items in Package	OSCT	Service Call Type

Object	Name	Object	Name
RPC9	A/P Credit Memo - Base Docs Details	OISR	Service Calls
RPD1	Goods Returns - Rows	CTR1	Service Contract - Items
RPD2	Goods Return Rows - Expenses	OCTR	Service Contracts
RPD3	Goods Return - Expenses	OENT	Shipping Types
RPD4	Goods Return - Document Tax Info.	USR1	Short Cut
RPD5	Withholding Tax Data	OSPP	Special Prices
RPD6	Goods Returns - Installments	SPP1	Special Prices - Data Areas
RPD7	Delivery Packages	SPP2	Special Prices - Quantity Areas
RPD8	Items in Package	OSPG	Special Prices for Groups
RPD9	Goods Returns - Base Docs Details	SRT1	SRT1
RTM1	Rate Differences	SRT2	SRT2
RTYP	Document Type List	OSQR	Standard Queries
SAL1	Salida - Rows	OCST	States
SCL1	Service Call Solutions	WTR9	Stock Transfer - Base Docs Details
SCL2	Service Call Inventory Expenses	WTR4	Stock Transfer - Document Tax Info.
SCL3	Service Call Travel/Labor Expenses	WTR3	Stock Transfer - Expenses
SCL4	Expense Documents	WTR6	Stock Transfer - Installments
SCL5	Service Call Activities	WTR2	Stock Transfer Rows - Expenses
SDEX	Dynamic Extensions	OWTR	Stock Transfers
SDIS	Dynamic Interface (Strings)	WTR10	Stock Transfers - Row Structure
SPP1	Special Prices - Data Areas	WTR1	Stock Transfers - Rows
SPP2	Special Prices - Quantity Areas	AIWZ	Summary Wizard
SPRG	Application Start	LOGN	System Login
SRI1	Serial No. Trans. for Item	OVTG	Tax Definition
SRT1	SRT1	VTG1	Tax Definition
SRT2	SRT2	WHT1	Tax Definition
STC1	Sales Tax Codes - Rows	VTR1	Tax Groups
TNN1	1099 Boxes	OVTR	Tax Report
TPI1	TPI1	HTM1	Team Members
TRA1	Transition - Lines	OHTR	Termination Reason
TRT1	Posting Templates - Rows	OTER	Territories
TSI1	TSI1	CTBR	Toolbars
TXD1	TXD1	TPI1	TPI1
UDG1	Defaults - Documents	OTRA	Transition
UDG2	Defaults - Credit Cards	TRA1	Transition - Lines
UDO1	User Object Children	OIND	Triangular Deal

Object	Name	Object	Name
UDO2	User Object Find Columns	TSI1	TSI1
UDO3	User Object Form Columns	TXD1	TXD1
UFD1	User Fields - Values Definitions	CUPC	Upgrade Control
UKD1	User Sub-Keys Description	ARI1	User Add-on Table
UPT1	Extend User Perm. Tree	USR3	User Authorization
USR1	Short Cut	OUPT	User Autorization Tree
USR2	Run External Application	OUDG	User Defaults
USR3	User Authorization	CUDC	User Display Cat.
VPM1	Payments - Check Rows	CUFD	User Fields - Descr.
VPM2	Payments - Invoices	UFD1	User Fields - Values Definitions
VPM3	Credit Vouchers	OUKD	User Key Description
VPM4	Payments - List of Accounts	CUMI	User Menu Items
VPM6	Payments - WT Rows	UDO1	User Object Children
VPM7	Payments - Document Tax Info.	UDO2	User Object Find Columns
VRT1	VRT1	UDO3	User Object Form Columns
VTG1	Tax Definition	UKD1	User Sub-Keys Description
VTR1	Tax Groups	OUTB	User Tables
WDD1	Documents for Approval - Authorizers	CUVV	User Validations
WDD2	Documents for Approval - Terms	OUDO	User-Defined Object
WHT1	Tax Definition	OUSR	Users
WHT2	WHT2	OVPM	Vendor Payment
WKO1	Work Instructions - Rows	VRT1	VRT1
WOR1	Production Order Lines	ODDG	W/holding Tax Ded. - Groups
WST1	Confirmation Level - Rows	DDT1	W/holding Tax Ded. - Hierarchy
WTM1	Confirmation Templates - Producers	ODDT	W/holding Tax Ded. - Hierarchy
WTM2	Confirmation Templates - Stages	OWHS	Warehouses
WTM3	Confirmation Templates - Documents	AWHS	Warehouses - History
WTM4	Confirmation Templates - Terms	OWGT	Weight Units
WTM5	Approval Templates - Queries	OINM	WH Journal
WTR1	Stock Transfers - Rows	WHT2	WHT2
WTR2	Stock Transfer Rows - Expenses	OWHT	Withholding Tax
WTR3	Stock Transfer - Expenses	ADO5	Withholding Tax Data
WTR4	Stock Transfer - Document Tax Info.	CIN5	Withholding Tax Data
WTR5	Withholding Tax Data	CPI5	Withholding Tax Data
WTR6	Stock Transfer - Installments	CPV5	Withholding Tax Data
WTR7	Delivery Packages	CSI5	Withholding Tax Data

Object	Name	Object	Name
WTR8	Items in Package	CSV5	Withholding Tax Data
WTR9	Stock Transfer - Base Docs Details	DLN5	Withholding Tax Data
ADO10	A/R Invoice - Row structure	DPI5	Withholding Tax Data
CIN10	Correction Invoice - Rows structure	DPO5	Withholding Tax Data
DLN10	Delivery - Rows structure	DRF5	Withholding Tax Data
DPI10	Down Payment In - Rows structure	IGE5	Withholding Tax Data
DPO10	Down Payment Out - Rows structure	IGN5	Withholding Tax Data
DRF10	Draft - Rows structure	INV5	Withholding Tax Data
IGE10	Goods Issue - Row structure	PCH5	Withholding Tax Data
IGN10	Goods Receipt - Row structure	PDN5	Withholding Tax Data
INV10	A/R Invoice - Row structure	POR5	Withholding Tax Data
PCH10	A/R Invoice - Row structure	QUT5	Withholding Tax Data
PDN10	Goods Receipt PO - Row Structure	RDN5	Withholding Tax Data
POR10	Purchase Order - Row structure	RDR5	Withholding Tax Data
QUT10	Quotation - Row Structure	RIN5	Withholding Tax Data
RDN10	Returns - Row Structure	RPC5	Withholding Tax Data
RDR10	Order - Row Structure	RPD5	Withholding Tax Data
RIN10	A/R Credit Memo - Row Structure	WTR5	Withholding Tax Data
RPC10	A/P Credit Memo - Row Structure	OWKO	Work Instructions
RPD10	Goods Returns - Row Structure	WKO1	Work Instructions - Rows
WTR10	Stock Transfers - Row Structure	CSTN	Workstation ID

Index